AN EXAMINATION OF ROLE THEORY

AN EXAMINATION OF ROLE THEORY

THE CASE OF THE STATE POLICE

JACK J. PREISS

HOWARD J. EHRLICH

UNIVERSITY OF NEBRASKA PRESS · LINCOLN

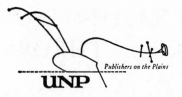

Publishers on the Plains

UNP

Copyright © 1966 by the University of Nebraska Press

Library of Congress Catalog Card Number 66–10874

Manufactured in the United States of America

1/27/67 *Bre· Dart* 8·50

To
May Frank
and
Herbert and Dorothy Ehrlich

Contents

Acknowledgments

THIS RESEARCH owes its greatest debt to the men of the Central State Police, and particularly to their Commissioner. We acknowledge our respect and our gratitude to all of them for their time and aid, but mainly for the opportunity they gave us to share in their ideas, their aspirations, and their experiences.

Initial financial and research assistance was given by the Highway Traffic Safety Center of Michigan State University through the offices of Mr. Gordon Sheehe, Director, and Dr. Theodore Forbes, Research Director. A United States Public Health Service Grant (No. M-2957) enabled us to elaborate and complete our studies.

We are indebted to Professors Duane Gibson, John Useem, and Ruth Useem for permitting us to adapt and use some of their research instruments and to Dr. Charles Proctor for his statistical advice. Dr. James W. Rinehart was our chief research assistant during most phases of the study, and Dr. John C. Howell assisted us administratively at the closing stages.

Dr. Benjamin Pasamanick, formerly Director of the Research Division of the Ohio State University Psychiatric Institute and Hospital, and later Dr. James G. Kelly, formerly Chief of the Community Projects Section of the Mental Health Study Center (National Institute of Mental Health), gave administrative support to Howard Ehrlich during our work on the book. We are obligated both for their support and for their encouragement.

Drs. William V. D'Antonio, James G. Kelly, and John R. Newbrough helpfully read portions of the manuscript. We are especially grateful to Dr. Sheila Feld for her critical and invaluable review of the entire manuscript.

Finally, we must acknowledge our special debt to Carol Ehrlich, who edited the manuscript through all of its drafts, coercing and cajoling us into clarity and readable English. Primary responsibility for the preparation of chapters 2 to 5 belongs to the first author, and primary responsibility for the preparation of chapters 6 to 9 belongs to the second author.

AN EXAMINATION OF ROLE THEORY

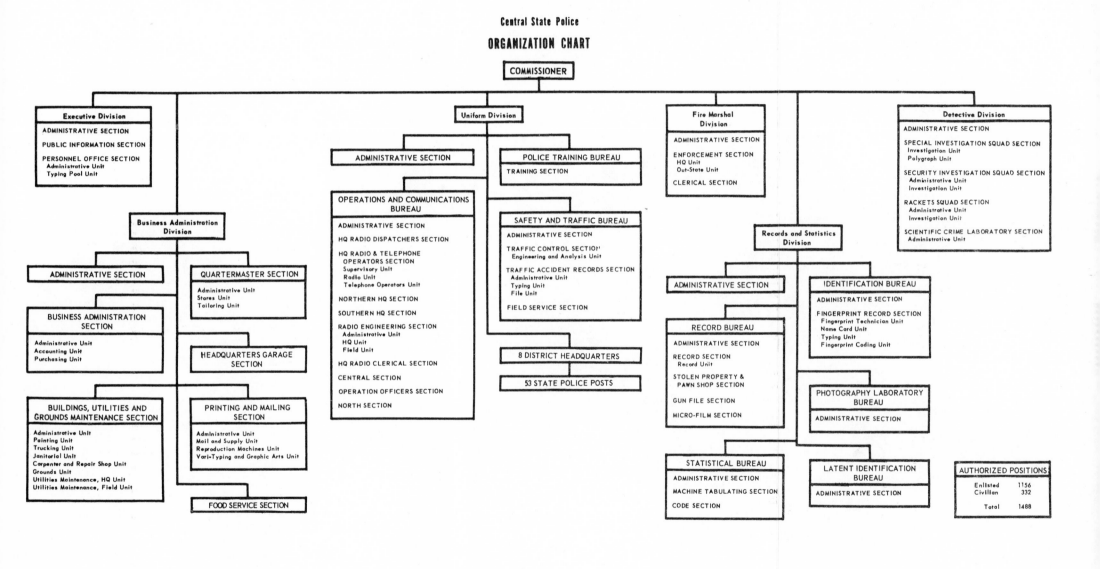

Central State Police

ORGANIZATION CHART

COMMISSIONER

Executive Division
- ADMINISTRATIVE SECTION
- PUBLIC INFORMATION SECTION
- PERSONNEL OFFICE SECTION
  - Administrative Unit
  - Typing Pool Unit

Business Administration Division

ADMINISTRATIVE SECTION

BUSINESS ADMINISTRATION SECTION
- Administrative Unit
- Accounting Unit
- Purchasing Unit

BUILDINGS, UTILITIES AND GROUNDS MAINTENANCE SECTION
- Administrative Unit
- Painting Unit
- Trucking Unit
- Janitorial Unit
- Carpenter and Repair Shop Unit
- Grounds Unit
- Utilities Maintenance, HQ Unit
- Utilities Maintenance, Field Unit

QUARTERMASTER SECTION
- Administrative Unit
- Stores Unit
- Tailoring Unit

HEADQUARTERS GARAGE SECTION

PRINTING AND MAILING SECTION
- Administrative Unit
- Mail and Supply Unit
- Reproduction Machines Unit
- Vari-Typing and Graphic Arts Unit

FOOD SERVICE SECTION

Uniform Division

ADMINISTRATIVE SECTION

OPERATIONS AND COMMUNICATIONS BUREAU
- ADMINISTRATIVE SECTION
- HQ RADIO DISPATCHERS SECTION
- HQ RADIO & TELEPHONE OPERATORS SECTION
  - Supervisory Unit
  - Radio Unit
  - Telephone Operators Unit
- NORTHERN HQ SECTION
- SOUTHERN HQ SECTION
- RADIO ENGINEERING SECTION
  - Administrative Unit
  - HQ Unit
  - Field Unit
- HQ RADIO CLERICAL SECTION
- CENTRAL SECTION
- OPERATION OFFICERS SECTION
- NORTH SECTION

POLICE TRAINING BUREAU

TRAINING SECTION

SAFETY AND TRAFFIC BUREAU
- ADMINISTRATIVE SECTION
- TRAFFIC CONTROL SECTION
  - Engineering and Analysis Unit
- TRAFFIC ACCIDENT RECORDS SECTION
  - Administrative Unit
  - Typing Unit
  - File Unit
- FIELD SERVICE SECTION

8 DISTRICT HEADQUARTERS

53 STATE POLICE POSTS

Fire Marshal Division
- ADMINISTRATIVE SECTION
- ENFORCEMENT SECTION
  - HQ Unit
  - Out-State Unit
- CLERICAL SECTION

Records and Statistics Division

ADMINISTRATIVE SECTION

RECORD BUREAU
- ADMINISTRATIVE SECTION
- RECORD SECTION
  - Record Unit
- STOLEN PROPERTY & PAWN SHOP SECTION
- GUN FILE SECTION
- MICRO-FILM SECTION

STATISTICAL BUREAU
- ADMINISTRATIVE SECTION
- MACHINE TABULATING SECTION
- CODE SECTION

IDENTIFICATION BUREAU
- ADMINISTRATIVE SECTION
- FINGERPRINT RECORD SECTION
  - Fingerprint Technician Unit
  - Name Card Unit
  - Typing Unit
  - Fingerprint Coding Unit

PHOTOGRAPHY LABORATORY BUREAU
- ADMINISTRATIVE SECTION

LATENT IDENTIFICATION BUREAU
- ADMINISTRATIVE SECTION

Detective Division
- ADMINISTRATIVE SECTION
- SPECIAL INVESTIGATION SQUAD SECTION
  - Investigation Unit
  - Polygraph Unit
- SECURITY INVESTIGATION SQUAD SECTION
  - Administrative Unit
  - Investigation Unit
- RACKETS SQUAD SECTION
  - Administrative Unit
  - Investigation Unit
- SCIENTIFIC CRIME LABORATORY SECTION
  - Administrative Unit

AUTHORIZED POSITIONS

Enlisted	1156
Civilian	332
Total	1488

CHAPTER 1

Introduction

THE INCREASED TEMPO of interest in role theory in the past decade has resulted in the development of a multiplicity of conceptual schemes for the analysis of both unambiguous and conflicted role behavior. Unfortunately, these attempts at theory construction typically have been executed with little regard to the empirical significance of the conceptualizations involved, and have been either untestable or untested. Although some of these theoretical statements have been provocative and stimulating (especially, for us, the formulations of G. H. Mead, Linton, and more recently Parsons), the concept of role has frequently been little more than an ambiguous device for describing ordered behavior in a group. Yet surely, at this stage in the development of sociological and social psychological theories, the assertion that a person's position or status in a system of social relationships affects his behavior in that system in some determinate manner is a weak proposition.

Those who have surveyed accomplishments of role theory, however defined, have generally made negative appraisals. Lindzey and Hall, for example, explaining their exclusion of role theory in their survey of theories of personality, say, "Role Theory, it seems to us, is less systematically developed than most of the other positions we elected to include. It is true that the theory contains *a leading idea of considerable value and importance* but this idea has not yet been incorporated into a network of concepts which deal comprehensively with human behavior."[1] Gross, Mason, and McEachern comment: "As we and others who have examined the use of the role concept in the social science literature have observed, despite its increasing involvement in conceptual schemes for explaining social behavior and cultural and social systems, it has yielded few significant hypotheses of theoretical importance ... it must be said that in current formulations the role concept has not proved its worth."[2] Biddle, after a systematic review of

[1] C. S. Hall and G. Lindzey, *Theories of Personality* (New York: John Wiley & Sons, 1957), p. viii, italics added.

[2] N. Gross, W. S. Mason, and A. W. McEachern, *Explorations in Role Analysis: Studies of the School Superintendency Role* (New York: John Wiley & Sons, 1958), pp. 319–20.

the role literature, asserts that "role theory, as a set of unified propositions, does not presently exist." Despite this deficiency, which he attributes primarily to inadequate and shallow theories, he concludes that "the field shows promise."[3]

Clearly, the net assessment of the concept of role and its empirical development, both by those who consider themselves "role theorists" and by those who respond to such theories, reflects doubt, tempered by hope—if not vacuous optimism. Apparently the idea of role as a fundamental explanatory construct of human behavior retains its appeal although its empirical validation has been little advanced. There are numerous reasons for this paradox, some of which we shall explore later in the book. Certainly among these has been the shibboleth of interdisciplinary integration. Few single concepts in contemporary social science have held the lure of conceptually bridging anthropology, psychology, and sociology that the concept of role has held.

To the present writers, one major reason for the impasse in empirical research here has been the failure to examine critically the key assumptions which have been made about role and role behavior. Certainly one of the pivotal constructs in role theories has been that of *expectations*. About this construct there has developed a complex of assumptions and strategy rules— the consequences of which are by no means easy to identify. One such outcome, for example, has been the failure to study the process of role acquisition. Instead of confronting this problem, many role studies have accepted a role as given, as a pre-established entity to be examined in some operational context. Their concern is primarily with role performance, role evaluation, and role conflict as processes *distinct* from role formulation. Analytically, these distinctions seem necessary, but they also serve either to misdirect or to beg the question of how a role image is developed and transmitted in the social environment. If the current symbolic interactionist conceptions of the socialization process are correct, then the expectations of "significant others" seem antecedent to the later steps of response, of implementation, and of maintenance. Consequently, it would be necessary (or at the least fruitful) to locate these "others," define their sets of expectations, and specify the relationship among these sets in terms of a total role image before analyzing those temporally subsequent dimensions of role behavior.

Another outcome of past research strategy has been the neglect of what we, at least, consider to be some crucial relationships among the variables of role analysis. Studies of role, for example, have been typically executed within a narrow framework of study of the *perceived* expectations of role

[3] B. J. Biddle, *The Present Status of Role Theory* (Columbia, Mo.: University of Missouri Press, 1961), pp. 100–101.

players, or occasionally their reports as to what their behavior might be in a given situation. Such a framework, however, has seldom considered the relationship between perceived role expectations and role performance. But an even more important neglect has been that of the consideration of the relationships among the *actual* expectations, the perceived expectations, and role performance. As we shall try to show later, when these three variables are considered synchronically, a quite different picture emerges from what would have been presented from a study of any two of these variables.

It should be clear that the difficulties, the assumptions, the alternative strategies of role research, and even the apparent optimism of those involved stems from a variety of meta-theoretical positions which have seldom been made explicit. Central to these meta-theoretical polemics are two interrelated questions. First, what kind of theory should role theory be? And second, should there at all be a *special* theory of role behavior? Gross and his associates argue, for example, "that it would be an unwise use of conceptual resources to limit . . . [the] application [of role concepts] to only one of the social science disciplines or to a selected problem area designated as 'role theory.'"[4] Sarbin, in contrast, seeks a special theory—albeit an eclectic one; and Parsons makes "status-role" a central construct in his functionalist conceptualization of the social system.

Other illustrations could, of course, be adduced, but these would be unnecessary. What is important here is the recognition that there are these many meta-theoretical positions, and that these positions all entail substantively different foci, hence different assumptions, different strategies, and the like. Our own position, assumptions, and strategy shall become apparent in the pages to follow; and we choose to unfold our statement as it developed through the research we are to report. In this fashion we hope to exhibit not only the findings and propositions of this study, but also the manner in which these came to be generated.

The intent of our research was to delimit the boundaries of role analysis: to explore—from a role theoretical perspective—the process of role acquisition, the interrelationships of the many dimensions of role expectations, and the procedures and mechanisms for the evaluation of role performance. Operationally, such a proposal entailed the selection of a role which offered favorable opportunities for supplying consistent and specific data. This eliminated, to our way of thinking, such broad general categories as father, leader, adolescent, and similar global designations. While these are certainly familiar role terms, their scope and ambiguity make controlled research extremely difficult. A more promising source seemed to lie in the area of work where, in complex organizations, the process of specialization has

4 Gross, Mason, McEachern, *op. cit.*, p. 326.

markedly increased the precision of job descriptions and expectancies.[5] Industrial specialization, for example, has narrowed some work patterns to a single requirement, although such minute specificity might be too limiting to yield variance in systems of role expectations. We decided to search, therefore, for an occupational pattern which had the following characteristics:

1. Being capable of technical differentiation by those close to the role, yet meaningful as a whole to the population in general.
2. Possessing a developmental cycle, as represented by a profession or specified bureaucratic career system in which the beginning and the end of the role could be encompassed within the study itself.
3. Having a designated formal period of training and preparation for the conscious transmittal of role expectations.
4. Providing the researchers with opportunities to observe and record role behavior and evaluation throughout the system in which the role was located.

Admittedly, most behavioral patterns and systems do not meet all of these conditions. Yet it was felt that the difficulties inherent in doing research in this area demanded optimum conditions for investigation. If it was not possible to examine role theory under such conditions, it would hardly be promising to do so in less favorable circumstances.[6] In keeping with this reasoning, it was fortunate that an occupational system was close at hand which seemed to have the desired characteristics. This was a state police department whose administration desired objective information about the structure and operation of its organization. There were, therefore, both practical and academic aims involved which appeared to be compatible.

The occupation of policeman, in the contexts of the department and of society-at-large, could be translated into the characteristics just enumerated:

1. The work of the policeman could be differentiated from that of other members of the system, such as corporals, sergeants, and officers. At the same time, policemen as policemen are highly visible to the public.
2. The career of the policeman was bounded by minimum and maximum age limits for entry and termination, and the department structure was clearly demarcated by ranks which could be entered only in sequence (i.e., entry is only at the bottom rank, and a promotion was rarely made by passing the succeeding rank). Our access to all ranks within the department, from recruit

[5] We make no claim to originality in selecting a work role as our research focus, although our choice of policemen was quite deliberate. Occupational settings and work roles have comprised perhaps the largest sector of role research. However, the emphasis of most of these studies has usually been upon the occupation rather than upon role theory per se.

[6] For a somewhat different perspective, see R. H. Turner, "Role-Taking: Process versus Conformity," in Arnold M. Rose (ed.), *Human Behavior and Social Processes* (Boston: Houghton Mifflin, 1962), esp. p. 22.

through retired groups, provided us with a fairly comprehensive and longitudinal profile of the police career.

3. The training of the policeman had a definite plan, comprising formal didactic instruction of recruits in a resident school program and followed by a probationary on-the-job period which resulted in final acceptance or rejection.

4. Access to the police department in all its aspects was provided us by the unstinting support of the department head. It was possible for us to observe every phase of department activity and to arrange interviews, questionnaires, and written tests with representatives of all ranks.

Having decided upon the site of the study, we considered the issues of research strategy. In reviewing past efforts, as well as our own initial attempts at theory construction, we felt that we had not yet developed sufficient clarity and precision of terms, ideas, and procedures to meet the requirements for an extensive testing of formal, theoretical hypotheses. We sought, therefore, to implement our study with such a *formulative design* that we might more properly describe the project as a series of interlocking studies. Our position was that not only can prematurity in the formalization of theory be misleading, but prematurity in formalizing the design of research operations may be equally misleading, especially where the sources of data cannot be subject to rigorous controls.

CHAPTER 2

The Social Organization of the Central State Police

IN THE FALL of 1957 we began our field work, this in the form of systematic and participant observation, first at headquarters and later at selected posts of the Central State Police (CSP). In this chapter we shall attempt to present an overview of the social organization of the CSP that is based almost entirely on our field notes. In subsequent chapters the role of policemen will be analyzed segmentally, chiefly with data obtained from a series of structured questionnaires, interviews, and formal test batteries.

This chapter, then, contains a distillation of our two major sources of observational data. The first, headquarters staff, represented all major phases of training, operations, and policy-making. The researchers spent hundreds of hours with all ranks assigned to headquarters. Obviously, this source was heavily weighted with commissioned officers. The second source was a sample of four posts, selected for variety of size, location, and performance rating, at which an investigator spent two to four weeks living on the post in intimate and direct involvement with a wide spectrum of police activities. This field experience was a kind of counterpoint to the headquarters environment, and the two sets of data permitted a comparative, depth view of the department which could not have been achieved from either source alone.

Most of the material reported here will be a summary of the values, attitudes, and behavior of several hundred persons with whom the researchers talked and lived. Although it is not possible for us to reproduce all the nuance and richness of these interactions, a number of central themes emerged, and these constitute the major concerns of this chapter. Naturally, the primary topics reflect the focus of the study upon role perception, role acquisition, and role performance.

The Setting

The existence of police organizations in a free society is a phenomenon of considerable interest. In one sense they can be viewed as an essentially alien factor, geared toward restricting the freedom of the individual and limiting his range of legitimate action. Further, the acceptance of police controls in American society—where there is a strong ideological aversion to individual authority—rests on a tenuous combination of trust and suspicion.

The policeman is not materially productive. His "business," at best, is to make it possible for other people to go about their business of producing and moving goods and services. His focus is chiefly upon the disruptions and aberrations of efficient human relationships.

In the type of services he performs, the policeman resembles the physician, the lawyer, and the nurse. Yet his lower status, as reflected by his relatively short role preparation and his comparatively meager rewards, accentuates the negative aspects of his work, which, in turn, tend to isolate him from other segments of the population. There is another important difference. Where contact with physicians and most other professionals is primarily a voluntary act on the part of the public, the policeman is usually the initiator of his contacts with others. He is the seeker rather than the sought, and even though a third person (complainant) may initiate his action, the main object (the criminal, the suspect, the violator) of his efforts strives for avoidance and disengagement.

Thus, while the apprehension of a criminal or the arrest of a traffic violator may be regarded as role fulfillment within the organization itself, and as de facto evidence of the efficiency and justification of police activity in the community at large, it tends to be unpalatable to those who are the direct recipients of the policeman's action. The cost, ranging from execution to payment of a nominal fine, results in a negative balance for the other parties involved. In short, the policeman's "profit" is usually someone's loss.

In a relatively free society, this likelihood of deprivation and loss in encounters with the police presents some fundamental problems in the attraction and retention of persons in this role. Although the similarity of the soldier and policeman seems obvious in terms of uniforms, armament, exposure to danger, discipline, etc., there are important differences. The primary one is that the soldier's object is the external enemy; he seldom takes punitive action against his own community. Thus his support is regarded as a matter of necessity, as a bulwark against alien threat. The investment in the soldier is regarded as insurance which may be expensive and little used but perilous to be without. The policeman, on the other hand, is the potential antagonist of every citizen, and, unlike the soldier, he is always at war. He is the public conscience, threatening the status and treasure of the wrong-doer. Since the citizen is committed to adherence to the community laws, he cannot challenge the right of the policeman to call him to account for his actions. Yet every law contains an implicit challenge of circumvention to a freedom-loving citizen (particularly when he did not participate in the law-making process). The element of the game, as we shall note later, has even become part of the pattern of law enforcement in which the policeman and the violator feel obligated to certain codes of "fair play."

The foregoing is not to imply that all perceptions of the policeman emerge as completely negative. We are aware of perceptions which present him as a protector of the community and the champion of the weak and the good. However, these positive images, we suspect, are more the product of conscious effort and institutional advertising by police agencies than of "natural" cultural response.

It is important to keep this kind of ideological and psychological setting in mind when we examine the general organizational characteristics of the Central State Police. Department leaders made strong efforts to deemphasize the punitive aspects of the organization and to foster an image of public service.[1] Recruits were constantly reminded of the public nature of their work and that the department's existence was at the discretion of the civil government.

General Organizational Characteristics

Within the CSP, considerable specialization can be observed. This becomes most apparent in the large urban posts, where detectives and other specialists handled most of the complaint and investigative work, and *policemen*[2] were confined mostly to traffic functions. A *policeman* assigned to a smaller rural post might have a relatively lighter or seasonal work load, but he would probably enjoy more variety than the more active but restricted *policemen* at a city post. Under such circumstances it was difficult for headquarters staff to make all of the eight field districts of the department seem equally desirable assignments. In addition to district differences, there was a clear hiatus between headquarters and field staffs, and, since headquarters was located in the populous southern region, it was usually identified with the districts containing most of the large posts.

Each district had its own regional headquarters, under a commander with the rank of captain, and included several other commissioned and non-commissioned officers. However, these units had a minimum of autonomy in policy matters and usually acted as relay and supervisory mechanisms for

---

[1] The CSP maintained a Public Information Office which was especially active. Its chief, a civilian, was directly responsible to the Commissioner and received a salary almost as high as the Commissioner's.

[2] As a matter of convention, we shall try to distinguish between "policemen" in general and "policemen" as the official job title of the lowest ranking uniformed officers in the CSP by italicizing the latter.

Central Headquarters programs. Though each of the districts was administratively equal, they were with respect to work volume, territory, and resource allocation most unequal. The status hierarchy of the department, as seen from the field, was simply put:

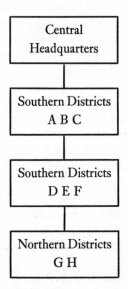

There was little doubt that increasing specialization and the proliferation of public and governmental demands for service were transforming the department into a number of semi-exclusive segments which had career consequences for recruits. If a man wished to concern himself mainly with the more diversified or the more glamorous aspects of police work, his main avenues of fulfillment would be to gain assignment to a northern district post as a *policeman* or to seek promotion into the Detective Bureau after the requisite years of service in the Uniform Division.

The *policeman's* view of headquarters was that it was "filled with brass," and, while this was literally true in terms of concentration, the implication was that this represented excessive centralization and fostered both arbitrariness and inertia in the upper echelons. Most high-ranked officers were sensitive on this point, and several took great pains to justify their work while at the same time expressing a preference for the more active life of the post environment.

The central unit of the department, and the most immediate and vital reference point for nearly every *policeman*, was the post. In all, there were 54 posts, ranging in size from the backwoods 7-man post to the 44-man post in Capital City. The number of posts within each district varied from 4 to 11.

On the organization chart all posts are "equal" insofar as functions and structure are concerned. Yet differences have already been noted in terms of location and size. We must now add to this a vast complex of variations which appear to stem principally from the personality and work patterns of the post commander. While central and district headquarters supply a framework of rules, regulations, and policies, there is evidence that no single work pattern applies across the board. All posts, of course, have virtually identical hierarchies of ranks (i.e., a corporal at one post is of equal standing in terms of pay and seniority with all other corporals of similar assignment and length of service) and keep identical basic records (radio logs, *policemen's* daily and monthly activity summaries, etc.).

Nevertheless, there were wide differences in the way in which these standard procedures were carried out and in the number and type of additional requirements expected of personnel. At one post, for example, *policemen* reported for shift duty one-half hour early to make sure they read the radio log and the previous two shifts' reports in the patrol area to which they were currently assigned. At another post *policemen* invariably washed their patrol cars at the conclusion of each patrol, and this would of necessity be done on the man's own time.

In most posts the noncommissioned officers do not participate in patrols, but they are responsible for making up the schedules. Usually this is a task of an assistant post commander, and, while rotation is generally prescribed, the men with least seniority, especially recruits, will frequently find themselves with a disproportionate amount of night work, assignments to the least desirable areas of post territory, and petty complaints.

Considerable variety was also noted in the interaction patterns among ranks. Some posts minimized rank distinctions and fostered camaraderie, while others maintained a fairly rigid social distance among ranks and preserved an impersonal form of address. As will be noted in other parts of the study, work procedures in such fundamental matters as enforcement and relationships with other police organizations were equally variable at the post level. Each post might view the others in its district as competitors in terms of patrol miles covered, arrests "closed out," and low frequency of equipment repair. If, for example, Central Headquarters decided to "push" for stricter enforcement of some issue in a given month, this directive would go down the line to district headquarters, to post commanders, and to the *policemen* themselves. Sometimes such an order would be read openly at a post meeting, while in other cases it would be conveyed informally in private chats or held out to the men as a personal incentive.

Many of the staff noted that the flow of communication was certainly greater out of headquarters than into it, and the output sometimes became garbled as it passed down through the ranks. Headquarters officers frequently stated that *policemen* in the field had misinterpreted many policy statements they had received, and that such misinterpretations were difficult to counteract once they had developed. With respect to input, it was obvious that very few ideas emanated from the *policeman* level, nor was there much desire among officers for a "suggestion box" approach. Most *policemen* showed little sense of involvement in policy-making. Probably, this scarcity of constructive feedback can be attributed to the semi-military structure of the department, which led to a fear that suggestions would be construed as criticisms and would result in punishment rather than approval. In addition, there was also a sense of passivity: the structure was perceived as too insensitive and inflexible to be altered by stimuli from the lower ranks. Thus there was fostered a tendency to take things as they came and not to waste energy in fruitless efforts to change the system. Certainly this last attitude, which was expressed by many *policemen*, reflected a kind of apathy with respect to organizational routines in a manner quite characteristic of bureaucratic organizations.

At the post level, the images of autonomy were somewhat contradictory. Headquarters officers generally felt that posts had considerable freedom to set their own patterns of behavior. Anything within reason would be approved, or at least permitted, if it got results. Post personnel, on the other hand, felt quite restricted by orders and directives. Autonomy in techniques was not regarded as noteworthy since the goals were prescribed arbitrarily from above. The "problems of the field" were continuously described as out of the ken and sympathy of headquarters staff. The generality of directives and policies was consistently viewed as evidence of a program of ignoring post differences and forcing an artificial uniformity upon the department.

Selection and Training

Like most specialized organizations, the CSP had recruitment problems which made the ultimate choice of a training class a risky and ambiguous task. The various stages of the selection process were subject to continuous discussion and tinkering at headquarters. At the time of the study, the sequence of steps for each applicant involved a Civil Service information and background form, an intelligence test, a character investigation by a field representative of the department, a medical examination and physical proficiency test, and an interview by a joint board of department officers and

Civil Service examiners.[3] If an applicant survived this sequence, he was placed on a roster of eligibles from which new classes were drawn. Due to variations in manpower needs and legislative appropriations there was no fixed schedule for recruit schools, although at least one class was needed each year to replenish losses by retirement. (Retirement was mandatory at age 56, and optional after 25 years of service.) Class size ranged between twenty-five and fifty recruits.

By law, of course, race and religion were not factors used for selecting recruits, and the roster of the department contained names which appeared to run the gamut of nationality and religion (except that there were no men who were known to be Jewish). Although exact figures were not available, a few Negroes had entered the department as recruits, but none made it through recruit school. Recruit candidates, then, were white, Christian, high school graduates between the ages of 21 and 29. Most of the recent recruits were below 25, and fewer than 10 per cent had attended college. For most men, this was their first or second full-time job, not counting their military service. Few entered with any well-developed occupational skills.

All recruits were residents of Central State, and all areas of the state were almost equally represented (the rural northern regions were slightly over-represented). Residential propinquity, as far as distance from a post or from Central Headquarters was concerned, had no bearing on recruitment.

In order to make some assessment of the socioeconomic background of the *policemen*, we obtained information on fathers' occupations for the members of the Uniform Division. The recruitment base shows an almost even split in fathers' occupations by a white-collar–blue-collar division (46 per cent vs. 54 per cent). If we compare fathers' occupations of recruits and *policemen* against those of commissioned officers and recently retired persons (a 20-year difference in recruitment), we find no significant differences. There is a tendency toward a shift to blue-collar recruitment, and the major differences can be found in the larger proportion of self-employed fathers and a smaller number of fathers in sales and clerical positions among the officers and retired members. The shift in recruitment is probably best summarized, then, as being away from entreprenurial toward "bureaucratic" occupational origins. This perhaps reflects the general societal trend and is not unique to the CSP, though it may carry with it problems which are unique to this organization.

Among recruits there seemed to be a central interest in job stability and economic security. Such factors as seniority, automatic pay increments, well-ordered career lines, and routinized evaluations seemed to hold greater appeal

[3] Tests of personality and job aptitude were sometimes employed as aids in screening applicants. There was generally a strong verbal commitment given to the discovery and adoption of standardized methods and instruments of screening and evaluation.

for the recruit than the opportunities for personal glory or a life of excitement and adventure. Job prestige was viewed more as a reflection of the status symbols assumed (the uniform, the patrol car, etc.) than as a result of role achievements.

At the commissioned officer level there was some concern expressed over what they saw as the increased motivational importance of security and stability. Many officers felt the department was formerly "more dynamic" and had higher "esprit de corps." They criticized the tendency of recruits to be interested in pay scales, work schedules, and retirement benefits. Several felt this began when married men were accepted as recruits, a change presumably necessitated by a dwindling pool of potential candidates. Early-marriage trends and the growing competition of education and other jobs underlay this shrinkage. Having a family accentuated the recruit's economic responsibilities and drew him out of the orbit of career primacy.[4]

Nevertheless, some training officers believed the security orientation provided major benefits for the department. These were a decrease in job mobility (which will be discussed later in this chapter) and a willingness to accept advancement "through channels." The ambitious man was seen as the impatient man, and impatience is not usually compatible with orderly bureaucratic procedures. This does not mean, of course, that the department was characterized by complacency. However, it does suggest that the men who entered their career with limited goals and modest expectations about the range and timing of their occupational achievement would be less likely to be disenchanted with their experience and progress in the CSP. Perhaps those officers who were disturbed about the security focus were clinging to an ideology of success which was unrealistic in the current, but not the past, organization of the department. The high ambition and high initiative which they sought in *policemen* could well be the qualities most conducive to internal friction, which, in turn, would probably intensify frustration and increase resignation rates.

The actual training process consisted of a series of courses in academic subjects, such as law, court procedures, and rules of evidence, along with the development of such skills as judo, marksmanship, and typing. The schools were planned and conducted by a training officer and his regular staff, supplemented by rotating groups of specialists (usually experienced *policemen*

---

4 One graphic illustration of this change in career orientation was that most of the older post buildings contained fairly extensive living quarters for the men. In recent years these facilities have been little used, and now serve as storerooms or are simply waste space. When the researchers lived at the posts during field work they were usually the only persons sleeping at the post other than a few unmarried *policemen*. Newer post buildings contained a much smaller proportion of space devoted to living quarters.

from various posts). Each rotating group would customarily serve for three consecutive schools. The program was held at headquarters, and all trainees lived and learned together. Each day of the six-week term was fully scheduled and was carried out in an atmosphere of discipline and austerity. In this sense it purposely resembled the military academy approach, which the staff felt was productive of high morale. The pattern of strict discipline did not encourage free discussion or criticism about training matters, and this itself was often seen as a worthwhile exercise in self-control. This crowded and pressurized training program was the first opportunity which the members of the department had to mold and to assess the recruits' performance. It was also the only period in which an entire class could be seen in terms of responses to a comparable set of experiences.

Because of differences among instructors as well as courses, the trainees found it necessary to discover quickly and to maintain a minimum perform-ance level for each subject. Since physical prowess (strength, stamina, boxing, etc.) and technical skill (pistol shooting, fingerprinting, typing) were highly regarded by most of the training staff,[5] a man who did very well in these areas could offset some deficiencies in academic measures (written exams, etc.), particularly if he exhibited willingness and enthusiasm. Such com-pensation was not usually applied, however, in the opposite direction.

CSP records revealed that of the recruits who did not complete school in a six-year period between 1952 and 1957, 36 per cent left because of failures in the physical training aspects of the work while only 6 per cent left because of academic deficiencies. While this does not support specifically the contention of one-way compensation, it indicates that physical ability is a more crucial variable for school survival than academic ability.

Physically, there were prescribed ranges of height and weight, and most recruits were closer to maximum than to minimum limits. It was obvious that physical prowess could not be established by exploits against persons,

[5] The rather extensive training in pistol shooting (in contrast with scant training in high-speed driving) belied the importance of this skill in police work. Recruits quickly realized that use of firearms in line of duty was a very rare occurrence, and they tended to lose interest in target practice. The department resorted to contests and competitions with other police departments to stimulate interest. However, these events were largely honorific for the participants and were seen as sport rather than part of the job. In this sense, shooting skill was more of an artifact of the role of *policeman*, and was mainly a form of conspicuous accomplishment and advertising which enhanced departmental prestige in the eyes of the public and other police agencies. Nevertheless, shooting ability was still considered by part of the training staff as one of the best criteria available for predicting success in the *policeman* role.

Likewise, boxing skill and judo seemed related to the "old days" of muscle, although the modern *policeman* could expect to use his hands much more often than his gun or blackjack. Furthermore, the department's growing sensitivity to public relations seemed more attuned to techniques of verbal suasion than to threats of physical force.

and a strong aversion was expressed against so-called "killer" and "sadist" types. Good physical condition and outdoor interests thus constituted legitimate proof of masculinity, though masculinity was continually being tested. Many of the staff in all ranks spent off-hours and vacations in camping, hunting, and fishing activities. As one highly placed officer summed up the point, "This is a rural police department." Clearly, the department could be described as a "masculine culture," with sports and physical prowess among the main avenues of personal identification.

In general, attitudes toward the department were most often characterized by some concept of loyalty, sometimes bordering on a demand for self-sacrifice and unquestioning acceptance of orders from above. Some officers professed their own adherence to this pattern. For instance, one division chief, who thinly disguised his personal misgivings about the research, remarked at the first interview, "What I think about this whole thing doesn't matter. If the boss says you're OK, then you must be OK. Now, what do you want to know?"

Yet, in spite of this emphasis upon self-subordination, some positive feeling was expressed for qualities of personal motivation and ambition. Usually, however, this was translated into such behaviors as volunteering for special duty and spending extra hours on reports and investigations. Taking correspondence courses in law, photography, and other relevant skills was also taken as evidence of the "right attitude." The opposite approach was complaint and criticism. Those who engaged in these forms of expression were suspect, and assessments of their work would tend to reflect this image. Recruits who were especially marked as complainers by the training staff were sometimes ranked low in the class despite evidence of considerable proficiency in several parts of the program. Some respondents seemed to have difficulty in finding a legitimate place for initiative, given the rather strong emphasis upon following orders and deferring to rank. There was also evidence that consistent independence of thought and action would be interpreted as disruptive or even insubordinate behavior.

Immediately after graduation from school, each recruit was assigned to a post as a probationary *policeman* for a period of six months. Assignment was governed chiefly by the operational needs of the department and secondarily by a matching of the needs and characteristics of recruits with those of post commanders and other supervisors. If possible, a recruit who had certain deficiencies would be sent to a post whose commander was known to be capable in such areas, and who would presumably contribute to the recruit's improvement.

During probation the recruit was paired with an experienced *policeman* who was designated his supervisor and was responsible for "breaking him in." This was clearly an apprenticeship for the recruit, and it was obvious that this work relationship was a pivotal phase of the entire training process.[6] Not only was the recruit trained and judged in the formal aspects of his work, but he also received part of the whole legacy of attitudes, habits, and goals of his career as seen by his supervisor. The hours spent in the patrol car and around the post, as well as off duty, provided abundant opportunities for the recruit to get the "inside dope" and discuss many aspects of the job. A twelve-item rating form was filled out monthly by the *supervisory policeman*, with post and district commanders adding comments if they chose. A final service rating was given at the conclusion of probation, and if all raters agreed that the recruit had done satisfactory work, he was recommended for confirmation by headquarters staff as a regular *policeman*.

As might be expected, the "washout" rate was considerably lower in the probationary phase than in the school phase of the program. Recent data from the CSP indicated that during the six years between 1952 and 1957 there were thirteen schools with a total of 874 recruits. School-phase washouts averaged 27 per cent, with a range of 19 to 44 per cent, while probation-phase washouts averaged 3 per cent, with a range of 0 to 9 per cent.

The probationary field training was succeeded by a return to school for a four-week program of instruction in law and police technology. This school was conducted in a relaxed atmosphere of teacher and "proven" pupils. Functionally, it provided the recruits with an opportunity to share their field experiences and develop some standards both for self-evaluation and for the evaluation of matters of police procedure and organizational policy.

In spite of the problems generated by the internal structure of the school and the traumas produced by the impact of its rigors upon those recruits who had little preparation for this kind of life (e.g., army service), the main issue concerning the training program was the relationship between the formal and the field phases. Discussions with all ranks of personnel indicated that many believed large discrepancies existed between school material and field practice. One factor emphasized repeatedly was that no two posts functioned alike and that any generalization learned in recruit school would necessarily be modified at any given post. Many post pundits suggested that probationary *policemen* should "forget everything they learned in recruit school," the implication being that the rejection of school material was not merely con-

---

[6] In spite of the importance of this relationship, it was not possible for us to examine it systematically since only four recruits (none of whom were members of the recruit class in the study) were in this phase at the posts where we did our field work. Therefore only general comments and post facto analyses by relatively new *policemen* could be used as sources of information about the probationary period. Any future study of role acquisition should certainly include a systematic investigation of this type of relationship.

venient but often necessary if one were to gain the approval of field supervisors. There were some indications that supervisors considered a debunking
of recruit school as a regular part of their work, and some appeared to do it
with considerable relish.

School training was identified as a headquarters product, and thus, by
definition, alien and unworkable in field situations. The "book" (formal
rules and procedures) rarely prescribed ways of dealing with family quarrels,
dog fights, female inebriates, and the similar situations which *policemen*
defined as distasteful and stressful. Therefore, at least by omission, training
was often deemed inadequate or unrealistic. In this regard, field personnel
sometimes described training as antiquated in that too much time was
devoted to some subjects—for example, target shooting, fingerprinting, and
memorizing statutes—and too little time to such matters as high-speed
driving, relations with other enforcement agencies, and photography. Many
field supervisors seemed convinced that recruit school training was superficial
and/or misleading and that the "real" education of the new *policeman* began
with the probationary phase.

For the recruit, the discrepancies outlined above posed immediate
dilemmas for his own role behavior. In most cases where a choice of behavior
was involved, the expectations of the field staff received priority. Although
such discrepancies rarely required an open choice between authority figures,
it was always necessary for the recruit to remain alert to such variables as the
nature of the work he was doing, who was observing its performance, and
how its success would be evaluated.

Rules and Discipline

One of the significant organizational dilemmas resided in the interpretation
of department "rules and regulations" and "special orders." Ostensibly,
these represented the explicit prescriptions and proscriptions for appropriate
behavior, and—as such—were given considerable emphasis in recruit school.

The recruit soon discovered that the appropriate response to many of these
rules was not at all clear-cut, even though the rule itself was unambiguous.
There were, for example, a number of regulations which governed off-duty
behavior, such as those dealing with drinking, outside employment, and the
contraction of debts. Typical on-duty rules covered such matters as getting
post desk permission to go "out of service" for meals or on personal errands
while on patrol, carrying shotguns on all patrols, and preparing an accurate
log of activities each day.

The general headquarters view was that a literal adherence to the rules was
dysfunctional: it dried up sources of information from within the ranks

about important breaches of discipline, and it set up an image of the department as "chicken."[7] This unwritten but universally recognized "soft" policy
on many rules operated in the following way. Any requirement or prohibition
of conduct on the books was considered to be technically in force. However,
many rules could be violated in practice as long as no negative consequences
occurred. Thus, a man who violated a regulation ran the risk of backfire. He
took this risk knowingly and was presumably prepared to pay penalties commensurate with the importance of the regulation he had chosen to ignore or
contradict. Since anyone who abused the soft policy threatened its contin-
uance for all, co-workers of chronic abusers felt obligated to whip an offender
into line, or even turn them in occasionally. Abusers who were caught usually
received little sympathy from their peers.

The functionalism of this principle can be partly illustrated by the
regulation involving use of alcoholic beverages. Consumption of these
beverages was denied to all personnel except within the privacy of one's own
home, and even there intoxication was prohibited. Excessive drinking was a
serious offense, usually handled by trial board (court-martial) procedures and
usually resulting in such drastic penalties as demotion and dismissal. Yet, in
deference to the social patterns of the larger society, the department did not
strictly enforce this regulation, and many men in all ranks consumed alcohol
in public as well as private surroundings. However, it was clear that if any
dereliction of duty—failure to meet a crisis, even if unexpected (while off
duty), or conduct unbecoming an officer (getting into fights, etc.)—could be
traced to drinking, the guilty party could be sure that he would receive the
full weight of punishment prescribed for the offense. He was not free to
plead general laxity of the rules or to expect clemency because of violations
by others which were unprosecuted. It was this tacit code which preserved
the operational integrity of many regulations in the face of consistent though
discreet violations by large segments of the department.

The more technical violations of work procedures were usually handled by
warnings and reprimands at the post level. However, major infractions—
such as sleeping while on night desk and stealing post property or goods
seized in an arrest—were likely to be reported to district or Central Headquarters as trial board offenses.

A ten-year review of trial board records revealed that more than two-thirds
of all trials were for "social" offenses, as contrasted with "job content"
offenses. The major social breaches were intoxication, sexual promiscuity,
and financial negligence. The primary job-oriented offenses were negligence

---

7 This, of course, is a derogatory term applied to organizations and persons who are zealous
about demanding conformity to rules and regulations, particularly those involving details
and minor aspects of the job.

in handling complaints and absence without leave. These findings emphasize the intimate tie between the *policeman* and his organization. Although some regarded such control as an infringement of their personal freedom while off duty, most conceded the right of the department to protect its public image whenever necessary. This concession was probably a reciprocal of the department's "soft" policy on many of the regulations regarding off-duty behavior.

Field observation revealed that veteran *policemen* were more inclined to risk breaking rules than were younger ones. This undoubtedly stemmed from a greater knowledge of the relative importance of the regulations, the attitudes held by post officers towards them, and the extent to which violations could be safely made. Since recruits on probation were assigned to experienced *policemen*, they gradually lost their anxiety about regulations and learned the post norms for handling them. Although the headquarters staff was positive that many infractions of regulations passed unnoticed in the field, they were not inclined toward witch-hunts or enforcement for its own sake. They were primarily interested in violations which demonstrably affected the department's performance record and its public image.

The Uniform

Probably no single symbol was of greater importance to the role of *policemen* than the uniform. It provided both external identification to the public and internal communality among all ranks in the department. Most recruits felt awe and excitement when they put on the uniform for the first time, and they continued to enjoy the sense of prestige and accomplishment which it signified. The uniform represented the department in the person of the wearer, and any unacceptable behavior was regarded as a failure to "live up to the uniform." It was not surprising, therefore, to find a strong departmental emphasis upon appearance, as exemplified by the condition of the uniform and the manner in which it was worn.

Obviously some recruits and a few *policemen* enjoyed the element of visibility in their work as much as anything else. Being noticed, even if this produced withdrawal or fear in the observer, was for some a concrete recognition of importance and an antidote to the general anonymity of everyday life. Nevertheless, after the first flush had worn off, the uniform was discovered, on occasion, to be a liability. When wearing it, the *policeman*—now in full view—became a target for a wide variety of petty tasks, inquiries, abuses, and annoyances which a plainclothesman could escape. People watched his movements intently, partly for clues to the legitimacy of their own behavior and partly to judge the competence of his behavior. Although self-consciousness in this respect was a rarity in the department, many *policemen* expressed relief from strain when off duty and in street clothes. More important, several *policemen* believed that the uniform was sometimes a handicap on complaint or criminal investigations because shy or frightened persons were often intimidated by the uniform, or occasionally afraid of being seen talking to a man in uniform.

Significantly, the Commissioner never wore a uniform, since it was thought desirable to demonstrate that the department was ultimately under civilian control. Although all ranks in the Uniform Division wore uniforms on duty, many of the commissioned officers said they chose to wear civilian clothes at civic and public functions where such dress was optional. "After all," said a corporal, "there is something about wearing a uniform that makes a man different."

Enforcement Practices and the Law

The recruit soon discovered that the law itself provided only a partial guide for carrying out his role. In the first place, a considerable portion of his on-duty time was devoted to preparatory and summarizing routines, such as checking equipment (firearms, patrol cars), reading logs and orders, and writing reports. Most of these activities often encroached upon his off-duty time. Secondly, many of his patrol hours were spent looking for and anticipating trouble rather than actually dealing with it. Contact with the public frequently took the form of providing information (travel directions, weather and road conditions, etc.) and performing special services (delivering emergency messages, checking property, acting as guards and escorts, assisting motorists who had breakdowns, etc.). Generally, the larger urban posts had more demands for information, while the smaller suburban or rural posts received more requests for special services.

The great bulk of time, of course, was spent patrolling the road networks of the post area. Most posts divided their area into geographical units, taking into account traffic flow, population, and land use. Technically, a *policeman* was responsible for anything which occurred in his patrol area, and post forces could be concentrated at any point in times of emergency. The focal control mechanism was the post radio desk, usually manned by corporals, and by a rotation of *policemen* at night in the smaller posts. The desk man had continuous radio contact with all post patrols, neighboring posts, district headquarters, and, through the latter, Central Headquarters. Contact could also be made with county and local police units via appropriate frequencies.

The *policeman* on patrol was directly accountable to his home base and was expected to follow orders given by the desk man. Shutting off radio communication was considered a serious breach of work responsibility, and permission of the desk man was necessary before contact was broken. Leaving the radio voluntarily was considered "going out of service" and had to be justified each time. Other than this communication link with the radio desk, the *policeman* was isolated from the department for most of his tour of duty, and he was not expected to return to the post until he was finished. Since nearly all day shifts were solo,[8] the structure of shift activity was a product of each individual's work methods. It was precisely the time spent on his own which nurtured some of the central dilemmas of the *policeman's* role.

Although his recruit school mentors had hinted that the law was only the framework in which he was going to function, the academic atmosphere of the classroom and legal material which he had to memorize created a sense of confidence in "the book." To the recruit, the efficacy of his own judgment seemed puny indeed beside the legal monolith he was trying to comprehend. Enforcement of the law seemed an inevitable consequence of knowing the law, and such ambiguities as "extenuating circumstances" and "intent of the violator" seemed to obscure this logic. One presumably judged acts, not people. This was the safeguard of the *policeman* and it protected him from misplaced sentiment and moral weakness. Armed with this objective code, the recruit on probation was rather unprepared for the attitudes of men in the field toward the law.

Part of the debunking process was to reorient the recruit to the law on the basis of local norms. This reorientation was frequently far more drastic and complex than training school references to "modification" had implied. For example, at small rural posts a double standard of law enforcement frequently existed. Since post personnel and local citizens were generally familiar to one another, it was deemed impolitic to arrest traffic violators or other misdemeanants on the same basis as the rest of the public, especially if the citizen in question was prominent. One dramatic instance of this was observed during a field observation when a *policeman* gave chase to a speeder who tried to shake him off. The chase, over treacherous roads, continued for fifteen minutes at a speed in excess of 100 mph. After overtaking and stopping the car, the *policeman* discovered that the driver, accompanied by several friends, was an off-duty deputy sheriff from a neighboring county. This identification resulted in a strained admonition to "take it easy" instead of a rather severe arrest. The driver made no apologies, taking this treatment as a matter of course. The *policeman*, obviously uncomfortable in the presence of an observer, justified his behavior as necessary by explaining, "We've got to

[8] After dark, all shifts were two-man patrols due to the extra hazards of night work. Since public activity usually lessened as night progressed, having a partner was also a valuable psychological antidote for isolation, boredom, and depression.

work with these people. If I had given him a ticket they would get back at us later. We can't afford to make enemies."

It was also recognized that local driving habits were difficult to change, and that people took considerable time to adjust to new speed zones, stop signs, and parking limits.[9] Under the pressure of making proper distinctions, the *policeman* soon found himself rationalizing his conscious failures to enforce the law in terms of other needs of the department as it functioned in the community. It was worth overlooking a traffic violation or inconsequential misdemeanor if this achieved goodwill for post personnel and led to local cooperation on more serious and difficult tasks in the future. Most veteran officers appeared as past masters in building up this kind of "capital."

While the norms of the local community can be, more or less, easily rationalized and accepted by the neophyte *policeman*, the vagaries of local community jurisprudence came as a shock.[10] Some *policemen*, we suspect, never recovered. Few escaped without some sense of impotence and cynicism. As they came to observe the unjust treatment of those they arrested, or the usurpation of "due process" by the inept or corrupt, some *policemen* became seriously involved with questions of social justice.[11] Others, unconcerned or unwilling to confront such involvement, attempted to develop a fixed and universalistic means for enforcement.

In addition to the difficulties of a "political" interpretation of the law and a developing concern with the meaning of justice, many new *policemen* experienced early pangs of conscience. These feelings were in part related to the realization that the behavior they were punishing in others was not too different from their own. One new *policeman* explained: "When I hand out tickets, sometimes I remember when I committed the same violation. I wonder if I have a right to sit in judgment when I'm not in the clear myself. It makes me feel uncomfortable, somehow." Most *policemen*, perhaps, never fully resolve their personal involvement, though the costs are great. As an

[9] One *policeman* recounted, for example, that soon after his confirmation he issued a ticket to a local resident for a stop-sign violation. The man complained to the post commander that the sign had been changed from a "yield" sign only two weeks previously. He had traveled this route to work for years and was not yet adjusted to the new sign. Since the ticket had gone through, the post commander admonished the *policeman* to take such factors into account before issuing future tickets. Then he contacted the Justice of the Peace, who sustained the conviction but waived the fine.

[10] The *policeman* at any given post area operates in a maze of different political-legal systems. In any given instance, the one in which he gets caught up may be out of his control, or it may depend on the law or charge he selects, and frequently on the geographic location of the offense. (The final disposition of the case is often completely out of his control.)

[11] One headquarters officer, for example, went so far as to write a general philosophical paper in which he attempted an explication of the concept "arrest."

older *policeman* said: "Nobody is perfect, and I can't let my own mistakes stop me from doing my job. You'd go crazy putting yourself in the other guy's shoes all the time."

Another emotional experience of the new *policeman* was a sense of remorse and responsibility for the families of persons arrested. "The worst part," said one seasoned veteran, "is seeing the families of some of the characters you arrest. When you see some decent wife or kid choke up it's about all you can do to keep from doing it yourself. You know these guys deserve what they're getting, but it burns you up to be put on the spot." A particularly upsetting type of complaint was the domestic quarrel, which led one *policeman* to remark: "I'd much rather take on an armed hood than answer a call about a family squabble." Without doubt, assignments focusing on emotional and family problems were stressful and distasteful for most *policemen*.

Enforcement Practices and Public Relations

One of the notable characteristics of the department was its sensitivity, sometimes bordering upon preoccupation, with public relations. There were few officers who were not vitally interested in creating an image of policemen as courteous, helpful public servants. The stereotype of the "cop" as a big, tough, and often crude individual was abhorred. As far as the CSP was concerned, the "cop" was a thing of the past. At headquarters, several individuals were responsible for keeping publicity files on the department and tracking down any unfavorable reports or comments in the press. Written and telephoned complaints and inquiries were given obsessive attention, and assiduous efforts were made to satisfy or mollify even the most truculent critics. Favorable reactions were similarly collected and were frequently quoted in the annual report of the department. Among other things, it was considered very important to be able to answer any queries from the state legislators regarding negative reports, whether originating in the mass media or in letters from irate constituents.

Traffic arrests were rarely occasions for physical methods of enforcement, or even threats of it. So-called "rough stuff" was condoned only as a last resort or to insure self-preservation. As the CSP shifted to an emphasis on traffic and service functions, the occasions for "muscle" decreased. Thus in practice it was possible to carry out one's police duties in a businesslike way, and to take almost an educational rather than a punitive attitude toward the average violator.

While the "velvet glove" had "paid off" in the increased prestige and comparative rating of the CSP, its "psychic cost" to the *policeman* was, at times, quite high. Even though the "customer" (violator) was usually wrong, one had to treat him almost as if he were right. Many *policemen* found this a rather difficult process, particularly if the violator attempted to challenge the *policeman's* judgment, or to argue or cajole his way out of the situation. There was, consequently, a good deal of "back-room" criticism of the public behavior encountered in the day's work, and some chafing at having to repress one's reactions to such behavior. Constant and extensive emotional control was required during all working hours, except in the privacy of the patrol car or the relative seclusion of the post dayroom. One had to be particularly circumspect in the small communities, where overt hostilities would be quickly noticed. Adding this kind of restraint to the intra-departmental pattern of "keeping the lid on," it was not surprising that many men accumulated considerable affect without adequate release.

In a very real sense, the enforcement of traffic law has become a kind of watchful game between two groups of antagonists. As in any game, certain rules and modes of conduct exist which stabilize the probability of either side winning. Factors which alter these probabilities generally arouse resentment and controversy. Thus, such innovations as radar and unmarked cars were originally viewed as "unfair" and as "loading the dice" in favor of the police. Their introduction was greeted with storms of protest and legal battles. These resulted, in Central State, in a new "rule" that the police had to post signs warning that radar equipment was being used at some specified distance in advance of the radar car. Similarly, the unmarked car was soon altered to a "semi-marked" car. Thus the odds were rebalanced.

Following the ethics of the game, a segment of the public has consistently claimed its right to an even chance. From the perspective of the toll in deaths, injuries, and property loss, adherence to the game seems misplaced, if not grotesque. Despite the department's commitment to traffic law enforcement, and despite the obvious necessity for new techniques of enforcement, some *policemen* opposed such innovations precisely because they believed the public would object. Some were opposed because they enjoyed the game, and others were clearly ambivalent and uncomfortable when facing this issue.

Although headquarters staff recognized the negative feelings of the public toward such technical aids, they strongly rejected the philosophy of the "game" as it was applied to traffic law enforcement. "A lot of people think we owe them some kind of built-in leeway to violate the law," said one high-ranking officer. "Of course, we have to allow for [errors of] speed measurement and things of that sort. But we certainly don't intend to limit ourselves to old methods of enforcement. Traffic law is sometimes a matter of life and death, and if things like radar will help catch violators it's not only our right but our obligation to use them."

Obligation or not, a sizable minority of *policemen* preferred not to be assigned to radar patrol or driving unmarked cars. As one said, "I like to be out in the open. . . . You always get more guff and arguments from people when you stop them on radar or in the unmarked cars. I get enough sad stories as it is."

Selling the department to the "local public" was construed as a general post responsibility. The *policeman* new to a post was frequently assigned first to learning the post area. Among other things, this meant distinguishing between the "transient public" and the "local public," as well as learning who the local "influentials" were. *Policemen* were expected to develop "contacts" and potential informants, and on all routine patrols they were expected to spend some time in visiting and politicking in their patrol area. Personnel at some posts were pointedly encouraged to participate in "extra-curricular" activities, such as playing in local bowling and baseball leagues and coaching children's teams. The noncommissioned officers were expected to accept almost all of the inevitable invitations to speak before women's clubs and service groups, and to assist in charity drives (though not fund-raising) and holiday celebrations.

As we indicated in a previous section, such community involvements entailed certain risks for the organization. A few individuals began to identify themselves so strongly with local persons and groups that they became, in a very real manner, separated from the department. One *police-man*, whom we observed, embittered by lack of promotion, became a lone wolf, shunning the post staff both on and off duty. Although his intimate knowledge of the community and extensive contacts were a great asset to the department during complaint and criminal investigations, he used this "grass roots" support for the purpose of insulating himself from head-quarters. "The brass at HQ don't like me a damn bit," he said, with some relish, "but they know I'm pretty valuable on complaints. They don't inter-fere with me too much and neither does the sergeant. As long as I get results they let me alone. I like it that way. If the brass started pushing me around they'd hear from plenty of people around here." Obviously capitalizing on the department's sensitivity to public relations, he was able to establish a deviantly independent work pattern.

Other law enforcement agencies constituted a problematic segment of the local public, and the CSP's relationships with them were highly variable. Since the CSP was a state agency, there was some generally negative reaction on the part of local officials to post personnel as outsiders—as persons in, but not of, the community. State *policemen*, in turn, disparaged the quality of the local police agencies, which they felt were envious and somewhat awed by the power and efficiency of the CSP. With over 2,500 police agencies in Central State (not counting federal and military units), the CSP's working relationships varied from fierce competition to joint action. Where in some post areas as many as forty agencies might have overlapping jurisdictions, the complexity of their relationships (legal-extralegal, formal-informal, competitive-cooperative, and the like) was truly incredible. The net result of the *policeman's* contacts with other enforcement agencies was seldom one of confidence and ease. "I was always worried whenever I had to be out on an assignment with a man from another police organization," said one top-ranking officer. "I never knew whether I could depend on him."

Evaluation and Promotion

The process of evaluation began as soon as an individual applied for entrance to recruit school. Impressions gained from interviews, test scores, and community inquiries provided an image of each man which preceded his arrival at headquarters.

Despite the fact that recruit school was the only time that members of a given class could be judged on a comparative basis, no systematic files were kept on individuals. Final recruit rankings in each class were kept in the Training Division at headquarters, although a special request could procure these data. Many staff members recalled early impressions about *policemen*, presumably stemming from the latter's recruit days, but the reliability of such information was always open to question. Individual files were started during the probationary phase, beginning with the monthly rating sheets. From that point on, every man had direct access to his own file and could discuss his performance ratings with the officers who made them.

Observation of the recruit school revealed that no regular evaluation procedure was followed. At the end of the training period, the teaching staff had an evening session to rank the class in order. This consisted of a general discussion about each recruit and the establishment of high, low, and average groupings. Further discussion was necessary for within-group rankings. There was rapid consensus upon the best and poorest men, but considerable wrangling over the middle groupings. No one possessed a comprehensive picture of the entire program. Although each staff man had the grade records and other scores made by all recruits, these data were not often crucial (or even consulted) in the final determination. The entire process was carried on in an informal manner, with much bantering and broad humor. Major differences were resolved by compromise, or by one side "giving in" from exasperation or impatience. (Although the class ranking, regardless of the way in which it was derived, was potentially a measure of the efficiency of the training program and the accuracy of evaluation methods, there was no indication that it was ever used for such purposes.)

Once the *policeman* was in the field, and physically separated from the rest of his class, the crucial judge of his performance was the post commander. There was, indeed, general agreement in the department that the favorable opinion of the post commander was the most important means to achieve high evaluation at headquarters. Although it was not difficult for a recruit to learn this, he still had the problem of discovering and meeting his superior's expectations. This was often a frustrating task because many post commanders were far from clear and concise about their requirements, partly because they wanted to remain flexible enough to respond to policy changes which might emanate from district or central headquarters.

Actually, an area of ambiguity seemed to exist in which some post commanders resisted efforts by *policemen* and corporals to pin them down specifically. Thus there was frequent anxiety among *policemen* as to whether they were "reading" the post commander accurately and whether their behavior was in line with his expectations. The less-sensitive men refused to worry about such matters and used compatibility with their peers and "keeping your nose clean" as criteria for success. There were, of course, those who gambled on what was important, and those who had very positive opinions about what really counted. As one man said emphatically: "Don't let anybody kid you about what counts around here. When you come down to it, the thing they look at is the tickets. They might talk about ambition and the rest of it, but the tickets talk the loudest."

The expansion of the department during the late 1950's put new pressure upon the evaluation system. For the first time it became clear that seniority alone would not ensure every *policeman* an eventual promotion. The manpower increases in the department raised the ratio of *policemen* to officers from 16 to 1 to 22 to 1. It was now likely that a sizable number of *policemen* would not advance as far as post commander, and that quite a few might not even become corporals. In the entire history of the department, only one man had retired at the *policeman* level.

Although the officers and training staff did not emphasize this lowered opportunity level, most *policemen* were aware of it. Some were satisfied with lesser goals, while others redoubled their efforts (frequently making their intent public) to make outstanding records. This latter drive for recognition was probably responsible for the belief that taking on new duties and tasks would enhance one's promotional stock. Recruits were particularly strong in this belief.

Since most of the in-grade rewards (principally salary increases based on service time) were prescribed by Civil Service procedures, a new *policeman* could not expect promotion until the completion of his fifth year. Everyone accepted this pattern as normal, but the length of the preparatory period after the fifth year was not fixed. Whenever a new roster was prepared to fill vacancies, competition increased and tension built up in the various ranks. Although monetary rewards were most desirable, it was promotion which remained the key to career success. One of the traditional barometers of the career time table was the position a man held vis-à-vis the majority of his recruit school class. The latter was the reference point which indicated whether he was or was not advancing at an acceptable rate. So salient was one's recruit class as a "comparison group" that twenty years later some men could tell you the present assignment and rank of every man who had been in their class.

The big promotional hurdle was the first one—from *policeman* to corporal. If this was not cleared within ten years of service it was generally believed that a *policeman's* future was not bright. If still a *policeman* at about the eighth year, a man would enter a traditional two- to four-year period of jitters during

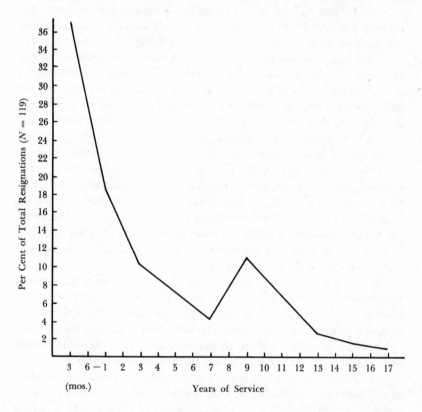

FIGURE 2–1

VOLUNTARY RESIGNATIONS BY YEARS OF SERVICE, 1949–58

which he "sweated out" his future. This is dramatically displayed in Figure 2–1, where the proportion of voluntary resignations takes a sudden and sharp upswing after the seventh year, not to return to that level for five more years.

Although resignations in the department had been highly concentrated in the first year, and are likely to remain so, future resignations during the seven- to twelve-year service interval might become more frequent. The officers at central headquarters were openly committed to a policy of merit promotion which would utilize seniority only if all other qualitative factors among candidates were about equal. Thus the competitive atmosphere might become intensified while the use of the recruit-class as a comparison group would probably diminish. Nevertheless, such changes as have occurred will probably not alter the basic fact that once a man has made a commitment to the department and gained a measure of identification with it he will be more inclined to adjust his goals than to totally reject the system (resign) if his personal expectations have not been achieved. Some evidence for this will be presented in the succeeding chapters.

In addition to the manifest ways in which work behavior affected evaluation, there were a number of beliefs which the men in the field held about the evaluation process which in turn affected their work behavior. For example, the assignment of recruits and the transfer of *policemen* were governed primarily by manpower needs and were not necessarily indicative of preferences by headquarters of some men over others. Yet there was an unmistakable conviction, in all ranks, that promotion assignments and transfers were not random. The gist of the belief was that the major avenue to achievement and promotion was through the large urban posts of the southern districts. The northern districts were considered something of a career dead end, and were frequently dubbed "Siberia." Long tenure at northern posts was therefore interpreted by *policemen* as indicative of a negative evaluation by headquarters. It was argued that commissioned officers were rarely selected from northern district post commanders.

It was quite true that the prospects of advancement for *policemen* were heavily dependent upon field promotion. Movement from staff assignments at district or Central Headquarters was slow and uncertain. It was not true, however, that promotions were biased by district assignment. As we shall show in our chapter on evaluation processes, the distribution of promotions from *policeman* to corporal and from corporal to sergeant manifested no significant relationship to district location.[12] We suspect that in large measure

12 It was extremely difficult to check the movement from sergeant to commissioned officer. From our limited data it appeared that the commanders of the twelve largest posts were more likely to be promoted than other commanders. The larger posts were all in the southern districts.

this discrepancy between fact and fiction is derived from the general ambiguity of evaluative criteria in the organization.

In the eyes of the new *policeman*, the whole evaluation system appeared as "a jungle with a few landmarks." The diversity of post practices and the ambiguities of policies on law enforcement made it necessary for him to "play it by ear" and to cultivate a kind of practiced opportunism with regard to matching others' expectations with appropriate behavior. In the final analysis, the payoff of high evaluation was promotion. Strategic informal contacts and skill in identifying and satisfying the expectations of superior officers were considered more important assets than formal Civil Service ratings and examination scores. "Getting an inside track" and "playing the game" were seen as the major techniques for achieving career success.

Our own experiences and observations suggest that *policemen* were not entirely unrealistic in their appraisal of the rating system. In general, evaluation seemed largely a product of agreement among raters by impressionistic methods rather than any measurement of performance by established standards. This was clearly the pattern employed by the recruit school training staff and, insofar as could be learned, by the committees charged with selection and promotion.

As competition for advancement is intensified, reliance upon these interpersonal techniques might be expected to increase. One mitigating element in the situation was that many men had entered the department with security and stability as their chief goals. A large number of these men probably would not adopt a vigorously competitive approach to promotion in favor of the automatic and purely bureaucratic rewards (i.e., seniority raises). Thus a group of ambitious go-getters might eventually dominate the promotional pattern, in contrast with a group of less-active (even apathetic) plodders who would achieve relatively few, if any, promotions in their department careers. In any event, restricted promotional opportunities could generate serious problems of recruitment. Recruit selectors might then have to consciously select men for each of several categories of career orientation, although given present methods of selection and evaluation this would seem a most difficult task.

In point of fact, many officers indicated that they were already classifying the *policemen* they knew in terms of advancement potential. An interesting aspect of this was the tendency for the evaluative image of a man to become solidified early in his career. If a *policeman* were low-rated on performance during his first two years, it was hard to alter his image in the eyes of others in spite of documentary evidence of improvement. This early "set" was advantageous for those who had a positive image and an obvious.handicap for those who did not. The long-range consequences of this remain to be seen.

Transfers and Mobility

Since the department operated over a rather large territory with a limited number of men, there was a considerable amount of internal mobility, especially in the *policeman* ranks. Many of these moves were in response to shortages of manpower, which might become acute at a post due to resignations, retirements, accidents, illness, or promotions. Other transfers within rank were made for disciplinary reasons or to remove a man with work problems or personality conflicts to a different environment. Most intra-rank transfers, however, were part of the general policy of the department to give *policemen* a variety of work experience at several types of posts. The steady volume of moving was high enough to support a regular van and crew. This service was supplied free by the department as its contribution to easing the financial hardships of transfers.

While headquarters staff was usually quite clear about the reason for a transfer, there was often uncertainty about such reasons among *policemen*. If a man received a notice that he was being transferred, he often began to think about the possible deficiencies of his performance. There was always some suspicion that a palatable given reason for a transfer might be a camouflage for a negative reason. The only transfer acceptable without qualms was the automatic one linked with a promotion.

Nearly all *policemen* conceded that transfers made "for the good of the department" were legitimate, even though this phrase was ill defined. This meant that the department was not obligated to justify transfers, and that this prerogative was accepted by recruits as one of the conditions of the job. Furthermore, the desire of many *policemen* for new and varied experience meshed well with the department's policy to provide it. It was recognized that one tended to "get into a rut" or become over-involved in the local community if he were stationed too long at the same post, especially a post in a small town.[13] In this sense, "the good of the department" and "the good of the individual" were jointly achieved by a continuous reshuffling, particularly on the *policeman* level. Thus if a man were at a post for four or five years, he could expect a transfer with increasing likelihood as his time at the post increased. If an additional man were needed at a post, he would frequently be selected from among those who had considerable tenure at other posts and were therefore "ripe" for a transfer. Obviously, some of these positions were filled by assignments of probationary *policemen* from recruit classes, but this did not meet needs arising between classes.

[13] Unlike the *policeman*, the post commander was indeed expected to become involved in the local community. Like the corporate manager, his involvement was seen as "good public relations," but precluded active participation in political or controversial matters.

In addition to these rather standardized channels for transfer, there were times when requests to be moved originated in the field. Such requests by *policemen* required the post commander's approval, and, for whatever reasons, fewer than half of the men who wanted to change posts had ever requested a transfer. No statistics were available on the number and kinds of requests made, nor the manner in which they were handled. It appeared that most requests were made for "personal reasons," which placed critical burdens upon the applicant. A distinction was drawn between acceptable reasons (e.g., illness in the family requiring a change of living conditions or proximity to medical facilities, or to be near to and support an aged or indigent parent) and unacceptable reasons (e.g., inability to "get along" at the post, desire to live in a rural or urban setting, or to return to one's home area). The fate of transfer requests was shrouded in mystery for most *policemen*. Although they acknowledged the right of headquarters to autonomy in dealing with their requests, they chafed under what they saw as the arbitrariness of many of the decisions and the cryptic manner in which they were conveyed.[14]

There was a general feeling among *policemen* that a transfer application should be granted unless there was a bona fide reason for rejecting it. The burden of justification would then fall upon reasons for rejection rather than upon those for acceptance. In essence, this would require the department to explain rejections in some detail. Headquarters staff resisted this point of view because it would eventually limit control over assignments and increase the chance of wrangling, appeals, etc.

Not all current factors, however, were in the direction of high mobility. The shift from single to married recruits, and their early establishment of families, tended to act as a brake on mobility. The desire for an adequate home life spurred *policemen* to build or buy houses even though faced with eventual and perhaps sudden transfer. Those who desired community ties were often reluctant to move, particularly with the attendant prospects of selling property hurriedly and uprooting children from school.[15]

It seemed that the adaptation of mobility patterns represented something

---

[14] Our questionnaire materials revealed that nearly half of all ranks accepted—and liked— transfer policies as they stood. The single major objection was to the use of transfers for disciplinary reasons.

[15] This does not mean that all *policemen* and their families disliked moving. Quite a few said they looked forward to moving about and that they felt the urge to change locations periodically. Furthermore, many of those who were not enthusiastic about moving accepted it as "part of the deal." One *policeman*, whose house had just been completed, said: "Well, we may only live in it a week but we sure enjoyed it. I'm just sorry we couldn't do [build] it earlier. When I'm assigned elsewhere, I'm not going to wait a day later than I can help it, and my wife agrees with me."

of a dilemma for department policy-makers. Although they wished to preserve their traditional control of transfers, they began to see that a fairly rigid system of periodic transfers was sometimes at variance with the practical requirements of middle-class family life, which they also regarded as desirable. While they wanted the men to have stable home lives and to fit in with the post community, they became aware that these objectives could interfere with the functional requirements of the department. In particular, high mobility gave *policemen* a broader base of police experiences, which, in turn, tended to make them not only better *policemen* but also more interchangeable. Further, routine transfers precluded the *policeman's* involvement with the community, and presumably fostered a greater involvement with and commitment to the organization. From all indications in the field, the clash of these orientations appeared likely to become even greater, until, at the very least, "localite" and "cosmopolite" orientations crystallized and both became accepted as legitimate.

Family Life

Although wives were not formally part of the department, their influence was recognized as powerful, and to some policy-makers ominous.[16] For a recruit in training, his wife was frequently a source of encouragement and incentive. At times she was also a producer of doubt and worry as she pondered a future as a *policeman's* wife. A majority of wives had no realistic preparation for the problems and issues to be faced in their new life.[17] While recruits were absorbed in an intense learning experience, their wives were left at home to wonder and speculate, gleaning only fragments of information from letters and short telephone conversations.

Most wives were willing to accept their husband's career choice without protest. The earliest worry was about the physical danger of the job. The

[16] We attempted no systematic investigation of the activities and attitudes of *policemen's* wives. Given the delicate tasks of participant observation and gaining the confidence of the *policemen* themselves during the limited time spent at each post, we considered it too problematic to attempt to interview wives formally. During field work, the researchers were invited into *policemen's* homes and they attended larger social gatherings at which wives were present. Many references to wives and families were also recorded in conversations with *policemen* on the job.

[17] Some time after our field notes had been compiled we discovered this almost elegant illustration—although from another state police agency—in this squib from the *New York Times*, July 19, 1962: "Faced with the problem of increasing numbers of state police recruits who quit because their wives object to their hours, Connecticut State Police Commissioner Leo J. Mulcahy last week issued an order: Henceforth, applicants will have to bring written permission from their wives."

presence of firearms was a constant reminder of this danger. The fear was intensified whenever a *policeman* in the department was involved in fatal gunplay. When such an event occurred during a training program, a subsequent resignation by a married recruit was not unusual, although the recruit's admission of such a connection was unlikely.

The first major family adjustment, after the recruit's two-month absence in school, was to the initial post assignment in a new community. Wives were immediately aware of being "special." Their conduct, and that of their children, was subject to above-average scrutiny, reflecting their husband's visibility. As one wife expressed it: "Whenever I go downtown shopping I feel like I'm wearing Bill's uniform. When people do special things for you, you're not sure if it's because they like you, or because you're a *policeman's* wife. It works the other way, too. If I park in the wrong place some people will talk about it. You live in a goldfish bowl." Like their husbands—but more slowly—most wives became accustomed to this visibility, and some unreservedly enjoyed any favored treatment they received.

The peculiarities of work schedules and the close work contacts among husbands practically ensured a good deal of interaction among post wives. Age and rank differences of husbands sometimes produced internal social stratification, especially in the larger urban posts. However, at most of the smaller posts, social life centered around department friendships, and there was a good deal of visiting among wives, particularly those whose husbands were working the same shift. At many posts, wives were organized as a kind of service auxiliary, which had regular meetings and whose activities were reported in department publicity. Some *policemen* felt that this kind of participation was a career asset for them, and at the same time increased their wife's identification with the department, as well as just keeping them busy. Under such conditions, few secrets could survive. Each wife was acutely aware of her husband's relative standing at the post in terms of his length of service and of the promotional picture for his recruit class as a whole.

Though not always successful in competing with the department for the time and attention of their husbands, wives extracted their "pound of flesh" in other ways. They usually could, and often did, apply steady pressure for promotion and higher economic rewards. The headquarters staff was agreed that many of the problems of promotion were traceable to the prodding and urging of wives. To most of the staff this was an irritating phenomenon, since they were accustomed to an era when wives were less numerous, and certainly less vocal, in the lower ranks.

One answer to the need for more income was the tempting prospect of part-time outside employment. Department rules were specific about not holding outside jobs without permission, and permission was difficult to get. A man wishing to take a part-time job was required to prove an emergency need. If he could do so, permission was usually granted for a specific period of time. Headquarters staff believed that an outside job detracted from the *policeman's* involvement and weakened their commitment to the department. In this sense, extra jobs posed the same competition as did wives. Although headquarters could be tough about such part-time jobs, it could not react in this way about marriage. Yet taking on extra work was often a direct result of wives' economic demands.

Despite these rules, there was—for some strange reason—a prevailing belief that many *policemen* currently held outside jobs which they had acquired without permission. Very little field evidence was discovered to support this belief. However, a kind of barter system was likely to emerge wherever several men had useful skills or resources. One might trade his masonry work for another's painting, and keep a rough account in terms of hours. Although eliminating expenditures rather than bringing in cash, trading services in this fashion represented a tangible economic gain to participants.

The variations in working periods resulting from the shift changes of the post schedule made it difficult to plan social engagements more than a week in advance, and a sudden emergency call, at any hour, took immediate priority. Even days off and vacations were not immune to such calls. Every home activity was harassed by this potential "24-hour call." In a sense, it was similar to the total availability of the physician, and, to some extent, the soldier. The following reaction was typical. "You have to live from day to day in this job; the schedule is the boss. If you plan anything in advance, it's an even bet you'll never get to do it. I never accept an invitation for us without telling people we might not show up."

Added to these uncertainties was the inevitable possibility of transfer. Whereas a promotional transfer could lessen the trauma of moving, it was hard to feel pleased about a move identified only as being "for the good of the department." One division chief commented bluntly: "Wives are the biggest headache we have on transfers. Even if they agree to move, they'll complain about the place they move to. If his wife doesn't accept this kind of life, a *policeman* ought to leave his job."

The strong career identification which characterized *policemen* resulted in obvious and pervasive conflicts between job and family loyalties. Few members of the department regarded job and family as well integrated. Most believed that they had to tailor their family lives to their job requirements, rather than the reverse. While most *policemen* were quite willing to adjust family to career, wives—on the whole—seemed less tractable. Some *policemen* actually said they would leave the job if it seriously jeopardized their family life. Few felt they would ever have to confront this choice.

Concluding Comments

In presenting this précis of our observational data we have attempted to provide an overview of the social organization of the Central State Police. For the moment, we seek a first approximation of the theoretical implications of these data.

It seemed to us—perhaps more clearly than this summary of our observations has displayed—that the role of *policemen* was characterized by considerable fluidity, by a lack of clarity and precision. Granting the correctness of this assessment, two plausible lines of explanation warrant comment. A first reaction to the findings of this chapter might be one of acceptance of these results as "expected" and "normal." It might be contended that any complex social system poses continuous behavioral dilemmas for individuals who function in it, and that trial-and-error learning is the basic "rule" of socialization. Constant changes in the environment require continuous behavioral adjustments to meet the needs of the moment, and here there is no substitute for experience. Certain dilemmas facing *policemen* may thus be seen and accepted as really part of the structure of the organization itself. The lack of uniform perceptions of the role (as represented, for example, by the divergent group evaluations of the formal training program) could be regarded as a natural consequence of group differences in status, in values, and in contact with the role segment under analysis. The phenomenon of "playing it by ear," which seemed so central, could thus be regarded as an intrinsic element of role behavior. This orientation would immediately raise the problem of identifiability of any significant uniformities in behavioral systems. It would certainly tend to limit the levels of role theoretical explanation, perhaps reducing role theory to a series of numerous low-order generalizations having narrow applicability.

On the other hand, if we had anticipated a more orderly and definitive pattern of role delineation and function, it might be argued that the confusions and dilemmas reported in the chapter were largely due to the method of investigation rather than the structure and content of the role itself. Given the assumptions that 1) role expectations are clearly defined by known "audience groups";[18] 2) perceptions of these expectations are accurately

[18] The term "audience group" refers to those groups by whom the actor sees his role performance observed and evaluated, and to whose expectations and evaluations he attends. For its obvious shorthand value, we shall make frequent use of the term.

From a theoretical perspective, the introduction here of the concept of audience group, however much refinement it may need, carries with it certain decided advantages: (*a*) Its

and uniformly perceived by incumbents of a particular position; and 3) the situational context in which role behavior occurs is essentially nonproblematic (i.e., normative), such an argument would be compelling.

If field observation represented the sole source of data about the role, there would be little prospect of successfully meeting this criticism. We have, however, adduced a great variety of data—derived chiefly from questionnaires, test protocols, and the formal records of the police department—which will permit comparisons with these observational materials. Beyond providing a cross-check of the field data, such comparisons constitute important indicators of the tenability of the theoretical assumptions themselves. In this connection, as we noted in the introductory chapter, role theory has not fulfilled its early promise in the eyes of many critics. We have suggested that the fault lies more with the conceptualization and assumptions of role theory than with research methodology. Perhaps an examination of these assumptions will prove so crucial that the comparative evaluation of data collection techniques will become a secondary issue. In either event, we have now presented the issues, both substantive and theoretical, which constitute the foci of the chapters to follow.

---

usage proscribes the arbitrary assignment of "counter-roles" ("alters," "role partners," etc.) by the observer. (b) Recognition of the symbolic character of an audience group helps emphasize that the physical presence of others is neither a necessary nor a sufficient condition for role performance. (c) The conception of audience group is flexible enough to encompass idiosyncratic sources of expectancies and evaluation, "significant others," "role models," etc. (d) This conception is further flexible in that it does not carry the implication that the actor necessarily conforms to the expectations of his audience. (e) Finally, the use of the concept of audience group, despite the nascent state of reference-group theory, hopefully directs attention to the possibility, or perhaps the necessity, of integrating reference-group theory and role theory. (Cf. R. H. Turner, "Role Taking, Role Standpoint, and Reference Group Behavior," American Journal of Sociology, 61 [1956], 316–28.)

CHAPTER 3

Perception of the Role: The Investigation of Consensus

Derivation and Application of Instruments

To BEGIN our formal role analysis we needed to determine whether the various expectations and evaluations involving the *policeman* role could be linked to specific audiences, and whether these expectations and evaluations had definable consequences for those who perform the role.

In order to hold the number of audience groups in bounds for the present study, we decided to limit ourselves to the hierarchy of ranks in the Uniform Division of the department. It was our guess that the major definition of the *policeman* role emanated from the uniformed rank groups. (In Chapter 6 we shall point out that in some situations the expectations of audiences outside the department—especially family and friends—were equally or more important than the rank groups.) For this reason the information we elicited from the rank groups furnished most of the raw material for our quantitative analyses here. The major sources of data were self-administered questionnaires filled out by current and past members of the Uniform Division. The following comprised the range of the rank variable, roughly covering a career pattern in the department: recruit; policeman; corporal; sergeant; officer; retired; resigned. (In Chapter 4 we shall further divide the recruit group into four stages, based upon "natural" breaks in the training process.)

While audiences (and researchers) may often agree about formal role requirements and specifications, they may differ or ignore the expressive and affective components of role behavior. Expressive elements are frequently treated as reactions to a role, and therefore as derivative phenomena. We suspect that these elements ought to be construed as part of the role and may have even greater influence upon some role performances than do the formal requirements.

The role requirements of the *policeman* were often clearly outlined in the department's regulations, and were systematically presented to recruits during the training period. These other, non-instrumental aspects of the role generally develop and are transmitted in a less formal manner. They entailed the challenge of having never been rigorously studied in a role theory framework; and we selected a set of *areas* utilized in a previous study, but in a different theoretical and occupational context. These role areas were:

Advancement Opportunity, the extent to which the job offers satisfactory career goals and adequate, impartial procedures for achieving them.

Social Value and Prestige, the extent to which the job fulfills important public services and the degree to which the public recognizes and values such services.

Freedom to Express Feelings, the degree to which the job permits the incumbent to convey his attitudes and emotions to others without incurring negative questions and responses from them.

Self-Realization, the degree to which the job provides the incumbent with opportunities to use initiative and develop his talents.

Job-Family Compatibility, the extent to which job requirements can be met without sacrificing family interests and obligations.

A series of questions for each area was designed to explore two dimensions, which we labeled *blockage* and *importance*. The blockage dimension focused upon the extent to which a respondent felt that *policemen* were thwarted or penalized in the area under consideration. The importance dimension focused upon the degree to which an area had or should have had personal significance and concern for *policemen*. These blockage and importance questions (see Appendix 1) provided the respondent with a series of graded choices, usually four.[1] The questions in each area were matched, so that for each blockage question there was a corresponding importance question.

Blockage Item	*Importance Item*
To what extent does your job cause you to neglect your family?	*How important is it to have a job that doesn't interfere with, or cause you to neglect, parts of your family life?*
1. —— To a great extent	1. —— Extremely important
2. —— To a considerable extent	2. —— Of considerable importance
3. —— To some extent	3. —— Quite important
4. —— Not at all	4. —— Of some importance

[1] The selected dimensions, and the questions which implement them, were developed by the Social Research Service at Michigan State University for a project studying stress in various occupational settings. The materials in the present study were adapted from the original instruments with the generous assistance and permission of Dr. D. L. Gibson and Dr. J. Useem, co-chairmen of the stress project. The choice of areas was made from a pool of more than twenty, and represented those which seemed to us to have most relevance for *policemen*. At first we anticipated that a group of scale types could be derived for each area since most sets of responses had scaled in the studies for which they had been developed. However, scalogram analysis was not successful enough to warrant its use in the present context. Nevertheless, an item analysis, using arbitrary weights and summated scores, indicated sufficient discriminatory power for us to retain all items.

We assumed that while some persons would experience practically no blockage on the above item, it would be rare for anyone to feel that his family relationships were completely secondary to work obligations. Therefore a more balanced range of alternatives is given for the importance variable. The use of a single dimension for a role component, as has usually been the case in studies where descriptive features of a role are the primary concern, appeared to us to be an oversimplification. Although multiple dimensions potentially complicate analysis and presentation, we believed that this type of analysis was empirically more valid. Furthermore, this approach offered a way of exploring not only the dimensions of blockage and importance but also those new dimensions which might be produced by the interplay of blockage and importance.

In all areas, questions were presented in simple terms. Response choices reflected realistic modes of expression rather than a fixed verbal or numerical scale. The reason for this variety of format was to minimize any temptation by respondents to answer all the questions with a single level of intensity in rote fashion. Since nearly all of these questionnaires were administered by mail, there would have been no opportunity for interviewers to overcome this kind of response set. (See Appendix 1 for testing details.)

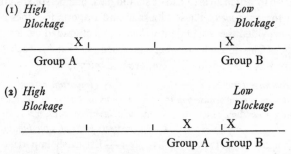

In example 1 there is an absolute difference between groups A and B which is statistically significant. In example 2 there is a much smaller difference between the two groups. Yet this may still be statistically significantly different. It is example 2 which illustrates the sort of situation we find in blockage scores. It is necessary to keep this relative comparison in mind to avoid the tempting error of treating the group differences per se as precise measures of the degree of blockage and importance.

After responses on the blockage-importance questionnaire were obtained from all of the rank groups in the Uniform Division, a frequency distribution of scores was derived for each group in each area. On this basis, each rank group could be compared with any other. In looking at the scores for each rank group in each area it is important to remember that these scores represent *relative* characterizations. By way of illustration, in the area of Social Value and Prestige *no* group actually feels blocked; however, some groups (officers and retired) think that *policemen* are significantly less blocked than other groups (*policemen* and recruits). What we are primarily interested in is the significance of group difference wherever we find it along the continuum. The above illustration may help dramatize this.

In this and the following chapter we shall be using several basic variables for comparative purposes. For orientation, we shall mention here the main variables and their relations to one another.

> *a*) *Rank*. Seven positions in the structural hierarchy of the department are identified, from "recruit" through "retired."
>
> *b*) *Area*. There are five constructed classifications of attitudes about the role.
>
> *c*) *Type*. There are four constructed modes of response in the several areas (which we shall introduce more systematically below). These modes are based upon scores representing relative amounts of blockage and importance perceived by respondents in each of the five areas. Blockage and importance scores, although computed independently, are combined to produce the types.

Essentially, all of the computations in these two chapters are cross-tabulations of these three variables. For example, since the areas reflect segmental dimensions of the role, we can see if rank accounts for any significant differences in these dimensions. Then, by holding rank constant, we can apply the type classification to the areas in a similar fashion. We can also examine type distributions among ranks, and so on.

Blockage and Importance: Area Comparisons by Rank

Table 3–1 shows what the different ranks report about blockage in the five areas. The groups in each cell are those whose perception in an area differs significantly in either direction from that expressed by the rank group in the left marginal column. The marginals show clearly that reports of blockage are not consistent across ranks. Corporals, sergeants, and resigned show considerably higher levels than the other groups. Officers and retired rarely show high levels, while recruits[2] and *policemen* fall between. The area

---

[2] The blockage and importance batteries were administered to recruits at three strategic points in the training process:

Recruit I, about halfway (one-and-a-half months) through the formal training program at headquarters. It was not given at the start because the group was already in training when we began the study. A delay would have meant at least a year's wait for the next class.

Recruit II, the end of the field assignment phase (about six months after the start of training). During this period the recruits had worked at assigned posts under supervisory *policemen*.

Recruit III, the end of the probationary phase (after twelve months after the start of training). This marked the official end of recruit status, culminating in formal appointment as a regular *policeman*.

marginals reveal fewer distinctions than do the rank marginals. Advancement Opportunity provided the most differences and Social Value and Prestige the least, with the remaining three areas falling between. Thus there is some evidence that different areas of a role may engender different degrees of consensus among audience groups. The data offer no guides for a systematic explanation of the occurrence of these variations.

Further interpretation of the blockage distribution is obtained by examining the cell distributions of the differences. For the total 30 differences displayed in Table 3–1 a distinct internal pattern is visible, obscured somewhat by the placement of the resigned and retired groups. Since our criterion here is rank, and almost all of the resigned group were recruits or *policemen* at resignation, we decided to consider the resigned as part of a "cluster" with recruits and *policemen*. Similarly, since almost all of the retired personnel held commissions at the time of their retirement, we classified them with officers. Thus we generated a threefold set of clusters which appears to parsimoniously account for rank variation: cluster A was comprised of recruits, *policemen*, and resigned personnel; cluster B contained the corporals and sergeants; and cluster C the officers and retired personnel. Only five significant blockage differences (about 16 per cent) occur *within* cluster groups; the remainder occur *across* clusters.

The distribution of importance by area indicates little in the way of clustering or consistency. Rank differences in importance follow the clustering observed for blockage, and the total number of importance differences among ranks is greater for importance (49) than for blockage (30).

The excess of importance differences over blockage differences is difficult to explain, but it points up the fact that neither of these dimensions can predict the extent or direction of the other. Within Table 3–1 there are only three cells which show differences involving the *same* groups for both blockage and importance.[3] Almost without exception, significant group differences in blockage were not accompanied by significant differences in importance. The meaning of this either/or phenomenon might be that avoidance of stress could be accomplished by compensating for relatively high emphasis on one dimension with a relatively low emphasis on the other. We shall

---

Although data were available for several time periods of recruit response, only Recruit III data is included here since it is the most mature phase of recruit experience. The other time periods will be included in the pattern of discussed intragroup change analyzed in the next chapter.

[3] These are Advancement Opportunity, recruits greater than officers; Self-Realization, corporals greater than *policemen*; and Job-Family Compatibility, resigned greater than officers.

TABLE 3–1
BLOCKAGE AND IMPORTANCE AREA COMPARISONS BY RANK

Rank Group	Advancement Opportunity (B)	Advancement Opportunity (I)	Social Value and Prestige (B)	Social Value and Prestige (I)	Freedom to Express Feelings (B)	Freedom to Express Feelings (I)	Self-Realization (B)	Self-Realization (I)	Job-Family Compatibility (B)	Job-Family Compatibility (I)	Total (B)	Total (I)	Cluster
Rec. III	Off.	Corp. Off.				Corp. Sgt. Off. Ret.				Corp.	1	7	A
Pol. ...	Off. Ret.			Rec. III		Corp. Sgt. Off. Ret.			Rec. III Off.	Ret.	4	6	A
Res. ...	Off. Ret.					Corp. Sgt. Off. Ret.	Rec. III Pol. Off. Ret.		Rec. III Off.	Pol. Corp. Sgt. Off. Ret.	8	9	A
Corp. ..	Off. Ret.			Rec. III Pol.	Pol. Ret. Res.		Pol. Off. Ret.	Rec. III Pol.	Rec. III Off.		10	4	B
Sgt. ...	Off. Ret.	Pol.	Off.	Rec. III Pol. Res.	Pol. Corp. Ret.			Rec. III Pol. Corp. Res.			6	8	B
Off. ...		Pol.		Rec. III Pol. Res.	Pol.			Rec. III Pol. Res.			1	7	C
Ret. ...				Rec. III Pol. Corp. Sgt. Res.				Rec. III Pol. Res.			0	8	C
Total B....	9		1		7		7		6		30		
I....		4		14		12		12		7		49	

NOTE.—The table can be read most easily with the following points in mind: 1) for each rank group in the left marginal column there is a row of cells for the five areas; 2) within each cell are a blockage item and an importance item; 3) a cell entry of a rank group is made for any area in which this group was found to have significantly *less* blockage and/or *less* importance than the rank group in the corresponding left hand margin. All cell entries are significant at $p < .05$ (Kolmogorov-Smirnov, two-tailed test).

EXAMPLE.—In the Advancement Opportunity cell for recruit III we find that officers showed less blockage while corporals and officers showed less importance in this area than did recruit III.

discuss this further when we consider the distribution of type responses in the next section.

Turning to Table 3–2, which is a recasting of Table 3–1 with areas collapsed, we can see more clearly that the blockage and importance differences in the five areas are not randomly distributed among the ranks. The cell entries indicate the number of areas in which there is a significant difference between two rank groups. For example, in the first row the *policemen* are significantly *higher* than recruits in one area of blockage and one area of importance. Looking at the row marginals for instances where each rank was significantly *lower* than any of the other ranks, we can see that cluster C accounts for most of the blockage differences, whereas cluster A accounts for most of the importance differences.

Table 3–3 offers additional evidence to suggest that *distance* between ranks is related to the frequency of significant differences between ranks. Only eight differences are within clusters while one-step cluster differences (between A and B or B and C) are more numerous. The proportionate incidence of significant differences (the ratio of the actual to the possible number of differences) clearly increases with distance and is greater for importance than for blockage.

The materials presented so far may be summarized in terms of the implica-

TABLE 3–2

AREA DIFFERENCES IN BLOCKAGE AND IMPORTANCE BY RANK PAIRS

HIGHER

Rank	Rec. III B	I	Pol. B	I	Res. B	I	Corp. B	I	Sgt. B	I	Off. B	I	Ret. B	I	Total B	I	Cluster
Rec. III			1	1	2	—	1	2	—	2	—	2	—	2	4	9	
Pol. ...	—	—			1	1	2	2	1	3	1	3	—	2	5	11	A
Res. ...	—	—	—	—			1	—	—	2	—	2	—	2	1	6	
Corp. ..	—	3	—	1	—	2			1	1	—	—	—	1	1	8	B
Sgt. ...	—	1	—	1	—	2	—	—			—	—	—	1	0	5	
Off. ...	1	2	2	1	3	2	3	—	2	—			—	—	11	5	C
Ret. ...	—	1	1	2	2	2	3	—	2	—	—	—			8	5	
Total ..	1	7	4	6	8	9	10	4	6	8	1	7	0	8	30	49	
Cluster	A				B				C								

NOTE.—Entries are the number of areas in which pairs differed significantly.

TABLE 3-3

CLUSTER DIFFERENCES IN BLOCKAGE AND IMPORTANCE

			Number of Significant Differences		
Cluster Distance	Blockage	Importance	Total Difference	Possible Differences	Percentage
Within A	4	2	6	30	20.0
Within B	1	1	2	10	10.0
Within C	0	0	0	10	0.0
Between A–B . . .	5	21	26	60	43.3
Between B–C . . .	10	2	12	40	30.0
Between A–C . . .	10	23	33	60	55.0
Total Differences . .	30	49	79		
Possible Differences .	105	105	210		
Percentage . . .	28.6	46.7	37.6		

Cluster A: Recruit   Cluster B: Corporals   Cluster C: Officers
        Policeman   Sergeants   Retired
        Resigned

tions they have for role analysis. Initially, by selecting non-instrumental aspects (the five areas) of the *policeman* role, and by measuring these on two dimensions (blockage and importance), we sought to investigate degrees of consensus among and within rank groups. The data indicated that (*a*) there are significant rank differences within these five areas; (*b*) there are area differences in addition to those of rank; (*c*) blockage and importance account for unequal portions of these differences, with importance displaying relatively more differences; and (*d*) there are significant differences by clusters of ranks based upon rank distance, with more differences being associated with greater distance. Despite the highly structured character of the CSP organization, there was a low order of consensus on these areas of the *policeman* role.

The Blockage-Importance Types

In the preceding analysis of ranks and areas we observed that blockage and importance responses displayed a low order of association. Since our aim was to deal with the interplay of these variables, we extracted from combined blockage–importance scores a fourfold set of *types*.

The index was derived in the following manner. First, the median scores for both the blockage and the importance instruments were computed for *policemen* in each of the areas. (Scores above the median we symbolized by a + and those below the median by a —. The first sign in each type refers to blockage and the second to importance.) Scores for all of the other rank groups were dichotomized on the basis of the *policeman* median in the appropriate area. Given the absence of any external norms for these blockage-importance measures, we chose the *policeman* medians; first, in order to provide an internal means of standardization, and second, because our questionnaires focused upon perceptions of the *policeman* role.[4]

Blockage-Importance Types

Type Code	Meaning
+ +	Conflict (stress, ambivalence)
+ —	Acceptance (adjustment, compromise)
— +	Satisfaction (accomplishment, ambition)
— —	Indifference (unconcern, withdrawal)

These types, quite obviously, are not direct empirical categories. As standardized constructs they facilitate the simultaneous comparison of blockage and importance by rank and by area; and despite their artificiality they may well be a more sensitive expression of role imagery than the blockage-importance variables taken one at a time. The meanings, as presented in the above typology, are attempts to translate the four types into attitudinal patterns. Although there is some arbitrariness about these translations, we felt that the accepted verbal meanings of blockage and importance are themselves consonant with the meanings suggested for the codes.

Frequency distributions were constructed for all ranks by area, and Table 3-4 summarizes these distributions. Each area grouping in Table 3-4 shows the relative prevalence of types by rank. Both frequencies and percentages are given in each cell, and the percentages are based on the original size of each group. The failure of percentages in four of the areas to total 100 per cent was due to the omission of the median interval. Again, it must be emphasized that we are using the distribution of the *policeman* group as a criterion upon which to base comparisons among rank groups. Thus the *policeman* distributions tend toward equality of type frequency, and in only two instances does any type contain more than 25 per cent of the total

[4] By this procedure each respondent was given a combined score, determined by his own blockage and importance scores in the area being tabulated. The *policeman* group, since it was the criterion group, showed a tendency toward equal distributions among the four types. However, when the median fell on a score interval rather than between two intervals, it was necessary to use the whole interval as midpoint. Scores falling within whole-interval medians were considered ambiguous, and all respondents having such scores for either variable were eliminated from rank comparisons in the area. Using this procedure, the total size of each rank group was reduced, but in most instances over four-fifths of each rank group were included in the computations.

TABLE 3-4
BLOCKAGE-IMPORTANCE TYPES BY AREA AND BY RANK

	Policemen f	%	Corporals f	%	Sergeants f	%	Officers f	%	Retired f	%	Resigned f	%
					Advancement Opportunity							
Conflict (++) . .	11	17	32	29	17	33	3	8	6	12	18	45
Acceptance (+−) .	15	23	10	9	1	2	2	6	1	2	3	8
Satisfaction (−+) .	16	25	31	28	18	35	21	58	30	59	10	25
Indifference (−−) .	11	17	16	15	8	15	6	17	6	12	4	10
		82		81		85		89		85		88
					Social Value and Prestige							
Conflict (++) . .	11	17	38	35	21	41	9	25	17	33	5	12
Acceptance (+−) .	18	28	19	17	9	17	3	8	5	10	10	25
Satisfaction (−+) .	22	34	36	33	22	42	21	59	26	51	13	33
Indifference (−−) .	13	21	16	15	0	0	3	8	3	6	12	30
		100		100		100		100		100		100
					Freedom to Express Feelings							
Conflict (++) . .	14	22	18	17	6	12	4	11	3	6	15	38
Acceptance (+−) .	10	16	46	42	24	46	20	57	18	35	5	13
Satisfaction (−+) .	11	17	5	5	0	0	0	0	2	4	9	23
Indifference (−−) .	13	20	17	16	12	23	6	17	13	26	5	13
		75		80		81		85		71		87
					Self-Realization							
Conflict (++) . .	6	9	39	36	22	42	8	22	15	29	14	35
Acceptance (+−) .	13	20	16	15	3	6	3	8	0	0	6	15
Satisfaction (−+) .	15	23	21	19	11	21	15	42	20	36	4	10
Indifference (−−) .	9	14	3	3	0	0	1	3	2	4	1	3
		66		73		69		75		69		63
					Job-Family Compatibility							
Conflict (++) . .	17	27	16	15	10	19	4	11	7	14	19	48
Acceptance (+−) .	9	14	25	23	9	17	5	14	12	23	5	13
Satisfaction (−+) .	10	16	22	20	13	25	16	44	11	21	8	20
Indifference (−−) .	16	25	32	29	13	25	10	28	17	33	4	10
		82		87		86		97		91		91

NOTE.—Where percentages do not total 100, scores falling within the median interval were excluded (see n. 4).

policeman distributions. No type contains more than one-third of the cases. Only in Self-Realization did there seem to be much attrition. However, this occurs within all ranks in this area, thus preserving comparability.

Looking first at the within-rank distributions of Figure 3-4, we see that only in five instances does any type contain more than 50 per cent of the total group—a figure which, for now, we shall arbitrarily employ to designate "consensus."[5] Only the officer and retired groups exhibited such a level of concentration. More common was the occurrence of bi-modality in which two types in an area would, in combination, account for high proportions of a rank total. It is difficult to assess the meaning of such bi-modality, but the type differences within rank groups suggest the existence of meaningful empirical types not yet identified.

As a practical problem, these type differences may at times produce ambiguities within a rank group whenever judgments about actual role performance must be made. For instance, a sergeant who perceives the *policeman* role as being (in our terms) a conflict type with respect to Advancement Opportunity may react to a particular *policeman's* work quite differently than a sergeant who perceives the role as satisfaction type. The data show that these two types displayed a bi-modal distribution for sergeants in this area. Thus, in a sense, either of these types could be interpreted by a *policeman* as having validity for the sergeant group as a whole. If a *policeman* were exposed to the perceptions of most of the sergeants in this area, he might well be confused. In essence, the accurate perception of the lack of consensus in an audience group could produce uncertainty and frustration in the perceiver. This would certainly occur if he were anticipating a high degree of consensus in that group.

We are not yet sufficiently confident about type meanings to make predictions from type to actual role behavior. Nevertheless, we might be willing to make predictions about role perceptions for the group as a whole if there were consensus within a rank group, say in the order of 75 per cent or better for a given type. If our present data accurately reflect the amount of consensus within rank groups, such predictions would not yield a high degree of success. With sufficient knowledge we might be able to predict for an individual respondent in a given area, but this would not encourage us to generalize to his rank group as a whole.

[5] An alternative criterion of consensus could require the percentage of any one type in an area to exceed the combined total of the other three. For example, in Table 3-4 conflict type for resigned in Advancement Opportunity and acceptance type for corporals and sergeants in Freedom to Express Feelings would then qualify as representing consensus, even though each contained less than 50 per cent of the group total. The drawback is that in distributions with pronounced bi-modality (as retired in Self-Realization) it is difficult to give much weight to a rather slight difference in favor of one type.

Our findings suggest that consensus about these non-instrumental aspects of the *policeman* role was weak or doubtful. In Table 3–4 we have seen that consensus (using our 50 per cent criterion) does not occur uniformly among the role areas or audiences in the department. Interactionist theory has usually assumed consensus within and among audience groups about a role, and has implied that successful learning of a role is dependent upon such consensus. We can now question these assumptions.

One might interpret this lack of consensus within and among audience groups as being evidence against any theory based upon the existence of uniformities of role imagery in social systems. Such an interpretation, however, is still tentative. If we examine the material further, we can locate several similarities of response patterns in the five areas. First of all, our clustering of rank groups seems to hold up, especially in clusters B (corporal-sergeant) and C (officer-retired). In the areas of Social Value and Prestige and Freedom to Express Feelings, the four rank groups in clusters B and C showed general similarity, with some tendency toward bi-modality. While bi-modality prevents a clear-cut pattern, it narrows the range of possibilities and permits better delineation of prevailing types. In Advancement Opportunity, for example, the combination of conflict type and satisfaction type would account for a high enough percentage of respondents to yield limited predictability in cluster B. Since these two orientations toward advancement may lead to sharp behavioral differences in role evaluation, they could be made the basis of further investigation to determine why this area is seen as relatively blocked by some and relatively unblocked by others. Unfortunately, this was not done in the present study because we were not in a position to follow up such a finding.

There is probably only a limited number of groups to which a role learner may be initially exposed. Where initial learning occurs in formal, organized settings, as in the case of *policemen*, the primary learning situations will probably reflect the attitudes of the special group(s) which the trainers represent and the grounds on which they are chosen. In the CSP, officers exercised direct control over training; they drew up the curriculum and assigned teaching functions. Secondly, training took place at Central Headquarters, where most of the officers were concentrated. Thirdly, most of the teaching staff, drawn from other rank groups, was regularly assigned to Central Headquarters, or to units in the immediate vicinity. From this combination of factors it was likely that the early recruit image of the *policeman* role would develop in the direction of the dominant type among officers. For example, Table 3–4 shows that among officers there was consensus on satisfaction with Advancement Opportunity. This might well mean that advancement potential would probably be presented to the recruits in very positive terms. Furthermore, since there were considerable numbers of men in other ranks who had the same orientation, it would not be difficult for a training staff with a satisfaction type consensus on Advancement Opportunity to be appointed. Even though there is some statistical possibility that those specifically charged with training would reflect more than one type, our observations of training indicate otherwise. Since we could identify officer protocols, this possibility was checked, and it was found that those officers specifically responsible for recruit training were unvaryingly satisfaction type in Advancement Opportunity. We do not contend that the selection of the training staff represented a sacrifice of technical proficiency for the sake of "right thinking," yet it seems unlikely that anyone would be selected as a trainer, regardless of his skills, if he held attitudes about the *policeman* role which were counter to those of the selecting officers. (We assume, of course, that officers were alert to such factors as our role areas and were able to screen candidates for the training staff accordingly.)

As a second order of analysis we attempted to explore the correlates of the blockage-importance types with some of our other materials. In particular, we were concerned with whether type consensus displayed any meaningful relationships to other role behavior dimensions. Our initial procedure was to sample the items in the Policy and Practices Questionnaire (Appendix 1) and cross-tabulate them with type distributions across rank groups. We did this for areas which seemed relevant for the particular item used. If these operations yielded significant differences, we then planned to do a more complete analysis of the type variable, using all area classifications and the full range of policy and practices data.

The items used were as follows (paraphrased for simplicity):

1. Should unmarked cars be used on patrol?
2. To gain a promotion or transfer, is it necessary to know someone at headquarters?*
3. What are the most important ways to gain a high evaluation by headquarters?
4. Should a *policeman* be allowed to earn an outside income?
5. May a *policeman* accept free meals, special discounts, etc.?
6. Would you like to see the department on a 40-hour week?*
7. Is there too much regulation of private life of the *policeman* by the department?
8. What do you like and dislike about the image of the *policeman* on radio, TV, etc.?*
9. Father's occupation.
10. The anomia scale.
11. The authoritarianism scale.
12. The minority attitudes scale.
13. What is the social position of the *policeman* in the community?
14. What percentage of jobholders does better economically than the *policeman*?

Using the same criterion of consensus employed in the preceding sections of this chapter (i.e., positing consensus in a group whenever more than half of its members fall in one type),[6] we were interested in whether (a) within-type consensus could be found in terms of the items selected, and (b) differences among types could be found where consensus occurred.

We found that area was rarely related to either (a) or (b). This suggested that the type variable functioned independently of area on the items selected.

TABLE 3–5

ILLUSTRATIVE RELATIONSHIP OF AREAS AND TYPES TO PERCEIVED NEED OF SUPPORT BY SOMEONE AT HEADQUARTERS IN ORDER TO GAIN PROMOTION OR TRANSFER (PER CENT)

	Area					
	Advancement Opportunity			Job-Family Compatibility		
	Need for Headquarters Support					
Type	Yes	No	Sometimes	Yes	No	Sometimes
Conflict (+ +) . .	77	6	16	71	8	21
Acceptance (+ −) . .	67	10	23	57	13	30
Satisfaction (− +) . .	41	31	28	48	33	20
Indifference (− −) . .	42	30	28	42	32	26

For only three of the items (those asterisked on the above list) did we discover that type consensus was present. Furthermore, in only one item exhibiting consensus was there a clear difference among types. This distribution is shown in Table 3–5 by means of illustrating the forms of relationships we had sought to investigate. Here we see consensus for two types and lack of it for the other two. Individuals who were conflict type and acceptance type, regardless of the area examined, showed high consensus that some kind of personal support was necessary for promotion or transfer. Apparently blockage, regardless of the level of importance, tended to foster the perception of headquarters support as a necessary factor in promotion.

As in our examination of consensus and rank, it is difficult to account for the scarcity of within-type consensus and between-type differences among the items selected for preliminary analysis. Certainly the results of our comparisons did not encourage further tabulations, and we did not analyze the data any further along these lines. Perhaps these findings support a need to delineate role components and group perceptions which are more pertinent and sensitive than those used here. However, at the moment, the analysis of

[6] Where some of the distributions contained only two choices or categories for an item, we decided that in those instances only a two-thirds concentration in one category would be necessary as a minimum for designating consensus.

our constructed type variable does not support the existence of prominent consensus within the department concerning these aspects of the *policeman* role any more than did our analysis of the empirical rank variable.

Summary

Let us now review the salient features of the various comparisons we have made and offer some limited assessment of their theoretical significance.

1. An examination of five selected areas pertaining to the *policeman* role yielded little consensus within and among rank groups on the extent or direction of blockage or importance within each area.
2. An examination of these five areas, using a combined index of blockage and importance that yielded four constructed types, also yielded little consensus.

At first glance this lack of consensus, particularly within rank groups, is puzzling. If we had uncovered well-formed but contrasting images within ranks or types in the various areas, we could have dealt with role congruency and conflict as clear-cut empirical facts. Yet the diffuse nature of this role imagery which we found raises serious questions about the relationship between the role perception of an incumbent and the corresponding role expressions of designated audiences. The fact that consensus, when it did occur, was usually a department-wide phenomenon strongly suggests that consensus is not simply a random occurrence but may well be a rare achievement in a behavioral system involving multiple groups.

While some aspects of roles may exhibit patterns of considerable homogeneity, this is not sufficient evidence to establish the proposition that perceptual or conceptual clarity is the basis of most role-oriented behavior. On the other hand, we do not claim that the ambiguity we observe is de facto evidence of conflict or stress for the actor or for the system. Certainly we may interpret this situation as having some positive consequences for role behavior. Where ambiguity exists, it is likely that considerable flexibility in role behavior is available to the incumbent. The low order of consensus within audience (rank) groups makes it less likely that uniform, stringent standards of performance will be demanded by these groups, or that deviations from a set of standards would be generally recognized and punished. Insofar as this ambiguity can obtain without destroying role identity, the chief problem for the actor becomes one of choosing behavioral alternatives which will satisfy situational and perhaps personal requirements for a given unit of role behavior. We do not doubt that those in the *policeman* role *did* have an holistic conception of some aspects of it, and that this conception was used extensively in their role relationships. Clearly, actual behavior was geared to *some* set of expectations, whether they were idealized self-images or the instrumental expectations of selected audiences.

CHAPTER 4

Acquiring the Role

Introduction

IN CHAPTER 3 we found little consensus within and among various groups of audiences within the CSP regarding several important aspects of the *policeman* role. While we did not conclude that learning and functioning in this role were necessarily impaired, it seems likely that ambiguous and diverse audience perceptions may affect the form and content of role acquisition. Since the CSP had an active formal program for training *policemen*, we undertook a special analysis of this program to explore the process of role acquisition in a developmental setting.

Our continuous access to a single recruit class permitted us a longitudinal analysis which we could not apply to the other rank groups. While the rank hierarchy in the department represented a longitudinal dimension, and would permit intergroup comparisons, the recruit group was the only one in which the role development process could be charted using a stable group of respondents. Within a single recruit class, then, we were able to observe and record shifts in patterns of role perception. These materials will be considered in the first part of the chapter.

In addition to the shift phenomenon, we also wished to explore further the relationship between a particular group's perception of a role and the perception of it held by other groups. This interest, stimulated by our findings in Chapter 3, can be expressed by two questions:

a) What was the extent of agreement between the perception of the *policeman* role expressed by recruits after their final stage of training and the perceptions expressed by the other rank groups?

b) What was the extent of agreement between the attributed and expressed role perceptions of the rank groups?

These two questions will be discussed in the second part of the chapter.

Shifts in Role Perception

Although recruits may be washed out any time during their initial year, separation by department action for reasons of discipline or competence becomes less likely as time goes on.[1] From a methodological standpoint, it was necessary to have periodic data on each recruit in order to trace changes in role perception. Due to the reduction of the original group of recruits from twenty-seven to twenty-three, the data of the following section are confined to the men who completed questionnaires for the first three stages.[2] Table 4–1 presents stage distributions for the recruit group by blockage-importance types. The fourth stage is included so that later trends can be identified. The following brief summaries for each area highlight the shifts in recruit perceptions of the *policeman* role.

Advancement Opportunity in the three-stage pattern does not show any conclusive shift. Conflict is the least frequent type, with indifference being modal at all stages. In general, one might say that the training experience produced no marked effect upon recruit perception of the *policeman* role in this area. By stage 4, a substantial change had occurred in the group. The low blockage types (satisfaction and indifference) decline, and the high blockage types (conflict and acceptance) increase. Apparently, then, the first year of regular experience carried with it a less optimistic view of advancement opportunities.

In Social Value and Prestige, acceptance begins as the modal type and becomes even more prominent with time. By stage 3, acceptance was larger than the other three combined, giving us the first distribution in which anything approaching group consensus (by our 50 per cent criterion) could be perceived. The stage 4 results did not show any dramatic reversals, except that conflict rose, and the group tended to revert to a distribution similar to stage 2.

In Freedom to Express Feelings, acceptance declined steadily and indifference increased. For the three-stage pattern there was considerable loss of blockage in the group as a whole. Stage 4 exhibited no unusual features, except to emphasize the relative absence of satisfaction.

Self-Realization has a trend pattern similar to that of Social Value and

---

[1] Voluntary drop-out is also highest in the recruit phase, and tapers off sharply in succeeding phases of the career. (See Chapter 2, Figure 2–1.)

[2] These time periods have already been noted in Chapter 3 (see p. 41). One man was separated from the department by disciplinary action, one left voluntarily, and two did not return questionnaires in the third battery. A year after the main portion of the study was completed, a fourth battery was sent to each member of the group at the end of his first twelve months as a regular *policeman*. Nineteen of the twenty-three eligible men responded. We felt that the loss of four additional men was too high to justify the extensive use of the fourth stage of the panel process. Therefore much of the shift data will focus upon the three-stage pattern. Nevertheless, the fourth-stage distributions will be included in several analyses when appropriate.

Prestige for the three-stage process, with acceptance beginning and remaining as the dominant type of orientation. Stage 4 reversals remained moderate, except that the indifference type, which was always rather small, disappeared completely from the group.

TABLE 4–1

BLOCKAGE-IMPORTANCE TYPE DISTRIBUTIONS IN THE RECRUIT GROUP BY ROLE AREA AND STAGE SUMMARY

Type	Stage			
	1 (1½ Mo.)	*2* (6 Mo.)	*3* (12 Mo.)	*4* (24 Mo.)
Advancement Opportunity				
Conflict (+ +) . .	2	3	2	5
Acceptance (+ −) . .	8	6	5	8
Satisfaction (− +) . .	5	6	8	3
Indifference (− −) . .	8	8	8	3
Social Value and Prestige				
Conflict (+ +) . .	6	4	1	4
Acceptance (+ −) . .	8	10	13	9
Satisfaction (− +) . .	5	4	3	2
Indifference (− −) . .	4	5	6	4
Freedom to Express Feelings				
Conflict (+ +) . .	8	6	6	7
Acceptance (+ −) . .	12	8	6	6
Satisfaction (− +) . .	2	5	4	1
Indifference (− −) . .	1	4	7	5
Self-Realization*				
Conflict (+ +) . .	6	3	1	3
Acceptance (+ −) . .	8	10	12	10
Satisfaction (− +) . .	8	8	6	5
Indifference (− −) . .	1	2	4	0
Job-Family Compatibility*				
Conflict (+ +) . .	7	1	3	7
Acceptance (+ −) . .	2	2	2	1
Satisfaction (− +) . .	13	16	11	6
Indifference (− −) . .	1	4	7	4

* One respondent did not furnish data in these areas in stage 4.

Job-Family Compatibility presents a unique constellation of change. This was the one role area which initially showed consensus. This consensus on satisfaction reached its peak at the end of formal headquarters training (stage 2). The pattern, however, changed markedly with field experience. Stage 3 displayed the development of indifference. By stage 4 there was a loss of consensus and a return to the original level of conflict. Thus, it would seem that field experience was directly related to the alteration of role imagery in this area.

Now that we have reviewed the stage summaries, do any overall consistencies emerge? Except for the rough similarity between Social Value and Prestige and Self-Realization, each sequence seems relatively idiosyncratic. Certainly the lack of within-type consensus is striking. Where such consensus developed it was only temporary. The stage 4 data, although incomplete, indicated trends involving some reversions to earlier stage distributions, but these were not conclusive. Obviously, a much larger number of subjects, and perhaps still more time, would be necessary to establish such trends.

TABLE 4–2
SUMMARY OF BLOCKAGE-IMPORTANCE TYPE CHANGE PATTERNS WITHIN
THE RECRUIT GROUP BY ROLE AREA

	Advancement Opportunity	Social Value and Prestige	Freedom to Express Feelings	Self-Realization	Job-Family Compatibility
A. Frequency of Changes					
No changes . .	6	5	9	7	7
One change .	11	11	11	12	11
Two changes .	6	7	3	4	5
Three changes .	6	7	3	4	5
B. Time of Changes					
Between stages					
1 and 2 . .	12	17	6	10	13
Between stages					
2 and 3 . .	11	8	11	10	8

One observation of interest is the consistent strength of the acceptance and satisfaction types across all of the stages. In most instances these types were more prominent than the other two. The relative rarity of conflict—as the level of acceptance and satisfaction indicates—supports our previous finding that it was rare for rank groups to be high on both blockage and importance in a single area (cf. Chapter 3, Table 1). However, as far as the type variable is concerned, we see little evidence of a crystallization of role perception by the recruit group within the five areas studied.

Although the stage summaries for recruits were not conclusive, we know that a variety of change patterns occurred during the training period. We shall now examine these patterns in some detail. Tables 4–2, 4–3, and 4–4 explore the internal character of change with respect to the amount of change and the stage time at which it occurred. Table 4–2 summarizes the number of recruits who changed from one type to another (A), and the times in the training program during which the changes occurred (B). This analysis is limited to the three-stage pattern for all of the areas.

We can see that most recruits change. In four of the five areas, fewer than one-third of the recruits displayed no changes of type, while approximately half of the recruits experienced one type change. Clearly, stability was not a dominant characteristic of role acquisition in these areas. The total number of changes which took place in each area can be compared by adding the two time categories in part B. For example, in Social Value and Prestige there was the highest number of changes (25), while Freedom to Express Feelings displayed the lowest (17). In general, the frequency of changes across areas is quite similar. In part B, however, we can observe greater variability in the time of changes by area than we can for the number of changes. This variation suggests that each area might have a relatively independent pattern of change for recruits.

From Table 4–2 we move to investigate the possible relationship between change patterns and type categories. These data are presented in Table 4–3. Once again we note the lack of similarity among areas. In two of the areas (Freedom to Express Feelings and Self-Realization) the number of recruits showing no changes is well dispersed among the types, while in two other areas (Social Value and Prestige and Job-Family Compatibility) recruits showing no changes were concentrated in the dominant type.

Indifference seemed to be the least stable type. For the recruits classified "indifference type" in all areas at stage 3, only six showed no change, resulting in a stability factor (i.e., number in "no change" over total number in type at stage 3) of 19 per cent for this type. This compares with 31 per cent stability for conflict, 32 per cent for acceptance, and 41 per cent for satisfaction. If we regard the reversion pattern (column D) as a trend toward stability, we could sum the reversions and the no-changes. The picture would then be altered to the extent that acceptance becomes about as stable (53 per cent) as satisfaction (47 per cent). Indifference remains lowest, at 22 per cent. This analysis of the contribution of the various change patterns to the stage 3 type distributions provides evidence that some types were considerably more stable than others.

It is clear that indifference expanded more than any other type. Between the stage 1 and stage 3 distributions over the five areas, indifference accounted for 45 per cent of the net changes—all in the direction of increasing indifference. In contrast, conflict accounted for 42 per cent of the net changes, and all of these changes were in the direction of decreasing conflict. There were practically no net changes in acceptance type and satisfaction type, where gains in some areas were balanced by losses in others. By stage 4, conflict increases while indifference and satisfaction show a marked decrease. In general, the areas do not exhibit any uniform pattern of change over the four stages.

TABLE 4–3

BLOCKAGE-IMPORTANCE TYPE CHANGES WITHIN THE RECRUIT GROUP
BY AREA CHANGE PATTERNS

Type	Distribution of Recruits at Stage 1	A Between Stages 1 & 2*	B Between Stages 2 & 3*	C Between Stages 1 & 2 2 & 3*	D Between Stages 1 & 2 2 & 3 (Reversion)*	Total Recruits Showing No Changes	Distribution of Recruits at Stage 3	Distribution of Recruits at Stage 4†
			Advancement Opportunity					
Conflict ...	2	1	0	1	0	0	2	5
Acceptance	8	1	0	2	1	1	5	8
Satisfaction	5	2	2	2	0	2	8	3
Indifference	8	2	3	0	0	3	8	3
Total ...	23	6	5	5	1	6	23	19
			Social Value and Prestige					
Conflict ...	6	1	0	0	0	0	1	4
Acceptance	8	5	1	2	1	4	13	9
Satisfaction	5	1	0	0	2	0	3	2
Indifference	4	3	0	2	0	1	6	4
Total ...	23	10	1	4	3	5	23	19
			Freedom to Express Feelings					
Conflict ...	8	0	2	0	1	3	6	7
Acceptance	12	0	1	0	2	3	6	6
Satisfaction	2	1	1	0	0	2	4	1
Indifference	1	2	4	0	0	1	7	5
Total ...	23	3	8	0	3	9	23	19
			Self-Realization					
Conflict ...	6	0	0	0	0	1	1	3
Acceptance	8	4	2	0	3	3	12	10
Satisfaction	8	2	2	0	0	2	6	5
Indifference	1	0	2	1	0	1	4	0
Total ...	23	6	6	1	3	7	23	18
			Job-Family Compatibility					
Conflict ...	7	1	0	1	1	0	3	7
Acceptance	2	1	0	0	1	0	2	1
Satisfaction	13	3	1	0	0	7	11	6
Indifference	1	3	2	1	1	0	7	4
Total ...	23	8	3	2	3	7	23	18

* Explanation of Change Patterns: *A*, recruits who changed type during first 6 months and did not change in second 6 months; *B*, recruits who did not change type during first 6 months and did change during second 6 months; *C*, recruits who changed type during first 6 months and during second 6 months; *D*, recruits who changed type during first 6 months and reverted to first type during second 6 months. Each cell contains the number of recruits gained in each type via each change pattern. The total number of recruits (for all change patterns) lost in each type is found by subtracting the No Changes entry from the Stage 1 entry.

† Stage 4 represents incomplete data given by the recruit group after 24 months of service. Four members of the group did not return questionnaires and one member did not furnish answers in two areas.

A comment should be made here concerning the time during which changes occurred. If we observe recruits who changed once regardless of area (columns A and B of Table 4–3), we note that there was a greater tendency for these recruits to change during the first six months rather than the second. Yet if we look at the column totals in each area, there is no uniformity among areas as to time of change. Two show early change tendencies, one shows a late change tendency, and two are about equal. Again we have limited evidence of pattern differences among areas in terms of role perception, although caution in interpretation is still necessary because of the small size of the recruit group.

Since we did not feel it was appropriate to make statistical tests of shifts in blockage and importance by using these constructed type categories, an analysis was made of these dimensions separately in each of the five areas. This is shown in Table 4–4. Part A presents the time and frequency of changes for the three-stage process. Part B shows the composition of the stage 3 distributions in terms of the shift patterns by which they were achieved. Part C indicates whether the differences in distribution for each dimension in each area, comparing stage 1 with stage 3, were statistically significant.[3]

We see immediately that significant changes occurred in only two of the areas, with two others showing changes slightly less than significant ($p < .10$). The fact that significant changes did not occur in both dimensions in any area is compatible with the finding in Chapter 3, where we found that significant differences between ranks rarely occurred in both variables in the same area. Thus, even though there might be considerable shifting by individuals in a group on blockage or importance, few of them would shift on both of these dimensions in an area. Furthermore, the group shifts rarely seemed to move in a single direction, since gains for some individuals often would be balanced by losses for others. The lack of significant net changes seemed due less to the rigidity of role perceptions than to randomized change within the group which produced no appreciable crystallization of perceptions. Table 4–2 showed that changes in type distribution occurred in all of the areas. Table 4–4 sharpens this picture by locating the sources of the type changes and by indicating whether the magnitude of change was statistically significant.

Both blockage and importance were involved in all of the shifts. Changes in role perception apparently occurred by either of two procedures. First, an individual might change his type by altering both blockage and importance orientations at the same time. For example, one might shift from conflict

[3] The statistic employed was the McNemar Shift Test. See S. Siegel, *Nonparametric Statistics for the Behavioral Sciences* (New York: McGraw-Hill, 1956).

type $(++)$ to indifference type $(--)$. However, our data strongly suggest that this double shift was rare. The reason for this is not clear. One might hypothesize that the extensive amount of cognitive reorganization required by a double shift was too traumatic for an individual in such a short time. A second hypothesis would invoke a principle of least effort. When group members responded to training and field experience which altered their role perceptions, they selected adaptive patterns requiring the least change from their previous state. Thus if a change in one variable produced functionally adaptive results, further alterations would be unnecessary, or even disruptive. Since we had not anticipated the nature of these changes during data-gathering, we were unable to investigate these hypotheses about change or to examine shifts within additional samples of similar recruit populations.

Let us now briefly examine each area in Tables 4–3 and 4–4 in terms of the shifts which took place between the first and third stages.

In Advancement Opportunity slight shifts occurred in opposite directions (with blockage going down and importance going up) but not enough to be significant. However, in stage-4 data we found a significant reestablishment of high blockage.[4] These gains were translated into a resurgence of both conflict and acceptance as dominant types, and marked this area as a probable growing source of stress for *policemen* who recently were recruits.

Social Value and Prestige showed that while blockage remained fairly high, importance declined significantly. Acceptance thus became modal. Conflict disappeared in stage 3, although it reappeared moderately in stage 4.

Freedom to Express Feelings provided a dramatic blockage decrease. This resulted in a shift from acceptance to indifference (rather than to satisfaction) as the modal type. There was a large number of non-shifting individuals in the high categories of both dimensions.

Self-Realization resembled the pattern of Social Value and Prestige, but its decrease in importance was of marginal significance. Acceptance became dominant, and there was a minor gain in indifference.

Job-Family Compatibility indicated some loss in both blockage and importance over the three-stage period, with importance showing a loss of borderline significance. The major type gain was in indifference. This was the only area of the five examined in which acceptance remained a consistently minor factor. The data suggest that conflict may eventually become the leading type, since the only gains in stage 4 were in this category. Of all the area patterns, this last one may hold the most stress potential—based on four-stage data—even though none of the shifts were as yet highly significant.

[4] This was the only area in which a significant shift ($p < .01$) occurred between stages 3 and 4.

TABLE 4–4

RECRUIT GROUP DISTRIBUTIONS AND CHANGES IN BLOCKAGE AND IMPORTANCE BY ROLE AREA

Blockage-Importance	(A) Time of Changes				(B) Change of Patterns				Distribution at Stage 4	(C) Significant Shift between Stages 1 & 3 McNemar Shift Test
	Distribution at Stage 1	Gain between Stages 1 & 2	Gain between Stages 2 & 3	Distribution at Stage 3	Between Stages 1 & 2	Between Stages 2 & 3	Between Stages 1 & 2	No Change		
Advancement Opportunity										
Blockage										
High ...	10	2	3	7	1	3	0	3	13	none
Low ...	13	3	5	16	3	4	1	8	6	
Importance										
High ...	7	6	4	10	3	3	1	3	8	none
Low ...	16	4	3	13	3	0	3	7	11	
Social Value and Prestige										
Blockage										
High ...	14	6	4	14	3	1	3	7	13	none
Low ...	9	6	4	9	3	1	3	2	6	
Importance										
High ...	11	2	0	4	1	0	0	3	6	decrease
Low ...	12	5	4	19	5	3	1	10	13	$p < .05$
Freedom to Express Feelings										
Blockage										
High ...	20	0	3	12	0	0	3	9	11	decrease
Low ...	3	6	5	11	3	5	0	3	8	$p < .02$
Importance										
High ...	10	1	2	10	0	2	0	8	7	none
Low ...	13	0	3	13	0	2	1	10	12	
Self-Realization										
Blockage										
High ...	14	4	2	13	4	0	2	7	13	none
Low ...	9	5	2	10	3	2	0	5	5	
Importance										
High ...	13	3	1	7	1	1	0	5	8	decrease
Low ...	10	5	5	16	6	3	2	5	10	$p < .10$
Job-Family Compatibility										
Blockage										
High ...	9	2	3	5	0	2	1	2	8	none
Low ...	14	7	2	18	6	1	1	10	10	
Importance										
High ...	20	2	3	15	0	0	2	13	13	decrease
Low ...	3	5	5	8	5	0	2	1	5	$p < .10$

In summarizing these analyses of recruit group shifts, we wish to emphasize two points. The first is the substantive observation that changes in role perception were not uniform among recruits within areas, nor were changes in one area consonant with changes in others. The one inter-area similarity over time (between Social Value and Prestige and Self-Realization) certainly could not be used as a basis for generalization. Whatever the factors were behind the recruit shifts, they did not function uniformly by areas. The diversity of these findings reemphasizes the complexity and the apparently unstable character of—at least—these categories of role perceptions. There was no evidence that a crystallization of role perception took place during training, although a slight gain in conflict occurred in all areas between stages 3 and 4.

The second point, with both theoretical and practical implications, derives from this diverse shifting in patterns of role perception. Although we cannot accurately delimit the range and patterns of such learning, it would still not be improper for us to ask how these findings might be linked to the formal training program. We realize that the five areas we have been discussing were not aspects of the role of *policeman* which were specifically incorporated in the program. However, their omission may have had direct consequences for the kind of self-perceptions in the role which a recruit would acquire. For example, their omission may have contributed to the diversity of role perceptions for the recruit group as a whole by permitting each recruit to develop his conception of the role with relative independence. It may thus have increased the potential of audiences outside the department to influence recruit role perceptions. These extra-organizational audiences (friends, wives, etc.) could then affect the outcome of the formal program in significant fashion, even to the extent of negating role patterns which the department was attempting to teach.

Attributed and Expressed Role Perceptions

We now focus our attention upon the relationship between the perceptions of the *policeman* role expressed by the rank groups and the perceptions attributed to these groups by the recruits. This was a rather elusive dimension with respect to data collection since it required recruits to consciously assign views to audience groups. Such assignment is rarely a conscious or formal process in daily behavior, yet this requirement would appear to be pivotal for demonstrating basic agreement between the perception of a role held by an actor and the perception of that role held by his audiences. Laboratory research in social psychology has strongly supported the proposition that under certain conditions individuals' perceptions of objects and events may be influenced by social group pressures. However, this type of research has rarely explored the ways in which the audiences' perceptions of a given role might be incorporated into the self-perceptions of the role player, particularly in natural social systems.

Data from Chapter 3 have already cast doubt upon the existence of much consensus concerning the *policeman* role in the perceptions of either rank groups or among those manifesting the same type of role area adjustment. This would not encourage us to expect agreement between attributed and expressed role perceptions involving these groups. However, it is possible that some patterns of congruence, perhaps reflecting hitherto unrevealed modes of agreement, might emerge from such comparisons. Conversely, these comparisons may further reinforce previous doubts that consensus in these aspects of role perception is present.

The procedure employed in making the comparisons was to ask the recruits at stage 4 to state their perceptions of the images held by the active rank groups in each of the five areas. After two years in the department, the recruits (now actually *policemen*) presumably had had sufficient opportunity to have on-the-job interaction with at least some members of all these groups. Therefore we felt that the rank groups could now be presented to recruits as manifest and identifiable audiences. Consequently, the final questionnaire distributed to the recruits contained options for the perceptions of the *policeman* role attributed by the recruits themselves to the *policeman*, corporal, sergeant, and officer groups in the five areas.

Table 4–5 (A to E) summarizes the percentage of types in each area by rank group, showing both attributed and expressed perceptions.[5] Because of the amount of data involved, tables are presented separately for each area. The major foci are the type variable and the rank group variable, represented by parts A and B respectively. The first column of part A shows the actual conception of the *policeman* role held by recruits according to the type distribution. Each succeeding column contains a percentage comparison between the perceptions of the *policeman* role expressed by a rank group and the perceptions of the *policeman* role attributed by the recruits to that rank group. Our chief interest here is the accuracy of attributed perceptions by the recruit group. In part B, the perceptions attributed to each rank group by the recruits are compared with the expressed perceptions by the rank groups for both blockage and importance.

In Advancement Opportunity (Table 4–5A) there was practically no congruence between attributed and expressed perceptions (part A). Acceptance was always overestimated and satisfaction always underestimated by recruits.

[5] The expressed rank group percentages of Table 4–5 are derived from Table 3–4. To facilitate the comparison in Table 4–5, the percentages were recomputed, using only those respondents who fit unambiguously in a given type.

Although the recruits displayed no consensus, they attributed consensus in the acceptance type to *policemen*. This consensus is barely achieved for the corporal group, and disappears for sergeants and officers. In part B we see that recruits uniformly overestimated blockage and underestimated importance among rank groups. Particularly in the blockage variable, rank trends are clearly visible for both attributed and expressed perceptions. Although blockage was consistently overestimated in absolute terms, the trend of decline by rank was rather accurately reflected. Thus, there was partial accuracy in recognizing rank differentials for this dimension in the

TABLE 4–5A

COMPARISON OF THE TYPE PERCEPTIONS ATTRIBUTED BY STAGE-4 RECRUITS TO RANK GROUPS WITH THE TYPE PERCEPTIONS EXPRESSED BY THE RANK GROUPS (PER CENT)

	ADVANCEMENT OPPORTUNITY								
	(A)								
	Recruit 4	Policeman		Corporal		Sergeant		Officer	
	Ex-	Attri-	Ex-	Attri-	Ex-	Attri-	Ex-	Attri-	Ex-
Type	pressed	buted	pressed	buted	pressed	buted	pressed	buted	pressed
Conflict . .	25	25	17	15	30	25	33	15	8
Acceptance .	40	55	33	50	19	30	7	20	8
Satisfaction .	15	10	25	10	28	10	35	30	59
Indifference .	20	10	25	25	23	35	25	35	25

| | (B) | | | |
| | High Blockage | | High Importance | |
Rank	Attributed	Expressed	Attributed	Expressed
Recruit 4 . .		65		40
Policeman . .	79	50	35	42
Corporal . .	65	49	25	58
Sergeant . .	55	40	35	68
Officer . . .	35	16	45	67

sense that the direction of these differentials was correctly assessed even though their magnitudes were not. This same pattern was discernible for importance, but with less consistency. By contrast, rank differences were not systematic in comparisons by type. This may well have been a consequence of the lack of consensus in the recruit group.

In Social Value and Prestige (Table 4–5B), the type and rank comparisons show patterns which are similar to those found in Advancement Opportunity. Freedom to Express Feelings (Table 4–5C), however, shows a marked contrast with the first two areas. Here, for the first time, we find a situation approaching congruence between attributed and expressed perceptions. This congruence occurred for both magnitude and direction in parts A and B.

Self-Realization (Table 4–5D) illustrates a clear tendency toward a uniform attribution of responses by recruits to the other rank groups. The picture here is one of major discrepancies between attributed and expressed perceptions. Part B indicates that the source of these discrepancies was the importance dimension, in which the discrepancies tended to increase with rank. Since personal success and satisfaction is involved, it is not surprising that part B patterns for this area were quite similar to those for Advancement Opportunity and Social Value and Prestige, which also reflected success potentials and status factors. Recruits seemed to continuously underestimate

TABLE 4–5B

COMPARISON OF THE TYPE PERCEPTIONS ATTRIBUTED BY STAGE-4 RECRUITS TO RANK GROUPS WITH THE TYPE PERCEPTIONS EXPRESSED BY THE RANK GROUPS (PER CENT)

	SOCIAL VALUE AND PRESTIGE									
	(A)									
	Recruit 4	Policeman		Corporal		Sergeant		Officer	
	Ex-	Attri-	Ex-	Attri-	Ex-	Attri-	Ex-	Attri-	Ex-
Type	pressed	buted	pressed	buted	pressed	buted	pressed	buted	pressed
Conflict . .	20	20	17	25	35	20	41	25	25
Acceptance .	50	50	28	45	17	35	17	30	8
Satisfaction .	10	5	34	10	33	20	42	25	59
Indifference .	20	25	21	20	15	25	0	20	8

| | (B) | | | |
| | High Blockage | | High Importance | |
Rank	Attributed	Expressed	Attributed	Expressed
Recruit 4 . .		60		30
Policeman . .	68	45	25	51
Corporal . .	70	52	35	68
Sergeant . .	65	58	40	83
Officer . . .	65	33	50	84

the expression of importance in these areas by most of the rank groups. Again, as might be anticipated, discrepancies were smallest between recruits and *policemen*.

Job-Family Compatibility (Table 4–5E) shows a distinct change in the type comparisons of part A. Here, acceptance was for the only time not a major attributed type. However, no other type replaced acceptance as dominant in the recruit group, and this area was one of high ambiguity. Since there was no consensus of expressed perceptions within rank groups in this area, the two instances of attributed consensus by recruits were bound to be inaccurate. There was a tenuous similarity between expressed recruit and attributed *policeman* perceptions which was consistent with findings in the other areas. The higher-rank groups showed the greater discrepancies with attributed perceptions by recruits. Part B indicates that the sources of discrepancy lay in underestimation of both blockage and importance. Therefore acceptance and satisfaction were expressed more often by the rank groups than they were attributed to these groups by recruits.

In summarizing the comparisons between attributed and expressed perceptions of the *policeman* role among the rank groups in the five areas, we find again that these role perceptions were quite variable. There were inter-

TABLE 4–5C

COMPARISON OF THE TYPE PERCEPTIONS ATTRIBUTED BY STAGE-4 RECRUITS TO RANK GROUPS WITH THE TYPE PERCEPTIONS EXPRESSED BY THE RANK GROUPS (PER CENT)

	FREEDOM TO EXPRESS FEELINGS								
	(A)								
	Recruit 4	Policeman		Corporal		Sergeant		Officer	
	Ex-	Attri-	Ex-	Attri-	Ex-	Attri-	Ex-	Attri-	Ex-
Type	pressed	buted	pressed	buted	pressed	buted	pressed	buted	pressed
Conflict . .	35	30	22	10	17	5	11	5	11
Acceptance .	35	40	25	55	50	55	58	60	65
Satisfaction .	5	5	20	10	5	5	0	10	0
Indifference .	25	25	33	25	28	35	31	25	25

| | (B) | | | |
| | High Blockage | | High Importance | |
Rank	Attributed	Expressed	Attributed	Expressed
Recruit 4 . .		70		40
Policeman . .	68	45	35	42
Corporal . .	65	67	20	22
Sergeant . .	60	69	10	11
Officer . . .	65	75	15	11

area differences, of which some were patterned and some were not; and some inter-area differences were related to the rank groups involved. There were also differences with respect to the emphasis placed upon blockage and importance in the role areas. Consensus was generally lacking in both the attributed and expressed perceptions of the *policeman* role. Whenever recruits consensually attributed a perception to a rank group they frequently were inaccurate.

Two patterns emerge from the comparisons, and these seem worthy of restatement. First, there was some evidence that the recruit group was beginning to identify itself with *policemen*. The recruit group's expressed perceptions were closer to those attributed to *policemen* and those expressed

ACQUIRING THE ROLE   67

by *policemen* than to those attributed to or expressed by any other group. Second, increases in rank distance were usually accompanied by increased differences in role perception. The farther each rank group was removed from the *policeman* role, the greater the discrepancies in both attributed and expressed perceptions. This is clearly consonant with the patterns of rank clusters which were examined in Chapter 3.

We have already offered some possible explanations of why there might be increasing discrepancies among perceptions of the *policeman* role as one moves through the department hierarchy (see Chapter 3). One was that the change of positions due to promotion carried with it a perception of the

TABLE 4–5D

COMPARISON OF THE TYPE PERCEPTIONS ATTRIBUTED BY STAGE-4 RECRUITS TO RANK GROUPS WITH THE TYPE PERCEPTIONS EXPRESSED BY THE RANK GROUPS (PER CENT)

SELF–REALIZATION

(A)

Type	Recruit 4* Ex-pressed	Policeman Attri-buted	Policeman Ex-pressed	Corporal Attri-buted	Corporal Ex-pressed	Sergeant Attri-buted	Sergeant Ex-pressed	Officer Attri-buted	Officer Ex-pressed
Conflict	15	15	19	20	45	25	46	25	31
Acceptance	50	50	38	50	31	45	27	40	19
Satisfaction	25	25	23	20	19	15	21	15	44
Indifference	5	5	20	5	5	10	6	15	6

(B)

Rank	High Blockage Attributed	High Blockage Expressed	High Importance Attributed	High Importance Expressed
Recruit 4		65		40
Policeman	72	57	40	42
Corporal	70	76	35	65
Sergeant	70	73	40	67
Officer	65	53	40	81

* $N = 18$; one recruit did not complete this area. Recruit percentages total 95% and are based on original $N = 19$.

earlier role in terms of the present role. This we presume to be a largely unintended displacement influenced by the structural and social distance between rank groups. Although we do not know fully the behavioral consequences of either the lack of consensus within rank groups, or the added discrepancies between attributed and expressed perceptions of rank groups, these were apparently insufficient to disrupt the CSP as a coherently functioning system. This does not mean, of course, that there was an absence of behavioral problems among *policemen*. Nevertheless, *policemen* seemed quite able to invoke mechanisms which made it possible for them to adapt to most role conflict situations with minimal psychological costs. As we have suggested earlier, this may well be due to the low levels of within-group consensus among rank groups. If such consensus were high, and if there were great discrepancies of role perception, the factor of personal stress would probably have increased, even (or especially) with accurate perception, for those in the *policeman* role.[6]

Another explanation was that the passage of years had so altered the circumstances and content of the role that the present conception bore little

TABLE 4–5E

COMPARISON OF THE TYPE PERCEPTIONS ATTRIBUTED BY STAGE-4 RECRUITS TO RANK GROUPS WITH THE TYPE PERCEPTIONS EXPRESSED BY THE RANK GROUPS (PER CENT)

JOB–FAMILY COMPATIBILITY
(A)

Type	Recruit 4* Expressed	Policeman Attributed	Policeman Expressed	Corporal Attributed	Corporal Expressed	Sergeant Attributed	Sergeant Expressed	Officer Attributed	Officer Expressed
Conflict	35	40	27	25	15	5	19	10	11
Acceptance	10	10	23	15	28	10	23	5	14
Satisfaction	30	25	16	20	20	20	25	25	44
Indifference	20	20	34	35	37	60	33	55	31

(B)

Rank	High Blockage Attributed	High Blockage Expressed	High Importance Attributed	High Importance Expressed
Recruit 4		45		65
Policeman	50	50	65	42
Corporal	40	43	45	35
Sergeant	15	42	25	54
Officer	15	25	35	55

* $N = 18$; one recruit did not complete this area. Recruit percentages total 95% and are based on original $N = 19$.

resemblance to earlier versions. These earlier conceptions might still be invoked, partly in nostalgia or partly in error. Certainly, the extent to which this imagery accounted for intergroup discrepancies needs to be examined systematically, particularly if such outmoded perceptions were themselves stable in a given system.

[6] It is important to point out again that the area perceptions we are considering are those which are not directly concerned with role performance, though performance would certainly be influenced by such perceptions. In Chapter 6, the problems of role conflict and its resolution will be treated in detail.

Turning again to the data, two additional tabulations were made. In the first of these, we checked the manner in which each recruit in stage 4 attributed role perceptions to the rank groups in each of the five areas. Table 4–6 summarizes the degree of uniformity with which recruits identified the role perceptions held by the various ranks. Many recruits attributed uniform perceptions to all rank groups in each area; and those who saw all rank group perceptions as having the same type across areas are shown in the first column.[7] Since we know that the expressed perceptions of the rank groups in a given area were not the same, the basis of this uniformity is unclear. What we possibly have here is a "perceptual set" in which a dominant perception is used for a number of audiences. The occurrence of this perceptual set varied slightly by area, and it averaged more than half the recruit group over the five areas. It cannot be inferred that those recruits who did not express a uniformity of attributed perceptions were more accurate

TABLE 4–6

UNIFORMITY OF ATTRIBUTED PERCEPTIONS OF RANK GROUPS
HELD BY STAGE-4 RECRUITS

Area	Uniformity of Attributed Perception	
	Total Agreement	One Different
Advancement Opportunity*	8	4
Social Value and Prestige*	11	5
Freedom to Express Feelings*	11	2
Self-Realization†	11	4
Job-Family Compatibility†	8	1

* $N = 19$.   † $N = 18$.

in their assessment of rank group perceptions. Such recruits were actually just as inaccurate in attributing correct type perceptions to rank groups as were those who followed a uniform pattern.

The second column of Table 4–6 adds support to the idea of a perceptual set for individual recruits. This column shows the number of recruits who attributed uniform perceptions to all but one rank in each area. Thus three of the four ranks were seen uniformly. If we then sum these two columns across the five areas, the proportion displaying such uniformity becomes rather impressive in four of the areas. Only in Job-Family Compatibility was there widespread diversity of attributed perceptions. This display of diversity in even one area is important to note. It provides evidence to

[7] A concrete example of total agreement would be a recruit who attributed acceptance type perceptions to all rank groups in Advancement Opportunity. The eight recruits comprising the total agreement group for Advancement Opportunity did not, of course, select the same type.

indicate that recruits were capable of attributing different perceptions to rank groups and it vitiates any argument of response set. We cannot explain this high incidence of individual uniformity, but it appears to be an intriguing, and perhaps important, matter to pursue in future research.

TABLE 4–7

COMPARISON OF EXPRESSED SELF-PERCEPTIONS AND ATTRIBUTED
POLICEMAN PERCEPTIONS BY STAGE-4 RECRUITS

	Area									
	Advancement Opportunity		Social Value and Prestige		Freedom to Express Feelings		Self-Realization		Job-Family Compatibility	
Recruit	Ex-pressed Self	Attri-buted Police	Ex-pressed Self	Attri-buted Police	Ex-pressed Self	Attri-buted Police	Ex-pressed Self	Attri-buted Police	Ex-pressed Self	Attri-buted Police
1	– –	– –	+ –	+ –	+ –	+ –	– –	– –	+ +	+ +
2	+ –	+ –	– –	– –	[+ +	+ –]	[– +	+ –]	+ –	+ –
3	[– –	+ –]	+ –	+ –	+ +	+ +	+ +	+ +	– +	– +
4	[– –	+ –]	+ –	+ –	+ –	+ –	[+ –	+ +]	[– +	+ +]
5	[– +	+ +]	+ –	+ –	– +	– +	– +	– +	– +	– +
6	– +	– +	– +	– +	– –	– –	– +	– +	– –	– –
7	+ –	+ –	– –	– –	– –	– –	+ –	+ –	– –	– –
8	– +	– +	– –	– –	– –	– –	– +	– +	– –	– –
9	– +	+ –	[+ +	+ –]	+ +	+ +	+ –	+ –	– –	– –
10	+ –	+ –	+ –	+ –	+ +	+ +	+ –	+ –	+ +	+ +
11	+ –	+ –	+ –	+ –	+ –	+ –	+ –	+ –	– +	– +
12	+ –	+ –	+ +	+ +	+ +	+ +	no response		no response	
13	+ +	+ +	[+ –	– –]	+ +	+ +	+ –	+ –	– +	– +
14	+ +	+ +	+ –	+ –	+ +	+ +	+ –	+ –	+ +	+ +
15	+ –	+ –	+ +	+ +	– –	– –	+ –	+ –	+ –	+ –
16	+ –	+ –	[– +	+ +]	+ –	+ –	+ +	+ +	+ +	+ +
17	– –	– –	– –	– –	– –	– –	– +	– +	– +	– +
18	+ +	+ +	+ –	+ –	+ –	+ –	+ –	+ –	+ +	+ +
19	+ +	+ +	+ +	+ +	+ –	+ –	+ –	+ –	+ +	+ +

[   ]:–Discrepancies.

Blockage-Involvement Types Key:

     + + = Conflict
     + – = Acceptance
     – + = Satisfaction
     – – = Indifference

Our final tabulation explored the relationship between the individual recruit's expressed self-perceptions and the perceptions he attributed to the *policeman* group. This relationship is shown in Table 4–7, using the cryptic form for each type. Each recruit is presented in a series of perceptual pairs for the five areas. Since self-perceptions among areas involved two dimensions for all recruits, the congruity within pairs is quite remarkable. Of ninety-three comparisons, only ten showed a discrepancy between the recruits' expressed and attributed responses. Although interpretation is difficult, one plausible explanation is that recruits were technically *policemen* in stage 4, and therefore may have already adapted the patterns attributed to *policemen* as an audience group. This would still be a valid explanation on the individual level, even though attributed perceptions on the group level were diversified and often inaccurate (as shown in Table 4–5).

Discussion

Our major efforts in this chapter have been directed toward analyzing the process of role acquisition in terms of the clarity and complementarity of role perceptions. Conducting a panel comparison of shifts in perceptions of the *policeman* role within the recruit group for the five areas, we found no orderly or consistent pattern of shifts. Similarly, an examination of the accuracy of role perceptions attributed by recruits to active rank groups revealed no overall pattern of either congruence or dissimilarity. In contrast, there was a marked tendency for many individual recruits to have uniform perceptions of rank groups regardless of the accuracy of such perceptions. There was some reason to suspect that recruits were now responding more like *policemen*, but even after two years the trend was not pronounced.

We have already pointed out that inaccuracies of role perception can occur in both audiences and actors. Evaluative reactions of audiences on an interpersonal level will call forth responses chiefly of psychological characteristics. On the other hand, the identification of self with role behavior might well ignore personality factors whenever performance of the role was evaluated. The question that this difference in perspective presents is which of these orientations governs the perceptions and evaluations of audiences to specific actors and role performances.

In Chapter 5 we shall try to assess the relative importance of personality criteria as compared with role content criteria in the evaluation of recruit role performance. Do audiences judge role behavior on the basis of individual or affective qualities, or do they employ a set of nonpersonal factors by which role performance may be impartially measured? If he were unsure which criteria were being used, a recruit might believe it more desirable to have his superiors think of him primarily as "well-rounded" and "personable" rather than as someone whose major characteristic is technical proficiency. This problem of choice presumes that these two images can be distinguished from one another and that they may also be incompatible.

CHAPTER 5

The Evaluation of Role Performance

AMONG THE central issues of role theory is the evaluation of role performance. It is here that the contingencies of self-expectations and the expectations of others are put by the actor to the behavioral test, for it is here that role performance is confronted with a test of its adequacy: adequacy for the actor in terms of his personal satisfaction, and adequacy for the audience in terms of the esteem accorded the actor's performance (i.e., the expression of their satisfaction). As evaluations are fed back into a system of role relationships they serve to institutionalize the existing sets of expectations and behaviors—to clarify and sharpen them, or to corrode and redefine the initial role relationship.

Our own explorations into the problems of evaluation were preliminary and hesitant—as is reflected in the tentative nature of the materials to follow. We have organized the chapter into three major sections. First, we attempt to describe the recruit evaluation procedures. Here evaluation is a formal and very prominent aspect of the training program, and most materials were available for this group. Second, we take up the problem of evaluating a work unit—in this case the police post. Third, we attempt to explore the organizational perceptions of current evaluation procedures.

Procedures for the Evaluation of Recruits

Certain ranges of age, height, weight, education, citizenship, physical fitness, and residence must be satisfied by all candidates in order to establish their eligibility for training. As long as an applicant fell within these ranges, no further comparative evaluations were made on these dimensions. With the exception of weight,[1] these initial screening criteria were of little consequence for an individual's subsequent career in the department.

[1] In the masculine culture of the CSP, being overweight became an obvious indicator of poor physical condition and the lack of self-discipline. Further, the obese *policeman* was viewed as a detriment to good public relations. While "weight" never became a formal category of evaluation, the choice between corpulence or a commission was not infrequent. Calorie-counting in the headquarters dining hall was a subject of grim humor. (See also Chapter 2.)

The major entrance variables used in *ranking* applicants were a written test "designed to determine applicant's intelligence and ability to learn," and an oral interview conducted by a panel consisting of two Civil Service examiners, one member of the department, usually the Personnel Officer, and an outside person, usually a psychologist selected by the department. Of the two variables, the oral interview had the least structure, and appeared to hinge largely on an assessment of the applicant's appearance, ease and productivity of interaction, and motivation for the career. According to general information derived from those who had been members of recent panels, the rating of applicants is quite independent in all of the above categories and no formal criteria were invoked. Subsequent to the interview, candidates were assigned a numerical rating, and the sum of their written examination score and their interview rating determined their ranking on an eligibility register. Recruit classes were composed of candidates drawn in order from this register in accord with manpower needs.

Since all Civil Service examinations were confidential, it was not possible for us to obtain a copy of the written test. We also made several attempts to obtain permission to attend the oral interviews of candidates, but the Civil Service Commission denied our requests on the grounds that the presence of outsiders was a violation of procedure and might penalize those who would be observed.

As far as we could determine, the written test was limited to a brief paper-and-pencil omnibus intelligence test. The criteria for the selection of this examination were not available to us. For that matter, the members of the Personnel Division were also uninformed both as to the rationale for the selection of the test and its scoring procedure.

The ratings of the screening panel, according to our informants, appeared to be quite uniform among members of any given panel. Such consensus, however, appeared from our reports to be generated within the panel during the screening sessions, though each panel member brought to the situation some image of what the necessary qualifications for *policemen* are, or at least ought to be.[2]

Thus, through this process not entirely clear to us, the recruit-applicants came to be rated and ranked in accord with their presumed eligibility for police work. From a pragmatic standpoint, these initial screening procedures

2 The potential for idiosyncratic individual and panel behavior is thus quite high. Illustrative of this is the report of one psychologist–panel member who, "not knowing what to kook for," decided that he didn't want *policemen* who were "overly aggressive, authoritarian, or punitively directed." To this end, he brought to the screening interview selected Rorschach cards, and on the basis of his on-the-spot administration and interpretation weeded out those applicants he deemed undesirable.

seem more likely to emphasize the acceptance of good candidates than the rejection of bad candidates. In any case, this Civil Service rating does not enter into a *policeman's* permanent record, but the ratings are communicated to the recruit school staff and have some influence on the subsequent evaluation of the recruits by some of the school staff.

During the eight-week recruit school, the recruits were evaluated 1) by their grade averages on written and performance examinations and 2) through formal discussion among the school staff which culminated in a final ranking of the class. Following the school was a six-month period of in-service training at posts throughout the state. The recruits were assigned, by post command, to work in apprenticeship to one or more veteran *policemen*. The *supervisory policemen* were then responsible for monthly service rating reports, a standard printed rating form comprised of such items as "attitude," "cooperation," "quality of work," "personal habits," etc., each scored on a four-point scale (see Table 5-2).

The major problem of the *supervisory policeman* ratings, from a research perspective, stemmed from the fact that the field phase of training dispersed the recruits throughout the department, with few posts having more than one recruit. Consequently there were numerous, isolated judges, each of whom evaluated only one or two individuals. At some posts, moreover, some recruits worked with only one supervisor, while at other posts a recruit may have been assigned alternately to two or three supervisors. Operationally, we assigned to each recruit a single rating by summing across the rating scale items and judges for all six (monthly) reports and then by computing a mean rating. The entire recruit group was then arrayed in rank order for the purpose of correlational analysis, from the recruit with the highest mean rating to the recruit with the lowest rating.

In addition to these standard organizational procedures, we introduced two ad hoc evaluation measures. First, we desired some indication, for comparative purposes, of how the post command staff would evaluate the recruits. Since no standard form was available for this, we constructed a simple form on which we asked the post commander (sergeant) and assistant post commanders (corporals) to compare the recruit with other men of the same rank on the basis of their past experience. The rating was requested on a four-point scale, both for present performance and for maximum potential. Since each recruit was under the scrutiny of between three and eight noncommissioned officers, dependent upon the size of the post at which he was stationed, a mean score for each recruit was again computed, and the entire group was ranked as a whole. In addition, comments were solicited from the raters concerning their conceptions of the major assets and liabilities of the recruits they were rating.

Second, since the formal evaluation procedures of the department focused so consistently upon matters of motivation, attitude, sociability, style, appearance, and the like, it seemed desirable to secure some measure of psychological adjustment. For reasons of relative brevity and substantial reliability in populations similar in background to the recruit class, the Heron-Maudsley Personality Measure was selected.[3] This two-part measure consists of a 110-item true-false behavioral inventory, of which 20 items are used as a basis for a score of emotional maladjustment and 12 items are used as a basis for a measure of sociability. The remaining items are buffers designed to obscure the intent of the test.

Using established norms, it was possible to determine which of the recruits were "probably well-adjusted," "doubtful," and "probably maladjusted"; while, for the second part, high, medium, or low sociability could be shown. It should be emphasized that these inventories alone are not claimed to be absolute clinical scales of neuroticism or other pathological conditions; they serve merely as a set of indirect indicators of the relative adjustment and sociability of an individual compared with norms of a test population.

It can be seen from the foregoing description of measures that an effort was made to utilize all of the actual criteria which were employed by the CSP to evaluate the performance of its recruits. The added measures were designed to assess dimensions of recruit performance which were not covered by department procedures. The major weakness in comparing all of these measures lies in the fact that some were applied uniformly to the recruit class by a single set of judges, while others represented only partial or segmented judgments by different sets of evaluators. Nonetheless, these measures encompass, reasonably well, the range of images which affect role behavior, and they are certainly exhaustive of the formal system of recruit evaluation.

Recruit Evaluation Measures Compared

We sought first to determine the degree and direction of association among the seven evaluation measures. This was accomplished by the rank order (rho) correlation matrix of Table 5-1. From a predictive standpoint we might first consider the time sequence of the evaluation measures. With prediction as an end, one would look for relatively high correlations between measures widely separated in time. Thus a high correlation—for example, between Civil Service scores and post command ratings—would have considerable practical value in that the earlier measure could be used to sift out unpromising recruits before expensive training was undertaken. However, we

[3] A. Heron, "A Two-Part Personality Measure for Use as a Research Criterion," *British Journal of Psychology*, 47 (1956), 243-51.

found that those measures displaying statistically significant rank correlations give no promise of accurate selectivity.[4] Indeed, considering the matrix as a whole, only five of the twenty-one correlations show any significant relationship (all in the positive direction), and only two of these are at all impressive. At the very least, it is clear that the measures used to determine recruit qualification do not reflect the criteria which determine later and final recruit evaluations.

TABLE 5-1
RANK ORDER CORRELATIONS (r_s) OF RECRUIT EVALUATION MEASURES

Measures	(7) Post Command Ratings	(6) Supervisory Policemen Ratings	(5) School Staff Ratings	(4) School Grade Averages	(3) Civil Service Ratings	(2) Emotional Adjustment Score
1. Sociability score	.02	.00	−.10	−.18	−.15	.64†
2. Emotional adjustment score . . .	−.19	.03	−.14	−.27	−.03	—
3. Civil Service ratings . .	.01	−.20	.02	.36*	—	
4. School grade averages . .	.17	.06	.38*	—		
5. School staff ratings . .	.62†	.21	—			
6. Supervisory policemen ratings . .	.35*	—				

* $p < .05$.   † $p < .005$.

From another perspective, the matrix may be analyzed by clustering the measures. In this instance, three clusters may be discerned in Table 5-1. The first cluster, consisting of measures 5-6-7, derives from the subjective judgments of the several audiences in the department who are specifically responsible for recruit evaluation. While the methods of rating are quite different, all three measures in fact focus upon the actual role performance of the recruits.

The second cluster, consisting of measures 3 and 4, emphasizes intellectual aptitude and functioning, and is based primarily on written examinations. These measures are the most precise of those used and are the least personalized and impressionistic. In this sense, they may be seen as more objective than those comprising the first cluster, though not necessarily more valid.

4 One must be careful to recognize that within this analysis the rank correlations serve only to delineate the relative standing of members of a recruit class, all of whom successfully completed the training program. It is quite conceivable that a predictive criterion could separate "successes" from "failures" without at the same time being able to differentiate within the group of successful persons.

The third cluster, a personality type, covering measures 1 and 2, is based upon emotional and relational factors which have little direct connection with the specific content of the role itself. They reflect general and individual qualities which presumably transcend any role situation. This type is important in that it represents a category of measures which has been extensively used in studies attempting to predict individual success and failure in occupational settings.

Considering the matrix on the basis of these clusters, we can see that four of the five significant correlations are of the *intra*-cluster variety. This finding lends support to the idea that these three types possess at least a partial integration which distinguishes them from one another.[5] To further test the meaningfulness of these three sets of evaluation measures we need to ask whether these types display internal consistency. Using Haggard's coefficient of intraclass correlation for ranks (R_r),[6] the following results were obtained:

	3 Measure	5 Measure	7 Measure
Type 1: Recruit school staff Supervisory policemen Post command staff	R_r .198		
Type 2: Civil Service ratings School grade average		R_r .117	
Type 3: Emotional adjustment Sociability			R_r .010

We can see from this analysis that the homogeneity and internal consistency of these measures is quite low; and, as each cluster is added, consistency decreases. It is clear that these organizational and ad hoc measures of recruit performance bear little relationship to each other singly or by cluster. Taking these measures at face value, we may conclude:

1. With respect to the cluster one measures, the low order of correlations suggests that the criteria used for recruit ranking were inadequate to achieve any

---

[5] The one instance of intertype correlation, between 4 and 5, can probably be explained by the fact that the independence of the measure is not absolute. In this instance, the grade average of the recruit is given some consideration by the Recruit School staff in the ranking of the class. However, attendance at the ranking sessions convinced the investigators that the grade average is given less weight than such factors as physical prowess, compatibility, pistol marksmanship, and so on.

[6] Basically, this coefficient is a measure of the relative homogeneity of the ranks within a class in relation to the total rank variation among all the classes. In terms of our problem, R_r is a function of a test statistic F_r, which indicates whether the sets of rankings are randomly distributed in terms of the measures used. As Haggard points out, R_r is similar to Kendall's W, and F_r is similar to Friedman's χ_r^2. For a full discussion of these procedures see E. A. Haggard, *Intraclass Correlation and the Analysis of Variance* (New York: Dryden Press, 1958).

impressive agreement, the primary source of disagreement being between the
supervisory policeman and both the post commanders and school staff.

2. With respect to clusters 2 and 3, the pattern of these findings suggests either
   that intellectual aptitude, adjustment, and sociability were not contributory to
   the actual or idealized role performance of police recruits, or that those who
   evaluate such performance do not give much weight to these factors.

In the following sections we shall explore the questions of evaluative
criteria and personality factors in greater detail.

Further Sources of Recruit Evaluation

The standard form used for recruit rating during their field probation was
a source of still further data which bear upon the evaluation of role performance. On this form the *supervisory policemen* rated the recruit, on a four-
point scale, on twelve items of performance. Space was also provided for the
rater to comment upon each of the twelve rating categories. In addition to
the *supervisory policeman*, the post commander and district commander—
both of whom reviewed the supervisor's rating—were provided with space to
write in comments. The ranking of the recruit class by the recruit school
staff similarly contained considerable voluntary comment about individual
recruits which was classifiable under the same categories used on the standard
form.

It seemed to us that these voluntary comments provided a valuable clue to
the kinds of factors which were salient to each of the rating groups. In this
regard, no distinction was made between positive and negative comments
since our interest is in the total emphasis placed on each category. Table 5–2
shows the several group distributions of comments by categories.

In attempting to analyze the rater comments on recruit performance one
may make at least two different kinds of assumptions about the nature of
these data. First, one could assume that the frequency of voluntary comments
by each rating group is an index of the importance of a category to a given
group. Or one could assume that the different group distributions of free
comments reflect not hierarchies of importance but rather differences in
perspective. Under this assumption we cannot say (as we could under the
first assumption) that, for example, the quality of the recruit's work is
unimportant to the school staff, or that *supervisory policemen* are not much
interested in the personal habits of recruits. What we could say under this
assumption, however, is that the recruit school staff and the *supervisory
policemen* have chosen to evaluate recruit performance from rather different
perspectives. We think that, within the confines of these data, this second
assumption is a more meaningful one.

TABLE 5-2

RATER COMMENTS ON RECRUIT PERFORMANCE

Comment Category	Per Cent of Rater Comments in Each Category				
	School Staff	Supervisory Policemen	Post Commanders	District Commanders	Overall Rank
Appearance . .	13.6	6.1	18.2	18.0	1.0
Personal habits .	32.3	3.1	17.0	10.3	5.0
Cooperation . .	3.4	4.6	5.3	0.0	11.5
Attitude . . .	18.6	5.2	18.9	15.4	2.0
Initiative . . .	5.1	11.5	3.0	5.0	8.0
Dependability .	0.0	9.6	1.7	0.0	11.5
Judgment . .	1.7	9.4	3.3	2.6	10.0
Public relations .	10.2	11.3	6.0	12.8	3.0
Progressiveness .	5.1	4.8	0.7	15.4	9.0
Knowledge . .	3.4	11.9	9.0	12.8	4.0
Work quantity .	6.8	7.3	10.3	0.0	7.0
Work quality .	0.0	15.2	6.6	7.7	6.0
No. of Comments	59	479	301	39	
No. of Raters .	8	36	19	7	

As we inspect Table 5-2 we can see that the school staff and the field command staff—as before—achieve a most modest consensus in perspective. The fundamental difference again seems to be centered in the *supervisory policemen*. This becomes especially apparent if we convert the distribution of comments in Table 5-2 to a matrix of rank-order correlations:

	Supervisory Policemen	Post Commanders	District Commanders
Recruit school staff	−.54	.64	.56
Supervisory policemen		−.19	−.09
Post commanders			.40

These rank correlations are comparable to those presented in Table 5-1, and the average agreement among all four groups, .13, is also approximately equal to the intraclass correlations we obtained earlier. Here, however, the differences between the *supervisory policemen* and the recruit's other audiences become most prominent. All of the negative correlations in the matrix involve the *supervisory policemen*.

The reason for this difference is not immediately clear. *Supervisory policemen* are, first of all, selected by their post commanders, and are generally veteran *policemen* of high standing at the post. Certainly it is plausible to expect that a commander would select a supervisor who would reflect his own standards and performance criteria. Yet even if the commander and his *supervisory policeman* shared the same evaluative criteria, two factors intervene in the application of such criteria. First, the commanders and supervisors interact with the recruits in different types of work situations. Thus the raters may be applying the same criteria to different segments of the recruit's performance, or they may be differentially emphasizing such shared criteria because of differences in recruit visibility. As we look at the substance of the voluntary comments given by the school staff and the field commanders we can see that their emphasis was primarily on those aspects of recruit performance which are most readily observable to them and which reflected on the nature of his *public image*: appearance, attitude, public relations skills, and personal habits. In contrast, the categories commented on most by supervisors appear to be primarily *work-oriented*: quality of work, knowledge of police work, initiative on the job, and public relations skills.

TABLE 5–3

PROGRESS AND FORECAST EVALUATIONS OF RECRUITS (PER CENT)

	Supervisory Policemen	Post Commanders	District Commanders	Recruit School Staff* Scholar- ship	Physical Skills
Progress Index					
Not satisfactory .	0.0	0.9	2.1	14.9	6.4
Satisfactory . .	0.0	52.3	66.0	27.7	29.8
Good	0.0	11.0	14.9	12.8	4.3
Excellent . . .	0.0	11.9	2.1	2.1	2.1
Improvement . .	0.0	23.9	14.9	0.0	0.0
Total Comments:					
$N =$	0	109	47	27	20
Forecast Index					
Satisfactory . .	(too	7.5	21.7	71.4	
Good	few	67.9	52.2	28.6	
Excellent . . .	comments)	24.5	26.1	0.0	
Total Comments:					
$N =$	3	53	23	21	

* Ratings were made during headquarters training period only, and percentages are based on a total of 47 comments.

The second factor that may contribute to these observed differences in the evaluative criteria selected by the rating groups may perhaps be found in the nature of the assumptions they make about recruit evaluation. We suspect that the school staff and the field commanders are less concerned about the immediate work performance of the recruits partly because they have successfully completed the first stage of their training (during which most of the drop-outs and failures occur) but primarily because the raters view the application of standards of professional police performance to such neophytes as premature. To the *supervisory policeman*, whose reputation and very life may depend on the adequate performance of his recruit-partner, there is nothing at all premature in his emphasis upon the work quality of the recruit.

That only low consensus can be achieved in recruit evaluation is in large measure a consequence of the inadequate specification of general criteria by which recruit performance can be reliably assessed independent of the direct visibility of such performance to a rater. It seems likely, too, that the evaluative criteria that have been specified are selectively emphasized by the raters, and that this selective emphasis appears as a consequence not only of recruit visibility but of variant assumptions made about recruit evaluation.

A final measure of evaluation gleaned from the standard rating form was derived from systematic statements of the progress of recruits made by the raters, along with their forecasts of eventual performance level. These statements were frequently utilized in the final "Recommendation for Confirmation," which officially transformed the recruit into a *policeman*. Although not made systematically for each recruit, the use of such index statements—"not satisfactory," "satisfactory," "good," "excellent," "improvement shown"—represents a kind of overall judgment of performance which suggests that raters are invoking some general scale of expectations along which they are grading the recruits in view.

The initial feature of interest in Table 5–3 is the almost complete absence of these overall progress and forecast evaluations by *supervisory policemen*. Their ratings were almost exclusively confined to the formal rating scale categories, and apparently they felt unable or unwilling to make such inclusive progress and predictive statements. The recruit school staff, by contrast, although not using the standard form, felt more able to make these gross judgments, to do so in detail, and to distinguish between scholastic performance and physical skills.

Looking first at the Progress Index, it is apparent that judgments of recruit performance tend to be moderate, and that work excellence was seen as relatively rare. The school staff stood almost alone in its reports of substandard performance among the recruits. The Forecast Index provided relatively fewer comments from all groups but showed a rather significant increase in optimism among the field commanders, while the school staff retained its caution by making no forecast of "excellence." It is clear, from even these crude data, that the field superiors of the newly confirmed *policemen* have a hopeful image of their role success even though judgments of actual performance would seem to indicate a less sanguine projection. The clearest finding of all is that the recruit school staff's more intimate knowledge of the recruits, plus the opportunity to see the entire class on a comparative basis, led to a more critical assessment of general role performance than did the field commander's more limited relationships with the recruits.

Although the data on these points are quite tentative, they suggest that the closer and more precisely role performance is evaluated the higher will be the proportion of criticism in the total distribution of evaluations. Apparently, when audiences make judgments of the behavior of novices at a distance in a formal organization, they tend to be more positive and optimistic in their assessments of future behavior the greater their distance from the role. Perhaps, as time goes on, the hope becomes part of subsequent perceptions.

Recruit Personality and Evaluation

At this point a further comment may be made concerning the Heron-Maudsley Emotional Adjustment and Sociability Scales described earlier in the chapter. Heron's applications of the Emotional Adjustment measure to several samples of "normal" populations and a sample of neurotic in-patients at a psychiatric hospital yielded a distribution of scores in which one standard deviation above the mean fell at a score of 9 for the normals taken as a group and one standard deviation below the mean fell at 9.5 for the hospitalized neurotics.[7] It seemed justifiable, then, to regard scores of 10 and over as "probably maladjusted," scores of 8 and 9 as "doubtful," and scores of 0–7 as "probably well-adjusted." Using these groupings with the recruit class, the distribution was 14 per cent, 21 per cent, and 65 per cent—which was roughly similar to the original test samples. Thus, while the recruits would appear to qualify as a "normal" sample, it also appears that the selection procedures of the department were not able to identify applicants whose emotional adjustment might be in doubt.[8]

The sociability measure, for which there were no norms, was scored on a basis of 0–3 as "high," 4–8 as "medium," and 9–12 as "low." The distribution of the recruit class was 19 per cent, 65 per cent, and 16 per cent.

It is clear from Table 5–1 that, while sociability and emotional adjustment scores manifest a moderately high correlation with each other, they bear no significant relationship to the other recruit rankings. A combined sociability-adjustment score similarly yielded only negligible correlations with the other measures. In fact, many recruits who scored well in both of the personality tests were ranked in the lower half of the class by the school staff. These findings certainly do not generate confidence in the ability of paper-and-pencil personality tests to predict the quality of role performance. However, the findings may also be indicative of real differences between those criteria used by evaluating groups and those incorporated in the majority of personality tests.

[7] Heron, *op. cit.*

[8] As a caution, it should be reemphasized that this measure does not denote pathology or normality but is simply an indicator of tendency based upon comparisons of nonclinical and clinical subjects.

From another perspective, we raised the question of whether or not *policemen* regarded themselves, as a group, as possessing distinctive personality characteristics. Accordingly, all respondents were requested to indicate those "qualities" which they felt most important for a *policeman* to have. This was asked in an open-ended question, with no limit on response. While we could discern seven broad categories of response, the two categories with the most frequent responses were those emphasizing "honesty and fairness" and "reliability and adaptability." It is obvious that these qualities are not role-related in any direct sense. They refer, rather, to personal attributes which anyone might expect to be dominant throughout the society. The *policeman* thus saw himself more as a member of this larger society than as a person having particular skills, functions, or distinctive personality characteristics.[9]

The Evaluation of Posts

In our concern with the evaluation of role performance we must necessarily give some attention to the problem of evaluating work units. Here we need to ask two important and interrelated questions.

1. To what extent are the criteria for the evaluation of work units independent of the criteria for the evaluation of the role performance of their members?
2. Given independence, to what extent does membership in a given work unit influence the evaluations of individual role performance?

We began, in our exploration of these questions, by asking all members of the department what they thought were the most important factors in evaluating a post; their responses appear in Table 5-4. Two things are apparent. First, there emerged a rather unidimensional criterion of post evaluation; over three-fourths of the responses stress the potential contribution of the post to the organization.[10] Second, it can be seen that these categories of *functional importance*—level of activity and increases in level, location, and size—emphasize factors which are relatively independent of the personnel assigned to the post. This is, of course, manifested more conclusively in the low proportion of nominations given the "combined

[9] Specific role-related attributes such as physical prowess, legal knowledge, public relations skills, etc., received only minor mention. Similarly, in our public samples—to be reported in the following chapters—there was little mention of any qualities which could be regarded as distinctive. For the public, the two categories with the most frequent responses were those emphasizing "courtesy, helpfulness, and friendliness" and "reliability and adaptability."

[10] Cf. W. S. Mason and N. Gross, "Intra-Occupational Prestige Differentiation: The School Superintendency," *American Sociological Review*, 20 (1955), 326–31.

ratings of *policemen*" or the "reputation of the post commander." Finally, we need to note that in our analysis of response by rank no rank differences appear. Thus, not only was there high consensus on evaluative criteria, but such consensus obtains independent of position within the organization.

It seems fair to ask, given such consensus, the extent to which a rating of posts in the department actually reflected these evaluative criteria. Accordingly, we asked all headquarters officers to sort the fifty-four posts into one of three categories—superior, average, and weak—and, in an attempt to minimize variation, we restricted their nominations to their first five choices in each of the categories. Some three months later we asked both headquarters and district officers to perform the same sorting operation, but this time on post commanders.[11] Both times we provided only a listing of the posts and the sorting directions, thus permitting the officers to invoke their own evaluative criteria. The results of these post and commander ratings appear in Table 5–4 (for simplicity, the "average" nominations have been omitted).

TABLE 5–4
NOMINATIONS FOR SUPERIOR–WEAK POSTS AND POST COMMANDERS

	Number of Nominations
Posts	
Designated as superior	12
Designated as weak	25
Designated as both	1
Not nominated	17
Post Commanders	
Designated as superior	29
Designated as weak	34
Designated as both	17
Not nominated	8
Post and Post Commander Combinations	
Superior post, superior commander . .	7
Superior post, weak commander . . .	1
Weak post, superior commander . . .	2
Weak post, weak commander . . .	9

It is clear that there is more agreement about superior posts than about weak posts. The almost complete absence of overlap shows that officers made a sharp distinction between the two categories. The picture is much less definitive of post commanders; there were many more nominations in both categories and considerable overlap. The extent of this ambiguity was rather unexpected, and perhaps officers have dissimilar standards for post commanders—as is suggested by the considerable contradiction in these ratings.

[11] The Policy Questionnaire, which contained the post evaluation and other evaluation questions, was administered about one month after the post ratings were completed.

On the other hand, the differential field experience of each officer might also have resulted in restricting his range of selections, particularly in judging individuals. Formal reports were available to all on post performance whereas such information was not routinely circulated on personnel.

The combination of these ratings yields considerable congruence between post and commander selections for both superiority and weakness. Without question, the larger, busier, urban southern district posts and their commanders received the most frequent superiority rating. Of the seven top combined ratings, only one was a middle-size post, and it was located in the southern district. On the other hand, the nine lowest combined ratings contained only one urban post, and five were very small northern district posts. The other three posts were middle-size and were located in surburban areas or small towns in the southern district. There were only three incongruent ratings, consisting of two weak posts with superior commanders and one superior post with a weak commander. Size and location of these posts varied.

TABLE 5-5

WHAT ARE THE MOST IMPORTANT FACTORS IN EVALUATING A POST?

	Number of Nominations	Per Cent
Level of activity (how busy a post is) . . .	228	33.0
Location of post	129	18.7
Amount of yearly increase in post activity .	96	13.8
Size of post (number of men)	88	12.8
Combined ratings of policemen at post . .	65	9.3
Assessment, reputation of post commander .	33	4.8
Rank in the district	13	1.8
All the other factors	40	5.8

NOTE.—Number of respondents, 282; number of nominations, 692.

These results indicate conclusively that officer judgments of superiority and weakness in posts and commanders were related, and that such ratings had considerable interchangeability at the extremes of the rating continuum. Further, it is quite apparent that expressed criteria of functional importance were indeed the actual criteria of post evaluation.

Given, then, this congruence in the evaluation of posts and post commanders, we must return to the second question posed at the outset of this discussion: To what extent is the evaluation of a *policeman* biased by the evaluator's assessment of where the *policeman* is assigned? If the judged quality of the post did indeed influence the rating given to *policemen*, then some indicator of discrimination should be manifest. At the very least, *policemen* from "superior" posts should be more favorably evaluated as a group than *policemen* from "weak" posts.

From the perspective of *policemen* themselves, our own field experiences had indicated that many *policemen* believed that promotion was linked to headquarters' favoritism for the larger posts, which were almost always in urban areas. Furthermore, this perception was generalized to the belief that men stationed in the sparsely populated northern districts were given less consideration than those in the heavily settled southern districts. These conceptions were further translated into an interpretation of post assignments which held that if a man were transferred from a large to a small post, or if he were to remain in the northern district for a considerable length of time, these facts could be taken as prima facie evidence of low evaluation, with consequent delay in promotion. Thus, even if such bias were not the case, it had all of the elements of a "self-fulfilling prophecy."

Clearly, the "hardest" criterion of evaluation is promotion, and if any evaluative bias existed it should have been manifested in the promotional record. Accordingly, a complete list of *policeman* promotions was assembled for the period August, 1957, to February, 1959. The eight administrative districts within the department provided our first test, since the districts ranged in size and level of activity from the highly urbanized and populous sections to the rural and sparsely settled ones, while the posts within each district were relatively homogeneous. A chi-square analysis, based upon proportionate promotions in terms of *policemen* populations, revealed no significant differences among these districts. Similarly, when northern and southern districts were compared it was observed for the period in question that promotions were received by 5.1 per cent of *policemen* in the northern districts and 5.06 per cent of *policemen* in the southern districts. Finally, a check was made of promotions from the top seven posts with a combined superior rating, and the bottom nine posts with a combined weak rating. Here the result was that 6.8 per cent of the *policemen* at superior posts and 7.1 per cent of those at weak posts received promotion. Thus, the evidence fails to support any belief that post reputations or location had any direct effect on *policemen* promotions.

Apparently then, *policemen* promotions were made on the basis of a combined weighting of post commander rating, examination performance (written and interview), seniority, and some more elusive impressionistic criteria which cannot be identified reliably. It is difficult to determine the organizational consequences of such a vague system of role evaluation. It is quite possible that, given the variability in the judgment of *policemen* performance by raters and the paucity of systematic rating instruments, a fair number of promotions can even be attributed to error and fortuitous circumstances. While this state of affairs may not provide encouragement of the highly ambitious individual, it may at least make the average (or even low) striver feel that his chances of promotion are as good as those of his peers, even if he judges his performance inferior to many of them. On the other hand, insofar as *policemen* define their promotional chances in terms of their post assignment, such self-definitions may have long-range consequences for their role performance.

Certainly, any large-scale organization is likely to reward some mediocrity as if it were high achievement, either through error or through weighting a nonperformance criteria such as age. If the ideology of the system specifically emphasizes achievement (as the CSP does), some frustration is bound to ensue if high-achievers, defined by self-evaluation, find themselves no more advantaged in terms of privilege, rank, and salary than relatively low achievers. Our field experience revealed that in the competition for promotion throughout the hierarchy some of the most talented men (as ascertained by the opinions of others) were often the most dissatisfied and impatient with their rate of progress in the department.[12]

Perceived Channels of Mobility

Once the recruit had been confirmed as a *policeman*, his performance was less intensively judged. Pay raises are generally a function of time spent in service, and promotions are made from the appropriate Civil Service register for each rank and division within the department. These registers were revised periodically by announced examinations, and they were taken by all men in grade who were eligible in terms of length of service and satisfactory yearly ratings by superiors.[13]

While the Civil Service selection of recruit candidates began in 1941, promotional examinations on the *policeman* level were not introduced until 1958. Promotions before then had been based on the field commander's recommendations and a formal interview by an ad hoc promotional board. It was general knowledge within the department that the outcome of promotional hearings was closely related to the sponsorship given applicants by influential members in the department. Since sponsors apparently did not seek to tie up all of the open positions, and since the sponsors themselves

[12] The extreme form of dealing with such dissatisfaction is, of course, resignation. Although department records of voluntary resignations were not very clear, our scrutiny of these records—as well as the replies we received from our mail-sample of resigned personnel —led us to two tentative observations. First, a large number of those resigning went into other police and protective service jobs. Second, resignees seemed to have disproportionately higher educational backgrounds.

[13] As with the recruit examinations, it was not possible for us to obtain copies of the written tests or to attend the oral interviews. The procedures for establishing these registers appeared to follow the same general procedure used in recruit selection.

had a vested interest in the merit of their candidates, the system operated with considerable success.

In spite of the new standardization and "objectivity" of the written examination, the general feeling still pervaded the lower ranks that informal factors weighed most heavily insofar as promotions and transfers were concerned. Accordingly, we asked respondents in all ranks whether they believed it was an advantage to know someone at headquarters in order to get a promotion or transfer. The results of this inquiry appear in Table 5–6.

TABLE 5-6

IN ORDER TO GAIN A PROMOTION OR DESIRED TRANSFER, IS IT AN ADVANTAGE FOR A "POLICEMAN" TO KNOW SOMEONE AT HEADQUARTERS WHO CAN SUPPORT OR SPEAK UP FOR HIM?

	Per Cent Responding, by Rank				
	Recruits (n = 25)	Policemen (n = 62)	Corporals (n = 99)	Sergeants (n = 50)	Officers (n = 29)
Yes	52.0	56.5	58.6	46.0	20.7
No	8.0	19.4	19.2	28.0	55.2
Possibly, sometimes	40.0	24.2	22.2	26.0	24.1

NOTE.—$\chi^2 = 25.94$; $df = 8$; $p < .01$.

Approximately 51 per cent of all ranks felt it was necessary to have a headquarters sponsor. The other half was equally divided between those who said "no" and those who thought it made a difference "sometimes." It is clear from Table 5–6 that the group distributions are significantly disparate. While recruits, *policemen*, corporals, and—to a lesser extent—sergeants felt that some "pull" was an asset, most officers—who are to be considered the main sources of sponsorship—deny its importance. This type of disparity emphasizes, markedly, the differential conception of the evaluation processes throughout the department. This is perhaps characteristic of organizations which have sharply differentiated hierarchies and diffuse standards of evaluation.

In a related question we asked our respondents what they thought were the most important ways for a *policeman* to gain a high evaluation by head-quarters. As can be seen in Table 5–7, the "post commander's rating" and the voluntary "taking on of new duties and activities" (e.g., pistol team, skin diving, taking college classes, etc.) accounted for 58 per cent of the ways nominated for a *policeman* to gain a high evaluation by headquarters. No doubt, taking on new duties was seen as a means of influencing the post commander's ratings. In line with this, "staying out of trouble," the third most frequently nominated, was a way of avoiding the commander's censure. There can be no doubt that the post commander's recommendation was viewed as crucial. Further, an analysis of these responses by rank showed no differences among ranks. Thus there was central agreement on the importance of the post commander for evaluation.

TABLE 5-7

THE MOST IMPORTANT WAYS FOR A "POLICEMAN" TO GAIN A HIGH EVALUATION BY HEADQUARTERS

	Number of Nominations	Per Cent
The opinion of his post commander . . .	214	31.2
Taking on new duties and activities . . .	183	26.7
Staying out of trouble	68	9.9
Quality of written reports	61	8.9
Popularity with fellow policemen	58	8.4
Number and kind of tickets written . . .	44	6.4
Getting a few big "knock-offs"	18	2.6
All other ways	41	5.9

In view of the responses to the preceding question on the advantages of a headquarters sponsor, had such a choice been included here our nominations might have followed a different pattern. On the other hand, we suspect that this latter question of how to gain a high evaluation reflects the realistic choices of *policemen* and is closer to the actual evaluation procedures that exist today. Thus, as can be seen in Table 5-8, the cross-tabulation of evaluation and sponsorship shows that the perceived manner of gaining a high evaluation was independent of a belief in sponsorship. Regardless of whether sponsorship was seen as necessary, the ways perceived for gaining a high evaluation remained constant. This was also true regardless of rank.

The presumed importance of sponsorship was, of course, a carry-over from an earlier day, but the persistence of that belief, coincidental with the more realistic appraisals (Table 5-7), perhaps reflected the *policeman's* disenchantment or disillusionment with the current procedures of evaluation and promotion. Certainly the belief in the necessity of sponsorship represented a kind of alienation from the normative procedures of promotion for merit. The genesis of such alienative feelings would be not only difficult to trace but beyond the scope of our present analysis.[14] However, a plausible hypothesis, using present data, was that those *policemen* who experienced high blockage in the five role areas explored earlier—particularly those related to advancement and free expression (Chapter 3)—would be more

[14] See, for example, L. I. Pearlin, "Alienation from Work: A Study of Nursing Personnel," *American Sociological Review*, 27 (1962), 314–26; M. Seeman, "On the Meaning of Alienation," *ASR*, 24 (1959), 783–91; and J. P. Clark, "Measuring Alienation within a Social System," *ASR*, 24 (1959), 849–52.

TABLE 5–8

EVALUATION AND SPONSORSHIP

Ways of Gaining a High Evaluation from Headquarters	For promotion or transfer, is it an advantage to know someone at headquarters?		
	Yes	Somewhat	No
How well liked by peers . . .	7.6	9.6	10.6
Number and kind of tickets . .	8.5	6.0	2.6
Opinion of post commander . .	32.9	31.1	29.8
Ambition, taking on extra duties .	23.8	28.7	27.8
Staying out of trouble	9.5	11.4	9.9
Quality of written reports . .	8.8	4.8	11.3
Getting a few big "knock-offs" .	3.0	3.6	2.0
All others	5.8	4.8	6.0

NOTE.—Number of "yes" responses, 328; "somewhat," 167; "no," 151.

likely to perceive sponsorship as necessary than those who did not feel constrained or blocked by the organization. In Table 5–9 we attempted to test this hypothesis by a cross-tabulation of the combined responses of recruits and *policemen*.

Though there was no unilateral relationship between blockage and "alienation" in these five areas, some of the expected and otherwise interesting relationships obtain. First, as we expected, feelings of blockage on Advancement Opportunities and Freedom to Express Feelings were directly related to the belief in sponsorship. Thus "pull" became an acceptable

TABLE 5–9

THE DISTRIBUTION OF AREA BLOCKAGE AND THE NEED FOR SPONSORSHIP

Area	Blockage	Need for Sponsorship						χ^2
		Number			Per Cent			
		Yes	No	Total	Yes	No	Total	
1. Advancement Opportunities	High	26	4	30	86.7	13.3	100.0	2.11
	Low	21	10	31	67.7	32.3	100.0	.20 > p > .10
2. Social Value and Prestige .	High	24	11	35	68.6	31.4	100.0	2.31
	Low	23	3	26	88.5	11.5	100.0	.20 > p > .10
3. Freedom to Express Feelings . .	High	28	5	33	84.8	15.2	100.0	1.61
	Low	19	9	28	67.9	32.1	100.0	.30 > p > .20
4. Self-Realization	High	26	8	34	76.5	23.5	100.0	0.35
	Low	21	6	27	77.8	22.2	100.0	.70 > p > .50
5. Job-Family Compatibility	High	31	4	35	88.6	11.4	100.0	˙4.73
	Low	16	10	26	61.5	38.5	100.0	.05 > p > .02

alternative—perhaps the only possibility perceived open—to those who saw themselves as blocked, presumably through normative channels, in their attempt to achieve advancement and freedom.

Second, though the findings with regard to Social Value and Prestige and Job-Family Compatibility seem to go in opposite directions, it seems likely that a single mechanism underlies both. The fact that the job can be seen as easily affording high prestige (low blockage) yet at the same time requiring "pull"—an "illegitimate" means of organizational advancement—suggests strongly that the means of organizational advancement had become, or was, less important than the end of public recognition. Thus, in a derivative manner the goal of public recognition had here replaced recognition within the organization as a primary goal. In a similar way, it seemed likely that the objective of a "normal" family life (which we saw in Chapters 2 and 3 as so important to the *policeman*) also became even more important than the means of organizational advancement. Thus in the case of both public prestige and family life, extra-organizational goals seemed to take precedence over the organizational norms. Perhaps, insofar as persons seek objectives outside those which are organizationally defined, their membership within the organization may become, itself, a means to their other ends. Organizational norms, where they conflict with such extra-organizational demands, may become irrelevant or less important. Our interpretation is certainly speculative, but it points up our previous suggestions that role perceptions and role behavior probably transcend the boundaries of the social systems in which the role is located. At least we may conclude that the perception of opportunity structures within the CSP is significantly related to the satisfaction or frustration of some role-related values, and that such values may be important alienative conditions within this organizational setting.

Discussion

In general, the evaluation measures employed formally in the CSP displayed a low order of correlation and homogeneity and a decided lack of predictive utility. Measures used to determine recruit qualification showed a negligible relationship to later and final evaluations; and evaluations of school performance similarly showed negligible relationships to evaluations of field performance.

The low consensus in recruit evaluation is made further apparent by the differential emphasis given performance categories by the various rating groups and by their differential perception of the current and projected success levels in the same recruit class. Operationally, the selective emphasis given the evaluative criteria that have been specified appears as a probable consequence of the limited visibility of recruit performance and variant assumptions made about performance quality among the several audiences. Generally, it appeared that the greater the direct involvement of the raters as role partners the higher the proportion of criticism in the total distribution of evaluations.

It is clear—from the vagueness of the evaluative criteria—that the role of *policeman* was not clearly distinguished from the other roles in which an individual was obviously engaged, or from the cultural definitions of human virtues and desired characteristics which apply throughout society. Thus a rater's general standard for a "man" appeared to strongly influence the conception he had of a *policeman* as a particular type of "man." Furthermore, the ambiguity of even these judgments made differentiation and evaluation a chancy matter.

Overt dissatisfaction with the evaluative process was demonstrated primarily in the increase of resignations between the seventh and twelfth year of service (see Chapter 2) and in the general comments of command staff personnel on the difficulties of evaluation. However, it is clear that, despite the nebulous quality of the evaluative process, most persons who completed recruit training remained within the organization for a full career, and that the CSP flourished as an organization highly esteemed by its public and its peers.

Given such conditions we may well wonder how any pattern of behavioral control within the organization could operate consistently. If we look for the "positive" consequences of what we have observed, a clue may be found in the very diversity of behavioral images. Since many of the *policeman's* audiences were not in agreement about their perceptions and expectations of him, they also varied in their evaluative criteria and their judgments of his performance. This variability could have lessened the impact that a precise and uniform evaluation procedure would have had on the role performance of a *policeman* by providing him with options and alternatives rather than one highly constraining set of role prescriptions. Perhaps, as Stouffer (among others) has noted, the existence of an acceptable *range* of permissible behaviors in a group provides the very flexibility which makes group survival possible.[15] If so, one would expect that increased pressures for conformity emanating from increasingly stringent standards of performance could become so great that group members could not follow a strict application of their own requirements. Under such pressure the structure of the group could crumble, by such channels as withdrawal, rebellion, or manipulation by group members.

[15] S. A. Stouffer, "An Analysis of Conflicting Social Norms," *American Sociological Review*, 14 (1949), 707–17.

If we regard consensus as a variable, we continue to face a difficult problem of measurement. We have already noted the potential for inconsistency for a role incumbent between his role perception and his actual behavior. Thus an actor may incorrectly perceive gross differences among audience expectations and consequently invoke negative sanctions from those audiences whose perceptions he misconstrued. In the same manner, his perceptions may be correct but the audiences may be imposing incompatible expectations and provoking similar consequences as before. In role behavior analysis, then, given the apparent probability of some lack of agreement among role definers, it would seem important to distinguish between these two types of behavior problems. Inaccuracy of perception can be laid at either the door of the perceiver himself or of the system which produces the role definitions. We have already presented considerable evidence that the several rank groups, as audiences, held different perceptions of the *policeman* role. At present, we are not sure of the importance of these differences in terms of their consequences both for actual behavior and for the evaluation of such behavior.

Gross has stated the research issues well at the conclusion of the theoretical and operational part of his study; namely, "investigate (1) degrees of consensus (2) among certain populations of role definers (3) on certain segments of a role (4) at given levels of generality (5) under given relational and situational specifications of the position."[16] Although these tasks are indeed imperative, they require measures—particularly in (4) and (5)—which are not yet adequate. What the precise organizational and behavioral consequences of "degrees of consensus" are, we do not yet know.

16 N. Gross, W. S. Mason, and A. W. McEachern, *Explorations in Role Analysis: Studies of the School Superintendency Role* (New York: John Wiley & Sons, 1958), p. 74.

CHAPTER 6

Role Conflict and Audience Expectations

THE STUDY of role conflict has been one of the promising areas of systematic research activity in role analysis. We were interested in role conflict in this study for three major reasons. The first was our belief that the constructs of role analysis are equally applicable to both conflicted and nonconflicted role behavior.[1]

Secondly, we viewed the framework of a role conflict study as most readily adaptable to the exploration of the relationships among *actual role expectations, perceived role expectations,* and *role performance;* and the explication of these relationships we regarded as crucial to the formulation of a theory of role behavior.

Finally, we viewed the analysis of the content of role conflict situations as an important technique for the understanding of organizational structure and its strains. We suspect that role conflicts, as we shall define them below, are generated primarily out of basic disagreements over organizational goals or out of discrepancies in group perceptions of these goals.

The Meaning of Role Conflict

Most definitions of role conflict seem to be in substantial agreement as to the core elements of such conflict. A conflict situation is generally described as one in which role expectations are *inconsistent, incompatible,* or *contradictory.* Unfortunately, this agreement appears to be superficial and tenuous. The elements of this core conception of role conflict have been sufficiently ambiguous as to permit the most diverse types of analyses to be lumped together under the rubric of role conflict studies. Typically, the terms "inconsistent," "incompatible," or "contradictory" are used with the

[1] Judson Brown, in his summary review of research on *intrapersonal* conflict, suggests that it may be necessary to reorient *its* study stressing the principle "that the important determinants of behavior in conflict-producing situations are indistinguishable from those in ordinary unambivalent situations and that no sharp dividing line can be drawn between the two kinds of behavior." See J. S. Brown, "Principles of Intrapersonal Conflict," *Journal of Conflict Resolution,* I (1957), 135–54.

implied meaning (and only an occasional qualification) that they are employed in a manner *analogous* to their usage in formal logic. However, since incompatible propositions in logic may be either contrary *or* contradictory, it is necessary to specify whether role conflict analysis will consider *all* incompatible expectations or only those which are contradictory.

A set of *contradictory* expectations is one in which all cannot be fulfilled *and* one in which all cannot be ignored. Thus, in the role conflict situation, any behavioral alternative selected by the actor, including inaction, will fail to fulfill the expectations of one or more audiences. Contradictory expectations, then, are *mutually exclusive* and are *exhaustive* of the universe of role behavior patterns which are acceptable (i.e., will not incur negative sanctions) to the relevant audiences. A set of *contrary* expectations cannot all be fulfilled, but *can* all be ignored. Thus while any selection among the given alternatives will not be congruent with *some* expectations, the selection of some other behavioral alternative (not inappropriate to the actor's status) may not be construed as "violating" the given expectations. Contrary expectations, then, like contradictory expectations, are mutually exclusive. However, contrary expectations are *not exhaustive* of the universe of role behaviors which will be acceptable to the audiences involved.

Sets of role expectations, then, may be viewed as compatible or incompatible. If incompatible, they may be either contrary or contradictory. Clearly, the two classes of incompatible expectations confront the incumbent with different problems. Further, while the techniques available for ameliorating contradictory expectations will be equally applicable to situations of contrary expectations, the reverse is not the case. As we suggested above, the incumbent has greater freedom to act in situations having contrary expectations. It appears necessary, therefore, to maintain a conceptual distinction between these two classes of situations. The term "role conflict" will be reserved for situations of contradictory expectations, and the term "role dilemma" for situations of contrary expectations.

Since we have been talking about empirically contradictory and contrary expectations, the conception of a conflict situation presented here refers solely to contradictory role expectations and does not imply that the actor either perceives them or experiences ambivalence as a result of them. It should be clear that the existence of a conflict situation should not be regarded as coterminous with its perception, nor should perception be construed as coterminous with effect. Conversely, the fact that a conflict situation does not exist should not be taken to mean that *no* persons will perceive the situation as one of conflicting expectations. Thus, to study only the objectively determined conflict situation (determined, that is, by the scientist-observer) necessarily precludes the researcher from making statements about conflict situations as perceived by the actors in the system under study, while the study of perceived conflict will not necessarily yield information about the actual conflict situations that exist.

The data for the first part of our role conflict analysis came from our purposive sampling of *policemen*. Concomitant with our participant-observation at the four posts selected for field work, we interviewed fifty-one of the fifty-three *policemen* assigned there. The interview schedule consisted, in part, of a series of five structured situations which represented potential conflict situations.[2] Each situation comprised three contradictory alternatives for behavior and a listing of eleven audience groups. Respondents were asked to indicate which of the alternatives each audience group would hold. If the respondent indicated that he would be confronted with contradictory expectations in such a situation, the interviewer probed with focused questions to ascertain the existence and degree of ambivalence (To what extent does this situation bother you?) and the mode of resolution (What do you do in this situation?). Finally, checks were made on the completeness of the schedule by attempting to elicit other audiences and other behavioral alternatives from the respondent. The relevant field command officers were then contacted—through a mail questionnaire that yielded complete returns —and asked to report what, in fact, they expected of *policemen* in these situations. The data thus collected were (*a*) perceived conflict situations, (*b*) perceived expectations of selected rank groups, (*c*) the reported degree of ambivalence engendered by the conflict situation, (*d*) the reported resolution of the conflict, and (*e*) the actual expectations of the field command staff. The various forms of the role conflict schedules appear in Appendix 1.[3]

Before proceeding with our analysis, some further comments on methodology are in order.

1. The interviews were conducted along with our observation and participation in post activities at our four field-sample posts. No interviews were begun during the first week, and most *policemen* were interviewed after we had worked with them on patrol for at least ten hours. Perhaps the most significant indicator of our rapport, though there were many, was that some

2 The interview schedule was modeled after the role conflict schedule designed by Gross, Mason, and McEachern and presented in their *Explorations in Role Analysis: Studies of the School Superintendency Role* (New York: John Wiley & Sons, 1958).

3 The interview schedule contained, in addition, questions dealing with legitimacy, obligation, and sanction. These materials, however, have been fully reported elsewhere, and these dimensions of role conflict analysis will be briefly summarized later. See H. J. Ehrlich, "The Analysis of Role Conflicts in a Complex Organization: The Police" (Doctor's thesis, Michigan State University, 1959), and H. J. Ehrlich, J. W. Rinehart, and J. C. Howell, "The Study of Role Conflict: Explorations in Methodology," *Sociometry*, 25 (1962), 85–97.

of the men engaged in activities at and beyond the periphery of acceptable and appropriate behavior in the presence of the writers with the apparently complete confidence that there would be no repercussions.

2. The interviews were conducted at four geographically separated and mutually isolated posts by the two authors. Analysis of variance indicated no significant differences in the responses obtained between interviewers or among posts, and the role conflict situation constituted the primary source of variation.

3. In three successive studies of role conflict—all utilizing modifications of our original procedure—we observed similar distributions of role conflict and role congruent responses. We introduce this here, though we shall discuss these studies below, to emphasize the stability of our findings and to indicate that the data-gathering procedures per se did not seem to be significant sources of variation in our findings.[4]

Situation 1: The Division of Labor

One of the fundamental tasks of a complex organization is the allocation of human and material resources in accord with the effective attainment of its objectives. Where an organization undergoes a rapid and extensive increase in both its human and material resources in conjunction with a large-scale turnover among those who determine its objectives and policies, one may anticipate a change in the allocation of statuses, duties, and obligations in the organization. The Central State Police was such an organization, as demonstrated by an approximately 40 per cent increase in police personnel, a 20 per cent increase in police posts, and an accelerating pace of experimentation with and adoption of technological innovations (e.g., patrol cars, radio systems, uniforms, record keeping) between 1956 and 1959. Further, in the last fourteen months of that three-year period, during which this study was conducted, about 44 per cent of the department's commissioned officers were replaced through retirement or were removed to different spheres of authority through transfer or promotion.

[4] The four studies are based on (a) the stratified-cluster sample of *policemen* who were personally interviewed; (b) a systematic random sample of *policemen* not included in study "a" by an abridged questionnaire form of the original interview schedule using an anonymous mail questionnaire; (c) our specimen recruit class (Chapter 4) in their fourth follow-up by the procedure employed in study "b"; and (d) a second recruit class in an extended questionnaire version of the original schedule which was group-administered.

Most of the details of the first three studies will be discussed above. Study "d" is reported extensively in J. W. Rinehart, "An Analysis of Selected Role Conflict Variables" (Master's thesis, Michigan State University, 1961). A comparison of studies "a" and "b" is to be found in Ehrlich, *op. cit.*, ch. 6; and comparisons between studies "a" and "d" are reported, in part, in Ehrlich, Rinehart, and Howell, *op. cit.*

TABLE 6-1

PERCENTAGE OF "POLICEMEN" REPORTING EXPOSURE TO CONGRUENT AND
CONFLICTING EXPECTATIONS IN EACH SITUATION

Situation	Per Cent Reporting Role Congruence	Role Conflict	N
1. Division of labor . . .	10	90	50
2. Occupational involvement .	32	68	50
3. Occupational secrecy . .	61	39	49
4. Role models	36	64	50
5. Rules and Regulations . .	29	71	51

Field work and questionnaires suggested a changing conception of the
policeman's role as a traffic patrolman and as a criminal investigator. Thus the
initial role conflict situation dealt with the *policeman's* perception of his
exposure to contradictory expectations in this context: Was he to concern
himself mainly with safety and traffic work, or mainly with complaint and
criminal investigation, or was he to spend equal time on both? As can be
seen in Table 6–1, 90 per cent of the men interviewed pictured themselves
as being confronted with contradictory role expectations here. Of the 10 per
cent (five men) who perceived themselves as being confronted with an
unambiguous situation, four reported they were exposed only to the "equal

TABLE 6-2

EXPECTATIONS OF THE AUDIENCE GROUPS AS PERCEIVED BY "POLICEMEN":
THE DIVISION OF LABOR SITUATION

Audience Groups	Percentage of Policemen Reporting			
	Safety- Traffic Expectation	Complaint- Criminal Expectation	Equal Time Expectation	Don't Know
1. Headquarters command .	52	2	44	2
2. District command . . .	55	8	37	—
3. Post commander . . .	54	2	44	—
4. Asst. post commanders .	22	2	76	—
5. *Policemen*	8	8	82	2
6. Wife-family	6	8	64	22
7. Personal friends . . .	20	10	10	60
8. Service clubs	36	4	34	26
9. Fraternal organizations .	26	2	46	26
10. The press	22	4	72	2
11. Local and county police .	34	6	58	2
12. Other*	33	8	59	—

* Twenty-four mentions of other audience groups were made, including "the public,
businessmen, legislature, safety council, schools, church groups, people stopped on the
road, colored groups, acquaintances, and wife's family." ("The public" accounted for
58 per cent of the total other mentions.)

time" expectation, while the fifth, a *policeman* who had assumed the role of the "post detective," perceived his audiences as holding the "investigator" expectation of him.

Table 6–2 presents the percentage of *policemen* who perceived their audience groups as holding the expectation that a person in the *policeman* role (*a*) concerns himself mainly with safety and traffic work, (*b*) concerns himself mainly with complaint and criminal investigation, and (*c*) spends equal time on both. The perspective of this table permits two immediate observations. First, that *policemen* seldom perceived themselves as being expected to emphasize criminal and complaint work. Second, that they were almost equally likely to report being confronted by the safety-traffic expectation as the equal time expectation. Not only can we infer that this was a situation of considerable conflict but also that it was one in which all of the *policemen's* audiences seemed to be involved.

Fifty per cent of the *policemen* for whom this was a conflict situation reported that they actually gave equal emphasis to both. Thirty per cent placed major emphasis on traffic work, while 9 per cent of the *policemen* adopted an expedient and pragmatic mode of behavior. (See Appendix 1, "Judges' Instructions.")[5] Illustrative of the latter were the following comments. "I do both, whichever is there. I would not neglect either to go to the other." "I feel that work should be adjusted to the situation. On holidays and weekends I can see the need for traffic emphasis. If there was a crime wave, I'd say drop traffic."

Situation 2: Occupational Involvement

Occupational roles could undoubtedly be cataloged according to the span of time encompassed by their performance.[6] At one pole we could conceive of segmental roles requiring limited time to enact, and, at the other, extended

---

[5] To determine the replicability of the classification of the role conflict resolutions, two independent judges with no previous connection with the project were employed. Each judge was presented with a brief set of instructions (see Appendix 1), a copy of the interview schedule, and the verbatim conflict resolutions as recorded by the interviewers—each of which was separately typed on 3 × 5-inch file cards. The average agreement between Ehrlich and the two judges was 89 per cent. One judge's classifications agreed with the author's 81 per cent of the time, the second 94 per cent of the time, and the two judges were in mutual agreement on 91 per cent of their classifications. We are indebted to Dr. D. L. Westby and Mr. J. R. Dove for their assistance in this matter.

[6] The temporal scope of role performance is a subject which has been afforded little formal discussion in the "role" literature. The distinction between segmental and general roles has its origination in A. Lindesmith and A. Strauss, *Social Psychology* (New York: Dryden Press, 1949), p. 171.

roles—the performance of which consumes, in the extreme, the entire waking day of the incumbent. In the CSP, and this probably holds true for most police agencies, the *policeman* was presented to the public, and especially to the recruit, as a 24-hour-a-day role.

Moreover, it was explicitly stated in the department rules and regulations and in the legislative statute creating the State Police that "Every member of [the] department shall be subject to orders at any time, the officers shall be deemed to be on duty at all times. . . ."

Since "being on duty at all times" is an expectation which is rarely invoked formally, it was necessary to keep the knowledge of its potential invocation continually alive. This was accomplished through a network of special orders, rules, and regulations that clearly proscribed the *policemen's* participation in a multitude of economic, political, and social relationships which might (even remotely) interfere with immediate recall to duty. By means of these restrictions the department thus attempted to restrict the *policemen's* access to any but highly segmental non-occupational roles.

TABLE 6–3

EXPECTATIONS OF THE AUDIENCE GROUPS AS PERCEIVED BY "POLICEMEN":
OCCUPATIONAL INVOLVEMENT

	Percentage of Policemen *Reporting*			
Audience Groups	*24-Hour Expectation*	*Leave Behind Expectation*	*No Expectation*	*Don't Know*
1. Headquarters command. .	98	2	—	—
2. District command . . .	98	2	—	—
3. Post commander . . .	94	2	4	—
4. Asst. post commanders .	88	6	6	—
5. *Policemen*	56	26	16	2
6. Wife-family	36	36	20	8
7. Personal friends . . .	28	41	31	—
8. Service clubs	30	18	38	14
9. Fraternal organizations .	32	14	38	16
10. The press	72	6	22	—
11. Local and county police .	73	12	15	—
12. Other*	67	14	19	—

* Nineteen mentions of other audience groups were made, including "the public, businessmen, neighbors, acquaintances, strangers, professional people, and colored groups."

Such a situation appeared to be a fertile area for the study of role conflict. Accordingly, the *policemen* interviewed were presented with the question as to whether they were expected to be a *policeman* twenty-four hours a day or whether they were, in fact, expected to leave their job behind when off duty. As depicted in Table 6–1, 68 per cent of the interviewees experienced this as a conflict situation. Those who did not, 32 per cent, were unanimous in their agreement that all audience groups were perceived as expecting them to be a *policeman* at all times.

The details of Table 6–3 indicate a marked difference in perception between authority and peer groups. Thus, while the headquarters, district, and post commanders were seen as in substantially complete agreement on the twenty-four–hour expectation (over 90 per cent), only 56 per cent of the *policemen* perceived their peers as holding this expectation. It is interesting to note also that almost three-quarters of the men interviewed perceived the local and county police as holding an "extended" role image. Those most closely associated with the non-occupational life of the *policeman*—his wife, family, and personal friends—were most likely to be seen as viewing his occupational role as an essentially segmental one, to be left behind when off duty.

Two-thirds of the men for whom this was a conflict situation adhered to a generally consistent theme of commitment to an extended occupational role. As one *policeman* expressed it: "I love police work. I feel we are public servants, and because we are, and do belong to the public, we owe them our time and effort as required. Personally, I can't get enough of police work. I am building a house now, so my off hours are tied up, but this is only temporary."

Eighteen per cent of the conflicted group responded in an expedient mode, stating that the police activities they might engage in when off duty would depend upon situational circumstances. By contrast, 26 per cent of the *policemen* "leave the post behind." Such a conflict resolution, reflecting disparity with the occupational ideology, carries with it a sense of disenchantment.

"Once I get out of my clothes, that's it. I don't think a man can be a *policeman* all the time. You've got to have a personal life. They ought to get us a five-day week. They've been promising us that for ten years. . . . They say you're supposed to be a *policeman* all the time. One time at a refresher school I asked about compensation to my wife if I were killed in uniform on the way to work. They said 'No.' What's a guy supposed to do? You tell me."

Situation 3: Occupational Secrecy

The importance of "secrecy" as a category of sociological analysis has long been recognized. Simmel, in 1908, in his last comprehensive statement on sociology, accorded extensive treatment to its analysis; and, half a century later, one can observe the dialectics of secrecy as a leitmotiv in the occupational sociology of Everett Hughes and his students.[7]

[7] G. Simmel, *The Sociology of Georg Simmel*, trans. K. H. Wolff (Glencoe, Ill.: Free Press, 1950), pp. 330–76; and E. C. Hughes, *Men and Their Work* (Glencoe, Ill.: Free Press, 1958).

The present impetus for considering secrecy as a potential component of a role conflict situation came from William Westley's report, "Secrecy and the Police."[8] As part of a larger study of a municipal police department in a midwestern industrial city, Westley sought to elicit the "policeman's orientation to secrecy." His procedure involved placing each officer interviewed in a hypothetical situation in which he had to decide whether or not to report his partner for stealing. The question was given to fifteen policemen, then dropped "because of large-scale cancellations of interviews." Twenty-seven per cent of the men stated that they would report other policemen for stealing, while 73 per cent said they would not. Through other data from interviews with trainees and experienced patrolmen, Westley was able to conclude that 1) the norm of secrecy was so important that it was made explicit to *every* trainee by *every* experienced man with whom he had been in contact, and 2) the majority of the experienced patrolmen considered adherence to this norm "the most desirable characteristic" in a new man, and one essential to a successful career. He generalized that such a collectively supported norm of secrecy "might be expected to fit most city police departments today."

TABLE 6–4

EXPECTATIONS OF THE AUDIENCE GROUPS AS PERCEIVED BY "POLICEMEN":
OCCUPATIONAL SECRECY

	Percentage of Policemen Reporting			
Audience Groups	Report Policemen Expectation	Keep Quiet Expectation	No Expectation	Don't Know
1. Headquarters command .	92	—	6	2
2. District command . .	92	—	6	2
3. Post commander . . .	94	2	2	2
4. Asst. post commanders .	82	6	10	2
5. *Policemen*	47	31	20	2
6. Wife-family	22	20	51	6
7. Personal friends . . .	45	12	39	4
8. Service clubs	41	2	39	18
9. Fraternal organizations .	41	2	39	18
10. The press	82	—	18	—
11. Local and county police .	68	14	16	2
12. Other*	60	10	20	10

* Ten mentions of other audience groups were made, including "the public, courts, strangers, acquaintances, businessmen, and professional people."

Initial observations in the CSP suggested that while Westley's generalization was not applicable to this organization, norms of secrecy might none-

[8] W. A. Westley, "Secrecy and the Police," *Social Forces*, 34 (1956), 254–57.

theless be a source of role conflict for some *policemen*. Accordingly, the following set of expectations was presented to the men interviewed: (*a*) Expect me to report any *policeman* whom I thought was not properly performing his police duties; (*b*) Expect me to keep quiet about this matter; and (*c*) Have no expectations of me on this matter. It should be noted that "not properly performing his police duties" is a "trial board" offense subject to the severest penalties of the department, including dismissal. Furthermore, failure to report to one's commanding officer "observation or knowledge" of such an infraction is itself a trial board offense.

As can be seen in Table 6-1, 61 per cent of the men defined this as an unambiguous situation. Of these, 93 per cent perceived their audience as expecting them to report their colleagues' infractions. The remainder (two men) viewed their audience as expecting silence.

The breakdown of Table 6-4 is especially interesting. Like the two preceding tables, it illustrates the ubiquitousness of contradictory expectations. Yet here, for the only time (cf. also Tables 6-5 and 6-6), we can observe three audiences which are not directly involved in the conflict situation. If a *policeman* perceives headquarters command, district command, and the press as holding a specific expectation of him in this situation, then—as Table 6-4 clearly shows—it will be expectation (*a*). In contrast to the unanimity of their perception of the staff commanders, *policemen* are more likely to view their fellow *policemen* as expecting secrecy more than any other audience. What, then, does the *policeman* confronted with this conflict do?

None of the men stated, unqualifiedly, that they would report their brother officer; and 16 per cent stated they would definitely "keep quiet." For 84 per cent, this situation elicited an expedient response. The criteria for assessing the advisability of reporting or not reporting a *policeman* can be seen in the following protocols.

"If it's not serious, I just look the other way. I have reported a man for drinking in uniform."

"It would depend on who he was and what he did. He'd almost have to do it twice before I'd say anything."

"It would have to be something that would seriously hurt other *policemen* or the department—or if the man was using the department for personal gain. If he were making unintentional mistakes, it would be up to someone higher in the department."

"Of course you owe some loyalty to the department, the public—if they're involved—and your brother *policemen*. What would be done depends upon the seriousness of what's involved. If the man is a bad *policeman*, you owe him no loyalty. If his actions involve the public or reflect on the department,

I'd report him. If what he did everybody was doing, or if it would reflect only on him and not involve anyone else, I'd keep quiet."

It is apparent that the decision about secrecy was often made in a climate which negatively sanctioned it. For 61 per cent of the *policemen* this was not a conflict situation. For the others, its resolution remained problematic—contingent upon situational factors. As will be shown later, this type of situation caused the *policeman* the greatest personal difficulty of the conflict situations studied.

Situation 4: Role Models

As a consequence of his status, the police officer—in his other statuses in the community—is often expected to play roles which are not expected of every member of the community and which are not formally part of the role definition of *policemen*.[9] This phenomenon, while closely related to the conception of occupational diffuseness introduced above, is yet something quite discrete. Everett Hughes exhibits its essential characteristic when he writes: "There tends to grow up about a status, in addition to its specifically determining traits, a complex of auxiliary characteristics which come to be expected of its incumbents."[10]

The extra-professional role of the *policeman* follows a pattern which is apparently typical of those formally designated agents of socialization and social control in society. The "license" granted such persons as "guardians of precious things" appears to be "chronically suspect."[11] Thus we demand that those granted such a license continually reaffirm their right to it, not merely in the "technical" performance of their occupational roles but morally in the performance of their extra-professional roles as exemplars of the socialized and socially controlled.[12]

The fourth potential role conflict situation was thus concerned with the perceptions of *policemen* as to their expected behavior in the community. As can be seen in Table 6–1, the issue as to whether a *policeman* was expected to be a model citizen setting an example for the community or a good citizen no different from others elicited conflict responses from 64 per cent of the men interviewed. The breakdown by expectation and audience group is given in Table 6–5.

9 Cf. W. I. Wardell and A. L. Wood, "The Extra-Professional Role of the Lawyer," *American Journal of Sociology*, 61 (1955–56), 304–7.

10 Hughes, *op. cit.*, p. 102.

11 *Ibid.*, p. 82.

12 Cf. K. Naegele, "Clergymen, Teachers and Psychiatrists: A Study in Roles and Socialization," *Canadian Journal of Economics and Political Science*, 22 (1956), 46–62.

Those who perceived themselves exposed to contradictory expectations and those who did not indicated approximately the same pattern of resolution. Fifty-nine per cent of the former and 67 per cent of the latter group chose the "model" resolution. There were no expedient resolutions. The contrast in methods of resolution is clearly displayed in the following statements of two *policemen*.

"It's a good thing to have to live up to. It has changed me considerably. I even cut the grass more often than my neighbors. It's good to be in this situation—it's a matter of pride, I guess."

"As long as I go home, mind my own business, don't create a disturbance, I think that's all right. If I want to drink a beer on the front porch, I'll do that. I'm not a model citizen; I'm not any god." [13]

TABLE 6–5

EXPECTATIONS OF THE AUDIENCE GROUPS AS PERCEIVED BY "POLICEMEN":
ROLE MODELS

	Percentage of Policemen *Reporting*			
Audience Groups	*Model Citizen Expectations*	*Good Citizen Expectations*	*No Expectations*	*Don't Know*
1. Headquarters command .	72	28	—	—
2. District command . . .	72	28	—	—
3. Post commander . . .	74	26	—	—
4. Asst. post commanders .	57	39	4	—
5. *Policemen*	35	63	2	—
6. Wife-family	46	46	2	6
7. Personal friends . . .	38	62	—	—
8. Service clubs	48	36	2	14
9. Fraternal organizations .	48	36	2	14
10. The press	74	26	—	—
11. Local and county police .	44	52	4	—
12. Other*	54	46	—	—

* Thirteen mentions of other audience groups were made, including "the public, acquaintances, neighbors, strangers, businessmen, and professional people."

Situation 5: The Rules and Regulations

The rules and regulations constituted the legal norms of the department. How an occupational group which has as its central task the enforcement of the legal norms of the larger society regards its own body of laws presents an

[13] Shortly after the interviewing was completed, the department's house organ reprinted the "Canons of Police Ethics," which had just been adopted by the State Association of Chiefs of Police. The section of this code dealing with "private life" concludes: "[the law enforcement officer] will so conduct his private life that the public will regard him as an example of stability, fidelity and morality."

intriguing question. More important for our purposes, however, is the effect that changing, unenforced, or unenforceable laws can have on the role behavior of those who must interpret such laws. It was noted during our field observations in the organization that some of the written rules and regulations had radically changed, though the changes themselves were not written; that some of the rules and regulations were not enforced; and that some were obviously unenforceable.

TABLE 6–6

EXPECTATIONS OF THE AUDIENCE GROUPS AS PERCEIVED BY "POLICEMEN":
RULES AND REGULATIONS

| | Percentage of Policemen Reporting | | | |
Audience Groups	To-the-Letter Expectation	Overlook Expectation	No Expectation	Don't Know
1. Headquarters command .	65	35	—	—
2. District command . . .	61	39	—	—
3. Post commander . . .	53	47	—	—
4. Asst. post commanders .	41	57	2	—
5. *Policemen*	17	81	2	—
6. Wife-family	14	64	16	6
7. Personal friends . . .	10	57	33	—
8. Service clubs	16	33	35	16
9. Fraternal organizations .	16	35	31	18
10. The press	43	31	26	—
11. Local and county police .	21	64	15	—
12. Other*	15	54	31	—

* Thirteen mentions of other audience groups were made, including "the public, businessmen, and professional people."

Given such a situation, what did the *policemen* believe they were expected to do? For 29 per cent this was an unambiguous situation (see Table 6–1). Approximately three-quarters of these perceived all audience groups as expecting them to occasionally overlook the rules and regulations, while one-quarter saw their audiences as expecting adherence "to the letter." The breakdown of expectations is presented in Table 6–6.

For the 71 per cent majority of *policemen* for whom this was a conflict situation, seven-eighths chose the "overlook occasionally" resolution. This is of particular significance in that the "occasionally" qualification built into the problem makes the choice of this resolution an expedient one. The gamut of responses is interesting to observe.

"I feel that the rules and regulations are good and should be followed to the letter. . . . I feel a rule is a rule and either it should be enforced or stricken from the books."

"I'm peculiar in that I feel if a regulation is made, it should be strictly adhered to. I overlook them occasionally, but I would try never to overlook the major ones."

"I try to follow the rules and regulations when reasonable."

"Above the post level they can't really tell you they expect you to overlook the rules and regulations, but they know. Every situation is different, and you've got to play it by ear."

"If you followed the rules and regulations to the letter, you'd be like a mummy in the patrol car."

Ambivalence and the Source of Conflicting Expectations

Ambivalence. The distribution of ambivalent responses provides us with an intriguing, and theoretically important, datum. Of the total number of responses made by *policemen* ($n = 163$), *56 per cent* were nonambivalent; that is, the *policeman* reported that he was "not at all" bothered by such a situation. Thus, as we suggested earlier, and contrary to the general assumptions that pervade the literature of role conflict and marginality, exposure to conflicting expectations is at best only one necessary condition of ambivalence. Six per cent of the responses to our probe (To what extent does this situation bother you?) were "very much" responses, while the remaining 38 per cent comprised the intermediate response, "to some degree."

Another view of the distribution of ambivalence can be found in Table 6–7. As before, in our analysis of the incidence of role conflict by post and by situation, analysis of variance shows that the situation, not the post, was the significant source of variation in ambivalent responses. Inspection of this table shows the situation of greatest ambivalence to the *policemen*, situation 3, was also the one which yields the lowest incidence of role conflict (Table 6–1). This suggested a possible relationship between the incidence of role conflict and ambivalence. Accordingly, a correlation was computed between the rank order of role conflict incidence, taken from Table 6–1, and the rank order of mean ambivalence as presented in the final column of Table 6–7. The obtained *rho* of $-.100$ is nonsignificant. In the context of this study, then, there is no relationship between the incidence of perceived role conflicts and ambivalence.

The Source of Conflict. In the interview schedule, respondents were asked to indicate what they perceived to be the expectations of eleven audience groups, plus an "other" category. The pattern of conflicting responses for those who saw these audiences in disagreement was, on the average, 9 to 3. That is, for each situation taken as a whole, approximately nine audience groups were perceived as expecting one alternative and three as expecting the second alternative. We shall arbitrarily label the numerically smaller expectation the "conflict-producing" response, and the audience perceived as holding this expectation the "deviant" audience. By enumerating, for every interview, the number of times an audience group was deviant—that is, was attributed with the conflict-producing expectation—we can determine the proportionate contribution of each audience group in the five situations to the role conflict. This material is presented in Table 6-8. Thus in situation 1, headquarters command was "responsible" for 10 per cent of the conflict-producing expectations, district command for 13 per cent, and so on. The average rank order of deviance for headquarters in all five situations was ninth.

TABLE 6-7

MEAN AMBIVALENCE RESPONSES BY POST AND BY SITUATION

| | Posts | | | | Situation |
Situation	A	B	C	D	Means
1. Division of labor . .	1.89	2.50	2.75	2.54	2.27
2. Occupational					
involvement . . .	2.82	3.00	2.50	2.90	2.82
3. Occupational secrecy .	2.10	2.00	1.00	2.00	2.00
4. Role models . . .	2.76	3.00	2.50	2.89	2.81
5. Rules and regulations .	2.39	2.00	2.40	2.70	2.46
Post Means . . .	2.41	2.53	2.44	2.66	(2.48)

NOTE.—1.00 = high ambivalence; 3.00 = low ambivalence.

Deviant audience groups remained relatively constant from situation to situation. Insofar as analysis of variance showed this to be the case and for there to be significant variation among audience groups, this means it was not the situation (or situational pressures) which were determinative of deviance but rather that audiences perceived as deviant were perceived as such in all situations. The rank order of deviant audience groups, moreover, shows us that the source of conflicting expectations was essentially outside the organization, and was composed of those others who constituted the primary groups of the *policeman*: personal friends, wife and family, fellow *policemen*, the local and county policemen (who were probably personal friends).[14]

We may now raise the question as to whether or not the degree of ambivalence was a consequence of which audience groups were perceived as deviant. In other words, did audience groups differentially engender ambivalence? The following array suggests such a differential.

[14] As part of our larger questionnaire, *policemen* were asked to list the occupations of their three closest friends. Thirty-two per cent of their choices were other policemen; and it is probably the case that this accounts for the high rank of local and county police.

Audience	Mean Ambivalence	Rank Order
Assistant post commanders .	2.28	1
Headquarters command . .	2.32	2
Post commander	2.33	3
District command . . .	2.38	4
Policemen	2.39	5
Fraternal organizations . .	2.43	6
Others	2.47	7
Personal friends	2.50	8
Local and county police . .	2.51	9
Wife-family	2.53	10
Service clubs	2.54	11
Press	2.57	12

As we can see, greater ambivalence was engendered when the deviant audience was part of the police organization. Furthermore, when the rank order of deviance (Table 6–8) is compared with this rank order of ambivalence, no significant relationship exists between the two (*rho* = −.156). Thus, although deviant expectations were perceived to emanate more frequently from audiences outside the formal organization, when the deviant audience was within the organization this was more likely to engender a greater degree of ambivalence.

TABLE 6–8

PROPORTION OF CONFLICT-PRODUCING RESPONSES BY AUDIENCE AND BY SITUATION

Audience Groups	Situations					Rank Order of Deviance
	1	2	3	4	5	
Headquarters command .	.10	.03	.00	.05	.12	9
District command . . .	.13	.03	.00	.06	.10	7.5
Post commander . . .	.11	.03	.03	.08	.06	5
Asst. post commanders .	.06	.03	.08	.08	.04	10
Policemen	.05	.15	.36	.14	.13	3
Wife-family	.06	.20	.20	.15	.12	2
Personal friends . . .	.15	.25	.12	.13	.11	1
Service clubs	.08	.09	.03	.06	.05	7.5
Fraternal organizations .	.08	.06	.03	.06	.06	6
The press	.06	.03	.00	.07	.09	11
Local and county police .	.08	.06	.12	.10	.07	4
Others	.04	.04	.03	.02	.05	12

We may summarize the findings of this section briefly.

1. The degree to which an audience group was perceived as holding deviant expectations was variable, and significant differences were observed among audiences in the extent of their deviance.

2. The degree to which audiences were perceived as deviant was not a function of the specific role conflict situation since the order of deviance remained the same across all situations.

3. The deviant audiences were essentially those which were not part of the formal organization but those which comprised the primary group network of the *policeman*: his wife, family, friends, and peers.

4. Ambivalence was found to be differentially distributed by situation and by audience; and those audiences which provoked most ambivalence were all of those contained within the boundaries of the formal organization.

5. There appeared to be no general relationship between the perception of role conflict and the experiencing of ambivalence, nor between the degree of ambivalence and incidence of role conflict or the extent of audience group deviance.

Reported Role Performance and the Accuracy of Perceived Expectations

The initial problem of this section is that of the veridicality of the *policemen's* perceptions of what the field command staff expected of them. Table 6–9 depicts the proportion of *policemen* whose perceptions of their field commanders' expectations of them were accurate.[15] As can be seen, the number of *policemen* who correctly reported the expectations of all three groups of commanders varied from 10 to 62 per cent. Thus in two situations, *90 per cent* of the *policemen* were *incorrect* in their perception of what was expected of them by at least one of these three audiences; and they were never correct, for all three, more than 62 per cent of the time.

TABLE 6–9

PROPORTION OF "POLICEMEN" ACCURATELY PERCEIVING THE
EXPECTATIONS OF THE FIELD COMMAND STAFF

		Per Cent of Accurate Responses			
Situation	*N*	District Command	Post Command	Asst. Post Command	*All**
1 . . .	50	40	46	78	10
2	50	70	94	88	62
3	48	71	79	83	44
4	50	46	72	24	10
Mean Per Cent . . .		57	73	68	31

* Refers to the per cent of *policemen* correctly reporting all three expectations.

The question now to be confronted is: What is it that *policemen* actually do, or report they do, in these situations? The data presented in Table 6–10

---

[15] In transforming the original role conflict interview schedule into a self-administering mail questionnaire, a clerical error resulted in the omission of the fifth role conflict situation ("rules and regulations").

are an attempt to answer this question. In the left-hand column the *expectations* of the three command groups have been combined, and the per cent of this combined group reporting they hold expectations A, B, or C has been presented for the four situations. In the right-hand column is the per cent of those *policemen* reporting their *actual selection* among the available alternatives, where X refers to the selection of an expedient form of action (i.e., the qualified report that one's selection among alternatives was inextricably linked to certain specified situational factors, as time, person, place, etc.). Close inspection of this table indicates a decided congruence between what the command staff expected of the *policemen* and what the *policemen* reported doing. This occurs 1) despite the fact that *policemen* were for the most part incorrect in their perception of what the command staff expected of them, and 2) despite the fact that their reported actual behavior was contrary to what they *perceived* they were expected to do. This latter point becomes even more apparent in Table 6–11.

To construct Table 6–11 it was necessary to deal with only those situations in which the command staff was unanimous in its expectations. If unanimity were not the case, then any perception of the *policeman* would in some measure be correct. Situation 4 (role models) was thus excluded. The left-hand column, then, indicates the per cent of *policemen* whose perception of the unanimous expectations of the command staff was accurate. The right-hand columns show the per cent of *policemen* who actually selected the behavioral alternative expected of them, as well as those who might possibly select it (i.e., who report an expedient mode of resolution). Thus in situation 1, while only 10 per cent of the *policemen* correctly perceived the expectations of the command staff, 53 to 63 per cent of the *policemen* complied with the expectations of this group. This means that 43 to 53 per cent of the men (the difference between the columns) were, in this instance, behaving contrary to what they perceived was expected of them by this audience group. Moreover, it is apparent from this table that 63 to 90 per cent of the *policemen* in these three situations were actually complying with the expectations of the command staff.

TABLE 6-10

EXPECTATIONS OF COMMAND STAFF AND THE SELF-REPORTED BEHAVIOR OF "POLICEMEN": SITUATION AND PER CENT REPORTING

Situation	Command Staff Expectations				Policemen Behavior				
	N	A	B	C	N	A	B	C	X
1	18	6	0	94	50	27	10	53	10
2	18	83	17	0	50	77	10	0	13
3	18	89	11	0	48	57	10	0	33
4	18	56	44	0	50	59	41	0	0

TABLE 6–11

DISCREPANCY BETWEEN ACTUAL EXPECTATION, ACCURACY OF ITS
PERCEPTION, AND SELF-REPORTED ROLE BEHAVIOR

Situation	% of Policemen Correctly Perceiving Expectations of Command Staff	% of Policemen Reporting Actually (A) and Possibly (P) Performing According to the Expectations of Command Staff	
		A	P
1 . .	10	53	10
2 . .	62	77	13
3 . .	44	57	33

The problem posed by these data can be succinctly stated and is of decided significance not only to role theory but to most theories of organization. How can we account for the reciprocity between expected and actual behavior, given this discrepancy between what is expected and what is perceived as expected? If role behavior is predicated on the perception of what is expected, then it would appear to follow that the incorrect perception of what is expected would lead to incorrect role performance.

It is here apparent that the incorrect role performance of *policemen* did not follow. *Policemen* did not always conform to their perceptions of audience group expectations, correct or not. This conclusion raises considerable doubt about the importance of the correct perception of role expectations as a determinant of role behavior. It seems to us reasonable to suggest, therefore, that some "compensatory mechanisms"—some structural features within this system of role relationships—operate, in part, so as to maintain this system. Such an assumption is, of course, well within the logic of functional analysis.[16]

At this juncture we have no clear indication of what these mechanisms might be in this organization, although we suspect that we may find our answer in the socialization process. The socialization of the *policeman* was apparently subject to many influences, some of which were inconsistent with one another. We suggested in earlier chapters that the diversity of expectations seemed to provide sufficient flexibility for the role to permit learners some freedom of choice. The pressure of negative sanctions was lessened thereby in many aspects of the role because there was no consensus as to their application. Therefore the *policeman* may have learned to interpret the requirements of his role in any given situation by assessing various expectations and then gearing his behavior to one expectation at the expense of another.

[16] For a discussion of the functional significance of compensatory mechanisms, see A. Gouldner, "Reciprocity and Autonomy in Functional Theory," in L. Gross (ed.), *Symposium on Sociological Theory* (Evanston, Ill.: Row, Peterson & Co., 1959).

As one policeman, discussing situation 1, put it: "My opinion of policemen was that they were out here to meet the public demands and to protect them. If you emphasize safety and traffic, you've got to let criminal and complaint work go by. I can't see that. . . . I don't think this is *really* what the Commissioner wants." (Emphasis supplied.)

Conformity to what are believed to be the ideals of police work may of course entail negative sanctions, and those selecting this course of action were not unaware of it: "I do what I think headquarters expects—not what some outpost commander wants. I've never been called down to district or Central Headquarters, but the . . . [post commander] has had me on the carpet."

Whether or not the mechanisms of adaptation and socialization were operative in this compensatory manner, our data are inadequate for any rigorous analysis. However, we believe that the area of adaptation to diverse role expectations is central to the establishment of any viable role theory.

A second problem inheres in these data. What produced the inaccuracy of perception? We have two perspectives for analysis here. The first is the accuracy of *policemen's* perception of the command groups and of their expectations in the four situations. The second is the extent of consensus among the command groups in the four situations. The findings of our analyses are summarized as follows.

a) There were no statistically significant differences in the accuracy of the *policemen's* perception of the field command group, or, for that matter, of headquarters command. The degree of accuracy was thus unaffected by status distance. The trend observed was for the *policeman* to be most accurate for the assistant post commander and district commander and least accurate for post command and headquarters command.

b) There were no statistically significant differences in the *policemen's* accuracy with respect to situations. The direction of the findings showed greatest accuracy in situations 3 and 4 ("occupational secrecy" and "role models").

c) There were no statistically significant differences in the extent of agreement among headquarters, district, post, and assistant post commanders. The expectations of the post commanders were most divergent from the other command groups, and the headquarters staff was second in its degree of divergence from the others.[17]

17 The pattern of consensus that obtained tended to follow status distance. Adjacent ranks (headquarters–district, district–post, post–assistants) displayed most agreement; one-step differences (headquarters–post and district–assistants) were next; and the two-step differences (headquarters–assistants) were the most widely separated.

d) There were no statistically significant differences among command groups with respect to their agreement by situation. Greatest consensus was displayed in situations 4 and 3 respectively.

While the two perspectives appear to be without significance when viewed independently, if we combine the order of the findings in each case our data take on added significance:

<table>
<tr><td align="center">*Rank Order of*
Policeman *Inaccuracy*</td><td align="center">*Rank Order of*
Command Staff Disagreement</td></tr>
<tr><td>S1—Division of labor
S2—Occupational involvement
S3—Occupational secrecy
S4—Role models</td><td>S1—Division of labor
S2—Occupational involvement
S4—Role models
S3—Occupational secrecy</td></tr>
<tr><td align="center">*Rank Order of*
Policeman *Inaccuracy*</td><td align="center">*Rank Order of*
Command Staff Disagreement</td></tr>
<tr><td>Headquarters command
Post commander
District command
Assistant post commanders</td><td>Post commander
Headquarters command
Assistant post commanders
District command</td></tr>
</table>

The association of the two sets of findings focuses upon the structural source of the *policemen's* inaccurate perception of their audiences' role expectations. It seems quite likely that their inaccuracy was a consequence of the lack of consensus. *Policemen* were most incorrect in those situations where there was greatest disagreement among their commander audiences, and most incorrect about those audiences who themselves were most divergent from the other command groups.

The Accuracy of Role Perception: Further Analysis

Some seven months after the role conflict interviews had been collected, but before their analysis had been completed, the researchers had an opportunity to mail out an abridged, self-administering form of the role conflict interview schedule to a 10 per cent, systematic random sample of *policemen* (see n. 4). The abridgement, coupled with the time lag, was in most respects unfortunate, and these data are only indirectly comparable with those obtained in the field phase of study. Finally, ten months after this mail survey we included the abridged questionnaire in our fourth follow-up with the recruit class. These two mail samples, then, are based on equivalent forms, and the time lapse here fortunately involved no major changes in the composition of the various audiences about whom the respondents were questioned. These comparative data, presented in Table 6–12A for *policemen* and in Table 6–12B for recruits, permit us to explore further the issue of the accuracy of role perceptions.

The abridged questionnaire contained the four role conflict situations and four audience groups—headquarters and post command, *policemen*, and the public. We also determined, by means of a separate mailing, the actual expectations of all of the command groups, and, from our survey (Chapters 7 and 8), the public. Examination of these data in Table 12 yields four major findings.

1. The pattern of consensus, as before, follows status distance. Adjacent ranks were in most agreement, and those furthest apart were in least agreement. The public's expectations were by far the most divergent. Contrary to our earlier observation, which was based on a small sample of the command personnel, these data based on virtually the entire command staff (96 per cent) show that the order of disagreement followed the status hierarchy. Headquarters staff showed the greatest discrepancy from the other members of the department, followed by the district, post, and assistant post commanders.

2. Recruits (who were now confirmed *policemen*) were more inaccurate than *policemen*. In terms of our analysis, they were 38 per cent more inaccurate, and especially so in their perception of headquarters and of district commanders. There were no differences with respect to the *policeman* and recruit perception of public expectations. Excluding the public, then, the order of inaccuracy for *policemen* and recruits follows the order of disagreement.

3. With respect to situations, the recruits were more inaccurate for all situations than are *policemen*. While they were both most incorrect for situations 1 and 4 ("division of labor" and "role models"), the order of disagreement among their audiences was somewhat different:

Rank Order of Disagreement	Rank Order of Inaccuracy Policemen	Recruits
S_4—Role models	S_4	S_1
S_2—Occupational involvement	S_1	S_4
S_3—Occupational secrecy . .	S_3	S_3
S_1—Division of labor . . .	S_2	S_2

Thus, it may be the case that the nonveridical component of role perception was less a matter of the specific situation and more a function of the generalized extent to which an audience group operated consensually. In other words, audiences who were typically divergent from others were less likely to be correctly perceived regardless of the situational context—much in the same manner that deviant audience groups tended to be perceived as deviant, independent of the situation.

4. The *policemen's* perception of the expectations of other *policemen* was quite divergent from their perception of the expectations of the command staff and the public. Recruits, more than *policemen*, perceived the *policemen's*

TABLE 6–12A

EXPECTATIONS OF THE AUDIENCE: PERCEIVED EXPECTATION OF "POLICEMEN" AND THE ACTUAL EXPECTATION OF THEIR ROLE PARTNERS

SITUATION 1—DIVISION OF LABOR

	(A) Safety and Traffic Per.	Act.	(B) Complaint Crim. Inves. Per.	Act.	(C) Both Equal Per.	Act.	No Answer or Other —	—
HQ command . .	43.8	18.2	4.7	9.1	43.8	72.7	7.8	0.0
District command .		18.8		6.3		75.0		0.0
Post command . .	43.8	11.1	6.3	1.9	45.3	83.3	4.7	3.7
Asst. post command		18.0		4.5		76.6		0.9
Policemen . . .	15.6		21.9		60.9		1.6	
Public	21.9	20.0	29.7	3.8	46.9	75.2	1.6	1.0

SITUATION 2—OCCUPATIONAL INVOLVEMENT

	(A) Policeman 24 Hrs. Day		(B) Leave Job Off Duty		(C) No Expectations		No Answer or Other	
HQ Command . .	95.3	90.9	0.0	9.1	3.1	0.0	1.6	0.0
District command .		75.0		25.0		0.0		0.0
Post command . .	84.4	74.1	4.7	24.1	4.7	0.0	6.3	1.9
Asst. post command		76.6		18.0		5.4		0.0
Policemen . . .	54.7		23.4		14.1		7.8	
Public	48.4	36.2	21.9	33.3	25.0	30.5	4.7	0.0

SITUATION 3—OCCUPATIONAL SECRECY

	(A) Report Policemen		(B) Keep Quiet		(C) No Expectations		No Answer or Other	
HQ command . .	87.5	81.8	3.1	18.2	4.7	0.0	4.7	0.0
District command .		93.8		6.3		0.0		0.0
Post command . .	76.6	77.8	4.7	7.4	10.9	13.0	7.8	1.9
Asst. post command		76.6		2.7		20.7		0.0
Policemen . . .	18.8		62.5		12.5		6.2	
Public	39.1	74.3	4.7	7.6	51.6	17.1	4.7	1.0

SITUATION 4—ROLE MODELS

	(A) Set Example Model Citizen		(B) Average Good Citizen		(C) No Expectations		No Answer or Other	
HQ command . .	65.6	27.3	29.7	72.7	1.6	0.0	3.1	0.0
District command .		68.8		31.3		0.0		0.0
Post command . .	46.9	66.7	45.3	33.3	1.6	0.0	4.7	0.0
Asst. post command		66.7		33.3		0.0		0.0
Policemen . . .	21.9		70.3		6.3		1.6	
Public	46.9	27.6	48.4	70.5	1.6	1.9	3.1	0.0

HQ Command $n = 11$	Post Command $n = 54$	*Policemen* $n = 64$
District Command $n = 16$	Asst. Post Command $n = 111$	Public $n = 105$

TABLE 6–12B
EXPECTATIONS OF THE AUDIENCE: PERCEIVED EXPECTATION OF RECRUITS AND THE ACTUAL EXPECTATION OF THEIR ROLE PARTNERS

SITUATION 1—DIVISION OF LABOR

	(A) Safety and Traffic Per. Act.		(B) Complaint Crim. Inves. Per. Act.		(C) Both Equal Per. Act.		No Answer or Other — —	
HQ command . .	85.0	18.2	5.0	9.1	5.0	72.7	5.0	0.0
District command .		18.8		6.3		75.0		0.0
Post command . .	80.0	11.1	10.0	1.9	10.0	83.3	0.0	3.7
Asst. post command		18.0		4.5		76.6		0.9
Policemen . . .	15.0		15.0		65.0		5.0	
Public	10.0	20.0	45.0	3.8	40.0	75.2	5.0	1.0

SITUATION 2—OCCUPATIONAL INVOLVEMENT

	(A) Policeman 24 Hrs. Day		(B) Leave Job Off Duty		(C) No Expectations		No Answer or Other	
HQ command . .	90.0	90.0	5.0	9.1	5.0	0.0	0.0	0.0
District command .		75.0		25.0		0.0		0.0
Post command . .	75.0	74.1	15.0	24.1	5.0	0.0	5.0	1.9
Asst. post command		76.6		18.0		5.4		0.0
Policemen . . .	35.0		55.0		10.0		0.0	
Public	45.0	36.2	25.0	33.3	25.0	30.5	5.0	0.0

SITUATION 3—OCCUPATIONAL SECRECY

	(A) Report Policemen		(B) Keep Quiet		(C) No Expectations		No Answer or Other	
HQ command . .	85.0	81.8	15.0	18.2	0.0	0.0	0.0	0.0
District command .		93.8		6.3		0.0		0.0
Post command . .	85.0	77.8	15.0	7.4	0.0	13.0	0.0	1.9
Asst. post command		76.6		2.7		20.7		0.0
Policemen . . .	20.0		75.0		5.0		0.0	
Public	35.0	74.3	10.0	7.6	55.0	17.1	0.0	1.0

SITUATION 4—ROLE MODELS

	(A) Set Example Model Citizen		(B) Average Good Citizen		(C) No Expectations		No Answer or Other	
HQ command . .	95.0	27.3	5.0	72.7	0.0	0.0	0.0	0.0
District command .		68.8		31.3		0.0		0.0
Post command . .	85.0	66.7	15.0	33.3	0.0	0.0	0.0	0.0
Asst. post command		66.7		33.3		0.0		0.0
Policemen . . .	30.0		70.0		0.0		0.0	
Public	30.0	27.6	70.0	70.5	0.0	1.9	0.0	0.0

HQ Command $n = 11$	Post Command $n = 54$	Recruits $n = 20$
District Command $n = 16$	Asst. Post Command $n = 111$	Public $n = 105$

expectations as even more divergent from the expectations they attributed to other audiences. Thus our earlier finding that of all the groups within the department the *policemen* were perceived as most deviant is again confirmed.

In this section, our further exploration of the accuracy of role perception has yielded two major propositions. First, the *policeman*-recruit comparisons indicate accuracy to be a function of experience in the role. Insofar as the trainees may be said to be "less socialized" into the organization than are the veteran *policemen*, we add further support to our hypothesis.[18] Second, accuracy varies directly with status distance and with consensus among the audience groups.[19]

The Prediction of Role Conflict Resolution

Many of the early attempts at predicting role conflict resolution entailed predictions based upon the personality characteristics of the persons exposed to the conflict situation. While yielding provocative results, such studies were never able to generate a successful predictive model. More current attempts at prediction have been based upon the perceived characteristics of the expectations held by an audience in a given situation. Here, such qualities as legitimacy, sanctions, obligations, and social distance have been used as predictors. None of these attempts, with the possible exception of the work of Gross and his associates, has been particularly successful; and no acceptable replication of their study has as yet been produced. Our own attempt at such study led us to the conclusion that:

None of the variables or possible combinations of variables—legitimacy, obligation, sanctions access, sanctions exercise, or personal preference—was dominant in regard to its relative efficacy as a predictor of role conflict resolution. The proportion of correct predictions of conflict resolution, utilizing the various and distinct operations reported, was found to be roughly commensurate, though a striking disparity is found between our studies and . . . that of Gross, Mason, and McEachern . . . .

[18] Our analysis, in effect, encompasses two interrelated hypotheses: first, that greater experience in the position leads to more appropriate behavior, and second, that greater experience leads to more accurate perception of role expectations. Our data, which are only applicable to a testing of the second hypothesis, are confirming. We should note, however, that experience or length of service can only be regarded as a first approximation of an indicator of socialization.

[19] In these data "status distance" and "agreement distance" have the same order, and both follow the order of *policeman* visibility. Further research will be necessary to determine their covariation. We shall have more to say about status distance and the visibility of the *policeman's* role performance in subsequent chapters.

It is our contention, that where our operations and procedures of analysis are comparable, the differences obtained between our findings and the findings of Gross and his associates are due in large measure to differences in the populations studied. Our research can by no means be taken as demonstration of this, but does indicate, at the very least, the necessity of further studies of the general applicability of these variables of role conflict analysis in other and diverse populations. . . .

The generally disappointing predictive accuracy reported by the authors seriously questions the efficacy of such variables as legitimacy and sanctions as predictors of role conflict resolution. Certainly the utilization of these variables did not appear in our studies as the most parsimonious technique available for prediction.[20]

In our exploration of new means of understanding and predicting role conflict resolution we came to see that at least one conceivable predictor, perhaps because of its all-too-obvious character, had not been given any significant attention: the audience group per se. Certainly we could anticipate, if only on the basis of introspective analysis, that the expectations of some audiences are of more importance to us than others. Corollary with this, it seems likely that, for those audiences who constitute an actor's "significant others," the actor will be more likely to conform to what he perceives to be their expectations than to the expectations of any other audience group.

We may easily subject this presumed predictor to test by taking every audience, and every possible combination of audiences, for each of the five role conflict situations and determining the number of times there is a correspondence between the actor's perception of what these audiences, or combinations of audiences, expect and what the actor reports doing. Thus, if in a given situation an actor perceives his wife to hold expectation A, and he reports doing A, we shall say we could have correctly predicted A from the prior knowledge of the wife's expectation.[21] Finally, to be most stringent in our test of this proposal, if an actor reports an expedient resolution, we shall count all of our predictions as being in error since he does not report that he perceives his audiences as expecting him to operate in an expedient manner. However, inasmuch as an expedient resolution may encompass, at times, the expectation of the significant others, we shall also indicate what improvement occurs in our predictions, if any, if we were to count the prediction as possibly correct. The results of this analysis appear in Table 6–13.

We took as our initial predictive criterion only those audiences who occupied formal positions within the police organization on the assumption that the expectations of these groups would be more important. Our predictions based on these audiences yielded approximately 57-per-cent-correct predictions. If we engage in a little post-factum analysis we can ascertain

20 Ehrlich, Rinehart, and Howell, *op. cit.*

21 For two or more audiences, the predictions are made on the basis of the most frequently mentioned expectations; and ties, expectations of equal frequency, are counted as an error.

which audience, or combination of audiences, is the best predictor. The best single predictor for all of the situations is the *policeman's* perception of what his peers—his fellow *policemen*—expect of him. *Policemen* are implicated as "best predictors" in four of the five situations; and we could have made, in fact, 55-per-cent-correct predictions on the basis of this knowledge.

All of our predictors, as can be seen in Table 6–13, enable us to make predictions at levels significantly beyond chance expectations, and to a degree of some considerable magnitude. Moreover, if we include the expedient responses as possibly correctly predicted, the proportion of correct predictions increases markedly. Though there is situational variability, we can obtain, through selective combinations of audiences, an average of 83-per-cent-correct predictions.

TABLE 6–13

PREDICTION OF ROLE CONFLICT RESOLUTION FROM SIGNIFICANT AUDIENCE GROUPS

Situation	Number of Predictions*	Best Predictors	Proportion of Correct Predictions		Proportion Expected by Chance
			Correct	Correct and Possibly Correct	
1	43	*Policemen*	62.8	74.4	
	34	Wife-family	61.8	76.5	.25
2	36	Headquarters, district, post, asst. post command and *policemen* combined	75.0	91.7	.33
3	11	Wife-family	18.2†	100.0	
	17	*Policemen*	17.6†	100.0	.33
4	29	HQ command	72.4	‡	
	29	District command	72.4	‡	.33
5	34	*Policemen*	82.4	‡	.33

* Differences in number of predictions result from differing frequencies of responses.
† All proportions except these differ significantly from the proportion of correct predictions expected by chance at $p < .01$.
‡ For these situations there were no expedient resolutions.

In sum, we have demonstrated that considerable prediction—or more properly, postdiction—can be achieved through a knowledge of the perceived expectations of the situationally significant audiences. The problem that remains, of course, is that of determining *in advance*, by some independent means, which of the audiences constitute the significant audiences in given situations. It is clear that further investigation into the nature of the audience group—and more generalized reference group processes—is in order.

Summary

The degree to which an audience group was perceived as holding deviant expectations is variable, and significant differences were observed among audiences in their extent of deviance. Moreover, the degree to which audiences were perceived as deviant was not a function of the specific role conflict situation; that is, the order of deviance remained the same across all situations. It was observed that the deviant audiences were essentially those who were not a part of the formal organization but those who comprised the primary group network of the *policeman*.

Ambivalence was found to be differentially distributed by situation and by audience; and those audiences which provoked most ambivalence were all those contained within the boundaries of the formal organization. Finally, there appeared to be no general relationship between the perception of role conflict and the experiencing of ambivalence, nor between the degree of ambivalence and the incidence of role conflict or the extent of audience group deviance.

To a great extent the *policemen* in our sample were inaccurate in their perception of command staff expectations. Despite this inaccuracy, their self-reported behavior conformed with the actual expectations of their commanders. Accuracy appeared to be related to the situation, to the audience, to the degree of consensus among the various audience groups, and to the experience of the *policeman*.

With respect to the prediction of role conflict behavior, the resolution of role conflict was shown to be a function of the audience perceived as holding a given expectation. Independent of attributions of legitimacy or sanctions, or of personal preference, modes of professed conflict resolution were successfully predicted from perceived expectations.

CHAPTER 7

The Public Image of the Police

THERE ARE many social techniques and mechanisms through which members of an occupational group may insulate their role performance from others. With respect to police-public relations, it is important to note that none of these techniques and mechanisms operate so as to achieve any high degree of insularity for the police. As a consequence, the expectations of the public, as well as the public's evaluation of the adequacy with which these expectations are met, are potent determinants of the occupational role performance of policemen. Though much evidence could be adduced in demonstration of the intimate dependency of the police on public opinion, we shall limit our discussion to what are perhaps the most salient structural features of this relationship. From there, we shall proceed to an examination of the public image of the Central State Police.

The Police and the Public

The growth of an urban industrial population carried with it the development of organized and uniformed police systems, though the status of police in a democratic society is a highly problematic and paradoxical one, and the license granted such formal agents of social control, reflecting these paradoxes, is both tenuous and vague.[1] It is, of course, most difficult to define the boundaries of any occupational license. If viewed from the complexity and ambiguity of law, with the continual repeal and redefinition of old laws and the constant passage of new ones, these difficulties are still further compounded when we attempt to delineate the specific activities which fall within the purview of a police license. Not only are we vague about the specific activities of the police, but the methods of police work—which also are continually changing—are constantly subject to popular and judicial review. Thus we are equally vague both in our conceptions of *what* ought to be done and *how* it may be done. The comment of one *policeman* mirrors the

[1] Our discussion here owes much to the insightful essay by E. C. Hughes, "License and Mandate," in his *Men and Their Work* (Glencoe, Ill.: Free Press, 1958).

dilemma of this situation eloquently: "The hardest thing I've had to learn is how to enforce the laws lawfully."

The activities of the police are chronically suspect—suspect, in part, because the enforcement of law needs to be constantly checked against its vague and changing social image. This is especially true since our traditional conceptions of criminal justice have become blurred with the breakdown in contemporary society of clear-cut distinctions between the violators and adherents of the law. Suspicion stems also from the very sacredness of the trust we place in the police. Few crimes reap more moral indignation than those committed by policemen in violation of this trust. Witness to this may be found in any daily city newspaper.

Members of occupational groups frequently attempt to claim a mandate as the primary arbiters of their own activities and standards of performance, and by this means to control the way in which outsiders may conduct themselves toward their work. Such mandates, however, can be legitimated only through collective actions, usually through professional associations or trade unions. No such associations have developed on any significant scale for policemen, and the likelihood for large-scale developments are dim. As current court decisions testing the limits of police prerogatives have noted:

The people, as the employer, have unilateral control of policy in the management of public police service. . . . Employment as a police officer does not constitute a right, but on the contrary is a privilege, subject to such control groups as boards of safety and civil service commissions, who may set conditions of employment.[2]

The structure of the relationship between the police and the public thus follows an intriguing pattern. The goals of a law enforcement agency are relatively diffuse, yet are no less important, for they encompass the truly sacred values of society. No less diffuse nor sacred are the means by which these objectives may be achieved. The achievement of any single legal objective may be accomplished by a multiplicity of means, but often the most efficient procedures, *in terms of time and money*, are precisely those which violate other important values and ends of (at least) a democratic society. Given the diffuseness of the laws (in terms of their complexity, vagueness, and scope), the diffuseness of the means by which enforcement of these laws may be achieved (in terms of the alternatives around which the police may be organized and the actual police procedures such organizations may utilize), and given the complexity of the relationship between these objectives and their means of accomplishment, it seems likely in a democratic society—and it is indeed the case—that the power to control police activities resides in the public.

2 Cited in D. L. Kooken and L. D. Ayres, "Police Unions and the Public Safety," *Annals of the American Academy of Political and Social Science*, 291 (1954), 152–58.

The power of the public is effective power. It is effective power because the role performance of policemen is both highly observable and easily confronted by public sanction. The observability of their role activities stems directly from their conspicuous occupational front—the uniform, the badge, and the marked car—and indirectly through public reports, courts of law, and legislative bodies. The visibility of role activities, however, is only a contributory factor to the effectiveness of sanction; and the issue of sanctions is a far more complex factor. To begin with, we must understand that a police organization is not to be construed merely as a body of individual practitioners. Each policeman, as a duly authorized representative of the organization, plays, in a significant measure, a role that is almost always that of a group representative.[3] For most occupational roles performed within the context of a formal organization, the improper performance of a role by an actor is primarily the responsibility of that actor and not the organization. For example, the patient who dies in a routinized surgical operation is less the responsibility of the hospital in which the operation was performed and more the responsibility of the individual practitioners involved in that operation, while, for the police, the death of a person in the course of routinized police activities is equally the responsibility of the department and the individual police officers concerned. One of the organizational consequences of this is the attempt on the part of the Central State Police Department to make all of the role activities of their *policemen* visible. This is attempted through the use of a maze of daily report forms on which all activities in which the officer is engaged are to be logged by time, place, location, persons involved, and so on. So numerous and complex are these forms, and so strained is the attempt to make these activities visible, that a majority of *policemen* indicate the writing of reports is one of the most unexpected and difficult aspects of their initial encounter with the field.

Public sanction is elegantly simple and effective in its method. Any communication, oral or written, about any member of the police department is subject to immediate investigation. Public complaints deemed unfounded by investigation are disposed of. Those which on investigation appear to be justified are entered into the individual officer's file and remain a permanent part of his record. Those complaints for which the evidence is inconclusive are typically placed in a special file, where they become inaccessible to the individuals implicated, but they may be used as contributory evidence in subsequent complaint investigations. Public praise and commendation

[3] On the concept of "representative roles," see E. Hartley, "Psychological Problems of Multiple Group Membership," in J. H. Rohrer and M. Sherif (eds.), *Social Psychology at the Crossroads* (New York: Harper & Brothers, 1951).

similarly are entered directly into the officer's file, and in each file is a "score card" on which the number of commending letters and public speaking appearances is tallied. All *policemen* may, on request, view the contents of their personal file folders, and it is common knowledge that all promotional boards study the contents of each individual's file.

Finally, it should be noted that the major disciplinary actions taken by the department involve police-public activities with significantly greater frequency than any other role relationships or activities.

Public Evaluation

Studies of the prestige rankings of occupations have yielded surprising consensus in the ranking of "police" as an occupational category. In general, the police are placed in the middle ranks. What is surprising is that these ratings of the police appear relatively stable through time, are relatively constant across national boundaries,[4] and seem relatively unaffected by differences in scaling techniques.[5]

The "police" category nevertheless encompasses a variety of jobs on all levels of government, and, in the United States, employees of an estimated 40,000 different and distinct police agencies. What, then, does the public

[4] Studies covering a time period from 1925 through 1961 and conducted in the United States of America, Great Britain, Australia, New Zealand, Japan, Canada, Germany, Poland, Indonesia, Brazil, and the Philippines have indicated extraordinary agreement in the placement of "policeman" in the third to fourth quintile of social prestige. Cf. G. S. Counts, "Social Status of Occupations," *School Review*, 33 (1925), 16–27; J. A. Nietz, "The Depression and the Social Status of Occupations," *Elementary School Journal*, 35 (1935), 454–61; M. Smith, "An Empirical Scale of Prestige Status of Occupations," *American Sociological Review*, 8 (1943), 185–92; National Opinion Research Center, "Jobs and Occupations: A Popular Evaluation" (1947), in R. Bendix and S. M. Lipset (eds.), *Class, Status and Power* (Glencoe, Ill.: Free Press, 1953); J. Hall and C. Jones, "Social Grading of Occupations," *British Journal of Sociology*, 1 (1950), 31–55; J. B. Montague, "Present Ranking of Occupations in an American City with Reference to Hall and Jones' Study," *BJS*, 5 (1954), 154–60; A. A. Congalton, "The Social Grading of Occupations in New Zealand," *BJS*, 4 (1953), 45–59; R. Taft, "The Social Grading of Occupations in Australia," *BJS*, 4 (1953), 181–87; B. Hutchinson, "The Social Grading of Occupations in Brazil," *BJS*, 8 (1957), 176–89; A. Inkeles and P. H. Rossi, "National Comparisons of Occupational Prestige," *American Journal of Sociology*, 61 (1956), 329–39; E. A. Tiryakian, "The Prestige Evaluation of Occupations in an Underdeveloped Country: The Philippines," *AJS*, 63 (1958), 390–99; C. E. Ramsey and R. J. Smith, "Japanese and American Perceptions of Occupations," *AJS*, 65 (1960), 475–82; A. Sarapata and W. Wesolowski, "The Evaluation of Occupations by Warsaw Inhabitants," *AJS*, 66 (1961), 581–91; and E. M. Thomas, "Reinspecting a Structural Position on Occupational Prestige," *AJS*, 67 (1962), 561–65.

[5] C. J. Bartlett, E. Heermann, and S. Rettig, "A Comparison of Six Different Scaling Techniques," *Journal of Social Psychology*, 51 (1960), 343–48.

think of the Central State Police?[6] And where do they stand relative to other police organizations serving the same area? Table 7–1 shows the answers to two questions: Capital City area residents were asked to "rate" the state police (1958); and Major City area residents were asked "how good a job" they thought the state police were doing (1959). As can be seen, Major City residents demonstrated a rather specific image of their police organizations and one which placed the state police at the top of the performance hierarchy. Not only do these two large urban centers show considerable agreement in their evaluation of the state police, but, in a third sample (not dealt with here) of all high school juniors and seniors in two rural counties, essentially the same pattern of results was obtained.[7] The

TABLE 7-1

COMPARATIVE RATINGS OF STATE, LOCAL, AND COUNTY POLICE IN TWO URBAN AREAS

	Capital City Area (n = 275)	Major City Area* (n = 764)				
	State Police %	State %	County %	Local %		
1. One of the best . . .	37	26	6	19 . .	Very good	1.
2. Better than average . .	35	48	35	44 . .	Good	2.
3. About average . . .	16	11	20	20 . .	Fair	3.
4. Below standard and poor	1	2	3	6 . .	Poor	4.
Not ascertained . . .	1	5	6	7 . .	Not ascertained	
Don't know	10	8	30	3 . .	Don't know	
Mean rating	1.78	1.87	2.33	2.15		

* Courtesy of the Survey Research Center, University of Michigan.

[6] The public survey materials reported here are based on two samples drawn in the metropolitan area of the capital city of Central State. The first sample was a systematic random sample, with a sampling fraction of approximately .001, drawn from the city directory. The scope of the sample was increased by a subsampling of the city's enumerated Mexican population. All persons were interviewed by sociology graduate students and Honors college undergraduates, all of whom underwent a short, intensive training program. The second sample was drawn from the universe of those Capital City residents who had received a traffic ticket from the local state police post during a specified one-month period. Through this means we were able to further expand the scope of the original sample. Respondents were here contacted by mail, and, with no follow-up, we received 36 per cent returns.

The two samples were then compared on the basis of background characteristics and on their response distributions for each item. The traffic violators' sample differed primarily by having had more contact with the police, and tended to be younger, unmarried, and better-educated (though this latter may be a function of return bias and the fact of contact, as we shall show later). Item by item comparisons yielded few differences between the samples, and they were thus combined for the remainder of the report.

In Appendix 2 we have included the background characteristics of the individual samples, and the distribution of responses to the public image questionnaire for the combined groups.

[7] We are indebted to Dr. H. F. Goldsmith for the acquisition and processing of these data.

rural youth, in general, tended to be slightly less favorable than their urban counterparts.

In our concern with the public's perception of the effectiveness with which the CSP discharges its role obligations we have thus far explored only one facet of occupational rankings, *esteem*. Other dimensions of equal importance are those of *functional importance, economic status,* and *social status.* Here we can call on data from not only the public but also from the police.

Table 7–2 presents a comparison between the public image of the functional or social importance of the job of *state policemen* and the *policemen's* perception of what this public image is. As we can see, there is high consensus within the public that such a role is an important one. Among *policemen* there is even less variability, for they significantly overestimate the public image.

TABLE 7–2

Social Importance: The Public Image and the "Policemen's" Conceptions of the Public Image

	Public		Policemen	
	f	%	f	%
Much more important than most jobs . .	81	29.8	71	66.4
Somewhat more important	128	47.1	33	30.8
About as important	62	22.8	2	1.9
Somewhat—much less important . . .	1	0.4	1	0.9

Note.—$\chi^2 = 48.65$; $df = 2$; $p < .001$ (bottom cells collapsed).

In our concern with the economic and social position of *policemen* in the community, we asked the *policemen* to report not what their conception of the public image of their respective positions was but rather what they themselves thought their positions were. Table 7–3 yields some interesting observations. To begin with, in both instances the public manifests a significantly lower placement of the state police. In other words, the *policemen* consistently overestimate both their economic and social status. Moreover, both the public and police indicate a significantly higher position for the *policemen* with respect to their social standing than with respect to their economic position. In general, then, the state police are seen as occupying a functionally important position in society, one which carries with it a high degree of social status and a high but somewhat lower degree of economic status. Finally, it can be seen that the public evaluation of the state police's role performance is high and higher than the evaluations given other police agencies in the same area.

For over 55 per cent of our samples, the job of state *policeman* is perceived as more desirable or about as desirable as the job of the person responding. The desirable features of the job as seen by the public are precisely those we

TABLE 7-3

How do you estimate the economic position of state policemen in your community?					How would you picture state policemen in your community with respect to their social standing?			
Public		Policemen				Public		Policemen	
f	%	f	%			f	%	f	%
10	3.8	4	3.0	. . . Very high . . .		43	15.7	21	15.9
18	6.8	7	5.3	. . . Quite high . . .		50	18.2	28	21.2
39	14.7	76	57.6	. . . Fairly high . . .		79	28.8	77	58.3
173	65.3	34	25.8	. . . Average . . .		98	35.8	5	3.8
22	8.3	10	7.6	. . . Fairly low . . .		4	1.5	1	0.8
2	0.8	1	0.8	. . . Quite low . . .		0	—	0	—
1	0.4	0	—	. . . Very low . . .		0	—	0	—

NOTE.—For all comparisons $p < .01$.

have been talking about. In answer to an open-ended question that asked why they considered the state *policeman's* job desirable, 70 per cent of the respondents who saw the job more desirable than their own answered in terms of social and economic prestige and the importance of the job to society. In contrast, the 45 per cent who perceived the job as less desirable selected different grounds for evaluation. In general, the rejection of the job was based on what they considered to be undesirable working conditions; in particular, the length of the working hours required, and—for one out of three respondents—the risk and danger involved in such an activity.

Most of our respondents knew how the state police were selected (74 per cent), though there was much less agreement as to what they thought the main job of the organization was. While one-half of all respondents thought that highway patrol and traffic law enforcement constituted its major objective, only 20 per cent thought it *ought* to constitute the main job. In answer to another query, 75 per cent of those questioned suggested that a balanced emphasis of traffic safety on the one hand and criminal and complaint investigation on the other was what they expected of the police. One can only conclude—in view of this discrepancy between what they say the police are doing, what they say they ought to be doing, and the high esteem with which they regard the state police—that the issue of traffic law enforcement is of relatively low saliency. In the following chapter, we shall pursue this finding further, and from some alternative perspectives.

An examination of some of the specific elements of public appraisal in Table 7-4 indicates an overwhelmingly favorable set of evaluations. The image that emerges is that of an honest, impartial, objective police organization whose job in general is about the same as most with respect to the time and effort involved, but one which involves frequent exposure to risk and danger. What they do is important and they do it well. Their rewards are an above-average income and high prestige standing in their community. Perhaps one further indicator of the prestige and esteem that accrue to this status can be seen in our data where 87 per cent of the responses describing the nature of public-police contacts depict that interaction as "friendly, helpful, and courteous." Moreover, and perhaps more significantly, the majority of those receiving a traffic summons by the Central State Police (57 per cent) report that their ticket was justifiable.

TABLE 7–4

THE PUBLIC EVALUATION OF THE STATE POLICE (N = 275)*

Percentage of respondents answering that the state police are:	
Well or exceptionally well dressed	98.6
Usually or unquestionably honest	93.3
Occasionally or often exposed to danger and risk .	90.9
Respectful of constitutional rights	87.3
Uninfluenced by type of car driven by traffic violators	85.1
Fair in treatment of minority groups	81.8
Unlikely to arrest the innocent	81.8
Uninfluenced by sex of traffic violators	77.5
Usually cooperative with other police agencies . .	76.7
Administered by competent and well-trained personnel	61.5
Working quite or exceptionally long hours . . .	42.2
Working on strenuous and demanding tasks . . .	20.7

* For full details, see Appendix 2.

The Determinants of the Public Image

In this section we shall attempt to dissect the public image through the use of standardized control variables such as age, sex, occupation, education, minority-group status, and the degree and kind of contact persons have had with the police. The configuration of these variables provides us with an interesting and heuristic composite. The pattern that emerges for a positive image of the police is found in the middle-age white female college graduate who has had no contact with the police and whose husband is engaged in a nonexecutive capacity in a white-collar occupation. In contrast, the negative image seems to stem from a somewhat younger, non-white male manual worker, with a grade school education or less, who has had some but not extensive contact with the police.[8]

[8] The relatively small size of our sample precluded a meaningful use of formal multi-variate analysis. We have employed in this section, two primary modes of statistical analysis. The first, Friedman's two-way analysis of variance by ranks; the second, the Sign Test. In the interpretation or reading of these tables, rank 1 always refers to the most favorable response; 2 to the second most favorable; 3 to the third most favorable, and so on; with the highest rank referring to the least favorable response. Where the Sign Test has been used, + always indicates a relatively favorable response and − a relatively unfavorable response. Though individual item analyses for all items by each of the control variables have been

Age and Sex. As can be discerned from Table 7–5, there is a direct, almost linear relationship between age and the relative favorableness of imagery. Younger persons are less favorable and older persons are more favorable with respect to this composite image of the police. By contrast, contact with the police shows an *inverse* linear relationship to age; while three-fourths of those over sixty-five had no police contacts in the past five years, only 4 per cent of those under twenty-one report no contacts. Despite their significantly more negative evaluation of the police, the younger respondent displays an interesting ambivalence in according the CSP relatively high esteem and social importance and in selecting the job as a highly desirable one. The negativism of the teen-ager is no doubt in part reflective of a realistic conflict in values between the "car culture" of the adolescent and the "traffic safety culture" of this police force.

TABLE 7-5

AGE DIFFERENCES IN THE EVALUATION OF THE STATE POLICE

	Rank Order of Favorableness by Age					
Item	Under 21 (n = 23)	21–29 (n = 67)	30–44 (n = 88)	45–54 (n = 41)	55–64 (n = 34)	Over 65 (n = 17)
3. Social importance	3	5	1	4	2	6
4. Social prestige	4	6	5	2	3	1
5. Economic position	6	1	4	2	3	5
6. Desirability of job	2	1	4	6	5	3
7. Rating	3	2	6	1	5	4
8. Public contact	6	5	3	2	4	1
10. Dress	4	3	5	2	6	1
11. Honesty	4	5	3	2	6	1
12. Selection	1	2	3	4	5	6
13. Arrest procedures	6	5	1	2	4	3
14. Minority groups	5	2	4	1	3	6
14a. Car bias	6	2	4	5	3	1
14b. Sex bias	6	5	3	2	4	1
16. Administrators	6	4	3	5	2	1
17. Cooperation	2	5	3	6	4	1
19a. Time	6	2	3	4	5	1
19b. Effort	2	6	4	5	1	3
19c. Exposure	6	3	2	4	5	1
Rank Sum	78	64	61	59	70	46
Mean Rank	4.33	3.56	3.39	3.28	3.89	2.56

NOTE.—$\chi_r^2 = 17.27$; $df = 5$; $p < .01$.

made, usually through the use of chi-square or Kolmogorov-Smirnov statistical tests, we felt that the total *pattern* of responses for all of the evaluation questions on our questionnaire was more important, and gave a more accurate picture, than individual item analyses. While the analysis of total questionnaires in this manner is somewhat novel, we think the results of such a pattern analysis have far more significance and validity than the more atomistic analysis. On the statistics employed, see S. Siegel, *Nonparametric Statistics for the Behavioral Sciences* (New York: McGraw-Hill, 1956).

TABLE 7–6

SEX DIFFERENCES IN THE EVALUATION OF THE STATE POLICE

Item	Direction of Relative Favorableness by Sex*	
	Male (n = 191)	Female (n = 81)
3. Social importance .	—	+
4. Social prestige . .	—	+
5. Economic position .	+	—
6. Desirability of job .	—	+
7. Rating . . .	—	+
8. Public contact . .	o	o
10. Dress	—	+
11. Honesty	+	—
12. Selection	o	o
13. Arrest procedures .	+	—
14. Minority groups . .	o	o
14a. Car bias	—	+
14b. Sex bias	—	+
16. Administrators . .	o	o
17. Cooperation . . .	—	+
19a. Time	—	+
19b. Effort	—	+
19c. Exposure	—	+

* $p = .058$, Sign test.

Women, more than any other category of respondents, manifest an idealized, almost stereotypic image of the police as an important, prestigeful, desirable, dangerous, and difficult occupation (Table 7–6). It is highly probable that our female respondents are evaluating the police from a quite different perspective than our male respondents. In this respect it is interesting to note that the woman's conception of the *policeman's* role seems quite different from that of the male. Women were twice as likely to view the police as primarily a *service* organization rather than one primarily responsible for criminal or traffic enforcement. The characteristics of the women in our sample, however, seem somewhat different from those of the men sampled. The women tend to be older and less educated, and are significantly more likely to have had no contact with the state police. For the almost seven out of ten women who have had no direct contact, it is interesting to observe— an observation about which we shall have more to say later—that their image of the police appears to stem from the mass media, and that they report on this image quite favorably. Among those who report being given a traffic summons by the Central State Police, women are more likely to describe the behavior of the *policeman* who gave them the ticket as *impersonal*, while men, in contrast, are more likely to describe the arresting officer's behavior as *friendly*. This probably reflects real differences in the treatment accorded the sexes by the *policeman*, and it is impressionistically corroborated by the field observations of the authors. This is quite interesting, for among women who report the affective tone of their role relationship with the police as impersonal we have a higher evaluation than among men who report the affective tone of their role relationship with the police as friendly.

TABLE 7-7

EDUCATIONAL DIFFERENCES IN THE EVALUATION OF THE STATE POLICE

		Rank Order of Favorableness by Education			
Item	Grade School (n = 41)	Some High School (n = 41)	High School Graduate (n = 94)	Some College (n = 41)	College Graduate (n = 49)
3. Social importance	2	4	5	3	1
4. Social prestige	1	4	2	3	5
5. Economic position	2	4.5	3	4.5	1
6. Desirability of job	1	2.5	2.5	4	5
7. Rating	5	4	2.5	2.5	1
8. Public contact	1.5	5	3.5	1.5	3.5
10. Dress	3.5	2	5	3.5	1
11. Honesty	3	4.5	2	1	4.5
12. Selection	5	1	4	2	3
13. Arrest procedures	4	3	1.5	1.5	2
14. Minority groups	5	4	1.5	3	1.5
14a. Car bias	3.5	5	3.5	3.5	3.5
14b. Sex bias	1	4	3	5	2
16. Administrators	2	4	1	3	5
17. Cooperation	1	5	3.5	3.5	2
19a. Time	3.5	5	1	2	3.5
19b. Effort	1	5	2	3	4
19c. Exposure	3	4.5	2	4.5	1
Rank Sum	48.0	68.0	48.5	54.0	49.5
Mean Rank	2.67	3.78	2.69	3.00	2.75

NOTE.—$\chi_r^2 = 0.53$; n.s.

Education and Occupation. Tables 7-7 and 7-8 show the rank patterns of results for education and occupation. The results are somewhat surprising. No matter how we look at the association between education and occupation with the evaluation of the state police, whether we subject the cross-tabulations to an intensive item by item analysis, or use the rank order analysis of variance as in these tables, and whether we use small discrete classes of occupational or educational achievement or large gross categories, the results remain the same. No meaningful pattern of relationship obtains for either variable; and the item analysis yields few items which show any statistically significant differences—other than the anticipated results that persons of low occupational and educational status see this as a desirable job and one which has high social prestige and economic position. The generalized image of the state police seems unrelated to these two variables.

Contact. The effects of intergroup contact on the attitudes and imagery

TABLE 7–8

OCCUPATIONAL DIFFERENCES IN THE EVALUATION OF THE STATE POLICE

Item	Rank Order of Favorableness by Occupation Professional Managerial Self-Employed ($n = 50$)	Other White-Collar ($n = 69$)	Manual ($n = 105$)
3. Social importance .	3	1	2
4. Social prestige . .	3	2	1
5. Economic position .	3	2	1
6. Desirability of job .	3	2	1
7. Rating	2	1	3
8. Public contact . .	1	3	2
10. Dress	1	3	2
11. Honesty	1	2	3
12. Selection	2	1	3
13. Arrest procedures .	2	1	3
14. Minority groups . .	2	1	3
14a. Car bias	3	1.5	1.5
14b. Sex bias	1	3	2
16. Administrators . .	3	2	1
17. Cooperation . . .	2	1	3
19a. Time	2	1	3
19b. Effort	3	2	1
19c. Exposure	3	2	1
Rank Sum	40	31.5	36.5
Mean Rank	2.22	1.75	2.03

NOTE.—$\chi_r^2 = 2.03$; $df = 2$; n.s.

of persons involved in the contact situations has been of long-standing interest to the sociologist. While it is difficult to summarize these studies— which have been done primarily in a context of minority–majority group relationships or cross-cultural contacts—it seems likely that contacts or contact situations where the persons in contact are of equal status, where the contacts are continuous and of relatively long duration, where the situation is either noncompetitive or where the members of both groups are working jointly towards the achievement of a common superordinate goal, will lead to more favorable intergroup imagery. Where majority-group members have had no contact with members of the minority group, they seem usually to accept the prevailing negative stereotypes about the minority group.[9]

The police in their own domain have been similarly concerned with the nature of the police–public contact situation. It was within this context of interest that we set out to explore the concomitance between contact with the police and images of the police. To do this we first enumerated the possible forms of contact that could occur between the public and the Central State Police. These involve such things as personal acquaintance with members of

[9] A summary of these materials appears in R. Williams, "Racial and Cultural Relations," in J. B. Gittler (ed.), *Review of Sociology* (New York: John Wiley & Sons, 1957).

the department, the seeking or receipt of information or personal services, involvement in complaint or criminal investigations, traffic violations, traffic accidents, searches and manhunts, etc.[10] We then constructed a fourfold index of contact types. *No contact:* persons who had had no contact in any form with members of the Central State Police department in the past five years. *Personal contact:* persons who reported acquaintance or friendship with members of the department and/or had had personal services performed for them by members of the department. (Of the persons placed in this category, about one-fourth had had no other form of contact with the police; slightly more than one-half had received one traffic citation in the past five years, and the remainder had received two or more. This type is our only nonexclusive type.) *Some negative contact:* included here are persons who had received one traffic citation in the past five years and had no other form of contact. *Considerable negative contact:* persons placed here were those who had received two or more traffic citations in the past five years. The mean number of tickets received in this category was three, and some persons had received as many as nine. All of the traffic citations spoken of here involve moving violations, with the vast majority being for speeding or disregarding stop lights or stop signs. The findings displayed in Table 7–9 are quite overwhelming.

Persons with no contact with the state police manifest a consistently more favorable image of the police than persons in any other contact category. Persons with personal contact are next most favorable, while those who have had considerable negative contact appear to be more favorably inclined than those with only some negative contact. There are three intriguing puzzles embedded in these findings. Why is it that persons with no contact at all manifest the most favorable image, and why is it that persons with personal contact seem less favorably inclined than persons who have had no contact? Third, why should considerable negative contact result in consistently more favorable evaluations than some negative contact?

By way of answering our first question, we might ask another: From what sources could persons who have had no contact with the police derive an image of the police? Within the confines of our data we can only answer this question indirectly. If we assume, however, that the source of this image might well reside within the mass media, then we could expect persons who have had no contact with the police to be more favorably disposed to the mass media image of the police than persons who have had contact of any form. Inspection of Table 7–10 confirms this expectation. Persons with no contact with the police are significantly more likely to report liking the mass media

[10] The specific questions in the questionnaire dealing with this are items 1, 2, 22*a*, 22*b*, 23, and 23*a*. See Appendix 2.

TABLE 7–9

THE EFFECT OF CONTACT WITH THE STATE POLICE ON THE IMAGES HELD
OF THE DEPARTMENT

	Rank Order of Favorableness by Type of Contact			
Item	None (n = 89)	Personal (n = 25)	Some Negative (n = 74)	Considerable Negative (n = 43)
3. Social importance	1	2	3	4
4. Social prestige	1	2	3	4
5. Economic position	1	2	3	4
6. Desirability of job	1	4	2	3
7. Rating	1	3	4	2
8. Public contact	2	1	4	3
10. Dress	1.5	3	4	1.5
11. Honesty	2	3	4	1
12. Selection	1	2	3.5	3.5
13. Arrest procedures	3	1	4	2
14. Minority groups	2	1	4	3
14a. Car bias	2	3	1	4
14b. Sex bias	2	3	4	1
16. Administrators	2	1	3	4
17. Cooperation	2	1	4	3
19a. Time	1	2	3	4
19b. Effort	1	3	2	4
19c. Exposure	2	1	4	3
Rank Sum	28.5	38.0	59.5	51.0
Mean Rank	1.58	2.11	3.31	2.83

NOTE.—$\chi_r^2 = 10.04$; $df = 3$; $p < .02$.

TABLE 7–10

EVALUATION OF THE MASS MEDIA IMAGE OF "POLICEMEN" AND CONTACT
WITH THE POLICE

	Per Cent Responding by Type of Contact			
	None (n = 89)	Personal (n = 25)	Some Negative (n = 74)	Considerable Negative (n = 43)
Like	37.0	20.0	20.3	18.6
Dislike	22.5	40.0	43.2	37.2
Ambivalent	4.5	12.0	4.1	4.7
Not ascertained	36.0	28.0	32.4	39.5

NOTE.—$\chi^2 = 10.57$, $p < .01$ (like–dislike by contact–no contact).

depiction of policemen than persons in any other contact type. When we probe further to determine the grounds for this evaluation, we find that those who report favorably on the mass media image regard it as a "good and fair portrayal," one which "upholds truth and reflects the ideals of society," while, by contrast, those who report unfavorably regard the mass media image as "exaggerated, stereotyped, untrue, and sensational." Thus persons with no contact seem to accept the prevailing and for them positive image of the police in the mass media, and this acceptance is reflected in their more favorable evaluation of the police.

Our next two questions are somewhat more complex, though there is an interesting parallel between them. As we go from no contact to personal contact, we get a decrease in favorableness, and as we go from some negative contact to considerable negative contact, we get an increase in favorableness. We can explain these two results parsimoniously, though without the requisite data, in the following manner. It seems to us quite likely that the situations of no contact and some negative contact involve situations of respectively unduly positive and unduly negative images of the police. As we moved in the first instance from no contact to some personal contact, this exaggerated favorable image becomes more realistic. Similarly, as we move from the situation of some negative contact (which means that the individual has received only one traffic citation and had only that contact with the police in five years) to the situation of considerable negative contact, we again find a movement to what is perhaps a more realistic evaluation. What we are suggesting, then, is that these two types of contact situations function so as to *clarify* the previously existing images of the police, to break down the existing stereotypes. Thus the person who has had more contact with the police, even though it has been negative contact, has a greater experiential basis for his images, and hence discards his older negative stereotypes. Similarly, the person who moves from an instance of no contact to an instance of personal contact discards his older exaggerated positive stereotypes. In both cases, then, we have a levelling effect which perhaps serves to clarify, to sharpen the police image.

Minority Groups and the Police

Minority-group relations have represented a chronic problem for law enforcement officials, and the formal literature on police–public relations has been much concerned with this important segment of the public. This concern stems realistically, with respect to Negroes and other low-status minorities, from the generally higher gross crime rates for them, especially in the large urban centers. The disproportionately high arrest rate has embroiled the police and minority-group agencies in a constant state of battle. While it is not the purpose of this section to explore in any exhaustive manner the complex relationships that obtain between the police and minority groups, we shall attempt to depict the minority-group image of the police (and here we shall have specific reference to Negroes and Mexicans) and, conversely, the police image of minority groups.

To begin with, it is necessary to point out certain limitations of a methodological nature in this analysis. First, we are dealing here only with Negroes and Mexicans. Secondly, the number of non-whites in our sample is 34, as compared to 233 whites. Our minority-group respondents, moreover, are a decidedly lower socioeconomic status group: 29 out of 34 are in manual occupations, and 24 out of the 34 did not complete high school. There is no doubt some interactive effect between minority-group membership and low socioeconomic status for which we cannot control. On the other hand, the combination of characteristics of our minority sample: manual occupation and low educational status—as well as the fact that the minority-group members here were significantly more likely to have had no contact with the police, and are significantly more likely to report liking the mass media image of the police—all of these characteristics are those most strongly associated with favorable imagery. Thus, given the direction of our findings, it seems quite likely that we are dealing with minority-group sensitivity per se.

With respect to a direct question as to how the Central State Police deals with minority-group members (Table 7–11), we can see that twice the proportion of our non-white sample answered negatively. Moreover, the pattern of results that obtains in Table 7–12 is almost that of a unilaterally negative picture. The state police is perceived as a prestigeful, well-paying, desirable job that requires hard work in a well-run organization; but the *policeman*, in general, is seen as tense, suspicious, and overbearing in his relationships with the public, as being likely to disregard constitutional rights, as using convenient methods without conscience, and as a man selected on the basis of political considerations or physical qualities. There can be little doubt—item by item and from the pattern of results that obtains—that the minority-group members sampled are significantly more likely to view the police in a relatively negative manner.

TABLE 7–11

THE PUBLIC IMAGE OF THE POLICE TREATMENT OF
MINORITY GROUPS BY MINORITY STATUS

	White %	Non-White %
Usually fair	82.8	73.5
Sometimes unfriendly . .	10.3	17.6
Often unfriendly	1.7	2.9
Prejudiced and antagonistic .	1.3	8.8
No answer	3.9	—

NOTE.—White = 233; Non-white = 34; No answer = 8.

What, then, is the *policeman's* image of the minority group? In attempting to answer this question, a note of caution—which appeared in another study similarly concerned with this problem—bears repeating here:

In the pages which follow it will soon become apparent that many white police personnel have, in varying degrees, unfavorable opinions about Negroes. It would have been most surprising had this not been the case, inasmuch as similar opinions are held by many persons of all occupational groups—be they lawyers, laborers, teachers, or baseball players. Whether police are more (or less) prejudiced against Negroes than are other occupational groups is not known to the writer—or to anyone else—and the present study should not be construed as an attempt to supply an answer. . . .

As a matter of record, it might be argued that a policeman who is "anti-Negro" probably has more reason to feel this way than a person engaged in almost any other occupation. With the exception of those few who have always been assigned to all-white areas, policemen probably have their opinions about Negroes at least partly shaped by their daily experience with them. The "them" in this instance represents the "bottom" Negro element: juvenile delinquents, drunks, dope addicts, sex offenders, thugs, thieves, and murderers. White policemen have comparatively little contact with the majority of Negroes who are self-respecting and law-abiding citizens. It is little wonder that to many police the Negro stereotype is that of an abusive Black who spells trouble.[11]

TABLE 7–12

MINORITY–NONMINORITY GROUP DIFFERENCES IN THE
EVALUATION OF THE STATE POLICE

Item	Direction of Relative Favorableness by Group*	
	White	Non-White
3. Social importance .	+	−
4. Social prestige . .	−	+
5. Economic position .	−	+
6. Desirability of job .	−	+
7. Rating	+	−
8. Public contact . .	+	−
10. Dress	+	−
11. Honesty	+	−
12. Selection	+	−
13. Arrest procedures .	+	−
14. Minority groups . .	+	−
14a. Car bias	+	−
14b. Sex bias	+	−
16. Administrators . .	−	+
17. Cooperation . . .	+	−
19a. Time	+	−
19b. Effort	−	+
19c. Exposure	+	−

* $p = .048$ (one-tailed sign test).

To arrive at some assessment, aside from our personal observations, two sets of questions were included in our mail sample of *policemen* and our third follow-up of the recruits. The first, two questions adapted from Kephart, was concerned with the reactions of *policemen* toward enforcement practices

[11] W. M. Kephart, *Racial Factors and Urban Law Enforcement* (Philadelphia: University of Pennsylvania Press, 1957), pp. 25, 77.

with respect to racial minorities and with their reactions to working with a Negro *policeman*.[12] Although a very small, and unknown, number of Negroes had been accepted as trainees, none in the department's history had ever finished the initial training cycle.

As a policeman, *what would have been your reaction toward working with a Negro* policeman *on patrol?*

	f	%
Would have refused	4	4.4
Strongly objected—done so under orders	28	31.1
Felt uncomfortable—would not have objected	35	38.9
Wouldn't have bothered me	21	23.3
Would like to have done so	1	1.1
No answer	1	1.1
	90	99.9

Do you feel that Negroes and other racial minority groups (Mexicans, Indians, etc.) require stricter enforcement procedures than the rest of the population?

	f	%
Definitely feel this way from experience	46	51.1
Feel this way—no direct experience	7	7.8
Definitely do not feel this way from experience	15	16.7
Do not feel this way—no direct experience	13	14.4
Don't know	9	10.0
	90	100.0

As we see, the two items yield somewhat independent distributions. Their cross-tabulation in Table 7–13 indicates that approximately one-fourth of the men who feel the need for stronger enforcement would refuse or strongly object to a Negro *policeman*, while another one-fourth, who do not feel stricter enforcement to be necessary, would not have objected to or been

TABLE 7–13

"POLICEMAN" REACTIONS TOWARD MINORITY-GROUP ENFORCEMENT PROCEDURES AND WORKING WITH NEGRO "POLICEMEN"

Reaction to Working with a Negro Policeman	Do Racial Minorities Require Stricter Enforcement?					
	Yes		No		Totals	
	f	%	f	%	f	%
Refused or strongly object to Negro policeman	21	26.3	9	11.3	30	37.5
Felt uncomfortable—no objection	22	27.5	10	12.5	32	40.0
Wouldn't have bothered me—would like to	9	11.3	9	11.3	18	22.5
Totals	52	65.0	28	35.0	80	100.0

12 *Ibid.*

bothered by a Negro patrol partner. Of the remainder, the majority (39 per cent) would have no objections to a Negro *policeman*, but they feel that racial minorities require stricter enforcement.

To help us further understand these findings, we turn to our second set of questions. These consisted of Srole's five-item "anti-minorities scale."[13] Of the five structured, agree–disagree questions (which appear in Appendix 1), two are specifically concerned with Negroes, one with Jews, one with unspecified "religious differences," and the last with foreign-born American residents. Of the 89 completed schedules, 71 per cent indicated a relatively unprejudiced, tolerant perspective—agreeing with no more than one of the five items.

TABLE 7–14

MINORITY ATTITUDES AND "POLICEMAN" REACTIONS TOWARD
MINORITY–GROUP ENFORCEMENT PROCEDURES AND WORKING
WITH NEGRO "POLICEMEN" ON PATROL

| Minority Attitudes Scale | Work with Negro Policeman | | | | | |
| | High Objection | | Low or No Objection | | Totals | |
	f	%	*f*	%	*f*	%
Prejudiced	16	61.5	10	38.5	26	100.0
Unprejudiced	16	25.4	47	74.6	63	100.0
Totals . .	32	36.0	57	64.0	89	100.0

| Minority Attitudes Scale | Minorities Require Stricter Enforcement | | | | | |
| | Yes | | No | | Totals | |
	f	%	*f*	%	*f*	%
Prejudiced .	18	78.3	5	21.7	23	100.0
Unprejudiced	35	61.4	23	39.6	58	100.0
Totals . .	53	65.4	28	34.6	81	100.0

NOTE.—Minority attitudes scale × work with Negro policeman, $\chi^2 = 8.96$, $p < .01$. Minority attitudes scale × minorities require stricter enforcement, $\chi^2 = 1.62$, n.s.

The relationships obtained between the minority attitudes scale score and the responses to the two earlier questions (presented in Table 7–14) further support our contention of independence. While minority attitudes are significantly associated with reactions to working with a Negro *policeman*— the prejudiced object to this, the unprejudiced do not—there is no significant association (at the .05 level) between the belief that minorities require stricter enforcement and the scale scores. If a *policeman's* attitude toward minority groups, then, is relatively independent of his belief about enforcement (or is at best no more than a contributory factor), what can account for the development of such a belief? Perhaps, as Kephart suggested, such a belief has its

[13] Leo Srole, "Social Integration and Certain Corollaries: An Exploratory Study," *American Sociological Review*, 21 (1956), 709–16.

roots in the white *policeman's* almost exclusive contact with the deviant members of the minority societies.

Since we asked the *policemen* to indicate their experiential basis for their feelings on strict enforcement, we may probe further by means of the analysis shown in Table 7–15. Two items stand out rather clearly: as we noted, there is 1) some tendency for prejudiced persons to be more prone towards strict enforcement, but 2) experience appears to be a more significant factor in the determination of the *policeman's* outlook on enforcement. Thus an interactive effect between minority attitudes—the feeling that racial minorities require stricter enforcement—and the report of the experiential basis of this feeling seems to exist, with experience possibly being the more important factor.[14]

TABLE 7–15
MINORITY ATTITUDES AND THE EFFECT OF EXPERIENCE ON "POLICEMAN"
REACTION TO MINORITY–GROUP ENFORCEMENT

Stricter Enforcement: Minority Attitudes Scale	Based on Experience				No Direct Experience			
	Yes		No		Yes		No	
	f	%	f	%	f	%	f	%
Prejudiced	14	60.9	2	8.7	4	17.4	3	13.0
Unprejudiced . . .	32	55.2	13	22.4	3	5.2	10	17.2

Experience × No experience	$.01 > p > .001$
Yes × Yes	$.50 > p > .30$
No × No	$.90 > p > .80$
Prejudiced–Experience × Unprejudiced–Experience . . .	$.50 > p > .30$
Prejudiced–No experience × Unprejudiced–No experience .	$.90 > p > .80$
Prejudiced × Unprejudiced	$.20 > p > .10$

By way of concluding this section we offer the following incident, which may further help reveal the complexities of analysis of police-race relations. It occurred with one of the authors while on a routine early-morning traffic patrol with a veteran *policeman.*

We had been proceeding north at a moderate rate of speed on a secondary road when we were passed by a southbound station wagon which was towing a small outboard motorboat on a boat trailer. The *policeman* braked the patrol car, executed a sharp U-turn, and took off in pursuit of this station wagon. We overtook them easily, and they came to a quick stop at our signal. The driver and his passenger, two Negro men in roughly their late thirties, were both visibly startled; and, as is routine in traffic investigations, the

14 We have, of course, no way of knowing whether the *policeman's* answer that his feeling is based on experience has, indeed, an objective basis. If it were the case, however, that the prejudiced respondents attempted to "rationalize" their answers in this manner, then the minority attitudes scale ought to have been a more powerful predictor than reports of experience. Finally, it should be noted that the percentage of those agreeing with the stricter enforcement thesis, 58.9, is approximately that obtained by Kephart—where 51.8 per cent of the 1,081 patrolmen surveyed similarly agreed.

policeman requested the driver's license and automobile registration of the driver. On inspecting these, he then requested the registration for the boat trailer and proof of ownership of the boat. These documents were furnished (after a long period of nervous fumbling) and were in order, and the officer thanked the men and graciously took leave. While the patrolman was logging the event, the writer asked what had caused him to take off in pursuit of this car. His reply was most interesting: "You seldom see a colored man with a boat. I thought maybe it had been stolen."

There can be no doubt that skin color was a contributory factor in this investigation: the probabilities that two white men under similar conditions would have been stopped are very low. It is indeed a moot question as to whether we are dealing here with an incident of racial discrimination or an incident of alert police practice. At the very least, we may conclude that much as contact with the police emerges as the single most important determinant of public imagery, so the *policeman*'s selective contact with minorities appears to be the major determinant of his image of them.[15]

[15] Gourley similarly concludes that contact, in his survey, emerges as the single most important variable. This is of considerable interest since his other data, with regard to age, sex, occupation, and education, are not entirely consonant with ours. See G. D. Gourley, *Public Relations and the Police* (Springfield, Ill.: Charles C. Thomas, 1953).

CHAPTER 8

Policy and Practice in the Role:
The Enforcement of Traffic Law

Introduction

UNLIKE MOST state police agencies whose authority is confined to highway patrol and offenses committed on the highway, the Central State Police is invested with a wide range of police powers throughout the entire state. Despite this warrant, functional restrictions emerged through the establishment of "working relationships" with the local police agencies. These restrictions represented a division of labor based upon the number, size, and mandates of the police agencies serving a given area. Episodes of competition among agencies were not uncommon, but the necessity of cooperation, particularly in emergencies, usually prevented any open rifts among police organizations. The effect of this coexistence of police systems in a given geographical area was that the extensive legal powers of the CSP were likely to be limited by the practical problems of overlapping jurisdictions and vested political interests. Thus the *policeman* in the CSP would have his widest latitude of functions in areas where few or no other police systems were present, most likely in the less urbanized areas of the state.

With its 58,000 square miles, Central State provided ample room for the annually recorded police vehicle travel of 22 million miles. The scope and diversity of the activities of the CSP were well beyond the knowledge of the citizenry they served. Among the activities for 1959 (the middle year of this study), for example, were:

Hazardous traffic violation arrests	199,633
Cars assisted	62,789
Cars investigated	168,332
Fire Marshal complaint investigations	9,710
Emergency relays of blood and serum	395
Liquor inspections	52,054
Juvenile offender arrests	11,343
Sex-motivated criminal cases investigated	847
Fraudulent checks investigated	1,698

Property inspections 450,384
Stolen items recorded 23,454
Requests by the public for delivery of emergency messages . 1,678
Polygraph examinations 2,358
Photographic prints processed 61,647

Though the scope of their activities was quite broad, as these limited examples indicate, the confinement of their activities to primarily the less urbanized areas of the state led the CSP to an emphasis on traffic patrol and enforcement. This safety-traffic focus is perhaps best exhibited by the departmental summary of arrests.

During the period covered by our study, approximately 87 per cent of all arrests were for traffic violations.[1] About 75 per cent of the total number of arrests were for "hazardous" violations (e.g., speeding, ignoring stop lights and stop signs, etc.) and the remaining 12 per cent were for "nonhazardous" violations, such as parking. Three out of every ten arrests were for speeding, and arrests for violations of speed laws occurred five times more frequently than any other single category of arrests in the department. Over 90 per cent of all traffic arrests resulted in conviction.

Thus the enforcement of traffic law, especially the speed law enforcement, constituted the major focus of the state *policeman's* daily activities. From our concern in preceding chapters with the non-instrumental and evaluative aspects of role performance, we now shift to a concern with the instrumental. Here we shall concentrate on traffic law enforcement, and especially speed law enforcement, as a specimen case.

Enforcement Policy and Practice

It is clear, if arrests are acceptable as the criterion of departmental practices, that "safety and traffic" constituted the predominant activity of the department. Certainly, we could not have expected or predicted this from the responses to our earlier inquiry: Do you expect *policemen* to emphasize safety and traffic or criminal and complaint investigation, or to give equal time to both? We observed in Chapter 6 (Table 12A) that three-fourths of all department members from *policemen* through officers, as well as three-fourths of our public respondents, selected the "equal time" expectation.

Perhaps a police organization ought to give equal time to both—or, more likely, is conceived of as doing both. At least we can say that the image that members of the CSP have of organizational practice and policy was generated through a delicate balance of myth and reality. This shall become even more apparent as we continue.

[1] This figure, however, provides no indication of nontraffic arrests which resulted from the search of persons and their vehicles as a result of being stopped for traffic violations.

With increasing urbanization of the state and the concomitant development of local community police agencies, the type and range of activities of the CSP had begun to change in the direction of safety and traffic. Accordingly, we asked the members of the organization: "Has there been an increased emphasis on safety and traffic compared with complaint work . . . within the last five years?" With almost no variation by rank, 95 per cent, from recruits through officers, said "Yes." Not only did everyone agree, then, that safety and traffic work had become increasingly emphasized, but few perceptions of organizational matters involved such high consensus as this. Indeed, only 6 out of 192 active members responding said that there had not been such a change.

What effect might this change have had upon the career goals and aspirations of *policemen*? We asked the recruits and *policemen* to select the divisions they would most and least like to enter.

| | *Which of these would you* | |
Division or Bureau	most *like* to enter?	least *like* to enter?
	%	%
Safety & Traffic Bureau . . .	8.6	14.7
Detective Bureau	77.3	4.7
Fire Marshal	9.4	8.5
Records & Statistics	—	53.5
Personnel & Training	3.1	11.6
Operations & Communications .	1.6	7.0

There can be no doubt that, despite the growing emphasis on safety and traffic, the idea of specialization here was, at best, an indifferent choice. Moreover, if the selection of the Detective Bureau was unrealistic from the perspective of the changing focus of departmental activities, it was even more unrealistic from the perspective of the availability of openings. The entire Detective Bureau, in fact, accounted for only 10 per cent of the positions within the department.[2]

A second order of changes that was under way and increasing was the "service" function of the CSP. As a state agency it provided centralized service to all other agencies as a clearing house of criminal records and statistics, for example, stolen property files, sex criminal files, firearms registrations, fingerprints, and the like. However, it was quite clear that, in spite of their growing importance, functions such as these were overwhelmingly rejected as career choices.

[2] Detective work is perhaps an irresistible objective for most *policemen*, and surely the keystone of the romantic image of police work. Kephart reports in his survey of Philadelphia patrolmen that, of those who prefer other duties, 90 per cent choose detective work: W. M. Kephart, *Racial Factors and Urban Law Enforcement* (Philadelphia: University of Pennsylvania Press, 1957), p. 87.

Let us attempt to bring together these seemingly disparate data. Nearly all members of the organization correctly perceived the changing focus of department functions. However, this change was not at all in keeping with their personal aspirations or desires in police work. Confronted, then, with specifying the primary obligations of the *policeman* in terms of his relative emphasis on safety-traffic or criminal-complaint work, they compromised. Thus "equal time" was largely professed as departmental policy, apparently generated through a conflict between organizational demands and personal objectives.

The implementation of such a policy, a matter clearly different from its origin, need not be categorically rejected as an organizational fiction. First, we should note that it would be factually possible to devote equal time to the two activities and still have an unequal number of arrests in each. Traffic arrests averaged one for every 2.9 man-hours (in daytime), while complaint investigations averaged 5.6 man-hours, and most of these did not call for, or result in, arrest.[3] Therefore it is theoretically possible, though unlikely, for the observed distribution of approximately 9 traffic to 1 nontraffic arrests to have occurred under conditions approaching equal time. The ideal of equal time persisted, then, as a blend of possibility and hope.

Secondly, the equal time expectation may have persisted because the policy-makers—headquarters command—were, as we shall show later in this chapter, more inaccurate in their perception of the actual law enforcement practices of the department than was any other group. Since these policy-makers were responsible for training and indoctrination, their views of time distributions may have been adopted by subordinates without regard to the accuracy of such views. This, again, would encourage an ideological rather than a realistic perception of the time factor.

The public, as we have seen, also accepted the image of the *policeman* as part detective and part highway patrolman. But, uncontaminated by concerns of organizational policy and the career aspirations of *policemen*, the public image of the "main job" of the state police departed considerably from the dominant image in the department. When our public respondents were asked, "As you see it, which of the following is the *main* job of the state policeman?" approximately 46 per cent chose "patrolling highways and enforcing traffic laws." Only half as many viewed "protection from criminal activity" as the major objective of the CSP. Thus, in a very real sense, the public image of the activities of the CSP appeared more congruent with the actual work of *policemen* than did the department's image.

---

[3] These figures came from official department statistics, which in these matters are not especially reliable. We suspect that the man-hours per traffic arrest are overstated.

Public and Police Perspectives on Enforcement

The enforcement of posted speed limits has been a matter of major concern to both the police and the public. While everyone may be "against" speeding —particularly in view of the beliefs that surround the relationships of accidents and injury to speed[4]—the perspectives of the enforced and the enforcers are not necessarily the same. Persons with similar evaluations of the consequences of "excess speed" frequently arrive at different objectives with respect to the enforcement of speed laws. And even persons who share the same objectives may not agree on the means appropriate to achieve those objectives.

Should everyone observed violating posted speed limits be arrested? If strict enforcement is not to be the case, then how much leeway is to be granted? Clearly, *policemen* do not arrest every observed law violator. As a distinguished jurist has noted:

The policeman's lot is indeed a difficult one. He is charged with applying and enforcing a multitude of laws and ordinances in a degree or proportion and in a manner that maintains a delicate balance between the liberty of the individual and a high degree of social protection. His task requires a sensitive and wise discretion in deciding whether or not to invoke the criminal process. He must not only know whether certain behavior violates the law but also whether there is probable cause to believe that the law has been violated. He must enforce the law, yet he must also determine whether a particular violation should be handled by warning or arrest. He is not expected to arrest every violator. Some laws were never intended by the enactors to be enforced, and others condemn behavior that is not contrary to significant moral values. If he arrested all violators, the courts would find it impossible to do their work, and he would be in court so frequently that he could not perform his other professional duties. Consequently, the policeman must judge and informally settle more cases than he takes to court. While the processes by which these settlements are made are not within the scope of his formal authority, they are not subject to judicial scrutiny, except in the unlikely event of a prosecution for misfeasance. There is very little data available as to how this discretion not to invoke the criminal process is exercised and controlled.[5]

Equally important to the problem of law enforcement is the issue of the means or facilities deemed proper for given objectives. While the facilities of traffic law enforcement have not generated the publicity and legal controversies as have the means of criminal law enforcement, the introduction of the

---

[4] For one of the few iconoclastic statements on these matters, see D. P. Moynihan, "Epidemic on the Highways," *The Reporter*, April 30, 1959.

[5] R. C. Donnelly, "Police Authority and Practices," *Annals of the American Academy of Political and Social Science*, 339 (1962), 90–110.

unmarked and semi-marked patrol cars, as well as the use of radar, has not escaped its share of controversy and public scrutiny. Certainly, then, inquiry into the grounds for the acceptance or rejection of such facilities is appropriate for our investigation.

We start first with the question, "Do you think state policemen should strictly enforce speed limits as posted?" As can be seen in Table 8–1, both the police and the public strongly opposed a regimen of strict enforcement. The significantly stronger opposition to strict enforcement on the part of the police is, in large measure, a consequence of their demand for "police discretion"—a dimension we shall explore later. For the public, the endorsement of a policy of strict enforcement is strongly related to contact and to socioeconomic position.

a) Fifty-eight per cent of those having no contact with the state police favored strict enforcement. Over 70 per cent of those having any form of contact opposed strict enforcement. (These differences are significant at $p < .01$.)

b) The higher the socioeconomic position of the respondent, as indexed by occupation and education, the lower the proportion of strict enforcement proponents ($p < .01$).

TABLE 8–1

DO YOU THINK STATE POLICEMEN SHOULD "STRICTLY"
ENFORCE SPEED LIMITS AS POSTED?

| | Public | | State Police | |
	f	%	f	%
Yes . . .	103	37.5	73	25.9
No . . .	166	60.4	208	73.8
No opinion .	4	1.5	1	0.4
No answer .	2	0.7	—	—

NOTE.—$\chi^2 = 10.29$; $df = 1$; $p < .01$
(Yes–No × Public–State Police).

What of the issues at hand? What claims are made for either a strict or "relaxed" policy of enforcement? In Tables 8–2 and 8–3 we have tried to summarize the arguments presented. For those of the police and the public who favor strict enforcement there is a high congruence of reasons. Both see strict enforcement as necessary for the reduction of accidents and for the protection and safety of other drivers. Secondly, they view a policy of close adherence to the legal limits as an end in itself. As many respondents stated, "All laws should be enforced. It is the policeman's job."

The opposing arguments, given in Table 8–3, present positions in keeping with the differential perspectives of each group. Both agreed that speed laws and enforcement should be adjusted to road and traffic conditions, for example, road surface width, time of day, weather, traffic flow, accident rate on the road, etc. But the public sought leniency, as suggested by their appeals to the "ease of unintentional transgression," "conditional necessity," and their charge of "unrealistic and outdated speed limits." The police, in contrast, were less concerned—though not unconcerned—with the intent of the violation. Their concern was with the "good pinch," the arrest where the motorist's violation is unquestionable to the arresting officer and, hopefully, to the violator himself. Speeding arrests where radar or other mechanical

TABLE 8–2

REASONS GIVEN FOR "STRICT ENFORCEMENT" BY THE PUBLIC AND STATE POLICE

	Public		State Police	
	f	%	f	%
Accident reduction, protection of others	34	32.4	25	33.8
Speed limits are reasonable, realistic .	20	19.0	14	18.9
For uniform enforcement	28	26.7	18	24.3
Other explanations	7	6.7	6	8.1
No answer	16	15.2	11	14.9

NOTE.—Frequencies and percentages refer to number of reasons given, not to number of respondents.

TABLE 8–3

REASONS GIVEN AGAINST "STRICT ENFORCEMENT" BY THE PUBLIC AND THE STATE POLICE

	Public		State Police	
	f	%	f	%
Speedometer error and difficulty of checking and pacing	29	18.0	73	28.2
Road and traffic conditions	62	38.5	91	35.1
Ease of unintentional transgression	33	20.5	29	11.2
Conditional necessity (e.g., when passing, to avoid accidents, etc.)	17	10.6	6	2.3
Unrealistic, outdated speed limits	10	6.2	10	3.9
Rigid enforcement is harassing, unfair, impossible, etc.	1	0.6	14	5.4
Departmental policy explanations	0	—	12	3.9
All others	9	5.6	14	5.4

NOTE.—Frequencies and percentages refer to number of reasons given, not to number of respondents.

timing devices were not employed entailed two problems. The first was the presence of speedometer variation and error; the second was the task of accurately pacing or estimating the speed of the car being pursued or observed. Thus, over one-fourth of the reasons presented by *policemen* in opposition to a strict enforcement policy emphasized this dual problem. Generally, where a conviction was unlikely, the motorist was given a verbal warning. Since traffic convictions occurred for 92 per cent of the traffic arrests made by the CSP, one can surmise that the decision to make an arrest was taken with care.[6]

If a policy of strict enforcement is to be rejected, then what alternatives are to be permitted? For the police, the answer is relatively clear-cut: the patrolmen should be permitted to use their own discretion. Such discretion, however, was not to be permitted to go unchecked. Three-fourths of the *policemen* opposed to strict enforcement indicated a preference for granting a specified leeway to those exceeding the posted speed limit. Ninety-three per cent of the police and 92 per cent of the public indicated that a leeway between 5 and 10 mph over the limit ought to be granted. On the average, the department tended to be a little more liberal than the public in their specification of a leeway.

Of all the facilities for traffic law enforcement, the unmarked car has perhaps precipitated more, and longer lasting, controversy than any other. While we questioned the police about semi-marked and radar cars as well as unmarked cars, we questioned the public sample only about their reactions to unmarked cars.[7]

TABLE 8-4

DO YOU THINK STATE POLICEMEN OUGHT TO
PATROL IN UNMARKED CARS?

	Public		State Police	
	f	%	*f*	%
Yes . . .	113	41.1	242	85.8
No . . .	140	50.9	29	10.3
No opinion .	22	8.0	10	3.5
No answer .	—	—	1	0.4

NOTE.—Department personnel were asked, "Do you think the department ought to maintain unmarked cars on patrol?" ($\chi^2 = 119.30$; $p < .001$; $df = 1$; Yes–No × Public–State Police.)

[6] Though this figure may appear high, the International Association of Chiefs of Police estimates the national conviction rate to be 95 per cent. For a discussion of this, and of traffic law violations in general, see, H. L. Ross, "Traffic Law Violation: A Folk Crime," *Social Problems*, 8 (1960–61), 231–41.

[7] The semi-marked patrol car was a standard police cruiser painted in stock car colors, with the red domelight and telltale radio antenna removed. It carried civilian license plates, making it unidentifiable as a police car when viewed from the front or rear. The CSP insignia was painted on the sides of the car and on a special hood ornament which is visible only from a side view. Such cars were used for traffic patrol only during the daylight hours (and have, since our study, replaced all unmarked cars in the CSP fleet). The unmarked car had no external identity—though most persons living in the post area were able to recognize it on sight. Both the semi-marked and the unmarked car had sirens under the hood and a red filter on the spotlight. The radar car was an unmarked car equipped with a radar speed-timing device. By state law, a sign indicating its presence had to be posted

Table 8–4 displays the sharp contrast between police and public. Eighty-six per cent of police but only 41 per cent of the public respondents were willing to accept the unmarked patrol car. Both agreed that the unmarked car is important, primarily because it is seen as a more effective means of enforcement, and, secondarily, because of its presumed deterrent value; for example, "It makes the public more alert and watchful."

Public opposition is built upon three claims, each made with equal frequency. The unmarked car was seen as a "deceitful," "dishonest," "underhanded" technique of enforcement, as lacking deterrent value, and as dangerous to use. Essentially, opposition to unmarked cars showed a significant association only with whether or not the respondent had received a ticket from the state police. Approximately 60 per cent who reported they had received at least one ticket in the past five years came out against the unmarked car. Only 37 per cent of those who had no negative contact were opposed to its usage. None of the other personal and social characteristics which were discussed in the preceding chapter were of significance here.

So few *policemen* were against the use of unmarked cars that an analysis of their responses was not fruitful. Interestingly enough, though, the largest single response was that the use of unmarked cars "creates ill will" and was "unacceptable to the public."

As we have seen in the preceding chapter, the generalized public image of the CSP was a favorable one, functionally related to the social characteristics and police contact experience of the respondents. Both the police and the public regarded the *policeman's* role as one of considerable importance to society, and the public gave the CSP more esteem than they did other police agencies.

Regarding the problem of traffic law enforcement, both police and public sought essentially the same objective—discreet enforcement of the speed limit. While they agreed on this objective, each group justified its claim from the perspective of its own position relative to the other. Important, though, is the fact that the grounds for such justification were almost identical, that is, the insulation of one's inadequate role performance from punitive sanctions. For the public, such insularity was sought by an appeal to "intent"; for the police it was through an attempt at arresting only those unquestionably in violation of the law. Similarly, the unmarked car as one means of traffic enforcement was disapproved by the public since it potentially increased their chances of arrest. For the police, approval reflected the fact that the

---

several hundred feet before the place at which it was parked. Radar cars were never used for patrol as such, and the pursuit or arrest of speeders was handled by a second patrol car stationed nearby.

unmarked car provided a potentially longer period for observing suspects, hence more certainty in arrests.

Given the vulnerability of the *policeman's* position and his pervasive concern with the "quality" of his arrest, few things could be more threatening to the *policeman* than for the public to reject his performance by proclaiming their innocence, by demeaning the officer's authority or judgment, or by seeking to undermine his position by refusing to cooperate. Thus, when we asked of *policemen*, "In your contacts with the public what sorts of things have you found particularly annoying?" the majority of responses emphasized precisely these characteristics.[8] The answers are displayed in Table 8–5.

TABLE 8–5

IN YOUR CONTACTS WITH THE PUBLIC WHAT SORTS OF THINGS HAVE YOU FOUND PARTICULARLY ANNOYING?

	Number of Nominations	%
Protestations of innocence and expressions of personal insularity from arrest	71	20.4
Status–demeaning reactions, lack of respect	57	16.4
Uncooperativeness and lack of understanding of police affairs	55	15.8
Seeking special considerations	46	13.2
Dirty work: having to deal with persons and offenses which are distasteful and/or status-degrading	37	10.6
All others*	82	23.6

* No other single response accounts for more than 5 per cent of the total responses.

The characteristics and outcome of this relationship can be explored still further. We observed earlier (Table 7–4) that 78 to 99 per cent of the public respondents viewed the state *policemen* as honest, unlikely to arrest the innocent, respectful of constitutional rights, and uninfluenced by the sex of traffic violators or the type of car driven. What of the more immediate reactions?

Some 7 per cent of the responses of our public sample depicted contact with the state police to be negatively toned. The *policeman* was seen as "overbearing," "tense," "suspicious," or "cold and distant." By contrast, the dominant response painted a picture of a "friendly," "helpful," and "courteous" officer. Among those who had just received a ticket (the sample of violators), 55 per cent described the behavior of the arresting officer as "friendly," while 22 per cent described him as "impersonal." Perhaps even

[8] Along these lines, Westley has shown that the illegal use of violence by the police (under conditions where their general community prestige is low) occurs primarily to coerce respect. See W. A. Westley, "Violence and the Police," *American Journal of Sociology*, 59 (1953), 34–41.

more important to an understanding of the *policeman*-motorist contact was the motorist's evaluation of the outcome. Was the ticket justified?

As can be seen below, six out of every ten persons felt the ticket was justified:

Do you feel the ticket was justified?

	f	%
Yes	85	56.7
No	47	31.3
Not ascertained .	18	12.0

Following through, to the final outcome:

What was your reaction to the penalty imposed by the court?

	f	%
Too lenient . .	0	—
Fair	80	55.6
Too severe . .	43	30.6
Pending . . .	2	1.4
Not ascertained .	25	12.5

Being arrested for even a minor traffic violation can scarcely be construed as a "satisfying" experience for most people. Nonetheless, the affective tone of contact with the arresting officer was characterized by our public sample as "warm"; and over half of those arrested saw not only the act as justified but also saw the court as having fairly upheld and evaluated the *policeman's* claims. We suspect that had we asked of the public whether or not the *policeman's* action was justifiable, many more persons would have responded affirmatively. That is, in view of the public's claims for control and their knowledge of the *policeman's* perspective, the *policeman's* action in issuing a ticket may well be construed as justifiable in principle though unjustified to the violator in its specific application to him at that time.

Both police and public agreed upon the basic objective of enforcement. Yet the intrinsic nature of their relationship, as enforcer to enforced, is predicated on conflict. With high consensus on their goals, they clash not so much on the means to be employed but on how and by whom control is to be maintained over these means. The respective interests of both were mirrored openly not only in the claims they made for discretionary law enforcement but also in the *policeman's* concern for an uncontestable arrest and the public's appeal for consideration of intent.

Organizational Perspectives on Policy and Practice

In the preceding section we sought to focus primarily upon the reciprocities between public and police perspectives on enforcement. Here, we shift our focus to an intra-organizational perspective and seek primarily to explore the organizational concomitants of enforcement policy and practice.

The issue of enforcement revolved about the degree of strictness of interpretation of speed limits and speeding. The concrete aspects of this issue were 1) the extent to which a *policeman* was free to exercise his own discretion in issuing tickets or verbally warning offenders and suspects, and 2) the special facilities, such as unmarked, semi-marked and radar cars, that the department may use in apprehending violators.

Clearly, no member of the CSP—and especially in the Uniform Division—escaped some confrontation with the problem of traffic law enforcement. Thus, when we raised the question of "strict enforcement," everyone queried responded, and only one man out of the 282 respondents said he had no opinion.

Though almost all of the issues of enforcement are clearly stipulated and recorded in the "general orders," "special orders," and the "rules and regulations" of the department—including legislative statute—it does not follow that all persons within the organization had full or accurate knowledge of these. For that matter, whatever knowledge they possessed, correct or not, may not necessarily have been the basis for their actions. From our general sociological knowledge of organizational behavior we know that matters of personal policy and the conceptions that may exist as to the actual practices of the organization will be, in large measure, influenced by one's position in the organization. In the CSP, the basic positional variable was *rank*. This is not to say that one's rank will be the exclusive determinant of one's law enforcement "ideology," but we suspect that rank *is* of primary importance. We begin our analysis, then, with three questions:

1. What personal practices were maintained by each rank?
2. To what extent was there consensus within each rank?
3. To what extent was there consensus across all ranks?

Finally, we need to ask: What were the relationships among rank, personal practices, and perceived departmental policies?

Table 8–6 displays the striking impact of rank on enforcement practices. The direction of percentaging and ranking is in line with a "hard" enforcement policy, that is, universalistic enforcement by all legitimate means. One thing should be made clear: personal practice on enforcement is a matter of high consensus. At least three-fifths of every rank were in agreement on every issue. Moreover, as we shall show later (Tables 8–7 and 8–8), for most persons their personal practice was in accord with "accepted department policies" (83 per cent), and most persons are in fact correct in their perception (72 per cent). Despite this high consensus on issues and the veridicality of their perception, rank differences remain distinctively and significantly different across the organization.

TABLE 8–6

AGREEMENT ON DEPARTMENT ENFORCEMENT POLICIES BY RANK

Percentage Agreeing on	Recruits	Policemen	Corporals	Sergeants	Officers
a) Strict enforcement . .	19.2	21.9	26.9	32.7	25.8
b) No patrolman discretion .	3.8	9.8	23.8	35.3	31.0
c) Use of unmarked cars .	87.5	88.1	89.1	94.0	89.7
d) Use of semi-marked cars .	68.2	81.0	78.8	73.5	92.9
e) Use of radar	68.2	81.0	78.8	73.5	93.1
Rank Orders of Agreement on					
a) Strict enforcement . .	5	4	2	1	3
b) No patrolman discretion .	5	4	3	1	2
c) Use of unmarked cars .	5	4	3	1	2
d) Use of semi-marked cars .	5	2	3	4	1
e) Use of radar	5	2	3	4	1
Rank Mean	5.0	3.2	2.8	2.2	1.8

NOTE.—$\chi_r^2 = 12.32$; $df = 4$; $p < .02$.

On the three major dimensions of a hard enforcement policy—strict enforcement, no patrolman discretion, and unmarked cars—sergeants were the hardest and recruits the softest. Overall, two observations seem warranted.[9] Recruits and *policemen* want considerably more autonomy than their superiors are willing to grant. Recruit-*policemen* autonomy seems to be a clear-cut function of status; and the post commanders (sergeants), who are accountable for post policy and practice, are least willing to grant their men autonomy in this sphere. This is reflected even in the arguments presented *against* strict enforcement. Recruits and *policemen* argue primarily in terms of "road and traffic conditions" while sergeants and officers argue primarily in terms of the difficulty for *policemen* to adequately "pace and check" speeds.

Secondly, and clearly related to this press for autonomy, is the issue of contact. Much in the same manner that no contact with the police resulted in public acceptance of a hard enforcement policy, so no contact with the public resulted in the police acceptance of a hard enforcement policy. Thus the

[9] From the standpoint of scientific analysis, the data of Table 8–6 presented an intriguing challenge. Clearly, there was demonstrably high agreement within and among rank groups concerning enforcement practices—a situation we rarely found in other aspects of the *policeman* role (see especially Chapters 3 and 4). We felt, however, that this was offset by differences in the degree of agreement. Thus, even though we might here use 75 per cent as a consensus criterion for the groups involved, it was still possible for us to observe significant group differences. Certainly, then, the establishment of consensus, using some percentage criterion, is not in itself a sufficient test of congruence in role perception among audiences. Had we failed to consider comparative degrees of consensus among groups, we would have neglected some rather important differences.

recruits' enforcement ideology is barely differentiated from that of the public; but the higher the *policeman's* rank the less his contact with traffic offenders, and the more he accepted a hard enforcement policy.

Since some three-fourths of the members of the department opposed strict enforcement and favored police discretion, it is instructive to observe how much tolerance they were willing to grant the motorist. We asked those opposed to strict enforcement of the speed limits to specify the "leeway" they would permit. As we observed before, recruits were the most liberal, favoring an estimated average leeway of 8 mph over the speed limit, and sergeants the least liberal—about 6 mph. *Policemen* and corporals were intermediate—being slightly under 8 mph for the former and slightly above 6 mph for the latter. Thus the order of leeway followed the rank hierarchy: recruits, *policemen*, corporals, sergeants. Officers fell on the mean estimated for all ranks, that is, 7 mph.

In Chapter 6 we found that the accuracy of perception of role expectations was relatively independent of the specific content of the situation and the expectation. Correct perception was a direct consequence of consensus: the greater the group consensus on role expectations, the more likely were those expectations to be correctly perceived. This finding is again replicated in Table 8–7. While in the role conflict study we observed low accuracy on matters of relatively low consensus, here we observe high accuracy on matters of high consensus.

A second finding of the role conflict studies was that the correct perception of role expectations was a function of rank distance. There we suggested that *policemen* were most correct about those audiences whose role behavior was more directly visible to them; that is, those who occupied adjacent ranks. Here again we achieve replication. The order of "correctness" displayed in Table 8–7 reflects precisely the visibility of patrol activities to each rank. The field commanders—sergeants and corporals—were most accurate; and officers—the district and headquarters command staffs—were the least accurate.

Thus, it is apparent that enforcement practices were correctly assessed by most members of the department. Yet, despite this high consensus and the small differences between ranks, rank differences still emerged as significant.

What, then, of the relationship between perceptual accuracy and personal practice? The question of who was correct in their perception of departmental policy cannot be answered merely by an analysis of rank variation. Certainly, most men—83 per cent—felt that their personal policy on enforcement was the same as accepted departmental policy, but only 72 per cent were in fact correct. More than that, however, some men with correct knowledge of actual policy were consciously deviant in their personal practices;

others didn't know they were right; and still others didn't know they were wrong. This can be seen below and in Table 8–8.

TABLE 8–7

CORRECT PERCEPTION OF DEPARTMENT ENFORCEMENT POLICIES BY RANK

Percentage Correct on	Recruits	Policemen	Corporals	Sergeants	Officers
a) Strict enforcement . .	80.8	80.3	82.7	88.2	79.3
b) No patrolman discretion .	80.8	80.3	82.9	88.2	79.3
c) Use of unmarked cars .	79.2	81.4	83.2	88.0	79.3
d) Use of semi-marked cars .	81.8	81.0	83.8	89.8	78.6
e) Use of radar	81.8	81.0	83.8	89.8	79.3
Rank Orders of Accuracy on					
a) Strict enforcement . .	3	4	2	1	5
b) No patrolman discretion .	3	4	2	1	5
c) Use of unmarked cars .	4	3	2	1	5
d) Use of semi-marked cars .	3	4	2	1	5
e) Use of radar	3	4	2	1	5
Rank Mean	3.2	3.8	2.0	1.0	5.0

NOTE.—$\chi_r^2 = 16.48$; $df = 4$; $p < .01$.

TABLE 8–8

PERSONAL PRACTICE, DEPARTMENTAL POLICY, AND THE ACCURACY OF PERCEPTION

		Is your opinion on enforcement the same as accepted practice in the department?					
		Number			Per Cent		
		Yes	No	Total	Yes	No	Total
Strict enforcement:	Yes .	62	9	71	22.9	3.3	26.2
	No .	162	38	200	59.8	14.0	73.8
	Total .	224	47	271*	82.7	17.3	100.0
Patrolman discretion:	Yes .	177	35	212	65.3	12.9	78.2
	No .	47	12	59	17.3	4.4	21.8
	Total .	224	47	271*	82.7	17.3	100.0
Use of unmarked cars:	Yes .	198	38	236	75.3	14.4	89.7
	No .	20	7	27	7.6	2.7	10.3
	Total .	218	45	263*	82.9	17.1	100.0
Use of semi-marked cars:	Yes .	176	26	202	68.8	10.2	78.9
	No .	38	16	54	14.8	6.3	21.1
	Total .	214	42	256*	83.6	16.4	100.0
Use of radar:	Yes .	177	26	203	68.9	10.1	79.0
	No .	38	16	54	14.8	6.2	21.0
	Total .	215	42	257*	83.7	16.3	100.0

* Difference between these totals and 282 equals the number of "no answer," "no opinion," and "don't know" responses.

	Correctly Perceived	Incorrectly Perceived	
Personal practice in accord with department policy	67.5% (a)	12.4% (b)	79.9%
Personal practice not in accord with department policy	4.5 (c)	15.5 (d)	20.1
	72.1%	27.9%	100.0%

To explore more fully the effects or rank, we took each cell (a, b, c, d) and executed four rank analyses of variance comparable to those executed in Tables 8–6 and 8–7. Only one of these yielded acceptably significant differences (cell b), but the remaining cells showed discernible trends by rank.

  a) For cell a the correct perception of the agreement between one's personal practice and accepted department policy was unrelated to rank ($p < .70$). While the correct perception of department policies was a consequence of rank, being correct *and knowing it* was not related to rank.
  b) Cell b refers to those men who, in effect, did not know that their personal practice was in accord with departmental policy. In Table 8–7 we observed that sergeants and corporals were most often correct in their perception of department policy. Here we observe that they are also the least likely to be ignorant of being right. Recruits and *policemen* were equally overrepresented in this subset of respondents who did not know they were correct. Differences are significant here at $p < .01$.
  c–d) Relatively few men (4.5 per cent) were consciously deviant; that is, maintained a practice that they knew to be contrary to department policy. Considerably more (15.5 per cent) were unknowingly deviant, holding to practices they incorrectly perceived to be in keeping with department policy. The sergeants, recruits, and *policemen* seemed most likely to be among those who knew they were deviant. By contrast, corporals and officers stood out as those who did not know they were wrong. In both cells, the direction of differences is only suggestive: $p < .30$.

Summary

The effects of rank on traffic law enforcement ideologies have been clearly delineated. All of the issues here were matters of high consensus, and such consensus was true of all ranks. Rank differences, nonetheless, stood out distinctively.

The elements that constituted an enforcement ideology all revolved about the universalistic-particularistic application of traffic laws and the legitimacy of the means employed for the enforcement of those laws. The adoption of personal enforcement practices was the outcome of two interrelated consequences of rank: the struggle for autonomy among ranks and the degree of contact between each rank and the public.

Personal practices were shown to be highly congruent with actual department policies. While this congruency itself was not a consequence of rank, the accurate perception of department policies was. The accuracy of perception, and most persons were here accurate, was a result of 1) the high consensus across ranks on what actually constituted department policy, and 2) the relative visibility of role performance to each of the ranks.

CHAPTER 9

The Prospects of Role Theory

The Traditionalist's Dilemma

WE HAVE delayed our overall discussion of role theory and its prospects until this final chapter because we chose to include our own work in such a discussion. We felt, furthermore, that an assessment of the key issues could be accomplished more effectively in one place than scattered throughout the earlier chapters. In this chapter we shall attempt to review both our own research and representative research of others in the field in order to point up these key issues as they have developed.

Role theory has produced a voluminous literature, as our Bibliography unquestionably demonstrates. As we observed in Chapter 1, while much of the material has been descriptive and declarative—as is consonant with the early stages of any scientific inquiry—a modest though continuous output of studies has analyzed particular roles or role situations through theoretically grounded empirical research. These studies have ranged from field examinations of "natural" roles and systems to the laboratory manipulation and observation of "artificial" systems under relatively controlled conditions. Regardless of the methodology, the theoretical frameworks utilized in these studies have generally been found inadequate *in the judgments of the researchers themselves*. Nevertheless, these inadequacies have rarely shaken the researchers' faith in their initial assumptions about role behavior and role theory. The strength of this attachment seems to us to derive from the very pervasiveness of role and cognate concepts in contemporary sociological and social psychological theories. Given such pervasiveness, the acceptance, reformulation, or rejection of contemporary role schemas is of prodigious importance. To reject role theory is to call for a revolution in social science, and such scientific revolutions demand the presentation of a new body of research or of a new paradigm which cogently reinterprets the existing body of relevant knowledge.[1] To seek reformulation, as is our objective, we need to recognize that the problems of role theory are inextricably bound with the

[1] See T. S. Kuhn, *The Scientific Revolution* (Chicago: University of Chicago Press, 1962).

general problems of sociology and social psychology. Thus we submit that the construction of a mature theory of role behavior must either wait upon the solution of the major problems endemic to all of the social sciences or be itself implicated as a partial solution to these problems.

The traditional framework for role theory received its earliest and historically most influential expression in the social psychology of George H. Mead. The general appeal of Mead to an interdisciplinary social psychology is perhaps best dramatized in this summary statement by Strauss:

Mead's writing offers a clear alternative to psychological theories based upon individualistic assumptions, principally through his insistence that individual acts are part of larger communal acts. In one way his stand is much like that of students of social organization (who also repudiate individualistic assumptions), but in another way it is not. Mead pictures social structures as somewhat less organized than do most sociologists and anthropologists.[2]

While Mead himself never elaborated a role theory, the two dominant approaches to such theory both lay claim to a derivation, in part, from Mead's writings. The *interactionists* focused on Mead's instrumentalism, on his definition of the social act in terms of process, and on his insistence of the uniqueness of the individual act. They saw in his metaphor of the game and in his introduction of a conception of role taking a beginning framework for the analysis of interpersonal behavior which gave primary emphasis to the actors and their actions.[3]

But others saw in Mead a way to focus upon the social context of interaction. Stryker ably summarizes this *social action* dimension:

In Mead's social psychology, social life is seen as highly organized. In stressing the "generalized other" and a universe of discourse, and in the ideal of a universe of discourse coterminous with humanity, Mead uses a model of social life in which the rules of the game are well defined, roles are precisely appropriate and neatly articulated, and goals are specific, consciously held, and unanimously accepted.[4]

Surely part of the tenacity of role theory stems from the intellectual power of the Meadian framework. As we proceed in this chapter, our own indebtedness to this tradition will be apparent. While we see no necessary incompatibilities between these two derivative frameworks, our own commitments

[2] A. Strauss (ed.), "Introduction," *The Social Psychology of George Herbert Mead* (Chicago: University of Chicago Press, 1956), p. xv.

[3] Among those presently working within this framework are Garfinkel, Goffman, Strauss, Turner, and Weinstein and Deutschberger.

[4] S. Stryker, "Conditions of Accurate Role-Taking: A Test of Mead's Theory," in A. M. Rose (ed.), *Human Behavior and Social Processes* (Boston: Houghton Mifflin, 1962), p. 58. Within this collection one can find a good representation of the divergence of "Meadian" social psychologists.

in the direction of action theory reflect our present inability to completely unite the two perspectives. Nevertheless, we feel ready to begin the task of specifying a program for the construction of role theory. Our program calls essentially for research to help us identify the complex relationships among the variables of role analysis such that we may begin to articulate a formalized theoretical system which has empirical grounding.

Let us first review some of the highlights of the preceding chapters. At the conclusion of Chapter 2 we commented that our field experience presented the role of *policeman* as lacking in clarity and precision when viewed from the perspectives of the various audiences of the Central State Police. Our findings in Chapters 3 and 4 support this conclusion. Using our role area and adjustment type variables, we found that comparisons within and among rank groups in the department failed to yield appreciable role consensus. Such consensus was the exception rather than the rule. While this result did not support some central tenets of role theory, we suggested another mode of interpretation. This was the obvious alternative that the diffuseness of role expectations may actually have positive adaptive value for role behavior. Thus a low order of consensus on role definition or specific expectations may provide considerable flexibility for individual style in role performance. Clearly, this line of reasoning needs more focused empirical investigation.

We had discovered that the training program at both school and post produced a variety of staff judgments about the applicability of the curriculum to the realities of field problems. Recruits were given formal instruction in police procedure, law, and department regulations. Certain skills, such as marksmanship, were emphasized in school yet rarely used in daily practice. Other skills, such as high-speed driving, were not taught but were a daily necessity. Strictness of law enforcement was also a situational variable which led to expediency of policy rather than consistency throughout the department. All in all, there was abundant evidence that the image of the *policeman* role reflected individual, positional, and systemic differentiation that was far from uniform or consistent. Furthermore, our longitudinal examination of a recruit class revealed no trend for increasing consensus within the non-instrumental role areas we had selected. (Although consensus did not appear to increase over time, our cross-sectional analyses show that the accuracy of role perception increased with experience in the role.)

The findings of Chapters 4 and 5 are consistent with this evidence. In Chapter 5 the disparities between recruit school demands and field imperatives were further emphasized by our finding that evaluations of school performance were negligibly correlated with evaluations of field performance. There was some inability of audiences to employ measures of evaluation which were specifically pertinent to the role of *policemen*. There was an even more marked inability of audiences to agree in role evaluations even when they presumably shared evaluative criteria.

In Chapter 6 we systematically examined the conflict potential in five situations of contradictory role expectations. Our most intriguing finding here was that the self-reported behavior of *policemen* conformed in large to audience expectations even though their perception of those expectations was notably inaccurate. In this chapter, too, we demonstrated the salience of reference group theory for understanding role behavior by the successful postdiction of role conflict resolutions.

When we pursued the matter of instrumental role expectations and behavior, in Chapters 7 and 8, we again found considerable variation in consensus on role expectations and in the accuracy with which expectations were perceived. We pointed out that some *policemen* had correct perceptions of the expectations of others, yet behaved contrary to those expectations. Others had incorrect expectations, and some of them acted accordingly while others acted in a correct manner—but unaware that their own perceptions of audience expectations were incorrect.

To be sure, these findings which we have highlighted represent only a small subset of the many findings reported in the preceding chapters. We have selected these because they seemed to us to be the most paradoxical and/or unexplainable by the traditional statements of role theory. Indeed, through our studies of the Central State Police we have attempted, particularly, to identify these crucial dilemmas within role theory. And through these studies we have come to feel ready to begin the task of specifying a program for the construction of role theory. Our program calls essentially for research to help us identify the complex relationships among the variables of role analysis such that we may begin to articulate a formalized theoretical system which has empirical grounding.

Specifying the Role Unit

In this report we have not, as a general policy, emphasized problems of terminology. Certainly, if one were simply to array all of the terms introduced into the literature of role theory, one would confront a rather sizable glossary of overlapping, vague, and imprecise terms. Nevertheless, we have assumed that the central terms of role theory are sufficiently known and communicable among social scientists to overcome whatever obscurities their usage in this report may contain. Terminological considerations are most important, and we do not mean to imply otherwise; however, the priority which ought to be assigned to terminological affairs is contingent upon the stage of theory at which one begins to operate. At this stage in the development of role theory we see this as a low-priority item. We could through rather simple linguistic conventions establish a delimited set of meanings to such central concepts as role, status, expectations, visibility, power, etc. But such a set of definitions, independent of a well-delineated theoretical scheme, would shed little light on the crucial problem of the relationships among the constituent terms. Although such beginning dictionaries often may be helpful, and sometimes reassuring, they will certainly be transitory.

The strategy decisions of role theorists converge upon the *problem of specifying the role unit.* This complex problem, which we shall now consider, is comprised of four interrelated but analytically separable problems: (*a*) the problem of identifying a role, (*b*) the problem of levels of generality in role analysis, (*c*) the problem of the situational context of role behavior, and (*d*) the problem of "the place of the person" in role analysis. We shall take these up in order and in some detail.

From an operational standpoint, establishing hard criteria for the identification of a role is perhaps the most elusive problem of role theory. If we were to exhibit a series of behavior episodes before a group of sociologists and social psychologists, we could probably get rather high agreement in their selection of those episodes which constituted role behavior. But if we asked them to specify the criteria by which they selected some behaviors and excluded others, we would probably discover that their decisions were more intuitive than specifiable, and that they could achieve little common agreement on criteria. At this level most role theorists have converged, regardless of orientation. Whether—like Parsons and Merton, or Gross, Mason, and McEachern—they accept a role as a "given" within some system of interaction, or whether—like Goffman, Strauss and Turner, or Weinstein and Deutschberger—they accept a role as emerging (and changing) within systems of interaction, role theorists have not provided a significant set of markers for distinguishing role behavior from non-role behavior.[5]

We suspect that few readers of this book, or at least few readers that have come this far with us, would reject "policeman" as a role title. Our acceptance was of course based on the current convention of accepting occupational titles (and social types) as role titles, though our choice of a police setting was beyond conventional criteria (see Chapter 1). Yet what are the alternative, identifying characteristics of the policeman role? Should we look toward the

---

[5] Some interesting attempts in this direction have come from two psychologists not normally identified as role theorists. See R. B. Cattell, "A Mathematical Model for the Leadership Role and Other Personality-Role Relations," in M. Sherif and M. O. Wilson (eds.), *Emerging Problems in Social Psychology* (Norman, Okla.: University of Oklahoma Book Exchange, 1957); F. Harary, "Status and Contra-status," *Sociometry*, 22 (1959), 23–43; and O. A. Oeser and F. Harary, "A Mathematical Model for Structural Role Theory," *Human Relations*, 15 (1962), 89–109.

behavior of those whom we designate as policemen, or should we look toward the expectations held by those audiences relevant to policemen? Clearly one ought to be able, through long and detailed observation, to record the behaviors of policemen and separate those behaviors of policemen as policemen from those behaviors which might be characteristic of any human, any member of this society, or any male. In a like manner, one ought to be able to isolate expectations. There can be no doubt that such detailed empirical specification would help us better understand the relationship between role as expected behavior and role as actual behavior. We might similarly develop further insight into the segregation of roles; that is, the process by which individuals manage the performance of roles which at different times appear incompatible. We might, given such a procedure, be able to enumerate with some precision the number of roles played by an individual and perhaps to observe whether or not individuals tend to play certain types of roles or whether certain types of roles tend to cluster.[6]

Certainly such study would bring an order and a precision to the designation of this role or any role so studied, and its accomplishment is, in principle, within the realm of present methodology. Yet the amount of time and the financial cost of such a routinized operation is clearly beyond the resources of most social science research budgets today.

Part of the problem of identifying roles is also the problem of specifying the level of generality at which the sociologist-observer chooses to operate. To be concerned with the generality of role performance is to be concerned essentially with whether the observed behavior is predominately status-centered or predominately, for want of a better term, situationally centered. We could say that role performance is predominately situation-centered if it existed in relatively few social systems in which the specific role studied is found and if it is nonexistent in the majority of instances. The implication drawn here is that if a specific behavior concomitant with a given role exists only in some small number of social systems in which that role is found, then it is somehow more related to its specific situation than it is to the general expectations appropriate to the status of which this role is a part. Thus, predominately status-centered role performance exists in the majority of systems in which the specific role studied is found, and is presumably related more directly to the components of that status than to the peculiarities of any given system.[7]

As should be apparent, the problem of generality has as its focus the degree

6 See some of the hypotheses proposed by T. R. Sarbin, "Role Theory," in G. Lindzey (ed.), *Handbook of Social Psychology* (Reading, Mass.: Addison-Wesley, 1954).

7 Cf. J. W. Getzels and E. G. Guba, "The Structure of Roles and Role Conflict in the Teaching Situation," *Journal of Educational Sociology*, 29 (1955), 30–40.

to which one can generalize from the observation of role behavior in a given system to (*a*) the existence of such behavior in similar systems which also encompass this status and role and (*b*) the degree to which one can generalize from the performance concomitant to a specific status to the performances attendant with other statuses which are *functionally analogous*.

In the Central State Police, by means of example, we observed approximately fifty-four posts. In studying the *policemen* at one post the researchers were faced with the question of the extent to which the expectations and the behaviors of the *policemen* at a given post are a resultant of the specific post conditions and the extent to which such expectations and performances may be found among all Central State *policemen* regardless of their post assignment. As one begins to re-focus research interests, one could ask the question: To what extent are such expectations and behaviors appropriate to all state policemen, to all policemen, to all law enforcement officials, or even to all formal agents of social control?

While the criteria for the identification of roles have been elusive, the problems of situational analysis have simply been ignored. The need for such analysis in social science is unmistakable. Roger Barker, in an intriguing paper, put it this way:

It seems to me that students of molar behavior might profitably emulate students of perception, and look at the ecological environment of the behavior with which they are concerned entirely aside from its connection with behavior. This, in fact, is the main point of my paper: We need a science, for which we as yet have no name, that stands with respect to molar behavior as the physics of light and sound stands with respect to vision and hearing. For students of role this means that role environment must be studied as carefully as role behavior.[8]

It ought to be clear that there are two problems of situational analysis. First, we have the discipline about which Barker speaks primarily, namely, the study of the properties of situations and their interrelationships. Secondly, we have the problem of the relationship of situational dimensions to role behavior. Certainly, we did not begin our research with any sophisticated concern for situational properties. Like most students of role behavior, we ignored such variables. In retrospect it is clear that we were remiss in doing so. Unfortunately, there are today few role theorists, properly speaking, who are either engaged with the problems of situational analysis or appear particularly concerned about these problems.[9]

[8] R. Barker, "Roles, Ecological Niches, and the Psychology of the Absent Organism" (paper presented to the Conference on the Propositional Structure of Role Theory, University of Missouri, March, 1962).

[9] Barker, following Lewin's conception of "psychological ecology," has been much concerned with the conceptualization and measurement of situational properties of

Much as the place of the situation in role theory has been neglected, so the place of the person in such theory has been confused. The resolution of the problem of the person depends, it seems to us, on the rational specification of the division of labor among sociology, social psychology, and psychology. Its more immediate solution, however, requires some tolerance of the ambiguous relationships that exist among these three fields of inquiry. To explore this problem we might first look at this lengthy but instructive statement from a critical review by Kaspar Naegele of the school superintendents study made by Gross, Mason, and McEachern:

In the end this work may be faithful to its subtitle. In a fashion it is a collection of unfinished studies—"of the school superintendency role." The school superintendents as such never appear. Surely a man is more than a collection of roles. Nor are roles just mass-produced clothes. Are they not played parts in a play that is partly being written in the act of being played? Do they not contain the marks of individuality? Is individuality not a social accomplishment par excellence? Is the very notion of "expectation," or of consensus, not predicated on what George Herbert Mead, awkwardly, described in the name of the "I"? Significantly enough, such an "I" is known only *after* it has acted. That is a weakness in Mead's argument. Yet, Gross's superintendents seem unpoised for superintending. They seem like hollow men, in the distance. I think the methods of this book, for all the richness of particular regularities that they yielded, dissolve, rather than explain, the phenomena they seek to unravel. Even half-alive men cohere and have some sort of center. An exploration unhaunted by this fact produces a false and incomplete image, falsely completed in the imagination of us, the readers. Nor is this a humanistic or clinical plea against abstraction. Quite the contrary, it is a plea for *appropriate* abstraction.[10]

Naegele goes on from there to indicate that Gross has ignored the dialectic between person and position, and that he has further ignored matters of the personal preferences of school superintendents for given role behaviors. We are not quite certain what Professor Naegele would accept as "appropriate abstraction," but if it means that Gross and his associates must necessarily include more details on the personality characteristics of superintendents, or if it means that greater details are necessary with respect to the interpersonal transactions of superintendents, we would disagree. We can readily accept a study of the role patterns of some selected occupation, organization, or the like, which does not refer to these more personalized concerns. We suspect,

behavioral relevance but not with their relationship to role behavior. Perhaps the earliest statement attempting to establish the nexus of role and situation is that by L. S. Cottrell, Jr., "The Analysis of Situational Fields in Social Psychology," *American Sociological Review*, 7 (1942), 370–82. But this focused primarily on role and self.

10 K. D. Naegele, "Superintendency versus Superintendents: A Critical Essay," *Harvard Educational Review*, 30 (1960), 372–93.

however, that Naegele's concern is shared by many and that it is based primarily on a discontent with what they see as the deterministic characteristic of role theoretical formulations.

Naegele goes on to say: "I have no objection if Gross treats school superintendents as though they were best described as marionettes. But I do object if he comes to assume this to exhaust the matter, simply because he has, in fact, not formulated a different possibility." If Gross had presented an exhaustive treatment of his school superintendents on the level of marionettes (which he did not), we would probably be satisfied. But Naegele would presumably like to move on to other levels of analysis. Certainly, if one wished to learn all there was to learn about school superintendents there would be no question of the need for other materials. But if one were concerned with the development of a theory of role behavior at a given level of analysis, then such additional research is extraneous.

We contend that role theory is, even in its present loosely formulated manner, an essentially deterministic theory. This is not to say that it precludes matters of individual difference, personal preference, personal style, and so forth. Whatever uniqueness may characterize the many individuals playing the same role as policemen, we need to underscore the fact that they all meet the minimal requirements necessary to maintain themselves in that role. We need to understand further that most of the characteristics of a role are highly determined. This is so both at the most abstract level (such that all policemen work to enforce the laws) and at the more atomistic levels (such that no policeman goes on traffic patrol without wearing his uniform).

We see no theoretical reason why a deterministic system cannot permit some element of personal preference or interplay between person and position. On the other hand, we think that role theory in the manner employed in the school superintendents study and in our study will work best, *if not exclusively*, in highly structured social systems where the goals of these systems are well elaborated. In such formal organizations, elements of personal expression are highly limited. We do not think that role theory can handle adequately expressive social systems, matters of primary group relations, or transitory collective behavioral phenomena. For these problems one must seek either a more general theory which will handle them *as well as* role behavior, or one must seek one or more specific theories to handle each of these problems.

Programming for Role Theory

It is our feeling that we have isolated almost all of the important elements for a theory of role behavior. This is not to say that all of the elements we shall present are irreducible. Rather, we suspect that, while there are no trivial elements in our program, only some of the elements will make up the axioms of our system. What we shall try to do now is to introduce these elements and briefly illustrate their operation through an analysis of the materials we have already presented. As a point of departure, we may classify our variables: first, as those which determine the *reference group matrix* for a given social system; second, those which characterize the *properties of system-specific role expectations*; and third, those concerned with the *articulation of roles* in the given social system. We shall take these up in order.

THE REFERENCE GROUP MATRIX

The process of socialization into any social system involves the determination of the reference group matrix appropriate to that system. This means the determination of those individuals, groups, or social categories which are and are not significant for one's role performance. To say that a person is socialized is to make the statement that he has learned both appropriate role behavior and the appropriate identification of the role-relevant reference groups.

Not all of those persons with whom an individual interacts are of significance to him in his role performance. There is clearly a class of role partners who are "neutral." Their presence or behavior must be taken into account in the performance of a role only in the same sense that one's physical surroundings need be taken into account. Turner has labeled this class of role partners an "interaction group."[11]

Thus the recruit must come to learn which of the available "potential" reference groups constitute his audience groups and which are merely the interaction groups. Over time, he must develop a hierarchy of audience groups. However important this process of learning the reference group matrix may be—and it may well be the crucial problem of socialization—it is clear that there is little integrated social science information on this subject.[12]

ROLE EXPECTATIONS

Role expectations refer to a set of systemic *specifications for role-appropriate behavior*. These specifications may be classified into 1) those concerned with the *content* of performance and the *evaluative standards* for that performance; 2) those which deal with the temporal and spatial location of performances; and 3) the conformity demands concomitant with the role expectations.

[11] R. H. Turner, "Role-Taking, Role Standpoint, and Reference Group Behavior," *American Journal of Sociology*, 61 (1956), 316–28.

[12] For an informal history, see H. H. Hyman, "Reflections on Reference Groups," *Public Opinion Quarterly*, 24 (1960), 383–96.

Generally speaking, little attention has been paid to the issue of evaluative standards in role theory, and most attention has been given to the content of role behavior. This comes, perhaps, because an expectation for role performance is seldom accompanied by an explicit statement of an evaluative nature. We suspect that the content of an expectation and the evaluative standards set for the expectation ought not be separated. Some contents and some standards are well-announced and quite clear. Others are neither well-announced nor clear. In our research we have shown that there is greater clarity and greater consensus on instrumental role expectations than on expressive role expectations. We have shown, further, that there is greater consensus on the content of role expectations than on their associated evaluative standards. Since the issues of content and evaluation are so inter-woven with matters of the articulation of roles in the social system, we shall postpone our discussion until we come to that section.

One independent aspect of role expectations is their variability with respect to the ease and degree to which the given expectations may be fulfilled. Some expectations may be easily fulfilled, and for others the conditions of fulfillment are indeterminate. Take, for example, the following set of expectations associated with traffic patrol:

All persons checked by radar as driving more than 10 mph over the posted speed limit are to be ticketed.
Use your judgment in arresting those exceeding the posted speed limit.
Cars transporting suspicious-looking persons should be stopped and investigated.
Patrol sector 5.
Investigate a breaking and entering at 2340 University Boulevard.
Arrest John Jones.

Now one can arrest Mr. Jones and be over and done with it, and the handling of that arrest will be competent or not. Yet these other expectations are not so easily fulfilled, and they vary rather considerably in the degree to which they can be fulfilled and in the specificity of the conditions for fulfill-ment. Clearly these "indeterminate expectations" represent an important class of role expectations. It may prove possible and fruitful to classify social systems, among other ways, in accord with the degree to which their role expectations can be fulfilled. Certainly the degree to which the conditions of fulfillment are known and the degree to which the conditions for fulfillment are indeterminate would have important consequences for the social system.[13]

The second set of specifications of role expectations deals with the temporal and spatial extension of these expectations. After all, all role performances are scheduled in time and placed in space. Scheduling and placement are

[13] Cf. J. Ladd, *The Structure of a Moral Code* (Cambridge, Mass.: Harvard University Press, 1957).

not random processes but are determined by the system in a manner as clear or unclear, or as determinate or indeterminate, as the content and evaluative standards of the expectations. Role expectations may well be construed as discrete or pervasive with respect to both time and space. By temporally discrete we mean that a given role performance is expected at some given time or time period. A temporally pervasive expectation would be one which would have no time binding, which is to say that it would be expected of an individual as long as he continues to play his role. In a like manner, spatially discrete expectations would be localized easily in space, and pervasive ones would apply to the role players in any location. (It seems likely that the more abstract and the more general an expectation, the more pervasive, both in time and in space, it may be. But this possibility has insufficient empirical confirmation and is one of many hypotheses that can be generated through this conceptualization.)

In the literature of role theory some writers have spoken of "segmental" as contrasted with "general" roles, by which they have implied a continuum of time and space involvement of an actor in a given role.[14] Thus roles that are relatively discrete with respect to their schedule and placement can be termed segmental roles, while roles that are pervasive with respect to their temporal and spatial extension can be termed general roles. It seems quite likely that the component roles in any social system may have different profiles in time and space and that such differences will have manifest consequences for the articulation of roles in that system.

The effects of this time-space dimension can be most cogently illustrated through a look at our role conflict reports (especially Chapter 6). First we ought to note that some of the conflict situations are themselves conflicts over the scheduling and placement of activities (situations 1, 2, and 5). This seems to be true of other role conflict research; namely, that conflicts over scheduling and placement are generally included in some listing of salient conflicts.

Aside from that, we can easily see that the pervasiveness-discreteness dimension does indeed contribute to an understanding of the role conflict situations we studied. The conflicts between emphasizing or balancing traffic work and criminal investigation, between leaving the job behind or preserving one's occupational role outside the job, between being a model citizen or being a good citizen—all of these appear to be pervasive conflicts. They have relatively no spatial or temporal limitations, entering into virtually all aspects of the policeman's role performance. This becomes especially apparent when we contrast these conflicts with those between reporting or not reporting a fellow policeman or between overlooking or not overlooking

[14] See, e.g., A. Lindesmith and A. Strauss, *Social Psychology* (New York: Dryden Press, 1956).

the rules and regulations. These two conflicts have behavioral relevance in highly limited contexts; that is, on the observation of someone not properly performing his duties or on those particularistic occasions when the rules and regulations are overlooked. Both of these situations, while recurrent, fall short of possessing the pervasive qualities of the other three.

If pervasiveness distinguishes these two groups of role conflict situations, is there anything else in our data which associates with this grouping and reflects on the utility of the pervasive-discrete distinction? Of course, our analysis is speculative and post factum, but if we review the data of Chapter 6 we can see that the two discrete conflict situations entail significantly greater ambivalence than do the pervasive conflicts.

If this, then, is a distinctive discriminant of these two classes of situations, how can we account for the greater association of ambivalence with discrete role conflict situations? Again we can only speculate; and here there appear to be two, quite complementary answers. First, it may well be the case that the very pervasiveness of a conflict situation *mitigates* against the retention of ambivalence. After the initial encounters with the conflict situation, it is quite likely that the actor subsequently chooses from among the available behavior alternatives in such a constant and/or habitual manner that the situation no longer (if it ever did) engenders an ambivalent reaction.[15]

Secondly, it seems equally likely that those who continue to experience ambivalence—given the pervasiveness of the situations and therefore the pervasiveness, and perhaps cumulative nature, of their ambivalence—either become so personally disturbed and/or ineffective in their role performance that they withdraw or are removed from their status incumbency. Thus those who remain are those for whom the situation is now relatively unambivalent.[16]

Time and space were not dimensions of our initial conceptualization of our research problems. As we have tried to illustrate, they now seem to us to be of considerable importance.

Every social system makes certain *conformity demands* on its actors in that certain role expectations must be fulfilled to some criterion. The failure of an actor to conform to certain expectations, *if not all expectations*, elicits some kind of negative sanction, and may ultimately lead to expulsion from the social system. But not all expectations need to be fulfilled, nor do they need

[15] Such an explanation is by no means new. Thus Cameron, in a different context, stated: "In many conflict situations, some extraneous factor reinforces one reaction, or annihilates the other, in such a way that what had been only a possible choice is now elevated to the position of an automatic, dominant habit." N. Cameron, *The Psychology of Behavior Disorders* (Boston: Houghton Mifflin, 1947).

[16] For example, Getzels and Guba (*op. cit.*) report that persons scoring high on their measure of ambivalence were significantly more dissatisfied with their job than those scoring low.

fulfillment at a satisfactory level. Some expectations, however, must be fulfilled at least at certain times and certain places. Probably some proscriptions may never be ignored or violated. Conformity demands may be expected to vary with the content of an expectation, with the adequacy of evaluative standards for its performance, with the clarity of the conditions for fulfillment of the expectation, and with matters of placement and scheduling. It should be clear that the adequate study of role behavior requires some clarification of the conditions under which failure to perform the role expected incurs sanctions. Certainly the number of times an actor has failed to perform a role as expected, the quality of his role performance, the character of personal evaluations made of the actor—as well as a variety of systemic factors that may have no direct link to the actor's history of role behavior—will all affect the likelihood of his being sanctioned for his failure at fulfilling his role expectations. Some actors, of course, may have high "idiosyncrasy credits," and other actors may not;[17] and some social systems may be highly tolerant of deviance and others not at all.

The complexity of conformity demands was made quite apparent in our role conflict interviews where we tried to ask the *policemen* what would happen if they didn't conform: "What would the audience do if you didn't do as they expect?" To our surprise, the *policemen* couldn't answer this question. Even when they knew that the audience group whose expectation they were not fulfilling demanded conformity, and that it would take some form of action, they were invariably uncertain as to what specifically it might do. Not only were the respondents unclear as to the informal sanctions that might be invoked by their fellow *policemen* or their wives or friends, they were equally unclear as to what the formal sanctions within the organization might be.

It may well be the case that, in attempting to elicit the specific sanctions which the actor anticipated, we were imposing upon our respondents the task of discriminating elements of their phenomenal world which they otherwise do not discriminate. This is not to say that persons are not aware of at least some of the specific sanctions which they encounter as a consequence of selecting among behavioral alternatives. This is to suggest, rather, that such knowledge in some groups and in some situations is relatively unimportant, and therefore there is no well-developed vocabulary for its articulation.[18]

[17] See E. P. Hollander, "Conformity, Status and Idiosyncrasy Credit," *Psychological Review*, 65 (1958), 117–27.

[18] In the school superintendent population, Gross, Mason and McEachern, asking a similar question, apparently encountered no such difficulties in eliciting responses nor in classifying them on an ad hoc scale of severity of sanctions. It seems quite likely that the school superintendents were much more sensitive to the sanctions their choice in role conflict situations may incur than are the policemen in our study, at least with respect to the situations under analysis.

THE ARTICULATION OF ROLES

Considering the problem of role behavior within the confines of complex organizations, we may now raise the question as to how the functional integration of roles is achieved. How is it that actors perform their roles more or less within the limits of expectations for their performance, and do so on schedule and in place?

The classic system problem is the problem of *consensus*. As a basic variable of sociological analysis, the concept of consensus has been incorporated into most theories of role behavior, as Gross and his colleagues demonstrated in their review of what they called the "postulate of consensus." Consensus up until then had been viewed as an unproblematic requisite for role behavior and as a characteristic that was either present or absent. We think it was one of the school superintendency study's signal contributions to emphasize (or better, reemphasize) the status of consensus as a variable and to raise the functional question of the implications of different degrees of consensus for role performance and for the social system.[19]

With respect to the articulation of roles in a system of interaction, the problem of consensus exists at two levels. First, there is the problem of consensus with respect to the ends and objectives of the system. Second, there is the problem of consensus with respect to specific roles and specific role expectations. Clearly, there is some requisite consensus, that is, some set of basic agreements minimally necessary for a social system to operate. Beyond that there must certainly be some further range of consensus for the system to operate efficiently, if not for the system to maintain itself in some adaptive or innovative manner.

The extent to which there is agreement on role definition within an audience group or between audience groups is a crucial question to which our data provide important and at times surprising answers. However, in our concern with consensus as a variable we think it necessary to understand that for certain field systems matters of degree may become matters of kind. Illustrations of this premise are redundant not only in the folk literature but in the natural and physical sciences. This excerpt from John Campbell's editorial, "A Matter of Degree," dramatizes quite appropriately the point at issue:

[19] Cf. N. Gross, W. Mason, and W. McEachern, *Explorations in Role Analysis: Studies of the School Superintendency Role* (New York: John Wiley & Sons, 1958), ch. 3. For general reviews of the concept of consensus, see O. E. Klapp, "The Concept of Consensus and Its Importance," *Sociology and Social Research*, 41 (1957), 336–42; T. M. Newcomb, "The Study of Consensus," in R. K. Merton *et al.* (eds.), *Sociology Today* (New York: Basic Books, 1959); and I. L. Horowitz, "Consensus, Conflict and Cooperation: A Sociological Inventory," *Social Forces*, 41 (1962), 177–88.

If the net gain due to the U–235 "neutron amplifiers" is exactly equal to the total loss of neutrons to all other components, the intensity of the nuclear reaction will be constant at whatever level it happens to be. The overall situation is, under this condition, that, on the average, the birth rate of neutrons in the system equals exactly the death rate, so that the neutron population is constant. The net neutron reproduction constant is, then, 1.000000. This neutron reproduction rate is referred to as the k-factor of the reactor.

However, if the k-factor is 1.0000001, each succeeding generation of neutrons is slightly more numerous; the neutron population is rising, and the level of activity of the reactor going up. In a reactor, the time per generation of neutrons is exceedingly short; the rate of rise of activity will be decidedly noticeable, even with so minute an excess over 1.000. . . .

On the inverse side, if k = 0.9999999 . . . , the rate of reaction is falling, the system is being damped, and will eventually settle down to zero reaction.

In such a system then, if k departs from exactly 1.000 . . . by even a minute degree, the system, as a whole, heads either for zero, or infinity. In the atomic bomb, we have a nuclear reactor with a high k-factor, and the system heads for an infinite rate of reaction at a spectacularly high rate. Yet the bomb is perfectly safe and stable until triggered, because the system has been so designed that, until triggered, the k-factor is held below 1.0000, and the reaction rate is, therefore, practically zero.

Now herein lies the peculiarity of this type of system-reaction; a minute difference in degree—the k-factor—produces, because of the chain interaction system, *a difference of kind*. If k is less than 1.0000, the reactor *does not* react; if k exceeds 1.0000, the reactor *does* react. A tiny difference of degree becomes, in a complexly interacting system of this type, an Aristotelian difference of Yes or No.[20]

While the qualitative effects of quantitative changes in social systems have received some attention in the social science literature, there has been no firm recognition of such occurrences in general, and certainly no application of these effects to role-related phenomena. Quite clearly, we need to ask what are the system consequences of different degrees of consensus. Is there perhaps some optimum degree of consensus for specified kinds of social systems or system-relevant tasks?

As we have suggested earlier, a moderate degree of consensus on role expectations provided the role player with a degree of flexibility that enabled him to select among alternative expectations and/or performances with low conformity demands. It seems to us unlikely that prescriptions or proscriptions upon which there is only moderate consensus can be defined as obligatory. Perhaps, given only moderate consensus, such expectations may not even be construed as legitimate, in the sense that Gross, Mason, and McEachern have used the term as meaning morally correct. However, where

20 J. Campbell, "A Matter of Degree," editorial in *Astounding Science Fiction*, 60, No. 2 (1957), 6–7, 161–62.

extremely high consensus exists we ought to expect to find an authoritarian system, that is, a highly constrained system of role relationships.

Flexibility in a system of role relationships occurs, we suspect, only where it is built into a system. Such adaptive mechanisms may entail 1) high consensus on optional or alternative expectations, 2) high consensus on expectations where no attempt is made to enforce conforming role performances, or 3) moderate or low consensus where actors have—by default—the same freedom as in (1).

At some point we must have some minimal consensus for a social system to cohere. We need, of course, to determine what such a point might be. Here we can see that consensus, as a matter of degree, may have implications for the maintenance and persistence of the social system (as in the illustration of our uranium pile). We suspect that where "too much" consensus obtains or where there is consensus about too many elements of behavior, the system also begins to break down.

Our next concern is with the mechanism of *involvement*. By involvement we mean essentially the degree to which audience groups are structurally articulated in the role performance of the actor.[21] Our concern is not with psychological involvement. It should be clear that the contact between actors performing their roles (as opposed to the informal or personal contacts of people within the social system) is not random and is *always*, to some large degree, regulated by the social system. Where involvement is systemically prescribed, the mutual relationships among role players are said to be *legitimate*. These relationships and the appropriate expectations for behavior may be construed as legitimate in the sense both that the relationships are organizationally *right* and that the role players are then *accountable* to each other for the adequate performance of their roles.

Legitimacy is not always a transitive occurrence. In some systems persons occupying superordinate positions are not organizationally accountable to their subordinates, while in others it is quite legitimate for the subordinates to question and/or evaluate matters of the role performance of their superiors. This seems particularly true in those organizations where technicians or professionals are integrated with nonprofessional administrative personnel.

As our conception of involvement implies, not all actors have direct access to each other in their role performance, and much of role involvement is determined by the social system. So too, *status distance* is not an entirely free or random matter. First, the system defines the permissible communica-

---

[21] What we mean by involvement appears much like Landecker's "functional integration," which he defines as "the degree to which there is mutual interdependence among the units of a system of division of labor." Cf. W. S. Landecker, "Types of Integration and Their Measurement," *American Journal of Sociology*, 56 (1951), 332-40.

tion links, and these links may facilitate or block direct communication among its role players. The channels of communication are almost invariably specified in any organizational blueprint, and so important is the established pattern or channels of communication that bypassing positions and establishing new communication links may frequently disrupt the organization.[22]

Access is often a function of status distance, and usually reflects the prestige or functional differences underlying the stratification of the organization. Not only is access a matter of the distance relationships prescribed by the system, it is also a matter of ecology (which may be prescribed, but is usually fortuitous). The segregation of role performances may occur both through the formal structure of communications and the structuring of the physical plant in which the interaction occurs.

Whether or not actors can confront their audience in order to seek clarification of their expectations or redress in the event of conflicting expectations seems to be a variable property of social systems. The ease or difficulty of confrontability, which is a part of the problem of status distance, seems intimately related to the system's ability to withstand internal stress and conflict, and possibly external stress.

The two most frequently discussed system mechanisms in the role literature are *visibility and power*. For this reason we shall discuss them here only briefly.[23] Visibility refers to the degree to which an actor's role performance can be observed by an audience group. The extremes of "complete" visibility or invisibility are rarely, if ever, permitted to occur in social systems. And it seems likely that there is some optimum range of visibility for types of role performances and for types of social systems. It is clear from our research that the application and specification of evaluative standards are related to the visibility of the actor's role performance to the audience and to the involvement of the audience in the actor's performance. We observed that the greater the status distance the more the audience focused upon the symbolic and superficial standards and the less it focused upon the content criteria in evaluating role performance. Similarly, the greater the visibility and the greater the involvement, the more the audience focused upon content criteria.

By power we mean the degree to which the audience group can exercise control over the actor's role performance. Such control may derive from the facilities and rights accorded the occupants of given statuses or from interpersonal skills and/or other nonsystemic factors. The former has been

22 This is well documented in E. L. Scott, *Leadership and Perceptions of Organization* (Columbus, O.: Ohio State University Bureau of Business Research Monograph No. 82, 1956).

23 Certainly the "classic" discussion, to which we can add very little, may be found in R. K. Merton, *Social Theory and Social Structure* (rev. ed.; Glencoe, Ill.: Free Press, 1957), ch. 9.

traditionally labeled "authority" and the latter "influence." In general, the smaller the status distance the less important are matters of authority and the more important are matters of influence. More precisely, we have observed that the greater the status distance and the lower the visibility and the involvement of an audience in a role performance, the greater the likelihood that conformity demands will be based on authority rather than influence. The consequence of authority-based conformity demands is to decrease the autonomy granted an actor in his role performance and to increase the likelihood of demands for autonomy by the actor. Thus the greater the power of an audience, the less visible is an actor's performance to them, and the more well-developed are the mechanisms for insulating role performance from visibility.

Although one might expect authority relationships to be relatively unambiguous in an organization such as the police (where rank insignia are conspicuously displayed), our field observations suggested that this was not the case. Where rank was high and status distance low, there seemed to be the greatest confusion of authority relations. Thus higher-ranking officers would occasionally preface their demands or requests with "Now, this isn't an order" or "I could order you to do this"—as if to increase distance or to display their potential power. Conversely, the junior officer might seek clarification directly: "Is that an order, sir?" or, more likely in a joking tone, "If you want to order me to do that, I'd be glad to do that, sir." Though we have no systematic materials here, we have introduced this consideration of the ambiguity of power relations in this kind of highly structured, quasimilitary organization to underscore the complexity of the problem of power.

Whereas visibility and power have been well-discussed components of role theories, the next two mechanisms we introduce have been ignored. Actors remain within social systems for a variety of reasons. Two such systemic mechanisms which operate to retain persons within the system we shall designate as *status commitment* and *system commitment*. By status commitment we refer to the degree to which factors other than those of psychological preference *prevent* the actor from withdrawing from his status.[24] By system commitment we mean the degree to which organizational norms

[24] This conception of "commitment" was adapted from J. Smith, R. C. Bealer, and F. Sim, "Research Design of Farmers' Use of Market News (Revised Preliminary Statement)" (East Lansing, Mich.: Social Research Service, Michigan State University, 1956 [dittoed]).

Goffman, in his concept of "role distance," combines both a notion of system commitment and status commitment (what he terms "commitment" and "attachment") with a conception of physical-motor involvement ("engagement"). In maintaining our own distinction, we are rejecting the strategy of combining logically independent types of commitment at such an early stage of inquiry. Cf. E. Goffman, *Encounters: Two Studies in the Sociology of Interaction* (Indianapolis, Ind.: Bobbs-Merrill, 1961).

prevent the system's members from expelling actors whose role performance is technically adequate. (Whether or not the qualification of "technical adequacy" is necessary is open to some question. Much may depend on how technical adequacy becomes defined, and here we would prefer further exploration. Certainly within some organizational settings it is most difficult to expel some actors whose role performance, while unsatisfactory, is not unsatisfactory to some stated criterion of ineptitude.) It is apparent that in some organizations, of which the CSP and college faculties are two examples, seniority systems and systems of tenure may take precedence over evaluations of role performance or over the personal preferences of the system's members. These, of course, are intended as "solutions" to problems of system commitment.

It is to be expected that in some instances system commitment is a matter of system survival. An exaggerated instance of system commitment might be divorce, where the rejection of a member results in the breakdown of the system. Another illustration is the case of the *policeman* who successfully declined promotion and transfer. He succeeded because the department expected that his involuntary transfer would so arouse community hostility that it would threaten the continued, efficient operation of his post.

The issue of status commitment is most graphically displayed through our data on the distribution of voluntary resignations of *policemen* over time. By the tenth year of service the likelihood of a *policeman's* advancement to sergeant is reasonably well determined. Although some men who are dissatisfied with these probabilities leave around that time period, most others, who also are presumably dissatisfied, remain and adapt more or less well. Given the youthful age of recruitment, and given the fact that most recruits enter the organization with few or no well-defined occupational skills, the *policeman* becomes committed to police work not necessarily for its psychological gratifications (which at the rank of *policeman* may have decreased considerably after ten years) but because he has few occupational alternatives. Further, he becomes committed because now—ten years later, with a young family, and possibly a mortgaged home—the social costs of changing jobs and moving exceed his material and psychological resources.

The Cognitive Map of Role Behavior

As sociologically trained social psychologists, we have constructed our program thus far at an essentially sociological level. Indeed, we have come to construe role theory as a part of the more general theory of social structure. There is a psychological homologue to this program for theory that we are developing, and we should like to explore some of its aspects.

We have now presented several sets of systemic mechanisms which can explain the regulation of role performance, and we endeavored to classify them in a threefold manner: those dealing with the reference group matrix, those dealing with the properties of system-specific role expectations, and those dealing with the articulation of roles in the social system. In asserting that there is a psychological homologue to our essentially sociological theory-program, we do not wish to derogate the importance of a psychologically framed role theory; neither should be construed as more important than the other. They constitute different levels of analysis, and one might theoretically be able to move in one direction and develop a cultural homologue, and in another direction and develop a biological homologue.

It should be clear that such reductionism does not dispense with the higher-level theory.[25] The question, for example, of how the distribution of power arrangements in a social system affects the performance of given roles within that system is quite a different question from that of how an individual's perception of the power of others affects his behavior in a given time and place. The understanding of either question will not necessarily increase our understanding of the other. While a single explanation may be possible, if we were to operate on such an assumption we might well preempt needed inquiry.

It is our contention that such mechanisms—for example, consensus, involvement, status distance, and so forth—have a determinative effect on the role performance of actors in the system and that this effect is *independent* of an actor's perception of these mechanisms. Thus, to stick with our example dealing with power arrangements, an individual's role performance is going to be at least partly determined by the structure of power within the system regardless of whether or not he perceives that power structure and regardless of the accuracy or inaccuracy of his perception. While many aspects of social structure are not perceived by actors—despite the significance of these structural features for their behavior—many aspects are perceived. We think it important to ask: How is it that certain features of a social system are more frequently or more readily perceived by the members of that system than others?

One proposal we should like to make is that some systemic elements have

[25] While we may insist that the problems of reduction should be clear, we discovered—after we wrote this—that the old confusions are still being promulgated. G. Homans in his presidential address to the American Sociological Association, for example, essentially disposes of most current sociological theories on the grounds that they are not appropriately psychological or they are easily reducible to psychological statements. See G. C. Homans, "Bringing Men Back In," *American Sociological Review*, 29 (1964), 809–18. For the antidote, see E. Nagel, *The Structure of Science* (New York: Harcourt, Brace & World, 1961), esp. ch. 11, "The Reduction of Theories."

the property of an "adequate stimulus." By this we mean that these elements are *invariably* perceived by actors within the system. Thus we propose that a dimension like power is one which is always incorporated into the cognitive maps of the individual performers within the system. Every actor comes to learn early that there exists within this interaction system a distribution of power, that some people in some positions can make some determinations about his own behavior, and that he too can influence the behavior of others. No actor, we insist, can escape this percept. Some may well be rather correct in their perception, and others may be rather inaccurate; some will have rather differentiated and well-defined knowledge of the power distribution, and others will have only limited, fragmentary knowledge.

Further, we should like to propose that while certain key elements of social structure will have this character of an adequate stimulus, an actor's cognitive map of the social system will itself be to some degree determined by his location within the system. We observed, for example, that there was a differential distribution of knowledge about enforcement policy and practices by rank within the organization, and we also observed that there was a differential distribution by rank of the accuracy and inaccuracy of this knowledge. There is, of course, more to the individual's cognitive map of the system than those elements which are the adequate stimuli—and more even than those which are more or less determinative of that mapping.

Which mechanisms, which components of social structure operate with this quality of an adequate stimulus, we do not know. Nor do we know what characteristics of social structure determine the distribution of knowledge and the differentiation of cognitions about the social structure. But clearly these problems constitute first-order problems for the psychological and social-psychological investigation of role phenomena. And one place to begin our search, which returns us to the original assertion of an homology, is to examine such variables as involvement, distance, visibility, power, commitment, and the like to determine their psychological counterparts.

Omega

One of the major deficiencies in the strategy of testing theory in sociology and social psychology has been the general unwillingness of researchers to seriously consider alternative conceptualizations. This is not to say that we feel that theorists are obligated to construct alternative theory or theories. But we do need to insist, either in the exposition or testing of new theories, that consideration be given to alternatives. In the case of role theory we might well ask—in the search for alternatives—what phenomena such a theory is meant to explain. What are the basic conceptual units employed to determine such an explanation? What would it mean if one were not to employ these units of analysis?

If we had a fully articulated theory, it would be relatively easy to determine the formal relationships among the propositions and the relative logical importance of the propositions. We could at least then begin to answer these questions on an analytic level. As for the empirical means for the testing of our theory and its alternatives, here too role theorists have been remiss. The number of times one theory has been pitted against another in empirical tests is hard to find in the literature. While the testing of hypotheses derived from role theories is no longer uncommon in sociology and social psychology, it is uncommon to observe a study design that entails the test of alternative hypotheses derived from alternative conceptualizations of the same phenomenon. How surprising or unsurprising are the materials we have presented may well depend on the sophistication of the reader and/or his willingness to grant that an otherwise "obvious" association was up until the time of its exhibition not *that* obvious to him. There have been—and we have tried to emphasize these—some rather surprising findings in this research. But we think it also correct to say that a great many of the findings of this research have not been surprising.

For further research and theory construction we see an enormous number of alternatives and possibilities now open. We have tried to present what we construe as the major determinants of role performance; and we have tried to indicate both what our research has had to say about these variables, and—directly or by implication—where we think further research ought to be aimed. While many will still continue to grind out abstract and occasionally elegant conceptual schemes for the analysis of role behavior—or will remain doggedly committed to previous ones—we see as the appropriate and the needed direction in this matter the exploration of the components of these variables, the rigorous testing of their interrelationships and their implications, and the establishment of empirically sound propositions concerning their operation. They read well, and we have provided some documentation for them; but this is clearly not enough. Beyond the problem of establishing the necessary research operations for their testing, we need also to consider, concomitantly, the development of alternative schemes and respective tests of these schemes.

Appendix 1

A Note on Research Operations

THIS RESEARCH may be viewed as taking place in four phases: (*a*) the observational phase, (*b*) the testing phase, (*c*) the recruit panel study, and (*d*) the public image study.

a) From October, 1957, through May, 1958, we systematically observed operations at Central Headquarters. Contact was sustained almost daily by one or both of the authors. From May through August, 1958, we lived and worked at four police posts as participant-observers. The results of our field work are presented primarily in Chapter 2.

b) From May through September, 1958, all of the formal questionnaire batteries and the role conflict interviews were administered. With the exception of headquarters personnel, the questionnaires were handled by mail and distributed to all members of the Uniform Division. Returns ranged from 90 per cent for *policemen* to 100 per cent for officers. The role conflict interviews were conducted at the posts where we worked. Further details are given in Chapter 6.

In addition to the current members of the Uniform Division, we attempted to contact by mail all of the living and known former members of the CSP who had resigned (voluntarily or otherwise) or who had retired. From the resigned we received 43 per cent returns, and from the retired 51 per cent. In view of this modest return and our inability to check on the representativeness of response, we have put these data to very limited use, primarily in Chapter 3.

c) The details of the recruit panel studies are presented in Chapter 4. The initial testing was in late November, 1957. At that time, and also in the second wave (May, 1958), the questionnaires were group-administered. For the third (November, 1958) and fourth (December, 1959) waves, the questionnaires were handled by mail.

d) The public image materials and the sample characteristics are presented in Appendix 2. This phase, including pre-testing, extended from late August to December, 1958.

Data analysis began in 1959 and was completed by mid-1960.

The Basic Questionnaires

BLOCKAGE-IMPORTANCE (*b-i*) INSTRUMENT: AREA I—ADVANCEMENT OPPORTUNITIES

1(*b*). Do you think that the State Police Department is the kind of organization that is generally considered to provide good opportunities for advancement?

   1 _____ It has excellent opportunities.

   2 _____ It has better-than-average opportunities.

   3 _____ It has about the same advancement opportunities as other organizations.

   4 _____ Advancement opportunities are poorer than in other organizations.

1(*i*). How important do you consider it to be to have a job which provides good opportunities for advancement?

   1 _____ Extremely important.

   2 _____ Quite important.

   3 _____ Of some importance.

   4 _____ Relatively unimportant.

2(*b*). Are the people who get promoted in your organization likely to be selected from among those who do the best work?

   1 _____ Yes, almost entirely.

   2 _____ Often.

   3 _____ Sometimes.

   4 _____ Seldom or never.

2(*i*). How much does it mean to you to be in the kind of position from which promotions are usually made?

   1 _____ I feel it is very important to be in that kind of position.

   2 _____ It means a great deal to me.

   3 _____ It is a relatively minor concern.

   4 _____ It is not important compared to other things about a job.

3(*i*). How do you feel about jobs where advancement is difficult?

   1 _____ I dislike them very much.

   2 _____ I would prefer not to have such a job.

   3 _____ Not a particularly important consideration to me.

   4 _____ Such a job would be a challenge to me.

4(*b*). Will the position of policeman be pretty much of a stopping point as far as promotion goes?

   1 _____ Practically everybody stops at this level.

   2 _____ Some people get beyond it but most do not.

   3 _____ Many people advance beyond this position.

   4 _____ Most people advance beyond this position.

4(*i*). How much would it bother you to be in a position which was a stopping point as far as promotion goes?

1 ＿＿ I would get very upset by it.

2 ＿＿ It would bother me quite a bit.

3 ＿＿ It would be somewhat disturbing.

4 ＿＿ It would hardly bother me at all.

5(*b*). Do you feel that you might be able to move up further if you were to go into another type of organization or company?

1 ＿＿ Yes, I very much feel this way.

2 ＿＿ I feel this way to some extent.

3 ＿＿ My organization is about the same as any other in this.

4 ＿＿ My chances are better here than they would be elsewhere.

7(*b*). Do you think you work for the kind of organization where anyone who really tries can be promoted?

1 ＿＿ This describes the organization I work for very well.

2 ＿＿ This describes the organization I work for fairly well.

3 ＿＿ This is hardly true of the organization I work for.

4 ＿＿ This is not at all true of the organization I work for.

7(*i*). Would you give up other good things in a job in order to get into another job where promotion would be faster?

1 ＿＿ Yes, because promotion is the most important thing.

2 ＿＿ I might be willing to change jobs.

3 ＿＿ No, I wouldn't. Promotion isn't that important.

8(*i*). How important is it to you to have a job which offers a future?

1 ＿＿ It's the most important aspect of any job.

2 ＿＿ It's a fairly important aspect of a job.

3 ＿＿ It's not too important.

4 ＿＿ Other things are much more important.

AREA 2—SOCIAL VALUE AND PRESTIGE

1(*b*). Do people in general think well of the *kind of job* you hold?

1 ＿＿ Yes, I believe they think very well of it.

2 ＿＿ Yes, I think so, but I'm not sure how well.

3 ＿＿ No, I don't believe they think much of it.

1(*i*). How important is it to you that people in general think well of your kind of job?

1 ＿＿ Extremely important.

2 ＿＿ Of considerable importance.

3 ＿＿ Of some importance.

4 ＿＿ Of little or no importance.

2(*b*). Do some people look down on the job of state policeman?

1 ＿＿ Yes, I'm sure they do.

2 ＿＿ Yes, I think they do but I'm not sure.

3 ＿＿ No, I don't think so.

3(*b*). Do other people recognize the value to society of the work policemen do?

    1 ＿＿ Most people do.

    2 ＿＿ Many do.

    3 ＿＿ Some do.

    4 ＿＿ Very few do.

3(*i*). How important is such recognition to you?

    1 ＿＿ It is of tremendous importance.

    2 ＿＿ It is very important.

    3 ＿＿ It is of some importance.

    4 ＿＿ It is of little importance.

4(*b*). Some people in your kind of work find that their jobs are not particularly respected by *the very persons* whom they would like to have think well of their jobs. To what extent do you think this to be true?

    1 ＿＿ This is very true in my case.

    2 ＿＿ This is generally true.

    3 ＿＿ This is somewhat true.

    4 ＿＿ This is not at all true in my case.

4(*i*). How strongly do you feel the need to have certain persons think well of your job?

    1 ＿＿ Very strongly.

    2 ＿＿ Fairly strongly.

    3 ＿＿ Not so strongly.

    4 ＿＿ Not strongly at all.

5(*b*). Do people outside your organization appreciate the value of the work policemen do?

    1 ＿＿ They always do.

    2 ＿＿ They generally do.

    3 ＿＿ They seldom do.

    4 ＿＿ They almost never do.

5(*i*). How important is such appreciation to you?

    1 ＿＿ Very important.

    2 ＿＿ Quite important.

    3 ＿＿ Of some importance.

    4 ＿＿ Of little or no importance.

7(*b*). Is your job considered to be one which is beneficial to humanity?

    1 ＿＿ Yes, very much so.

    2 ＿＿ To a considerable extent.

    3 ＿＿ To some extent.

    4 ＿＿ Not to any degree.

7(*i*). How important is it to you that your job be thought of as one which benefits humanity?

    1 ＿＿ It is of extreme importance.

    2 ＿＿ It is of considerable importance.

3 ____ It is somewhat important.

4 ____ It really doesn't matter.

8(*b*). Some positions are respected because they provide important and worthwhile services for people. Is your position one which others might like to have for this reason?

1 ____ Yes, it is very much this kind of job.

2 ____ It is largely this kind of job.

3 ____ To some extent it is this kind of job.

4 ____ No, it's not that kind of job.

8(*i*). How important is it to you to have a job which is respected because of the important and worthwhile services it provides for people?

1 ____ Very important.

2 ____ Of considerable importance.

3 ____ Of little importance.

4 ____ Of almost no importance.

9(*b*). Do you feel that people look down on your kind of job because of some of the things you will have to do?

1 ____ Many people do.

2 ____ Some people do.

3 ____ Perhaps a few do.

4 ____ I feel certain no one does.

10(*b*). Is your job considered an important one by other people?

1 ____ Yes, I believe people consider it very important.

2 ____ Yes, I think people feel it is rather important.

3 ____ I suppose they think it is as important as most jobs.

4 ____ No, I don't think people consider it important.

10(*i*). Do you like to have people feel that your job is important?

1 ____ Yes, I care very much.

2 ____ Yes, I care considerably.

3 ____ Yes, but it doesn't matter too much.

4 ____ No, I don't care how they feel.

AREA 3—FREEDOM TO EXPRESS FEELINGS

1(*b*). In your work, do you have to soft-pedal your feelings when dealing with others?

1 ____ Yes, always.

2 ____ Quite often.

3 ____ Occasionally.

4 ____ Very rarely, if at all.

1(*i*). How do you react to having to do this?

1 ____ It hardly bothers me at all.

2 ____ It's a little annoying.

3 ____ I find it quite frustrating.

4 ____ I get very upset.

2(*b*). Does your work prevent you from acting like a human being with feelings and emotions?

1 _____ It never does.

2 _____ It seldom does.

3 _____ It sometimes does.

4 _____ It frequently does.

2(*i*). How frustrating is it when you feel prevented from acting like a human being with feelings and emotions?

1 _____ Extremely frustrating.

2 _____ Very frustrating.

3 _____ Somewhat frustrating.

4 _____ A little frustrating.

3(*b*). Does your job require you to work with and be friendly toward people even if you don't like them?

1 _____ Most of the time.

2 _____ This is often necessary.

3 _____ Sometimes find I have to.

4 _____ Rarely does this happen.

3(*i*). If this is necessary, what is your reaction?

1 _____ It bothers me greatly.

2 _____ It bothers me considerably.

3 _____ It bothers me somewhat.

4 _____ It bothers me not at all.

4(*b*). In your work, are you often in the position of having to quietly put up with actions of others that are distasteful to you?

1 _____ Yes, a great deal of the time.

2 _____ Yes, much of the time.

3 _____ Sometimes this is the case.

4 _____ Only rarely is this the case.

4(*i*). How much does it bother you to have to put up with the distasteful actions of others?

1 _____ I get very upset by it.

2 _____ It bothers me quite a lot.

3 _____ It's somewhat disturbing.

4 _____ It doesn't bother me at all.

5(*b*). In your work, are you able to say what you think?

1 _____ Always.

2 _____ Generally.

3 _____ Sometimes.

4 _____ Seldom.

5(*i*). How much does it bother you not to be able to say what you think?

1 _____ Very much.

2 _____ A good deal.

3 _____ Somewhat.

4 _____ Very little.

6(i). How do you feel about having to control your temper when you are irritated?
    1 ____ It disturbs me tremendously.
    2 ____ It bothers me a great deal.
    3 ____ It bothers me a little.
    4 ____ It doesn't disturb me.

7(i). How important is it to you to be frank with others?
    1 ____ Very important.
    2 ____ Of considerable importance.
    3 ____ Of some importance.
    4 ____ Of little or no importance.

8(b). Does it endanger your position to say what you think?
    1 ____ Yes, very much.
    2 ____ To a considerable extent.
    3 ____ Somewhat.
    4 ____ Hardly at all.

8(i). How important is it to you to be able to say what you think?
    1 ____ Very important.
    2 ____ Of considerable importance.
    3 ____ Of some importance.
    4 ____ Of little importance.

9(b). Jobs vary in the way people have to hide their emotions and feelings. What is your job like in this respect?
    1 ____ I will be required to hide my feelings and emotions at all times.
    2 ____ It will usually be necessary to hide my feelings and emotions.
    3 ____ I will seldom need to hide my feelings and emotions.
    4 ____ I will never have to hide my feelings and emotions.

9(i). How much does it bother you to have to hide your emotions and feelings?
    1 ____ Very much.
    2 ____ Considerably.
    3 ____ A little.
    4 ____ None at all.

AREA 4—SELF-REALIZATION

1(b). Does your work give you a feeling of accomplishment?
    1 ____ Very much so.
    2 ____ To a considerable extent.
    3 ____ To some extent.
    4 ____ Little or not at all.

2(b). Are there other jobs you might have chosen that would give you more opportunity to do the things you can do best?
    1 ____ Yes, there are jobs that would give me a much greater chance to do these things.
    2 ____ There are jobs that would give me considerably more chance.
    3 ____ There are jobs that would give me some more chance to do these things.
    4 ____ There is no other job that would give me more chance to do these things.

2(*i*). How important is it to you that your work allow you to do those things you can do best?

    1 _____ Extremely important.

    2 _____ Of considerable importance.

    3 _____ Of some importance.

    4 _____ Of little or no importance.

3(*b*). Do you feel that your work provides adequate opportunities for you to express initiative?

    1 _____ Entirely adequate.

    2 _____ Fairly adequate.

    3 _____ Not very adequate.

    4 _____ Not adequate at all.

4(*b*). Does your job allow you opportunities to do the kind of things you like to do?

    1 _____ Generally.

    2 _____ To a considerable extent.

    3 _____ To some extent.

    4 _____ Hardly at all.

4(*i*). How important is it to you in your work to be able to do the kind of things you like to do?

    1 _____ It is extremely important.

    2 _____ It is quite important.

    3 _____ It is of some importance.

    4 _____ It is a minor matter.

5(*b*). To what extent does your work give you a feeling of self-fulfillment?

    1 _____ To a great extent.

    2 _____ To a considerable extent.

    3 _____ To some extent.

    4 _____ Very little, if any.

5(*i*). How important is it to you that your work give you a feeling of self-fulfillment?

    1 _____ It is very important.

    2 _____ It is of considerable importance.

    3 _____ It is of some importance.

    4 _____ It is of little, if any, importance.

6(*i*). In selecting a job, is the amount of mental energy required an important consideration?

    1 _____ Yes, very important.

    2 _____ Of considerable importance.

    3 _____ Of some importance.

    4 _____ Of little or no importance.

7(*b*). Does your work make use of your particular abilities and capabilities?

    1 _____ Yes, fully.

2 ____ For the most part it does.

3 ____ Not to a great extent.

4 ____ It doesn't make use of them at all.

8(*b*). How interested are you in your work?

    1 ____ Very much interested.

    2 ____ Considerably interested.

    3 ____ A little, but not much.

    4 ____ Not interested at all.

8(*i*). How important do you consider it to have a job which interests you?

    1 ____ It is of primary importance.

    2 ____ It is quite important.

    3 ____ It is of some importance.

    4 ____ It is of little or no importance.

9(*b*). One man says of his job: "I have *no* chance to accomplish and build—to be creative." Is this true of your job?

    1 ____ Yes, this is very true of my job also.

    2 ____ In general it is true.

    3 ____ To some extent it is true.

    4 ____ My job is not like that at all.

9(*i*). How important is it to you to have work which gives you a chance to be creative?

    1 ____ It is an absolute necessity.

    2 ____ It means a great deal to me.

    3 ____ This is of some importance.

    4 ____ I don't consider this to be very important.

AREA 5—JOB–FAMILY COMPATIBILITY

1(*b*). Would you say that, in practice, your work comes before your family?

    1 ____ Yes, this is very often the case.

    2 ____ This is quite often the case.

    3 ____ This is seldom the case.

    4 ____ This is almost never the case.

1(*i*). Does or would it bother you to have to place your work before your family?

    1 ____ Yes, extremely.

    2 ____ Considerably.

    3 ____ Somewhat.

    4 ____ To a limited degree.

2(*b*). To what extent does your job cause you to neglect your family?

    1 ____ To a great extent.

    2 ____ To a considerable extent.

    3 ____ To some extent.

    4 ____ Not at all.

2(i). How important a consideration is it to have a job that doesn't interfere with, and cause you to neglect, parts of your family life?

    1 _____ Extremely important.
    2 _____ Of considerable importance.
    3 _____ Quite important.
    4 _____ Of some importance.

3(b). Do you have as much opportunity to be with your family as people in other types of work?

    1 _____ Much more opportunity.
    2 _____ A little more.
    3 _____ About the same.
    4 _____ A little less.
    5 _____ Much less opportunity.

3(i). How important a factor is this to you?

    1 _____ Very important.
    2 _____ Of considerable importance.
    3 _____ Of some importance.
    4 _____ This is not an important consideration.

4(b). Do you think your work uses up all your time and energy?

    1 _____ Yes, completely.
    2 _____ To a very large extent.
    3 _____ To some extent.
    4 _____ No, not at all.

4(i). How do you feel about work that takes up all your time and energy?

    1 _____ I very much dislike this kind of work.
    2 _____ I somewhat dislike it.
    3 _____ I rather prefer it.
    4 _____ I very much prefer this kind of work.

5(b). Do you feel that you fall down on your obligations to your family because of your work?

    1 _____ Yes, very frequently.
    2 _____ Often.
    3 _____ Sometimes.
    4 _____ Seldom or never.

5(i). If this occurs, how much does it bother you?

    1 _____ Very much.
    2 _____ Considerably.
    3 _____ Somewhat.
    4 _____ Not too much.

7(b). Does your type of work fit in well with being a family man?

    1 _____ Very well.
    2 _____ Fairly well.
    3 _____ Not too well.
    4 _____ Very poorly.

7(*i*). How important is it for you to have the type of work which fits in well with being a family man?

    1 _____ Very important.

    2 _____ Of considerable importance.

    3 _____ Somewhat important.

    4 _____ Not very important for me.

8(*b*). Do you ever fail to do what your family expects of you because of the demands of your work?

    1 _____ Yes, very frequently.

    2 _____ I often do.

    3 _____ I sometimes do.

    4 _____ I almost never do.

8(*i*). How much does it bother you if such a situation arises?

    1 _____ Very much.

    2 _____ Considerably.

    3 _____ Somewhat.

    4 _____ Not too much.

9(*b*). Does your work draw you away from your family?

    1 _____ Very much.

    2 _____ Somewhat.

    3 _____ Not at all.

    4 _____ It will bring us closer together.

9(*i*). What should one do in such a situation?

    1 _____ He should leave such work.

    2 _____ He should want to leave such work.

    3 _____ He should be quite dissatisfied.

    4 _____ He should just try to make the best of it.

Please list the most important qualities a state policeman should have. List as many as you like, but put the most important first, the next second, and so on down the line.

The Policy and Practices Series

1. Has there been an increased emphasis on safety and traffic as compared with complaint work in the Uniform Division within the last five years?
   ____ Yes. ____ No.

2. Should there be a relationship between number of traffic arrests and number of verbal warnings given by a policeman?
   ____ a) He should use his own discretion primarily since there is no relationship.
   ____ b) These should be more or less kept in a ratio to one another (50–50, 2 to 1, 3 to 1, etc.) Give the ratio you feel should generally be maintained: ____ verbal warnings to ____ traffic arrests.
   ____ c) Post areas vary and policemen should follow accepted practices at his post.
   ____ d) Other _____
   _____
   _____

3. Do you think policemen should strictly enforce the posted speed limits?
   ____ Yes.
   ____ No. (If "no," what leeway above the limit should be allowed?)
   _____
   _____

   ____ No opinion.

4. What are the main reasons for your answer above?

5. Is your opinion on enforcement the same as accepted practice in the department? ____ Yes. ____ No.

6. Do you think the department ought to maintain unmarked cars on patrol?
   ____ Yes. ____ No. ____ No opinion.
   Comments:

7. Do you think the department ought to maintain semi-marked cars on patrol?
   ____ Yes. ____ No. ____ No opinion.

8. Do you feel the department ought to maintain radar units? _____ Yes. _____ No. _____ No opinion.

9. What are the most important factors in evaluating a post? Select one or more. (If more than one, mark in order of importance "1," "2," "3," etc.)
   _____ a) Size of post (number of men).
   _____ b) Level of activity (how busy a post is).
   _____ c) Its ranking in the district.
   _____ d) Assessment and reputation of post commander.
   _____ e) Combined rating of policemen at the post.
   _____ f) Amount of increase in post activity from year to year.
   _____ g) Location of the post.
   _____ h) Other _____
   _____
   _____

10. In order to gain promotion or a desired transfer, is it an advantage for a policeman to know someone at headquarters who can support or speak up for him?

11. Which of the following are the most important ways for a policeman to gain a high evaluation by headquarters? If more than one choice, please *number* choices in order of importance.
    a) _____ How well he is liked by fellow policemen.
    b) _____ The number and kind of tickets he issued.
    c) _____ The opinion of his post commander.
    d) _____ His ambition, as indicated by taking on new duties and activities (pistol team, skin diving, taking courses, etc.).
    e) _____ Staying out of trouble (no public complaints, bad publicity, etc.).
    f) _____ The quality of his written reports.
    g) _____ Getting of few big "knock-offs."
    h) _____ Other: (Specify)_____
    _____
    _____

12. What percentage of policemen would you estimate has an outside income not officially approved by the department? _____%.

13. Under what circumstances should a policeman be allowed to earn an outside income?

14. Is it all right for policemen to accept free meals, trade discounts, etc., as long as it does not obligate them? ___ Yes. ___ No.

15. Would you like to see the department on a 40-hour week? ___ Yes. ___ No. Comment:

16. Do you think there is too much regulation of the private lives of policemen by the department?
    a) ___ Yes.
    b) ___ No.
    c) ___ Undecided.

17. What are the main reasons for your answer above?

18. One can't help being annoyed occasionally by the behavior of policemen. As you think back, what things have you found particularly annoying?

19. In your contacts with the public, what sorts of things have you found particularly annoying?

20. What kinds of procedures covered during the policemen's training period are most likely to be altered or modified in actual experience?

21. Under what conditions are policemen's applications for transfer now
    Granted:

    Denied:

22. Under what conditions are policemen transferred without having requested one?

23. What do you feel ought to be the policy on transfers?

24. What do you like or dislike about the way in which policemen are pictured in radio, TV, movies, books, etc.?

25. What are the occupations of your three closest friends? (Do not list their names, just their occupation.)
    1. ———————————————
    2. ———————————————
    3. ———————————————

26. Father's occupation. (If deceased, list what his major occupation was before he died.)

What would be your reaction toward working with a Negro policeman on patrol?*

_____ a) Would refuse.

_____ b) Strongly object but do it under orders.

_____ c) Feel uncomfortable but would not object.

_____ d) Wouldn't bother me at all.

_____ e) Would like to do so.

Do you feel that Negroes and other racial minority groups (Mexicans, Indians, etc.) require stricter enforcement procedures than the rest of the population?*

_____ a) I definitely feel this way from experience.

_____ b) I feel this way although I haven't had direct experience.

_____ c) I definitely do not feel this way from experience.

_____ d) I do not feel this way although I haven't had direct experience.

_____ e) I don't know.

ANOMIA (*a*), AUTHORITARIANISM (*f*), AND ANTI-MINORITIES (*m*) SCALES

The following are a series of questions concerning a number of important social and personal matters. The best answer to each statement below is *your personal opinion.* We have tried to cover many different points of view; you may find yourself agreeing strongly with some of the statements, disagreeing just as strongly with others. Whether you disagree or agree with any statement, you can be sure that many other people feel the same as you do.

1(*f*). The most important thing to teach children is absolute obedience to their parents. Agree _____. Disagree _____.

2(*m*). It is better for a child if he keeps to playmates of the same religious background as his own. Agree _____. Disagree _____.

3(*a*). There's little use in writing or complaining to public leaders because often they aren't really interested in the problems and feelings of the average man. Agree _____. Disagree _____.

4(*f*). Any good leader should be strict with people under him in order to gain their respect. Agree _____. Disagree _____.

5(*m*). There are a good many people in the U.S. who ought to go back to the countries they came from. Agree _____. Disagree _____.

6(*a*). Nowadays a person has to live pretty much for today and let tomorrow take care of itself. Agree _____. Disagree _____.

* Asked only of *policemen.*

7(*f*). There are two kinds of people in the world: the weak and the strong. Agree _____. Disagree _____.

8(*m*). It would be better all around if white children had swimming pools for themselves. Agree _____. Disagree _____.

9(*a*). In spite of what some people say, the lot of the average man is getting worse, not better. Agree _____. Disagree _____.

10(*f*). Prison is too good for sex criminals. They should be publicly whipped or worse. Agree _____. Disagree _____.

11(*m*). Refugees from Nazi Germany should have been kept out of the United States and sent to Israel instead. Agree _____. Disagree _____.

12(*a*). It's hardly fair to bring children into the world with the way things look for the future. Agree _____. Disagree _____.

13(*f*). No decent man can respect a woman who has had sex relations before marriage. Agree _____. Disagree _____.

14(*m*). In the South they have had pretty much the right slant about having separate colleges for white students. Agree _____. Disagree _____.

15(*a*). These days a person doesn't really know whom he can count on. Agree _____. Disagree _____.

THE PRESTIGE RATINGS SCALES

1. How would you picture the job of state policeman in your community at the present time? (Make a check in the spaces to indicate your answer.)

   a) With respect to the general prestige of the position:

   |_____|_____|_____|_____|_____|_____|

   | Very High | Fairly | Moderately | Quite Low |
   | in Prestige | High | Low | in Prestige |

   b) With respect to the degree of influence policemen have in community affairs:

   |_____|_____|_____|_____|_____|_____|

Very High	Fairly	Moderately	Quite Low
Degree of	High	Low	Degree of
Influence			Influence

   c) With respect to the social position of policemen in the community:

   |_____|_____|_____|_____|_____|_____|

Very High	Fairly	Moderately	Quite Low
Social	High	Low	Social
Position			Position

   d) With respect to the economic position of policemen in the community:

   |_____|_____|_____|_____|_____|_____|

Very High	Fairly	Moderately	Quite Low
Economic	High	Low	Economic
Position			Position

2. From an economic standpoint, what per cent of income earners in the community would you estimate is doing better than the average policeman? ____%.

EXPERIENCE–CHANGE–ASPIRATIONS SERIES

[Administered to Recruits and Policemen only]

1. As compared with your feelings when you first started out in the department, what is your present feeling about your job? (Check one in each column.)

At First	Today
a) ____ Very enthusiastic.	a) ____ Much more enthusiastic.
b) ____ Quite enthusiastic.	b) ____ Somewhat more enthusiastic.
c) ____ Fairly enthusiastic.	c) ____ About the same.
d) ____ Not particularly enthusiastic.	d) ____ Somewhat less enthusiastic.
e) ____ Not at all enthusiastic.	e) ____ Much less enthusiastic.
f) ____ Not sure.	f) ____ Not sure.

2. Who *helped* you most in learning and adjusting to your work when you first started out? (Mark two in order of importance: Place the number "1" next to the most important; the number "2" next to the second most important.)

a) ____ The regular policemen with whom I have been teamed.

b) ____ My own efforts (reading, studying, keeping alert, etc.).

c) ____ Post personnel in general.

d) ____ One particular policeman (if not the one described in "a").

e) ____ The post commander.

f) ____ My wife.

g) ____ Other relative or friend (specify _____).

h) ____ No one in particular.

3. Who has *hindered* you most in learning and adjusting to your work when you first started out? (Mark two in order of importance: Place the number "1" next to the most important; the number "2" next to the second most important.)

a) ____ The regular policemen with whom I have been teamed.

b) ____ Post personnel in general.

c) ____ One particular policeman (if not described in "a").

d) ____ The post commander.

e) ____ My wife.

f) ____ Other relative or friend (specify _____).

g) ____ No one in particular.

4. What *important* problems or procedures have you encountered which were *omitted* in your initial training?

5. What materials or procedures which were covered in the initial training period have turned out to be *inadequate* or *contradicted* by your experiences?

6. What other things have happened to you on the job which you had *not expected*?

7. Would you like to be at some post other than the one to which you are now assigned?
   a) ____ Yes.
   b) ____ No.
   c) ____ Don't know.
   d) ____ It makes no difference.

8. What are the main reasons for your answer above?

9. The various specialities within the department correspond to different interests and talents among personnel: Safety and Traffic, Fire Marshall, Detective, Special Investigation, Security Investigation, Crime Lab, Records and Statistics, Personnel, Training, Operations and Communications.
   a) Which of these would you *least* like to enter? _____
   _____
   b) Which of these would you *most* like to enter? _____
   _____

10. Do you think there is too much regulation of the private lives of policemen by the department?
    a) ____ Yes.
    b) ____ No.
    c) ____ Undecided.

11. What are the main reasons for your answer above?

12. One can't help being annoyed occasionally by the behavior of fellow policemen. As you think back, what things have you found particularly annoying?

13. In your contacts with the public, what sorts of things have you found particularly annoying?

14. What do you like or dislike about the way in which policemen are pictured in radio, TV, movies, books, etc.?

15. What are the occupations of your three closest friends? (Do not list their names, just their occupation.)

    1. _____
    2. _____
    3. _____

16. Father's occupation. (If deceased, list what his major occupation was before
    he died.) _____

The Role Conflict Study Materials

THE ROLE CONFLICT INTERVIEW SCHEDULE

I. Here are three attitudes which various groups and persons might take about
    you as a policeman:
    A) Expect me to concern myself mainly with safety and traffic work.
    B) Expect me to concern myself mainly with complaint and criminal investiga-
       tion.
    C) Expect me to spend equal time on both.
    For each group or person listed below, please check the lines which most
    nearly represent what they think you should do about this.

	A	B	C	Lr	La	Oi	Os
1. Headquarters command	—	—	—	—	—	—	—
2. District command	—	—	—	—	—	—	—
3. Post commander	—	—	—	—	—	—	—
4. Asst. post commanders	—	—	—	—	—	—	—
5. Policemen	—	—	—	—	—	—	—
6. My wife-family	—	—	—	—	—	—	—
7. Personal friends	—	—	—	—	—	—	—
8. Service clubs	—	—	—	—	—	—	—
9. Fraternal organizations	—	—	—	—	—	—	—
10. The press	—	—	—	—	—	—	—
11. Local and county police	—	—	—	—	—	—	—
12. Other	—	—	—	—	—	—	—
	—	—	—	—	—	—	—

(A) To what extent would (or does) a situation like this bother you?
    1. ____ Very much.   2. ____ To some degree.
    3. ____ Not at all.   4. ____ Don't know: (why)

(R) What would or do you do in such situations?

II. Here are three attitudes which various groups and persons might take about you as a policeman:
  A) Expect me to be a policeman twenty-four hours a day.
  B) Expect me to leave my job behind when I am off duty.
  C) Have no expectations of me on this matter.
  For each group or person listed below, please check the lines which most nearly represent what they think you should do about this.

	A	B	C	Lr	La	Oi	Os
1. Headquarters command	——	——	——	——	——	——	——
2. District command	——	——	——	——	——	——	——
3. Post commander	——	——	——	——	——	——	——
4. Asst. post commanders	——	——	——	——	——	——	——
5. Policemen	——	——	——	——	——	——	——
6. My wife-family	——	——	——	——	——	——	——
7. Personal friends	——	——	——	——	——	——	——
8. Service clubs	——	——	——	——	——	——	——
9. Fraternal organizations	——	——	——	——	——	——	——
10. The press	——	——	——	——	——	——	——
11. Local and county police	——	——	——	——	——	——	——
12. Other	——	——	——	——	——	——	——
	——	——	——	——	——	——	——

(A) To what extent would (or does) a situation like this bother you?
  1. —— Very much.　　　　　　　　2. —— To some degree.
  3. —— Not at all.　　　　　　　　4. —— Don't know: (why)

(R) What would or do you do in such situations?

III. Here are three attitudes which various groups and persons might take about you as a policeman:
  A) Expect me to report any policeman whom I thought was not properly performing his police duties.
  B) Expect me to keep quiet about this matter.
  C) Have no expectations of me on this matter.
  For each group or person listed below, please check the lines which most nearly represent what they think you should do about this.

	A	B	C	Lr	La	Oi	Os
1. Headquarters command	—	—	—	—	—	—	—
2. District command	—	—	—	—	—	—	—
3. Post commander	—	—	—	—	—	—	—
4. Asst. post commanders	—	—	—	—	—	—	—
5. Policemen	—	—	—	—	—	—	—
6. My wife-family	—	—	—	—	—	—	—
7. Personal friends	—	—	—	—	—	—	—
8. Service clubs	—	—	—	—	—	—	—
9. Fraternal organizations	—	—	—	—	—	—	—
10. The press	—	—	—	—	—	—	—
11. Local and county police	—	—	—	—	—	—	—
12. Other	—	—	—	—	—	—	—
	—	—	—	—	—	—	—

(A) To what extent would (or does) a situation like this bother you?

1. ___ Very much.   2. ___ To some degree.

3. ___ Not at all.   4. ___ Don't know: (why)

(R) What would or do you do in such situations?

IV. Here are three attitudes which various groups and persons might take about
you as a policeman:

A) Expect me to be a "model citizen," always setting an example for everyone
in the community.

B) Expect me to be a "good citizen," but not any different from anyone else
in the community.

C) Have no expectations of me regarding what sort of citizen I should be.

For each group or person listed below, please check the lines which most
nearly represent what they think you should do about this.

	A	B	C	Lr	La	Oi	Os
1. Headquarters command	—	—	—	—	—	—	—
2. District command	—	—	—	—	—	—	—
3. Post commander	—	—	—	—	—	—	—
4. Asst. post commanders	—	—	—	—	—	—	—
5. Policemen	—	—	—	—	—	—	—
6. My wife-family	—	—	—	—	—	—	—

    7. Personal friends   ___ ___ ___   ___ ___ ___ ___
    8. Service clubs   ___ ___ ___   ___ ___ ___ ___
    9. Fraternal organizations   ___ ___ ___   ___ ___ ___ ___
   10. The press   ___ ___ ___   ___ ___ ___ ___
   11. Local and county police   ___ ___ ___   ___ ___ ___ ___
   12. Other   ___ ___ ___   ___ ___ ___ ___

                          ___ ___ ___   ___ ___ ___ ___

(A) To what extent would (or does) a situation like this bother you?

    1. ___ Very much.   2. ___ To some degree.

    3. ___ Not at all.   4. ___ Don't know: (why)

(R) What would or do you do in such situations?

V. Here are three attitudes which various groups and persons might take about you as a policeman:

    A) Expect me to follow the rules and regulations to the letter.

    B) Expect me to overlook the rules and regulations occasionally.

    C) Have no expectations of me on this matter.

    For each group or person listed below, please check the lines which most nearly represent what they think you should do about this.

	A	B	C	Lr	La	Oi	Os
1. Headquarters command	___	___	___	___	___	___	___
2. District command	___	___	___	___	___	___	___
3. Post commander	___	___	___	___	___	___	___
4. Asst. post commanders	___	___	___	___	___	___	___
5. Policemen	___	___	___	___	___	___	___
6. My wife-family	___	___	___	___	___	___	___
7. Personal friends	___	___	___	___	___	___	___
8. Service clubs	___	___	___	___	___	___	___
9. Fraternal organizations	___	___	___	___	___	___	___
10. The press	___	___	___	___	___	___	___
11. Local and county police	___	___	___	___	___	___	___
12. Other	___	___	___	___	___	___	___
	___	___	___	___	___	___	___

(A) To what extent would (or does) a situation like this bother you?

    1. _____ Very much.   2. _____ To some degree.

    3. _____ Not at all.   4. _____ Don't know: (why)

(R) What would or do you do in such situations?

GUIDE FOR ROLE CONFLICT INTERVIEW SCHEDULE

· Respondent is to be given the schedule, instructed to read Question I, then told to check the appropriate lines (1–12) in the appropriate columns (A–B–C).

· Interviewer is to probe for other possible audiences (line 12), and to instruct respondent to write these in on the schedule.

· If in any question (I–V) respondent places all of his checks in a *single* column, interviewer is to skip that question and go on to the next.

Question I is different from all others, being the only one where three alternatives are presented. In Question I, then, if respondent checks at least one line in more than one column, interviewer is to continue interviewing on that question.

In Questions II–V, column C is to be ignored by interviewer. Interview is to continue here only if respondent checks at least one line in *both* columns A and B.

· Column Lr: Interviewer is to ask a question of the general form, "Which of these persons do you feel has the right to expect you to do this?" Respondent is then to check those lines where he feels the person involved "has a right" to such an expectation.

· Column La: Respondent is to be asked question of the general form, "Are you accountable to these persons for what you actually do?" and to check only those to whom he holds himself accountable.

· Column Oi: Respondent is to be asked question of the general form, "Would they insist or demand that you do as they expect you to?" and to check only those who would insist that he conform to their expectations.

· Column Os: Interviewer is to ask questions of the general form, "What would they do if you didn't do as they expect?" so as to elicit whether or not respondent anticipated being negatively sanctioned. Interviewer is to indicate in space provided the respondent's answer.

· In Questions A and R, interviewer is to probe as to ascertain the extent to which the respondent is bothered by such a situation (degree of ambivalence) and the manner in which respondent resolves or would resolve such a situation; i.e., what he would or does do in that situation.

JUDGE'S INSTRUCTIONS FOR CONFLICT RESOLUTIONS CODE

Familiarize yourself with the role conflict situations and this set of instructions. To acquaint yourself with the resolutions of the conflict situations, and to better prepare yourself for the task at hand, read over all of the response cards at least once before attempting to code them. Code each situation separately.

Please note that the categories are not all applicable to every situation, and that every response is to be placed in one of the five categories.

Category	Description
A, B, or C	Responses are to be adjudged A, B, or in the case of situation one, C, if the respondent indicates: 1) That he does, or would do A, B, or C; OR, in the *absence* of such a statement, 2) that he attempts to do, or prefers to do A, B, or C.
X—(expedient)	Responses are to be adjudged X if the respondent indicates that what he does or would do is dependent upon situational requirements, or aspects of the situation as person, time, place, personal consequences, or group consequences, or his judgment of the situation. (This category is not to be used for situation five.)
?	Uncertain, can't decide, insufficient data.

ABRIDGED FORM FOR "POLICEMEN" AND RECRUITS

The following four items represent expectations which various groups and persons may have about *policemen*. For *each* item check the attitude which *most nearly* represents the one held. Be sure to make a check for *every* group and person listed.

ITEM I

A. Expect a *policeman* to concern himself mainly with safety and traffic work.
B. Expect a *policeman* to concern himself mainly with complaint and criminal investigation.
C. Expect a *policeman* to spend equal time on both.

	A	B	C
Headquarters command	——	——	——
Post commander	——	——	——
Policemen at my post	——	——	——
The public	——	——	——

ITEM II

A. Expect a *policeman* to be a *policeman* twenty-four hours a day.
B. Expect a *policeman* to leave his job behind when off duty.
C. Have no expectations of a *policeman* on this matter.

	A	B	C
Headquarters command	——	——	——
Post commander	——	——	——
Policemen at my post	——	——	——
The public	——	——	——

ITEM III

  A. Expect a *policeman* to report another *policeman* whom he thought was not properly performing his police duties.

  B. Expect a *policeman* to keep quiet about such matters.

  C. Have no expectations of a *policeman* about such matters.

	A	B	C
Headquarters command	—	—	—
Post commander	—	—	—
Policemen at my post	—	—	—
The public	—	—	—

ITEM IV

  A. Expect a *policeman* to be a "model citizen," always setting an example for everyone in the community.

  B. Expect a *policeman* to be a "good citizen" but not any different from anyone else in the community.

  C. Have no expectations of a *policeman* regarding what sort of citizen he should be.

	A	B	C
Headquarters command	—	—	—
Post commander	—	—	—
Policemen at my post	—	—	—
The public	—	—	—

ABRIDGED FORM FOR COMMAND STAFF

Please check one:

  ___ Captain   ___ Sergeant

  ___ Lieutenant   ___ Corporal

The following four items represent expectations which one may have about policemen. For *each* item check the attitude which *most nearly* represents the one *you* hold. Be sure to make a check for *every* item.

ITEM I

___ A. Expect a *policeman* to concern himself mainly with safety and traffic work.

___ B. Expect a *policeman* to concern himself mainly with complaint and criminal investigation.

___ C. Expect a *policeman* to spend equal time on both.

ITEM II

___ A. Expect a *policeman* to be a *policeman* twenty-four hours a day.

___ B. Expect a *policeman* to leave his job behind when off duty.

___ C. Have no expectations of a *policeman* on this matter.

ITEM III

___ A. Expect a *policeman* to report another *policeman* whom he thought was not properly performing his police duties.

___ B. Expect a *policeman* to keep quiet about such matters.

___ C. Have no expectations of a *policeman* about such matters.

ITEM IV

___ A. Expect a *policeman* to be a "model citizen," always setting an example for everyone in the community.

___ B. Expect a *policeman* to be a "good citizen" but not any different from anyone else in the community.

___ C. Have no expectations of a *policeman* regarding what sort of citizen he should be.

Appendix 2

The Public Image Questionnaire:
Sample and Response Distributions (Per Cent)

1. Do you personally know any policemen, officers, or detectives in the Central State Police Department?
   0—No Answer
   1—Yes 28.0
   2—No 72.0

2. Have the State Police ever performed any personal services for you?
   0—No answer
   1—Yes 23.6
   2—No 76.4

3. Compared with other kinds of jobs, how do you rate the job of State Policeman in terms of its importance to society?
   0—No answer 1.1
   1—Much more important than most jobs 29.5
   2—Somewhat more important than most jobs 46.5
   3—About as important as most jobs 22.5
   4—Somewhat less important than most jobs 0.4
   5—Much less important than most jobs 0.0

4. How would you picture State Policemen in your community with respect to their social standing?
   0—No answer 0.4
   1—Very high in prestige 15.6
   2—Quite high 18.2
   3—Fairly high 28.7
   4—Average 35.6
   5—Fairly low 1.5
   6—Quite low 0.0
   7—Very low in prestige 0.0

5. How do you estimate the economic position of State Policemen in your community?
   0—No answer 3.6

1—Very high in economic position 3.6
2—Quite high 6.5
3—Fairly high 14.2
4—Average 62.9
5—Fairly low 8.0
6—Quite low 0.7
7—Very low in economic position 0.4

6. In terms of all-around desirability (income, hours, type of work, etc.), how does the job of State Policeman compare with your own job? (If you are not working, how does it compare with your former job; if you are a housewife, how does it compare with your husband's job; if you are still in school, how does it compare with the job you expect to hold?)
0—No answer 2.2
1—Much more desirable 8.7
2—Somewhat more desirable 13.8
3—About equal 26.9
4—Somewhat less desirable 38.2
5—Much less desirable 10.2

What are the main reasons for your choice?
Less Desirable (4 or 5) (N = 133):
0—No answer 6.0
1—Hours (irregular, long, changing, on-call) 18.0
2—Risk, danger, excitement 19.5
3—Salary 19.5
4—Low status, status-demeaning imputations 3.8
5—Low or negative interest in police work 9.0
6—Too much regimentation and responsibility 3.0
7—Working conditions and job characteristics 15.0
8—Unclassifiable 6.0

Equal (3) (N = 74):
0—No answer 14.9
1—Same hours 17.6
2—Same salary 6.8
3—Same interest, working conditions, type of job . . .   9.5
4—More pay 0.0
5—More interesting or desirable 0.0
6—Poorer pay 0.0
7—Poorer hours 1.4
8—Don't know, uncertain 4.1
9—All other reasons 23.0
x—Positive and negative reasons balanced 23.0

More Desirable (1 or 2) (N = 62):
0—No answer 8.1
1—Status, prestige, and respect 16.1

2—Value to society 21.0
3—Income and security 17.7
4—Personally satisfying type of work 11.3
5—Desirable working conditions 16.1
6—All other reasons not classifiable above 9.7

7. How would you rate the Central State Police Department?
0—No answer 0.7
1—One of the best in the country 37.5
2—Better than average 35.3
3—About average 16.0
4—Below standard 0.4
5—Poor 0.4
6—Don't know 9.8

8. Which of the following characteristics best describe State Policemen in their
contact with the public? (Mark "1," "2," etc., in *order of importance*.
Mark *only* those which you feel apply.) (Number of Nominations = 711)
0—No answer 0.1
1—Overbearing 1.4
2—Friendly 28.6
3—Tense 1.0
4—Suspicious 2.0
5—Helpful 29.3
6—Cold and distant 2.2
7—Courteous 29.4
8—Cocky 1.8
9—Don't know 4.2

9. What personal qualities do you think it most important for a State Policeman
to have? (List in order of importance.)
0—No answer 1.7
1—Intelligence, judgment, common sense, education . . .   9.7
2—Courteous, helpful, friendly, gets along well with others,
easy going, cheerful, sense of humor, understanding,
kind, patient, considerate, personality 38.8
3—Physically fit, strong, courageous, tough, appearance, neat-
ness 10.1
4—Impartiality, objectivity, fairness, honesty, integrity,
veracity 16.9
5—Ability, competence, efficiency, conscientious, hard-work-
ing, ambitious, dependable, reliable, stable, initiative,
resourcefulness, adaptability, alertness 10.3
6—Knowledge of work, departmental procedures, and law;
communication and public relations skills; willingness
and desire to be a policeman, loyalty 3.2

7—Self-controlled, self-directed, disciplined, able to carry out
     orders, strict, firm, reputation, morality, and character   8.2

8—Unclassified 1.1

10. The Central State Police dress:

   0—No answer 0.0

   1—Exceptionally well 51.3

   2—Well 47.3

   3—Fairly well 1.5

   4—Sloppily 0.0

11. Most State Policemen are:

   0—No answer 2.2

   1—Unquestionably honest 37.8

   2—Usually honest 58.5

   3—Often dishonest 1.1

   4—Usually dishonest 0.4

12. Policemen are selected chiefly on the basis of:

   0—No answer 4.7

   1—Physical qualities and appearance 11.3

   2—Written tests and personal background information . . 63.9

   3—Political considerations and outside influence 1.5

   4—Not having been successful in other types of jobs . . . 0.4

   5—*1* and *2* checked together 18.2

13. In general, Policemen:

   0—No answer 2.5

   1—Respect the constitutional rights of suspected law violators 87.3

   2—Use whatever methods are found convenient 8.0

   3—Are often without conscience and brutal in performing
     their duties 2.2

14. In dealing with minority groups, Policemen are:

   0—No answer 3.6

   1—Usually fair 81.8

   2—Sometimes unfriendly 10.9

   3—Often unfriendly 1.8

   4—Definitely prejudiced and antagonistic 1.8

14*a*. In dealing with traffic violators, Policemen:

   0—No answer 5.1

   1—Give more favorable treatment to people driving new
     expensive cars 8.7

   2—Give more favorable treatment to people driving older cars 1.1

   3—Give the same treatment to all classes of drivers . . . 85.1

14*b*. In dealing with traffic violators, Policemen:

   0—No answer 4.0

   1—Are more lenient with men 2.9

2—Are more lenient with women 15.6
3—Treat everyone about the same 77.5

15. In terms of arresting procedures, Policemen:
    0—No answer 6.9
    1—Rarely arrest innocent persons 43.3
    2—Sometimes arrest innocent persons 38.5
    3—Frequently arrest innocent persons 1.1
    4—Are indifferent about whether persons arrested are innocent
        or not 10.2

16. Administrators and supervising officers of the State Police Department are
    generally:
    0—No answer 1.5
    1—Highly competent and well trained 61.5
    2—Of average ability and competence 17.5
    3—Incompetent and untrained 0.4
    4—Don't know 19.3

17. In their work, state, local and county police:
    0—No answer 0.7
    1—Usually cooperate 76.7
    2—Occasionally cooperate 6.5
    3—Seldom cooperate 0.7
    4—Can't get along together 0.0
    5—Don't know 15.3

18. As you see it, which of the following is the *main* job of a State Policeman?
    (List one only.)*
    0—No answer 0.0
    1—Protection of persons and property from criminal activity   30.5
    2—Performing services (locating persons, rendering assistance
        in emergencies, preventive work with youth and civic
        groups, etc.) 11.3
    3—Patrolling highways and enforcing traffic laws 44.7
    4—*1* and *2** 1.5
    5—*1* and *3** 4.4
    6—*2* and *3** 1.1
    7—*1, 2,* and *3** 5.5
    8—Other 1.1

19. The following are three characteristics of Policemen's work. From *each* group
    select the item which is closest to your opinion.
    A. Time required:
       0—No answer 0.4
       1—Exceptionally long hours 4.4

* Although the original question calls for selecting only one of the first three choices,
many respondents insisted upon the modifications as noted.

2—Quite long hours 37.8
3—Average hours 45.1
4—Less hours than most jobs 0.4
5—Don't know 12.0

B. Effort required:
0—No answer 0.7
1—Strenuous and demanding 20.7
2—Average physical and mental demands 63.3
3—Relatively easy 8.4
4—Don't know 6.9

C. Exposure:
0—No answer 0.7
1—Often dangerous and risky 30.9
2—Occasionally dangerous and risky 60.0
3—Not particularly dangerous 4.0
4—Rarely dangerous or risky 1.5
5—Don't know 2.9

20. Do you think Policemen ought to patrol in unmarked cars?
0—No answer 0.0
1—No opinion 8.0
2—Yes 41.1
3—No 50.9

If yes (2) ($N = 113$):
0—No reasons stated 1.8
1—More effective means of enforcement (including, e.g.,
   people on the watch for a marked car; catches the
   habitual violator; a necessary means for protection and
   prevention; any and all effective measures should be
   used). 68.1
2—Deterrent value (places additional pressure on public;
   makes public more alert and watchful) 22.1
3—To a limited degree (daytime only; in high accident speed
   areas; in small numbers). 0.0
4—Other 8.0

If no (3) ($N = 140$):
0—No reasons stated 13.6
1—Dishonest, underhanded, sneaky, gestapo-like, etc. . . 22.9
2—Lacks deterrent value 20.7
3—Creates ill will and is unacceptable to the public . . . 2.1
4—Not identifiable to those seeking police assistance . . . 11.4
5—Dangerous to use—possibility of misrepresentation or
   misidentification 21.4
6—Other 7.9

21. Do you think Policemen should *strictly* enforce speed limits as posted?

    0—No answer 0.7

    1—No opinion 1.5

    2—Yes 37.5

    3—No 60.4

If yes, then ($N = 105$):

    0—No answer 15.2

    1—For the reduction of accidents and the protection and
        safety of other drivers 32.4

    2—Speed limits and zones are reasonable and realistic . .   19.0

    3—For uniform enforcement (all laws should be enforced—it
        is the policeman's job) 26.7

    4—Other explanations 6.7

If no, then what leeway ($N = 166$):

    0—Leeway, but not specified 13.3

    1—Under 5 mph 5.4

    2—5 mph 44.6

    3—5 to 10 mph 21.7

    4—10 mph 13.3

    5—Over 10 mph 1.8

Why? ($N = 161$):

    1—Speedometer error and variation *and* difficulty of accurate
        checking and pacing 18.0

    2—Road and traffic conditions (e.g., road surface width, time
        of day, weather, traffic flow, posted limits, accident rate
        on road, etc.) 38.5

    3—Ease of unintentional transgression 20.5

    4—Conditional necessity (e.g., when passing, to avoid
        accidents, slowing without braking, etc.) 10.6

    5—Unrealistic and outdated speed limits and zones . . .   6.2

    6—Rigid enforcement is harassing, persecutory, unfair,
        impossible, etc. 0.6

    7—Departmental explanations: department policy, tickets
        used for mobility purposes, etc. 0.0

    8—All other explanations 5.6

22. How many times in the last *five* years have you been stopped in your car by
Central State Police? Circle number of times.

    0—Zero, none 31.6

    1—Once 33.1

    2—Twice 17.5

    3—3 times 10.2

    4—4 times 2.9

    5—5 times 1.5

    6—6 times 0.4

7—7 times 0.7
8—8 times 0.7
9—9 times 0.0
x—More than nine times 1.5
y—No answer 0.0

a. For what reasons were you stopped? (Write in number or closest estimate in each category which applies to you.)

Traffic violation or traffic accident:

o—No answer 37.8
1—Once 37.8
2—Twice 16.0
3—3 times 4.4
4—4 times 1.1
5—5 times 0.4
6—6 times 1.1
7—7 times 0.4
8—8 times 0.4
9—9 times 0.7

Search or manhunt:

o—No answer or inapplicable 86.5
1—Once 8.0
2—Twice 0.0
3—3 times 4.7
4—4 times 0.4
5—5 times 0.4

Give information:

o—No answer or inapplicable 94.2
1—Once 3.6
2—Twice 1.5
3—3 times 0.4
4—4 times 0.4

Other:

o—No answer or inapplicable 90.0
1—Once 6.9
2—Twice 1.5
3—3 times 0.4
4—4 times 0.0
5—5 times 0.0
6—6 times 0.4

In terms of your *most recent* ticket:

b. List the *specific* traffic violation (speeding, crossing yellow line, etc.) for which you received the ticket ($N = 150$).

oo—No answer 10.0
o1—Don't know 0.0

02—Speeding—excessive speed 43.3
03—Improper turns 1.3
04—Improper passing 8.0
05—Improper use of lanes 3.3
06—Defective equipment: brakes or lights 2.0
07—Defective muffler—excessive noise 3.3
08—Disregarded stop-and-go light 2.7
09—Disregarded stop sign or signal 8.7
10—Reckless driving 2.0
11—Drunk driving, drinking on the highway 0.0
12—Unsafe starting 1.3
13—Driving without lights 0.0
14—Violation of financial responsibility laws 0.0
15—Operators license: expired, not on person, has none . . 4.0
16—Violator of operator license restrictions 0.0
17—Plates: no plates, improper plates 1.3
18—Allowed minors to drive 0.7
19—Parking on highway 0.7
20—All other motor vehicle offenses 4.7
21—All nontraffic offenses erroneously mentioned . . . 2.7

c. Do you feel the ticket was justified? ($N = 150$)
   0—No answer 7.3
   1—Yes 56.7
   2—No 31.3
   y—Denied receiving ticket 4.7

d. How would you describe the behavior of the policeman who gave you the ticket? (Select *one*.) ($N = 144$)
   0—No answer 5.6
   1—Impersonal 22.2
   2—Friendly 54.9
   3—Antagonistic 5.6
   4—Suspicious 0.7
   5—Other 11.1

e. What was your reaction to the penalty (fine, license revocation, etc.) imposed by the court? ($N = 144$)
   0—No answer 12.5
   1—Too lenient 0.0
   2—Fair and justifiable 55.6
   3—Too severe 30.6
   4—Pending 1.4

23. During the past five years have you ever had contact with the Central State Police during the course of an investigation? (As one who might have been involved, a witness, etc.)
   0—No answer 2.5

1—Yes 7.3
2—No 90.2

24. What do you like or dislike about the way in which policemen are pictured in radio, TV, movies, books, etc.?

0—No answer 26.9
1—Like 24.7
2—Dislike 35.6
3—Both like and dislike 5.1
4—Unable to infer from answer given 7.6

Favorable comments ($N = 79$):

1—Good and fair portrayal 34.2
2—Of educational value to children 8.9
3—Ability—get their man 12.7
4—Upholds truth—reflects ideals 13.9
5—Like a specific program, book, etc. 2.5
6—All other favorable comments which are relevant and clear 10.1
7—Unclassifiable, nothing specific 13.9
8—No answer 3.8

Unfavorable comments ($N = 112$):

1—Presents an *exaggerated positive image* of the police: glorified, overrated, superhuman, too perfect, etc. . . 31.3
2—Presents an *exaggerated negative image* of the police: brutal, cocky, illiterate, stupid, musclemen, crooked, etc. . . 12.5
3—Presents both extremes: exaggerated positive image and exaggerated negative image 6.3
4—Generalized assertion that the police are depicted in an untrue manner 20.5
5—Speedy success—doesn't show tedium and hard work . 5.4
6—Specific program or character named 0.9
7—Sensational and over-dramatic 8.0
8—All other unfavorable comments which are relevant and clear 9.8
9—Unclassifiable 4.5
x—No answer 0.9

Information about respondent:—

Sex:
0—No answer 1.1
1—Male 69.5
2—Female 29.5

Age:
0—No answer, not ascertained 1.8
1—Under 21 . . . . 8.4

2—21–25 . . . . 13.1
3—26–29 . . . . 11.3
4—30–34 . . . . 9.8
5—35–39 . . . . 13.8
6—40–44 . . . . 8.4
7—45–49 . . . . 8.0
8—50–54 . . . . 6.9
9—55–59 . . . . 9.5
x—60–64 . . . . 2.9
y—65 and over 6.2

Marital status:
0—No answer 2.5
1—Married 72.0
2—Single 16.4
3—Divorced 2.5
4—Separated 1.1
5—Widowed 5.5

Education:
0—No answer, not ascertained 2.9
1—No elementary school 0.4
2—Some elementary school 5.8
3—Graduated elementary school 9.1
4—Some high school 14.9
5—Graduated high school 34.2
6—Some college 14.9
7—Graduated college 9.5
8—Some graduate training 8.4

Race:
0—No answer, not ascertained 2.9
1—White 84.7
2—Negro 9.1
3—Mexican 3.3

Occupation:
0—No answer, not ascertained 6.5
1—Professionals and executives 8.4
2—Middle management: other managers and officials . . 4.4
3—Self-employed: small business 5.5
4—Other white-collar: sales, clerical, technical . . . 25.1
5—First-line supervisors and skilled 14.2
6—Semi-skilled 10.2
7—Unskilled 13.8
8—Police and police-related occupations 2.9
9—Student 9.1

Contact Index :

1—No contact 32.4
2—Personal contact 9.1
3—Some negative contact 26.9
4—Considerable negative contact 15.6
5—Miscellaneous other contacts 16.0

RANDOM AND VIOLATOR SAMPLE CHARACTERISTICS

TABLE AP2–A
RANDOM AND VIOLATORS' SAMPLE CHARACTERISTICS

Age	Random Sample f	Random Sample %	Violators' Sample f	Violators' Sample %
Age				
Under 21	1	0.8	22	14.7
21–29	20	16.0	47	31.3
30–44	39	31.2	49	32.7
45–54	26	20.8	15	10.0
55–64	25	20.0	19	6.0
Over 65	14	11.2	3	2.0
N.A.	0	—	5	3.3
Sex				
Male	68	54.4	123	82.0
Female	57	45.6	24	16.0
N.A.	0	—	3	2.0
Marital Status				
Married	97	77.6	101	67.3
Single	7	5.6	38	25.3
Divorced, separated	7	5.6	3	2.0
Widowed	14	11.2	1	0.7
N.A.	0	—	7	4.7
Education				
Elementary School				
Not complete	16	12.8	1	0.7
Complete	11	8.8	14	9.3
High School				
Not complete	14	11.2	27	18.0
Complete	50	40.0	44	29.3
College				
Not complete	9	7.2	32	21.3
Complete	12	9.6	14	9.3
Post graduate	10	8.0	13	8.7
N.A.	3	2.4	5	3.3
Occupation				
Professionals, executives	7	5.6	16	10.7
Middle management	8	6.4	4	2.7
Self-employed	7	5.6	8	5.3
White collar	33	26.4	36	24.0
Skilled and first-line supervisors .	20	16.0	19	12.7
Semi-skilled	15	12.0	13	8.7
Unskilled	24	19.2	14	9.3

TABLE AP2–A (*cont.*)
RANDOM AND VIOLATORS' SAMPLE CHARACTERISTICS

	Random Sample		Violators' Sample	
	f	%	*f*	%
Police, police-related	5	4.0	3	2.0
Students	2	1.6	23	15.3
N.A.	4	3.2	14	9.3
Minority Status				
White	96	76.8	137	91.3
Non-white	29	23.2	5	3.3
N.A.	0	—	8	5.3

The Effects of Contact:
Some Additional and Selected Characteristics

TABLE AP2–B
COMPARISON OF SAMPLES BY CONTACT WITH CENTRAL STATE
POLICE IN THE LAST FIVE YEARS

Number of Contacts	Random Sample		Violators' Sample	
	f	%	*f*	%
None . .	80	64.0	7	4.7*
1 . . .	29	23.2	62	41.3
2 . . .	7	5.6	41	27.3
3 . . .	5	4.0	23	15.3
4 . . .	2	1.6	6	4.0
5 . . .	1	0.8	3	2.0
6 . . .	1	0.8	0	—
7 . . .	0	—	2	1.3
8 . . .	0	—	2	1.3
9 . . .	0	—	0	—
Above 9 . .	0	—	4	2.7

* We may assume that these respondents did not know that they were stopped by the State Police, misunderstood our question, or were lying.

TABLE AP2–C
CONTACT WITH THE STATE POLICE, BY OCCUPATION

	Number of Contacts in Last 5 Years					
	0		1		2 and Over	
	f	%	*f*	%	*f*	%
Professional, managerial, self-employed	13	26.0	16	32.0	21	42.0
Other white-collar	23	33.3	20	29.0	26	27.7
Manual workers	43	41.0	36	34.3	26	24.8

NOTE.—$\chi^2 = 6.26$; $df = 4$; $p = .10$.

TABLE AP2–D

CONTACT WITH THE STATE POLICE, BY EDUCATION

| | Number Responding by Type of Contact | | | |
	None (n = 89)	Personal (n = 25)	Some Negative (n = 74)	Considerable Negative (n = 43)
Grade school . .	24	1	9	5
Some high school .	11	4	11	7
High school graduate	35	7	21	15
Some college . .	5	6	16	7
College graduate .	12	7	13	8

NOTE.—χ^2 = 19.70; df = 4; p < .01 (contact–no contact by education).

TABLE AP2–E

CONTACT WITH THE STATE POLICE, BY SEX

| | Male | | Female | |
Contact Type	f	%	f	%
No contact	42	27.5	47	62.7
Personal contact . . .	18	11.8	7	9.3
Some negative . . .	53	34.6	18	24.0
Considerable negative .	40	26.1	3	4.0

NOTE.—χ^2 = 31.0; df = 3; p < .001.

TABLE AP2–F

CONTACT WITH THE STATE POLICE, BY AGE

| | Age | | | | | |
Number of Contacts	Under 21 (n = 23)	21–29 (n = 67)	30–44 (n = 88)	45–54 (n = 41)	55–64 (n = 34)	Over 65 (n = 17)
	Per Cent Reporting					
0 . .	4.3	19.4	28.4	41.5	52.9	76.5
1 . .	47.8	25.4	34.1	39.0	29.4	17.6
Over 2 .	47.8	55.2	37.5	19.5	17.6	5.9

NOTE.—χ^2 (H-test) = 0.12; n.s.

TABLE AP2–G

CONTACT WITH THE STATE POLICE, BY MINORITY STATUS

| | Number of Contacts in Last 5 Years | | | | | |
| | 0 | | 1 | | 2 and Over | |
	f	%	f	%	f	%
White . .	68	29.2	75	32.2	90	38.6
Non-white .	19	55.9	10	29.4	5	14.7

NOTE.—χ^2 = 11.31; p < .01; df = 2.

TABLE AP2–H
DO YOU THINK "POLICEMEN" SHOULD STRICTLY ENFORCE SPEED LIMITS AS POSTED?

	Per Cent Responding by Type of Contact			
	None (n = 89)	Personal (n = 25)	Some Negative (n = 74)	Considerable Negative (n = 43)
Yes	58.4	24.0	27.0	23.3
No	40.4	76.0	71.6	69.8
No opinion	1.1	—	1.4	7.0

NOTE.—χ^2 = 23.25; p < .001 (Yes–No × Contact–No contact).

TABLE AP2–I
DO YOU THINK "POLICEMEN" OUGHT TO PATROL IN UNMARKED CARS?

	Per Cent Responding by Type of Contact			
	None (n = 89)	Personal (n = 25)	Some Negative (n = 74)	Considerable Negative (n = 43)
Yes	51.7	52.0	32.4	30.2
No	37.1	36.0	62.2	58.1
No opinion	11.2	12.0	5.4	11.6

NOTE.—χ^2 = 6.13; p < .01 (Yes–No × Negative–No negative contact).

TABLE AP2–J
THE EFFECT OF CONTACT ON THE RATING OF THE SOCIAL IMPORTANCE OF THE STATE POLICEMAN'S JOB. (HOW DO YOU RATE THE JOB OF STATE POLICEMAN IN TERMS OF ITS IMPORTANCE TO SOCIETY?)

	Per Cent Responding by Type of Contact			
	None (n = 89)	Personal (n = 25)	Some Negative (n = 74)	Considerable Negative (n = 43)
Much more important . . .	40.4	28.0	21.6	18.6
Somewhat more	38.2	64.0	52.7	55.8
About the same	21.3	8.0	20.3	25.6
Somewhat less	—	—	1.4	—
No answer	—	—	4.1	—

TABLE AP2–K
THE EFFECT OF CONTACT ON ESTIMATES OF THE SOCIAL STANDING OF STATE POLICEMEN IN THE COMMUNITY

	Per Cent Responding by Type of Contact			
	None (n = 89)	Personal (n = 25)	Some Negative (n = 74)	Considerable Negative (n = 43)
Very high social standing . . .	28.1	12.0	9.5	9.3
Quite high	15.7	28.0	17.6	11.6
Fairly high	36.0	20.0	24.3	37.2
Average	19.1	40.0	44.6	39.5
Fairly low social standing . . .	1.1	—	2.7	2.3
No answer	—	—	1.4	—

TABLE AP2-L

THE EFFECT OF CONTACT ON THE ESTIMATES OF THE STATE POLICEMAN'S
ECONOMIC POSITION IN THE COMMUNITY

	Per Cent Responding by Type of Contact			
	None (n = 89)	*Personal* (n = 25)	*Some Negative* (n = 74)	*Considerable Negative* (n = 43)
High economic position . . .	29.2	20.0	23.0	25.6
Average	56.2	76.0	63.5	62.8
Low economic position . . .	11.2	4.0	8.1	9.3
No answer	3.4	—	5.4	2.3

Bibliography

Role Behavior and Role Theory and Related Materials
through 1963

List of Abbreviations

Acta Psychologica	*Acta Psychologica*
Acta Sociologica	*AS*
Administrative Science Quarterly	*ASQ*
Agricultural Experiment Station Research Bulletin	*AESRB*
Alpha Kappa Deltan	*AKD*
AMA Archives of Neurology and Psychiatry	*AMAANP*
American Anthropologist	*AA*
American Catholic Sociological Review	*ACSR*
American Journal of Nursing	*AJN*
American Journal of Orthopsychiatry	*AJO*
American Journal of Psychiatry	*AJ. Psychiatry*
American Journal of Psychology	*AJ. Psychol.*
American Journal of Sociology	*AJS*
American Political Science Review	*APSR*
American Psychologist	*AP*
American Sociological Review	*ASR*
American Teacher	*AT*
Archives of General Psychiatry	*AGP*
Archives of Psychology	*Arch. Psychol.*
Australian Journal of Psychology	*Australian J. Psychol.*
Behavioral Science	*BS*
British Journal of Sociology	*BJS*
California Management Review	*CMR*
Canadian Journal of Economics and Political Science	*CJEPS*
Catholic University of America Studies in Sociology	*CUASS*
Child Development	*CD*
Clearing House	*CH*
College of Education Quarterly	*CEQ*
Econometrica	*E*
Education, Administration and Supervision	*EAS*
Educational and Psychological Measurement	*EPM*
Genetic Psychology Monographs	*GPM*
Group Psychotherapy	*GP*

Harvard Educational Review	*HER*
Human Organization	*HO*
Human Relations	*HR*
Industrial and Labor Relations Review	*ILRR*
International Journal of Social Psychiatry	*IJSP*
Journal of Abnormal and Social Psychology	*JASP*
Journal of Aesthetics and Art Criticism	*JAAC*
Journal of Applied Psychology	*JAP*
Journal of Child Psychiatry	*J. Child Psychiatry*
Journal of Child Psychology	*JCP*
Journal of Clinical Psychology	*J. Clin. Psychol.*
Journal of Conflict Resolution	*J. Conflict Resol.*
Journal of Consulting Psychology	*J. Consult. Psychol.*
Journal of Criminal Law and Criminology	*JCLC*
Journal of Educational Psychology	*J. Educ. Psychol.*
Journal of Educational Sociology	*JES*
Journal of Experimental Education	*JEE*
Journal of Experimental Psychology	*JEP*
Journal of Genetic Psychology	*JGP*
Journal of Health and Human Behavior	*JHHB*
Journal of Medical Education	*JME*
Journal of the National Association of Women Deans and Counselors	*JNAWDC*
Journal of Pediatrics	*J. Pediatrics*
Journal of Personality	*J. Pers.*
Journal of Politics	*J. Politics*
Journal of Psychology	*J. Psychol.*
Journal of Religion	*JR*
Journal of Social Issues	*JSI*
Journal of Social Psychology	*JSP*
Journal of Teacher Education	*JTE*
Journalism Quarterly	*JQ*
Marriage and Family Living	*MFL*
Mental Hygiene	*MH*
Merrill-Palmer Quarterly	*MPQ*
Midwest Sociologist	*MS*
New South	*NS*
Nursing Research	*NR*
Pacific Sociological Review	*PSR*
Pastoral Psychology	*Pastoral Psychol.*
Pedagogical Seminary	*PS*
Personnel	*P*
Personnel Guidance Journal	*PGJ*
Personnel Psychology	*Pers. Psychol.*
Philosophical Review	*Phil. R.*
Philosophy and Phenomenological Research	*PPR*
Phylon	*Phylon*
Proceedings of the Lifemanship Academy	*PLA*
Psychiatry	*Psychiatry*
Psychoanalytic Review	*Psychoanal. R.*
Psychological Bulletin	*PB*
Psychological Monographs	*PM*
Psychological Review	*Psychol. R.*
Public Health Reports	*PHR*

Public Opinion Quarterly	*POQ*
Public Personnel Review	*P. Pers. R.*
Religious Education	*RE*
Research Studies of the State College of Washington	*RSSCW*
Review of Educational Research	*RER*
Revista Internacional de Sociologia	*RIS*
Rural Sociology	*RS*
School and Society	*SS*
School Review	*School R.*
Science	*S*
Social and Economic Studies	*SES*
Social Forces	*SF*
Social Problems	*SP*
Social Science Research Monograph	*SSRM*
Sociatry	*Sociatry*
Sociological Quarterly	*SQ*
Sociological Review	*Sociol. R.*
Sociologus	*Sociologus*
Sociology and Social Research	*SSR*
Sociometry	*Sociom.*
Southwestern Social Science Quarterly	*SSSQ*

Pre-1940

ADAMS, H. F. The Good Judge of Personality. *JASP*, 22:172–181, 1927.

ALLPORT, F. The J-curve Hypothesis of Conforming Behavior. *JSP*, 5:141–183, 1934.

ARCHER, W. *Masks or Faces?* N.Y.: Longmans, Green, 1888.

BEALE, H. K. *Are American Teachers Free?* N.Y.: Scribner's, 1936.

BENEDICT, R. Continuities and Discontinuities in Cultural Conditioning. *Psychiatry*, 1:161–167, 1938.

BOOK, W. F. The High School Teacher from the Pupil's Point of View. *PS*, 12:239–288, 1905.

BROWN, J. F. *Psychology and the Social Order.* N.Y.: McGraw-Hill, 1936.

CHAMPLIN, C. D. Attributes Desired in College Instructors. *SS*, 33:89–90, 1931.

CHAPMAN, D. W., and J. VOLKMANN. A Social Determinant of the Level of Aspiration. *JASP*, 34:225–238, 1939.

CHARTERS, W. W., and D. WAPLES. *The Commonwealth Teacher-Training Study.* Chicago: University of Chicago Press, 1929.

CLINTON, R. J. Qualities College Students Desire in College Instructors. *SS*, 32:702, 1930.

COOK, L. A., and R. B. ALMACK. The Community Participation of 2,870 Ohio Teachers. *EAS*, 25:107–119, 1939.

COOK, L. A., et al. Teacher and Community Relations. *ASR*, 3:167–174, 1938.

COOLEY, C. H. *Human Nature and the Social Order.* N.Y.: Scribner's, 1902.

Pre-1940 (cont.)

COREY, S. M. Attitudes Toward Teaching and Professional Training. *EAS*, 23:521–527, 1937.

DAVIES, J. E. What Are the Traits of the Good Teacher from the Standpoint of Junior High School Pupils? *SS*, 38:649–652, 1933.

DONOVAN, F. *The School Ma'am*. N.Y.: Frederick A. Stokes, 1938.

FARIS, E. The Social Psychology of George Mead. *AJS*, 43:391–403, 1937.

FORD, C. S. The Role of a Fijian Chief. *ASR*, 3:541–550, 1938.

FRANK, L. K. The Father's Role in Child Nurture. *Child Study*, 16:135–137, 1939.

GORDON, K. A Device for Demonstrating Empathy. *JEP*, 17:892–893, 1934.

HUGHES, E. C. Institutional Office and the Person. *AJS*, 43:404–413, 1937.

———. Personality Types and the Division of Labor. *AJS*, 33:754–768, 1928.

———. Position and Status in a Quebec Industrial Town. *ASR*, 3:709–717, 1938.

LINTON, R. *The Study of Man*. N.Y.: Appleton-Century-Crofts, 1936.

MEAD, G. H. *Mind, Self, and Society*. Chicago: University of Chicago Press, 1934.

MEAD, M. *Sex and Temperament in Three Primitive Societies*. N.Y.: Morrow, 1935.

MILES, C. C. Sex in Social Psychology, in C. MURCHISON (ed.), *Handbook of Social Psychology*. Worcester, Mass.: Clark University Press, 1935.

PARK, R. E. Human Migration and the Marginal Man. *AJS*, 33:881–893, 1928.

SHERIF, M. *Psychology of Social Norms*. N.Y.: Harper, 1936.

STONEQUIST, E. V. *The-Marginal Man*. N.Y.: Scribner's, 1937.

SULLIVAN, H. S. A Note on Formulating the Relationship of the Individual and the Group. *AJS*, 44:932–937, 1939.

THOMAS, W. I. *The Unadjusted Girl*. Boston: Little, Brown, 1923.

VERNON, P. E. Some Characteristics of the Good Judge of Personality. *JSP*, 4:42–58, 1933.

WALTON, W. E. Empathic Responses in Children. *PM*, 48:40–67, 1936.

WATSON, D. L. On the Role of Insight in the Study of Mankind. *Psychoanal. R.*, 25:358–371, 1938.

WINSLOW, C. N. A Study of the Extent of Agreement Among Friends' Opinions, and Their Ability to Estimate the Opinions of Each Other. *JSP*, 8:433–442, 1937.

1940–1944

ALLPORT, G. W. The Ego in Contemporary Psychology. *Psychol. R.*, 50:451–478, 1943.

AMES, V. M. On Empathy. *Phil. R.*, 52:490–494, 1943.

ANDERSON, W. A. Family Member Roles in Social Participation. *ASR*, 8:718–720, 1943.

ASCH, S. E. Studies in the Principles of Judgments and Attitudes: II. Determination of Judgments by Group and by Ego Standards. *JSP*, 12:433–465, 1940.

BARKER, R. G. The Social Interrelations of Strangers and Acquaintances. *Sociom.*, 5:169–179, 1942.

BENOIT-SMULLYAN, E. Status, Status Types, and Status Interrelations. *ASR*, 9:151–161, 1944.

BERNARD, J. Biculturality: A Study in Social Schizophrenia, in I. GRAEBER and S. BRITT (eds.), *Jews in a Gentile World*. N.Y.: Macmillan, 1942.

——. Normative Collective Behavior. *AJS*, 47:24–38, 1941.

BROOKOVER, W. The Social Role of Teachers and Pupil Achievement. *ASR*, 8:389–393, 1943.

CANNON, W. B. "Voodoo" Death. *AA*, 44:169–181, 1942.

CHAPPLE, E. D. Measuring Human Relations: An Introduction to the Study of the Interaction of Individuals. *GPM*, 22:1–147, 1940.

CHILD, I. L. The Use of Interview Data in Quantifying the Individual's Role in the Group. *JASP*, 38:305–318, 1943.

COTTRELL, F. *The Railroader*. Stanford, Calif.: Stanford University Press, 1940.

COTTRELL, JR., L. S. The Adjustment of the Individual to His Age and Sex Roles. *ASR*, 7:617–620, 1942.

——. The Analysis of Situational Fields in Social Psychology. *ASR*, 7:370–382, 1942.

DAVIS, K. A Conceptual Analysis of Stratification. *ASR*, 7:309–321, 1942.

——. The Sociology of Parent-Youth Conflict. *ASR*, 5:523–534, 1940.

FESTINGER, L. Wish, Expectation, and Group Standards as Factors Influencing Level of Aspiration. *JASP*, 37:184–200, 1942.

GOLDBERG, M. A Qualification of the Marginal Man Theory. *ASR*, 6:52–58, 1941.

HULETT, JR., J. E. The Person's Time Perspective and the Social Role. *SF*, 23:155–159, 1944–45.

——. The Social Role of the Mormon Polygamous Male. *ASR*, 8:279–287, 1943.

HYMAN, H. The Psychology of Status. *Arch. Psychol.*, No. 269, 1942.

ICHHEISER, G. Structural Dynamics of Interpersonal Relations. *ASR*, 8:302–305, 1943.

IRWIN, F. W. The Realism of Expectations. *Psychol. R.*, 51:120–126, 1944.

KATONA, A. Comment on Brookover: Social Role of Teachers. *ASR*, 9:108–109, 1944.

KAY, L. W. Relation of Personal Frames of Reference to Social Judgments. *Arch. Psychol.*, 283:1–53, 1943.

——. Social Norms as Determinants in the Interpretation of Personal Experiences. *JSP*, 19:359–367, 1944.

LINTON, R. Age and Sex Categories. *ASR*, 7:589–603, 1942.

MERTON, R. K. Bureaucratic Structure and Personality. *SF*, 18:560–568, 1940.

1940–44 (cont.)

MORENO, J. L. Psychodramatic Treatment of Psychoses. *Sociom.*, 3:115–132, 1940.

NEWCOMB, T. Community Roles in Attitude Formation. *ASR*, 7:621–630, 1942.

PARSONS, T. Age and Sex in the Social Structure of the United States. *ASR*, 7:604–616, 1942.

SARBIN, T. R. The Concept of Role Taking. *Sociom.*, 6:273–285, 1943.

SCHEUTZ, A. The Stranger: An Essay in Social Psychology. *AJS*, 49:499–507, 1944.

SOLBY, B. Role Concept in Job Adjustment. *Sociom.*, 7:222–229, 1944.

STONEQUIST, E. V. The Marginal Character of the Jews, in I. GRAEBER and S. BRITT (eds.), *Jews in a Gentile World*. N.Y.: Macmillan, 1942.

THOMPSON, C. The Role of Women in This Culture. *Psychiatry*, 4:1–8, 1941.

THORNER, I. Pharmacy: The Functional Significance of an Institutional Pattern. *SF*, 20:321–328, 1942.

TREUDLY, M. B. The Concept of Role in Social Work. *ASR*, 9:665–670, 1944.

WALLER, W. The Teacher's Roles, in J. S. ROUCEK (ed.), *Sociological Foundations of Education*. Bridgeport, Conn.: University of Bridgeport, 1942.

WILSON, L. *The Academic Man*. N.Y.: Oxford, 1942.

ZNANIECKI, F. *The Social Role of the Man of Knowledge*. N.Y.: Columbia University Press, 1940.

1945–1949

ANDERSON, W. A. Family Social Participation and Social Status Self-Ratings. *ASR*, 2:253–258, 1946.

ARNOLD, M. B. On the Mechanism of Suggestion and Hypnosis. *JASP*, 41:107–128, 1946.

ASCH, S. E. The Doctrine of Suggestion, Prestige, and Imitation in Social Psychology. *Psychol. R.*, 55:250–276, 1948.

BARNARD, C. I. Functions and Pathology of Status Systems in Formal Organizations, in W. F. WHYTE, *Industry and Society*. N.Y.: McGraw-Hill, 1946.

BENNE, K. D., and P. SHEATS. Functional Roles of Group Members. *JSI*, 4:41–50, 1948.

BENNETT, J. W., and M. M. TUMIN. *Social Life: Structure and Function*. N.Y.: Knopf, 1948.

BIBER, B., and C. LEWIS. An Experimental Study of What Young Children Expect of Their Teachers. *GPM*, 40:3–97, 1949.

BOWMAN, C. C. Role-Playing and the Development of Insight. *SF*, 28:195–199, 1949.

CAMERON, N. *The Psychology of Behavioral Disorders, A Biosocial Interpretation*. Boston: Houghton Mifflin, 1947.

CONN, J. H., and L. KANNER. Children's Awareness of Sex Differences. *J. Child Psychiatry*, 1:3–57, 1947.

COOK, W. W., *et al.* Predicting Teacher-Pupil Relations, in State Teachers College Yearbook, ch. 4, *The Evaluation of Student Teaching*. Lock Haven, Pa: The Association for Student Teaching, State Teachers College Yearbook, 1949.

COTTRELL, JR., L. S., and R. F. DYMOND. The Empathic Response: A Neglected Field for Research. *Psychiatry*, 12:355–359, 1949.

COUTU, W. *Emergent Human Nature*. N.Y.: Knopf, 1949.

CURLE, A. Transitional Communities and Social Reconnection: Part I. *HR*, 1:42–68, 1947.

——— and E. L. TRIST. Transitional Communities and Social Reconnection: Part II. *HR*, 1:240–288, 1947.

DAVIS, K. *Human Society*. N.Y.: Macmillan, 1949.

DYMOND, R. F. A Preliminary Investigation of the Relation of Insight and Empathy. *J. Consult. Psychol.*, 12:228–233, 1948.

———. A Scale for the Measurement of Empathic Ability. *J. Consult. Psychol.*, 13:127–133, 1949.

FESTINGER, L. The Role of Group Belongingness in a Voting Situation. *HR*, 1:154–180, 1947.

FRENCH, J. Role Playing as a Method of Training Foremen. *Sociom.*, 8:410–425, 1945.

GEBHARD, M. E. The Effect of Success and Failure upon the Attractiveness of Activities as a Function of Experience, Expectation and Need. *JEP*, 38:371–388, 1948.

GOUGH, H. G. A Sociological Theory of Psychopathy. *AJS*, 53:359–366, 1948.

GREEN, A. A Reexamination of the Marginal Man Concept. *SF*, 26:167–171, 1947.

HAAS, R. B. A Role Study from Pupil Motivations: Students Evaluate Their English Instructors. *Sociom.*, 10:200–210, 1947.

HARTLEY, E., and D. KRUGMAN. Notes on Children's Social Role Perception. *J. Psychol.*, 26:399–405, 1948.

HARTLEY, E., M. ROSENBAUM, and S. SCHWARTZ. Children's Perceptions of Ethnic Group Membership. *J. Psychol.*, 26:387–398, 1948.

———. Children's Use of Ethnic Frames of Reference: An Exploratory Study of Children's Conceptualizations of Multiple Ethnic Membership. *J. Psychol.*, 26:367–386, 1948.

HELSON, H. Adaptation-Level as a Basis for a Quantitative Theory of Frames of Reference. *Psychol. R.*, 55:297–313, 1948.

HENRY, W. E. The Business Executive: The Psychodynamics of a Social Role. *AJS*, 54:286–291, 1949.

HILLER, E. T. *Social Relations and Social Structures*. N.Y.: Harper, 1947.

HUGHES, E. C. Dilemmas and Contradictions of Status. *AJS*, 50:353–359, 1945.

1945–49 (cont.)

HUGHES, E. C. Social Change and Status Protest: An Essay on the Marginal Man. *Phylon*, 10:58–65, 1949.

KAY, L. W. Variation in Role and Group Identification as Frames of Reference. *JSP*, 27:63–78, 1948.

KLAPP, O. E. The Fool as a Social Type. *AJS*, 55:157–162, 1949.

KOMAROVSKY, M. Cultural Contradictions and Sex Roles. *AJS*, 52:184–189, 1946.

LAWLER, G. Two Aids to the Analysis of Role Behavior. *Sociatry*, 2:407–418, 1948.

LEE, L. L. A Brief Analysis of the Role and Status of the Negro in the Hawaiian Community. *ASR*, 13:419–437, 1948.

LEWIS, O. Husbands and Wives in a Mexican Village: A Study of Role Conflict. *AA*, 51:602–610, 1949.

LINTON, R. Concepts of Role and Status, in T. NEWCOMB and E. HARTLEY (eds.), *Readings in Social Psychology*. N.Y.: Holt, 1947.

———. Problems of Status Personality, in S. S. SARGENT and M. W. SMITH (eds.), *Culture and Personality*. N.Y.: Viking Fund, 1949.

———. *The Cultural Background of Personality*. N.Y.: D. Appleton-Century, 1945.

LIPPITT, R., and L. BRADFORD. Role-Playing in Supervisory Training. *Personnel*, 22:3–14, 1946.

MEAD, M. *Male and Female*. N.Y.: Morrow, 1949.

MERTON, R. K. Role of the Intellectual in Public Bureaucracy. *SF*, 23:405–415, 1945.

MURPHY, G. *Personality*. N.Y.: Harper, 1947.

NAESS, A. *Objectivity of Norms*. Oslo: Universitetets Studentkontor, 1948.

NOTTINGHAM, E. K. Toward an Analysis of the Effects of Two World Wars on the Role and Status of Middle Class Women in the English Speaking World. *ASR*, 12:666–675, 1947.

REISSMAN, L. A Study of Role Conceptions in a Bureaucracy. *SF*, 27:305–310, 1949.

SEWARD, G. *Sex and the Social Order*. N.Y.: McGraw-Hill, 1946.

SHERIF, M., and H. CANTRIL, *The Psychology of Ego Involvements*. N.Y.: Wiley, 1947.

SIMMONS, L. W. *The Role of the Aged in Primitive Society*. New Haven, Conn.: Yale University Press, 1945.

STEINMETZ, H. C. Directive Psychotherapy: Measuring Psychological Understanding. *J. Clin. Psychol.*, 1:331–335, 1945.

STOUFFER, S. An Analysis of Conflicting Social Norms. *ASR*, 14:707–717, 1949.

TURNER, R. The Navy Disbursing Officer as a Bureaucrat. *ASR*, 12:342–348, 1947.

WARREN, R. L. Cultural, Personal, and Situational Roles. *SSR*, 34:104–111, 1949.

———. Social Disorganization and the Interrelationship of Cultural Roles. *ASR*, 14:83–87, 1949.

WHYTE, W. F., and B. B. GARDNER. The Man in the Middle: Position and Problems of the Foreman. *AA*, 4:17–28, 1945.

WILLIAMS, J. Patients and Prejudice. *AJS*, 51:283–287, 1946.

WIRTH, L. Consensus and Mass Communication. *ASR*, 13:1–15, 1948.

WRAY, D. E. Marginal Men of Industry: The Foreman. *AJS*, 54:298–301, 1949.

YOUNG, K. Sex Roles in Polygamous Mormon Families, in T. NEWCOMB and E. HARTLEY (eds.), *Readings in Social Psychology.* N.Y.: Holt, 1947.

ZANDER, A. Role Playing: A Technique for Training the Necessarily Dominating Leader. *Sociatry*, 1:225–235, 1947.

1950

BALES, R. F. A Set of Categories for the Analysis of Small Group Interaction. *ASR*, 15:257–263.

———. *Interaction Process Analysis: A Method for the Study of Small Groups.* Reading, Mass.: Addison-Wesley.

BELL, G. B., and R. L. FRENCH, JR. Consistency of Individual Leadership Position in Small Groups of Varying Membership. *JASP*, 45:764–767.

BENDER, I. E., and A. H. HASTORF. The Perception of Persons: Forecasting Another Person's Responses on Three Personality Scales. *JASP*, 45:556–561.

BUGENTAL, J. F. T., and S. L. ZELEN. Investigations into the "Self Concept": 1. The W-A-Y Technique. *J. Pers.*, 18:483–498, 1949–50.

CAMERON, N. Role Concepts in Behavior Pathology. *AJS*, 55:464–467, 1949–50.

CHARTIER, B. The Social Role of the Literary Elite. *SF*, 29:179–186.

COTTRELL, JR., L. S. Some Neglected Problems in Social Psychology. *ASR*, 15:705–712.

DALTON, M. Conflicts between Staff and Line Managerial Officers. *ASR*, 15:342–351.

DEVEREUX, G., and F. WEINER. The Occupational Status of Nurses. *ASR*, 15:628–634.

DYMOND, R. F. Personality and Empathy. *J. Consult. Psychol.*, 14:343–350.

FESTINGER, L. Informal Social Communication. *Psychol. R.*, 57:271–282.

——— et al. *Social Pressures in Informal Groups.* N.Y.: Harper.

GIBB, C. A. The Sociometry of Leadership in Temporary Groups. *Sociom.*, 13:226–243.

GOLOVENSKY, D. I. The Marginal Man Concept: An Analysis and Critique. *SF*, 30:333–339.

HAIRE, M., and W. F. GRUNES. Perceptual Defences: Processes Protecting an Organized Perception of Another Personality. *HR*, 3:403–412.

HITES, R. W., and D. T. CAMPBELL. A Test of Ability of Fraternity Leaders to Estimate Group Opinions. *JSP*, 32:95–100.

1950 (cont.)

HOMANS, G. C. *The Human Group*. N.Y.: Harcourt, Brace.

JENNINGS, H. H. *Leadership and Isolation*. N.Y.: Longmans, Green.

KOMAROVSKY, M. Functional Analysis of Sex Roles. *AJS*, 15:508–516.

MOTZ, A. B. Conceptions of Marital Roles by Status Groups. *MFL*, 12:136–162.

NEWCOMB, T. M. Role Behaviors in the Study of Individual Personality and Groups. *J. Pers.*, 18:273–289.

———. *Social Psychology*. N.Y.: Dryden Press.

ORT, R. B. A Study of Role Conflicts as Related to Happiness in Marriage. *JASP*, 45:691–699.

PARK, R. E. Human Migration and the Marginal Man, in *Race and Culture*. Glencoe, Ill.: Free Press.

RABBAN, M. Sex Role Identification in Young Children in Two Diverse Social Groups. *GPM*, 58:31–158.

RADKE, M., and H. G. TRAGER. Children's Perceptions of the Social Roles of Negroes and Whites. *J. Psychol.*, 29:3–33.

SARBIN, T. R. Contributions to Role-Taking Theory: Hypnotic Behavior. *Psychol. R.*, 57:255–270.

SIMMEL, G. The Stranger, in *The Sociology of Georg Simmel*. Glencoe, Ill.: Free Press.

THOMPSON, C. W., and K. BRADWAY. The Teaching of Psychotherapy Through Content-Free Interviews. *J. Consult. Psychol.*, 14:321–323.

WALLIN, P. Cultural Contradictions and Sex Roles: A Report Study. *ASR*, 15:288–293.

WILLIAMS, J. The Woman Physician's Dilemma. *JSI*, 6:38–44.

1951

ACKERMAN, N. Social Role and Total Personality. *AJO*, 21:1–17.

ARROW, K. Alternative Approaches to the Theory of Choice in Risk-Taking Situations. *E*, 19:404–437.

ASCH, S. E. Effects of Group Pressures upon the Modification and Distortion of Judgements, in H. GUETZKOW, *Groups, Leadership, and Men*. Pittsburgh: Carnegie Press.

BACK, K. W. Influence Through Social Communication. *JASP*, 46:9–23.

BALES, R. F., and F. L. STRODTBECK. Phases in Group Problem-Solving. *JASP*, 46:485–495.

BECKER, H. S. The Professional Dance Musician and His Audience. *AJS*, 57:136–144.

BRUNER, J. S., *et al.* Expectation and the Perception of Color. *AJ. Psychol.*, 64:216–227.

CAMERON, N., and A. MARGARET. *Behavior Pathology*. Boston: Houghton Mifflin.

COUSINS, A. N. Social Equilibrium and the Psychodynamic Mechanisms. *SF*, 30:201–209.

COUTU, W. Role Playing vs. Role-Taking: An Appeal for Clarification. *ASR*, 16:180–187.

EMERY, F. E., and F. M. KATZ. Social Theory and Minority Group Behavior. *Australian J. Psychol.*, 3:22–35.

FENICHEL, G., *et al.* Subjective Status and the Equilibration Hypothesis. *JASP*, 46:476–479.

FESTINGER, L., and J. THIBAUT. Interpersonal Communication in Small Groups. *JASP*, 46:92–99.

FIEDLER, F. E. A Method of Objective Quantification of Certain Countertransference Attitudes. *J. Clin. Psychol.*, 7:101–107.

FOOTE, N. N. Identification as the Basis for a Theory of Motivation. *ASR*, 16:14–21.

GYR, J. Analysis of Committee Member Behavior in Four Cultures. *HR*, 4:193–202.

HACKER, H. Women as a Minority Group. *SF*, 30:60–69.

HARTLEY, E. Psychological Problems of Multiple Group Membership, in J. ROHRER and M. SHERIF (eds.), *Social Psychology at the Crossroads*. N.Y.: Harper.

HUGHES, E. C. Mistakes at Work. *CJEPS*, 17:320–327.

———. Studying the Nurse's Work. *AJN*, 51:294–295.

———. Work and the Self, in J. ROHRER and M. SHERIF (eds.), *Social Psychology at the Crossroads*. N.Y.: Harper.

JACOBSON, E., W. CHARTERS, and S. LIEBERMAN. The Use of the Role Concept in the Study of Complex Organizations. *JSI*, 7:18–27.

KORBER, G. Comments on "Role Conflict and Personality." *AJS*, 57:48–49.

LEWIN, K. *Field Theory in Social Science*. N.Y.: Harper.

MCCLELLAND, W. A. A Preliminary Test of Role-Playing Ability. *J. Consult. Psychol.*, 15:102–108.

MILLS, C. W. *White Collar*. N.Y.: Oxford.

NEIMAN, L. J., and J. W. HUGHES. The Problem of the Concept of Role—A Resurvey of the Literature. *SF*, 30:141–149, 1951–52.

NOTCUTT, B., and A. L. M. SILVA. Knowledge of Other People. *JASP*, 46:30–37.

OFSTAD, H. Objectivity of Norms and Value-Judgements According to Recent Scandinavian Philosophy. *PPR*, 12:42–68.

PARSONS, T., and E. A. SHILS. *Toward a General Theory of Action*. Cambridge, Mass.: Harvard University Press.

PARSONS, T. Illness and the Role of the Physician: A Sociological Perspective. *AJO*, 21:452–460.

PARSONS, T. *The Social System*. Glencoe, Ill.: Free Press.

1951 (cont.)

PHILLIPS, E. L. Attitudes Toward Self and Others: A Brief Questionnaire Report. *J. Consult. Psychol.*, 15:79–81.

QUEENER, E. L. *Social Psychology*. N.Y.: William Sloane.

ROSE, A. M. The Adequacy of Women's Expectations for Adult Roles. *SF*, 30:69–77.

SARGENT, S. Concepts of Role and Ego in Contemporary Psychology, in J. H. ROHRER and M. SHERIF (eds.), *Social Psychology at the Crossroads*. N.Y.: Harper.

SCHACTER, S. Deviation, Rejection, and Communication. *JASP*, 46:190–207.

STOUFFER, S., and J. TOBY. Role Conflict and Personality. *AJS*, 56:395–406.

TOBY, J. Some Variables in Role Conflict Analysis. *SF*, 30:323–327, 1951–52.

ZELENY, L. D. Status and Role among Fifth Grade Children. *SSR*, 35:425–427.

ZETTERBERG, H. L. The Religious Conversion as a Change of Social Roles. *SSR*, 36:159–166, 1951–52.

1952

ABERLE, D. F., and K. D. NAEGELE. Middle-Class Fathers' Occupational Roles and Attitudes toward Children. *AJO*, 22:366–378.

ARGYLE, M. The Concepts of Role and Status. *Sociol. R.*, 44:39–52.

ASCH, S. E. *Social Psychology*. N.Y.: Prentice-Hall.

BATES, A. P. Some Sociometric Aspects of Social Ranking in a Small Face-to-Face Group. *Sociom.*, 15:330–341.

BECKER, H. S. Social Class Variations and Teacher-Pupil Relationships. *JES*, 25:451–465.

BERGER, E. The Relation between Expressed Acceptance of Self and Expressed Acceptance of Others. *JASP*, 47:778–782.

BLOCK, J. The Assessment of Communication: Role Variations as a Function of Interactional Context. *J. Pers.*, 21:272–286.

BROWN, J. C. An Experiment in Role-Taking. *ASR*, 17:587–597.

BROWNFAIN, J. J. Stability of the Self-Concept as a Dimension of Personality. *JASP*, 47:597–606.

CHOWDRY, K., and T. M. NEWCOMB. The Relative Abilities of Leaders and Non-Leaders to Estimate Opinions of Their Own Groups. *JASP*, 47:51–57.

COPELAND, M. T. *The Executive at Work*. Cambridge, Mass.: Harvard University Press.

FARIS, R. E. *Social Psychology*. N.Y.: Ronald Press.

FESTINGER, L., *et al.* Some Consequences of De-Individualization in a Group. *JASP*, 47:382–389.

———. The Influence Process in the Presence of Extreme Deviates. *HR*, 5:327–346.

FIEDLER, F., *et al*. Unconscious Attitudes and Sociometric Choice in a Social Group. *JASP*, 47:790–796.

FILER, R. J. Frustration, Satisfaction, and Other Factors Affecting the Attractiveness of Goal Objects. *JASP*, 47:203–212.

GATTLING–FENN, G. F. Are Eskimo Women Frigid: A Study on the Climatological Bases of Role Performance. *PLA*, Yeovil University, Great Britain.

GETZELS, J. W. A Psycho-Sociological Framework for the Study of Educational Administration. *HER*, 22:235–246.

GOFFMAN, E. On Cooling the Mark Out: Some Aspects of Adaptation to Failure. *Psychiatry*, 15:451–463.

GOLD, R. L. Janitors vs. Tenants: A Status-Income Dilemma. *AJS*, 57:486–493.

HARE, A. P. A Study of Interaction and Consensus in Different Sized Groups. *ASR*, 17:261–267.

HARTLEY, E., and R. HARTLEY. *Fundamentals of Social Psychology*. N.Y.: Knopf.

HASTORF, A. H., and I. E. BENDER. A Caution Respecting the Measurement of Empathic Ability. *JASP*, 47:574–576.

JACOBSON, A. H. Conflict of Attitudes toward the Roles of the Husband and Wife in Marriage. *ASR*, 17:146–150.

KELLEY, H. H. Two Functions of Reference Groups, in G. E. SWANSON, T. M. NEWCOMB, and E. L. HARTLEY (eds.), *Readings in Social Psychology*. N.Y.: Holt.

―――― and E. H. VOLKART. The Resistance to Change of Group—Anchored Attitudes. *ASR*, 17:453–465.

KILLIAN, L. M. The Significance of Multiple-Group Membership in Disaster. *AJS*, 57:309–313.

LEVY, JR., M. *The Structure of Society*. Princeton, N.J.: Princeton University Press.

LU, YI–CHUANG. Predicting Roles in Marriage. *AJS*, 58:51–55.

――――. Parent-Child Relationship and Marital Roles. *ASR*, 17:357–361.

McCORMACK, T. H. The Motivation and Role of a Propagandist. *SF*, 30:388–394.

MOTZ, A. B. The Role Conception Inventory: A Tool for Research in Social Psychology. *ASR*, 17:465–471.

RILEY, M., *et al*. The Measurement of Consensus. *SF*, 31:97–106.

SARBIN, T. R. Contributions to Role-Taking Theory: A Preface to a Psychological Analysis of the Self. *Psychol. R.*, 59:11–22.

―――― and N. FARBEROW. Contributions to Role-Taking Theory: A Clinical Study of Self and Role. *JASP*, 47:117–125.

STRAUSS, A. L. The Development and Transformation of Monetary Meanings in the Child. *ASR*, 17:275–286.

TAFT, R. Minority Group Behavior and Reference Group Theory. *Australian J. Psychol.*, 4:10–23.

TAGIURI, R. Relational Analysis: An Extension of Sociometric Method with Emphasis upon Social Perception. *Sociom.* 15:91–104.

1952 (cont.)

TASCH, R. J. Role of the Father in the Family. *JEE*, 20:319–361.

TIMASHEFF, N. The Basic Concepts of Sociology. *AJS*, 58:176–186.

TURNER, R. Moral Judgment: A Study in Roles. *ASR*, 17:70–77.

ULRICH, R. On the Role of Teacher. *AT*, 36:9–14.

VON WIESE, L. Role Playing as a Method of Academic Education. *GP*, 5:73–77.

WALTERS, J., and R. H. OJEMANN. A Study of the Components of Adolescent Attitudes Concerning the Role of Women. *JSP*, 35:101–110.

WARDELL, W. I. A Marginal Professional Role: The Chiropractor. *SF*, 30:339–448.

1953

ADAMS, S. Status Congruency as a Variable in Small Group Performance. *SF*, 32:16–22.

BECKER, H. S. The Teacher in the Authority System of the Public School. *JES*, 27:128–141.

BENDER, I. E., and A. H. HASTORF. On Measuring Generalized Empathic Ability. *JASP*, 48:503–506.

BIERI, J. Changes in Interpersonal Perceptions Following Social Interaction. *JASP*, 48:61–66.

BIRDWHISTELL, R. L. *Introduction to Kinesics.* Louisville, Ky.: University of Louisville Press, 1953.

BORGATTA, E. F., and R. F. BALES. Task and Accumulation of Experience as Factors in the Interaction of Small Groups. *Sociom.*, 16:239–252.

BOVARD, JR., E. W. Conformity to Social Norms and Attraction to the Group. *S*, 118:598–599.

BRACHFELD, F. O. Sobre La Necesidad De Una Nueva Teoria De La "Marginalidad Social" Y Del Concepto De "Minoria" En Sociologia. *RIS*, 11:287–334.

CRONBACH, L. J. Correlation between Persons as a Research Tool, in O. H. MOWRER (ed.), *Psychotherapy: Theory and Research.* N.Y.: Ronald Press.

DWYER, R. J. The Negro in the U.S. Army, His Changing Role and Status. *SSR*, 38:103–112.

ESSELSTYN, T. C. The Social Role of a County Sheriff. *JCLC*, 44:177–184.

FENSTERHEIM, H., and M. E. TRESSELT. The Influence of Value Systems on the Perception of People. *JASP*, 48:93–98.

FICHTER, J. H. The Marginal Catholic. *SF*, 32:167–173.

FIEDLER, F. E. The Psychological-Distance Dimension in Interpersonal Relations. *J. Pers.*, 22:142–150.

FIELD, M. G. Structural Strain in the Role of the Soviet Physician. *AJS*, 53:493–502.

GAGE, N. L. Accuracy of Social Perception and Effectiveness in Interpersonal Relationships. *J. Pers.*, 22:128–141.

GOLDSTEIN, S. I. The Roles of an American Rabbi. *SSR*, 38:32–37.

GREER, S. Situational Pressures and Functional Role of the Labor Leader. *SF*, 32:41–45.

GROSS, N., and W. MASON. Some Methodological Problems of 8-Hour Interviews. *AJS*, 59:197–204, 1953–54.

GROSSACK, M. M. Cues, Expectations, and First Impressions. *J. Psychol.*, 35:245–252.

HALL, H. E., and G. B. BELL. The Relationship between Two Tests of Empathy: Dymond's and Kerr's. *AP*, 8:361–362.

HARDING, C. F. A Plea for an Anthropological Approach to the Study of Personality. *HO*, 12:13–16.

HARVEY, O. J. An Experimental Approach to the Study of Status Relations in Informal Groups. *ASR*, 18:357–367.

HEINICKE, C., and R. F. BALES. Developmental Trends in the Structure of Small Groups. *Sociom.*, 16:7–38.

IRWIN, F. W. Stated Expectations as Functions of Probability and Desirability of Outcome. *J. Pers.*, 21:329–335.

LINDGREN, H. C., and J. ROBINSON. An Evaluation of Dymond's Test of Insight and Empathy. *J. Consult. Psychol.*, 17:172–176.

MATHEWS, R. C., C. HARDYCK, and T. R. SARBIN. Contributions to Role-Taking Theory: Self Organization as a Factor in the Performance of Selected Cognitive Tasks. *JASP*, 48:500–503.

MISHLER, E. G. Personality Characteristics and the Resolution of Role Conflicts. *POQ*, 17:115–135.

MORENO, J. L. *Who Shall Survive?* N.Y.: Beacon House.

NEWCOMB, T. M. An Approach to the Study of Communicative Acts. *Psychol. R.*, 60:393–404.

SCODEL, A., and P. MUSSEN. Social Perception of Authoritarians and Nonauthoritarians. *JASP*, 48:181–184.

SEEMAN, M. Role Conflict and Ambivalence in Leadership. *ASR*, 18:373–380.

SHERIF, M. The Concept of Reference Groups in Human Relations, in M. SHERIF and M. O. WILSON (eds.), *Group Relations at the Crossroads*. N.Y.: Harper.

STEPHENSON, W. *The Study of Behavior*. Chicago: University of Chicago Press.

STERN, E., and S. KELLER. Spontaneous Reference Groups in France. *POQ*, 17:208–217.

STRAUSS, G., and R. LEONARD. Leadership Roles in Labor Unions. *SSR*, 38:96–102.

TAFT, R. The Shared Frame of Reference Concept Applied to the Assimilation of Immigrants. *HR*, 6:45–56.

1953 (cont.)

TANTUM, J. R. Changing Roles of Professional Personnel in the Field of Medical Care. *Nursing Outlook*, 1:694–696.

TOBY, J. Universalistic and Particularistic Factors in Role Assignment. *ASR*, 18:134–141.

VAN LENNEP, D. J., and R. H. HOUWINK. Projection Tests and Overt Behavior. *Acta Psychologica*, 9:240–253.

WARDELL, W. I. Social Integration, Bureaucratization, and the Professions. *SF*, 33:356–359.

YABLONSKY, L. An Operational Theory of Role. *Sociom.*, 16:349–354.

1954

ALLPORT, G. W. The Historical Background of Modern Social Psychology, in G. LINDZEY (ed.), *Handbook of Social Psychology*. Cambridge, Mass.: Addison-Wesley.

BARKER, R. G., and H. F. WRIGHT. *Midwest and Its Children*. Evanston, Ill.: Row, Peterson.

BERKOWITZ, L. Group Standards, Cohesiveness, and Productivity. *HR*, 7:509–519.

BLAKE, R. R. Social Standards and Individual Conduct. *SSSQ*, 35:11–24.

BOGEN, I. Pupil-Teacher Rapport and the Teacher's Awareness of Status Structures within the Group. *JES*, 28:104–114.

BOTT, E. The Concept of Class as a Reference Group. *HR*, 7:259–285.

BRUNER, J. S., and R. TAGIURI. The Perception of People, in G. LINDZEY (ed.), *Handbook of Social Psychology*, Cambridge, Mass.: Addison-Wesley.

BURCHARD, W. W. Role Conflicts of Military Chaplains. *ASR*, 19:528–535.

BURNS, T. The Directions of Activity and Communication in a Departmental Executive Group. *HR*, 7:73–97.

CARTER, L. F. Evaluating the Performance of Individuals as Members of Small Groups. *Pers. Psychol.*, 7:477–484.

CHEIN, I. The Environment as a Determinant of Behavior. *JSP*, 39:115–127.

CHINOY, E. *Sociological Perspective*. N.Y.: Doubleday.

DAVIS, F. J. Conceptions of Official Leader Roles in the Air Force. *SF*, 32:253–258.

———, R. HAGEDORN, and J. R. LARSON. Scaling Problems in a Study of Conceptions of Air Force Leader Roles. *POQ*, 18:279–286, 1954–55.

DREYER, A. S. Aspiration Behavior as Influenced by Expectation and Group Comparisons. *HR*, 7:175–190.

EDWARDS, W. The Theory of Decision Making. *PB*, 51:380–417.

EISENSTADT, S. M. Reference Group Behavior and Social Integration: An Exploratory Study. *ASR*, 19:175–185.

EISENSTADT, S. M. Studies in Reference Group Behavior—1. Reference Norms and the Social Structure. *HR*, 7:191–216.

EMERSON, R. M. Deviation and Rejection: An Experimental Replication. *ASR*, 19:688–693.

FESTINGER, L. Theory of Social Comparison Processes. *HR*, 7:117–140.

—— *et al.* Self-Evaluation as a Function of Attraction to the Group. *HR*, 7:161–174.

FIEDLER, F. E. Assumed Similarity Measures as Predictors of Team Effectiveness. *JASP*, 49:381–388.

FORD, T. R., and D. D. STEPHENSON. *Institutional Nurses: Role Relationships and Attitudes in Three Alabama Hospitals.* University, Ala.: University of Alabama Press.

GETZELS, J. W., and E. G. GUBA. Role, Role Conflict, and Effectiveness: An Empirical Study. *ASR*, 19:164–175.

GOLDBERG, S. C. Three Situational Determinants of Conformity to Social Norms. *JASP*, 49:325–329.

GRACE, H. A. Conformance and Performance. *JSP*, 40:333–335.

GUSTAFSON, J. M. An Analysis of the Problem of the Role of the Minister. *JR*, 34:187–191.

HAVIGHURST, R. J. Flexibility and the Social Roles of the Retired. *AJS*, 59:309–311.

JANIS, I. L., and B. T. KING. The Influence of Role-Playing on Opinion Change. *JASP*, 49:211–218.

KENDALL, P. *Conflict and Mood: Factors Affecting the Stability of Response.* Glencoe, Ill.: Free Press.

KERR, W. A., and B. J. SPEROFF. Validation and Evaluation of the Empathy Test. *J. General Psychol.*, 50:269–270.

KIRKPATRICK, C., and C. HOBART. Disagreement, Disagreement Estimate, and Non-empathic Imputations for Intimacy Groups Varying from Favorite Date to Married. *ASR*, 19:10–20.

KLAPP, O. E. Heroes, Villains and Fools, As Agents of Social Control. *ASR*, 19:56–62.

KUHN, M. H., and T. S. MCPARTLAND. An Empirical Investigation of Self Attitudes. *ASR*, 19:68–76.

LAULICHT, J. Role Conflict, The Pattern Variable Theory, and Scalogram Analysis. *SF*, 33:250–254, 1954–55.

MACRAE, JR., D. Role of the State Legislators in Massachusetts. *ASR*, 19:185–194.

NEIMAN, L. J. The Influence of Peer Groups upon Attitudes toward the Feminine Role. *SP*, 2:104–111.

NORMAN, R. D., and P. AINSWORTH. The Relationships among Projection, Empathy, Reality and Adjustment, Operationally Defined. *J. Consult. Psychol.*, 18:53–58.

1954 (cont.)

OLMSTED, M. S. Orientation and Role in the Small Group. *ASR*, 19:741–751.

POLLACZEK, P. P., and H. D. HOMEFIELD. The Use of Masks as an Adjunct to Role-Playing. *MH*, 38:299–304.

RIECKEN, H. W., and G. C. HOMANS. Psychological Aspects of Social Structure, in G. LINDZEY (ed.), *Handbook of Social Psychology*, Vol. II. Cambridge, Mass.: Addison-Wesley.

RIESMAN, D. *Individualism Reconsidered*. Glencoe, Ill.: Free Press.

———. Marginality, Conformity, and Insight, in D. RIESMAN, *Individualism Reconsidered*, ch. 10. Glencoe, Ill.: Free Press.

———. Some Observations Concerning Marginality, *Individualism Reconsidered*, ch. 9.

RILEY, M. W., and J. W. RILEY, JR. Notes on a Conceptual Model, in RILEY *et al.*, *Sociological Studies in Scale Analysis*. New Brunswick, N.J.: Rutgers University Press.

ROMMETVIET, R. *Social Norms and Roles*. Akademisk Forlag, Oslo, Norway, 1953, and University of Minnesota Press, 1954.

SAUNDERS, L. The Changing Role of Nurses. *AJN*, 54:1094–1098.

SARBIN, T. R. Role Theory, in G. LINDZEY (ed.), *Handbook of Social Psychology*. Cambridge, Mass.: Addison-Wesley.

SOMMER, R., and L. KILLIAN. Areas of Value Difference: 1. A Method for Investigation. *JSP*, 39:227–235.

SPIEGEL, J. P. The Social Roles of Doctor and Patient in Psychoanalysis and Psychotherapy. *Psychiatry*, 17:369–376.

STRAUSS, A. L. The Development of Conceptions of Roles in Children. *CD*, 25:193–208.

TURNER, R. Self and Others in Moral Judgement. *ASR*, 19:249–259.

1955

BALES, R. F., and E. F. BORGATTA. Size of Group as a Factor in the Interaction Profile, in HARE *et al.*, *Small Groups: Studies in Social Interaction*. N.Y.: Knopf.

BALES, R. F., and P. SLATER. Role Differentiation in Small Decision Making Groups, in T. PARSONS and R. F. BALES, *Family, Socialization and Interaction Process*. Glencoe, Ill.: Free Press.

BENNETT, E. B. Discussion, Decision, Commitment, and Consensus in "Group Decision." *HR*, 8:251–273.

BENSON, L. G. Family Social Status and Parental Authority Evaluations among Adolescents. *SSSQ*, 36:46–54.

BERG, J. Cooperation without Communication and Observation. *JSP*, 41:287–296.

BERNBERG, R. E. A Measure of Social Conformity. *J. Psychol.*, 39:89–96.

BIRDWHISTELL, R. L. Background to Kinesics. *ETC*, 13:10–18.

BLAKE, R. R., *et al.* Gift-Giving as a Function of Group Standards. *HR*, 8:61–73.

BOEK, W. E., and H. E. HILLEBOE. Role of a Social Scientist in Public Health. *HO*, 14:25–27.

BORGATTA, E. F. Analysis of Social Interaction: Actual, Role-Playing. and Projective. *JASP*, 51:394–405.

———. Attitudinal Concomitants to Military Statuses. *SF*, 33:342–347.

BOSSARD, J. H. S., and E. S. BOLL. Personality Roles in the Large Family. *CD*, 26:71–78.

BOTT, E. Urban Families: Conjugal Roles and Social Networks. *HR*, 8:345–384.

BOULDING, E. The Cooperative Nursery and the Young Mother's Role Conflict. *MFL*, 17:303–305.

BROOKOVER, W. Research on Teacher and Administrator Roles. *JES*, 29:2–13.

BURGESS, E. W. The Sociologic Theory of Psychosexual Behavior, in J. HIMELHOCH and S. FAVA (eds.), *Sexual Behavior in American Society*. N.Y.: Norton.

BURNS, T. The Reference of Conduct in Small Groups: Cliques and Cabals in Occupational Milieux. *HR*, 8:467–486.

CHASE, F. S., and E. G. GUBA. Administrative Roles and Behavior. *RER*, 25:281–298.

CLINE, V. B. Ability to Judge Personality Assessed with a Stress Interview and Sound Film Technique. *JASP*, 50:183–187.

CONNER, R., T. B. JOHANNIS, JR., and J. WALTERS. Family Recreation in Relation to Role Conceptions of Family Members. *MFL*, 17:306–309.

CRONBACH, L. J. Processes Affecting Scores on "Understanding of Others" and "Assumed Similarity." *PB*, 52:177–193.

DALLOLIO, H. C. Teachers on Trial: Group of Pupils Tell What They Like in Teachers. *CH*, 29:497–499.

DAVITZ, J. R. Social Perception and Sociometric Choice of Children. *JASP*, 50:173–176.

FOLEY, A. S. The Status and Role of the Negro Priest in the American Catholic Clergy. *ACSR*, 16:83–93.

FOOTE, N. N., and L. COTTRELL. *Identity and Interpersonal Competence*. Chicago: University of Chicago Press.

GAGE, N. L., and L. J. CRONBACH. Conceptual and Methodological Problems in Interpersonal Perception. *Psychol. R.*, 62:411–422.

GETZELS, J., and E. GUBA. Role Conflict and Personality. *J. Pers.*, 24:74–85.

———. The Structure of Roles and Role Conflict in the Teaching Situation. *JES*, 29:30–40.

1955 (cont.)

GLICK, C. E. Social Roles and Types in Race Relations, in A. W. LIND (ed.), *Race Relations in World Perspective*. Honolulu: University of Hawaii Press.

GORDON, W. The Role of the Teacher in the Social Structure of the High School. *JES*, 29:21–29.

GROSSACK, M. M. Effects of Variation in Teacher Role Behavior on Student-Teacher Relationships. *J. Educ. Psychol.*, 46:433–436.

GULLAHORN, J. T. Measuring Role Conflict. *AJS*, 61:299–303, 1955–56.

HABENSTEIN, R., and E. A. CHRIST. *Professionalizer, Traditionalizer, and Utilizer*. Columbia, Mo.: University of Missouri Press.

HAIRE, M. Role Perceptions in Labor-Management Relations. *ILRR*, 8:204–216.

HALL, R. L. Social Influence on the Aircraft Commander's Role. *ASR*, 20:292–299.

HALPIN, A. W. The Leader Behavior and Leadership Ideology of Educational Administrators and Aircraft Commanders. *HER*, 25:18–31.

HASTORF, A. H., I. E. BENDER, and D. J. WEINTRAUB. The Influence of Response Patterns on the Refined Empathy Score. *JASP*, 51:341–343.

HETZLER, S. A. Variations in Role-Playing Patterns among Different Echelons of Bureaucratic Leaders. *ASR*, 20:700–706.

HUGHES, E. C. The Making of a Physician. *HO*, 14:21–25.

JACKSON, W., and A. CARR. Empathic Ability in Normals and Schizophrenics. *JASP*, 51:79–82.

JAMES, J. M. The Social Role of the Priest. *ACSR*, 15–16:94–103.

KATZ, E., and P. LAZARSFELD. *Personal Influence*. Glencoe, Ill.: Free Press.

KELLY, G. A. *The Psychology of Personal Constructs*. N.Y.: Norton.

KERCKHOFF, A., and T. McCORMACK. Marginal Status and Marginal Personality. *SF*, 34:48–55.

KERR, M. The Study of Personality Deprivation through Projection Tests. *SES*, 4:83–94.

MILLER, H. Role-Awareness as an Object of Group Work in Teacher Education. *JTE*, 6:128–133.

PARSONS, T., and R. BALES. *Family, Socialization and Interaction Process*. Glencoe, Ill.: Free Press.

PEPITONE, A. P., and R. G. HAYDEN. Some Evidence for Conflict Resolution in Impression Formation. *JASP*, 51:302–307.

ROSEN, B. Conflicting Group Membership: A Study of Parent-Peer Group Cross-Pressures. *ASR*, 20:155–161.

————. The Reference Group Approach to Parental Factors in Attitude and Behavior Formation. *SF*, 34:137–144.

SAENGER, G. Male and Female Relations in the American Comic Strip. *POQ*, 19:195–206, 1955–56.

Sarbin, T. R., and C. D. Hardyck. Conformance in Role Perception as a Personality Variable. *J. Consult. Psychol.*, 19:109–111.

Sarbin, T. R., and D. S. Jones. An Experimental Analysis of Role Behavior. *JASP*, 51:236–241.

———. The Assessment of Role Expectations in the Selection of Supervisory Personnel. *EPM*, 15:236–239.

Sarbin, T. R., and B. G. Rosenberg. Contributions to Role-Taking Theory: IV. A Method for Obtaining a Qualitative Estimate of the Self. *JSP*, 42:71–81.

Shepherd, C., and I. R. Weschler. Relation between Three Interpersonal Variables and Communication Effectiveness: A Pilot Study. *Sociom.*, 18:103–110.

Sherif, M., *et al.* Status in Experimentally Produced Groups. *AJS*, 60:370–379.

Shibutani, T. Reference Groups as Perspectives. *AJS*, 60:562–569.

Slater, P. E. Role Differentiation in Small Groups. *ASR*, 20:300–310.

Stanton, H. R., and E. Litwak. Toward the Development of a Short Form Test of Interpersonal Competence. *ASR*, 20:668–674.

Steiner, I. D. Interpersonal Behavior and Accuracy of Social Perception. *PB*, 62:268–274.

Stogdill, R. M., and C. L. Shartle. Methods in the Study of Administrative Leadership. Columbus, O.: Ohio State University *Bureau of Business Research Monograph No. 80.*

Strodtbeck, F. L. Husband-Wife Interaction Over Revealed Differences. *ASR*, 16:468–473.

Taft, R. The Ability to Judge People. *PB*, 52:1–23.

Terrien, F. The Occupational Roles of Teachers. *JES*, 29:14–20, 1955–56.

Thomas, E., N. Polansky, and J. Kounin. The Expected Behavior of a Potentially Helpful Person. *HR*, 8:165–174.

Turner, R. Reference Groups of Future Oriented Men. *SF*, 34:130–136.

Wardell, W. I. The Reduction of Strain in a Marginal Social Role. *AJS*, 61:16–25, 1955–56.

——— and A. L. Wood. The Extra-Professional Role of the Lawyer. *AJS*, 61:304–307, 1955–56.

Whiting, J. F. Q-Sort: A Technique for Evaluating Perceptions of Interpersonal Relationships. *NR*, 4:70–73.

Wispe, L. G. A Sociometric Analysis of Conflicting Role-Expectancies. *AJS*, 61:134–137.

——— and K. Lloyd. Some Situational and Psychological Determinants of the Desire for Structured Interpersonal Relations. *JASP*, 51:57–60.

Zelditch, M. Role Differentiation in the Nuclear Family: A Comparative Study, in T. Parsons and R. F. Bales, *Family, Socialization and Interaction Process.* Glencoe, Ill.: Free Press.

1956

ANTONOVSKY, A. Toward a Refinement of the Marginal Man Concept. *SF*, 35:57–62.

ASCH, S. E. Studies of Independence and Conformity: I. A Minority of One against a Unanimous Majority. *PM*, 70 (No. 416).

AUBERT, V. The Housemaid—An Occupational Role in Crisis. *AS*, 1:149–158.

BAKER, B. O., and T. R. SARBIN. Differential Mediation of Social Perception as a Correlate of Social Adjustment. *Sociom.*, 19:69–83.

BARRON, M. J. The Dynamics of Occupational Roles and Health in Old Age, in J. E. ANDERSON (ed.), *Psychological Aspects of Aging*. Wash., D.C.: American Psychological Association.

BATES, A., and J. CLOYD. Toward the Development of Operations for Defining Group Norms and Member Roles. *Sociom.*, 19:26–39.

BATES, F. L. Position, Role, and Status: A Reformulation of Concepts. *SF*, 34:313–321.

BECKER, H. Empathy, Sympathy, and Scheler. *International Journal of Sociometry and Sociatry*, 1:15–22.

BECKER, H. S. The Elements of Identification with an Occupation. *ASR*, 21:341–348.

———. The Development of Identification with an Occupation. *AJS*, 61:289–298.

BECKER, H. S., and A. STRAUSS. Careers, Personality, and Adult Socialization. *AJS*, 62:253–263.

BERKOWITZ, L. Group Norms among Bomber Crews: Patterns of Perceived Crew Attitudes, "Actual" Crew Attitudes, and Crew Liking Related to Air-Crew Effectiveness in Far Eastern Combat. *Sociom.*, 19:141–153.

———. Personality and Group Position. *Sociom.*, 19:210–222.

BOTT, E. Urban Families: The Norms of Conjugal Roles. *HR*, 9:325–342.

BROWN, E. L., and S. FLECK. Role of the Public Health Nurse in Mental Health. *AJ. Public Health*, 46:745–754.

CAMPBELL, D. T. Leadership and Its Effect upon the Group. Columbus, O.: Ohio State University *Bureau of Business Research Monograph No. 83*.

CAUDILL, W. Perspectives on Administration in Psychiatric Hospitals. *ASQ*, 1:155–170.

CLARK, B. R. Organizational Adaptation and Precarious Values: A Case Study. *ASR*, 21:327–336.

COHEN, E. Stimulus Conditions as Factors in Social Change. *AP*, 11:407.

COSER, L. A. *The Functions of Social Conflict*. Glencoe, Ill.: Free Press.

DAVIS, J. A. Status Symbols and the Measurement of Status Perception. *Sociom.*, 19:154–165.

DEUTSCHER, I., *et al. Public Images of the Nurse*. Kansas City: Community Studies Publication 96.

DEXTER, L. Role Relationships and Conceptions of Neutrality in Interviewing. *AJS*, 62:153–157.

DITTES, J. E., and H. H. KELLEY. Effects of Different Conditions of Acceptance upon Conformity to Group Norms. *JASP*, 53:100–107.

FARBER, B., and L. S. BLACKMAN. Marital Role Tensions and Number and Sex of Children. *ASR*, 21:596–601.

FAULS, L. B., and W. D. SMITH. Sex Role Learning of Five-Year-Olds. *JGP*, 89:105–117.

FRENCH, JR., J. R. P. A Formal Theory of Social Power. *Psychol. R.*, 63:181–194.

GHISELLI, E. E., and R. BARTHOL. Role Perceptions of Successful and Unsuccessful Supervisors. *JAP*, 40:241–244.

GOFFMAN, E. The Nature of Deference and Demeanor. *AA*, 58:473–502.

———. Embarrassment and Social Organization. *AJS*, 62:264–271.

GOWMAN, A. G. Blindness and the Role of Companion. *SP*, 4:68–75.

GROSS, E. Symbiosis and Consensus as Integrative Factors in Small Groups. *ASR*, 21:174–179.

HAAS, E. Role, Position, and Social Organization: A Conceptual Framework. *MS*, 19:33–37.

HALPIN, A. W. *The Leadership Behavior of School Superintendents.* Columbus, O.: Ohio State University, College of Education.

HAYTHORN, W., A. COUCH, D. HAEFNER, P. LANGHAM, and L. F. CARTER. The Behavior of Authoritarian and Equalitarian Personalities in Groups. *HR*, 9:57–74.

HELFAND, I. Role Taking in Schizophrenia. *J. Consult. Psychol.*, 20:37–41.

HENRY, A. F. Family Role Structure and Self-Blame. *SF*, 35:34–38.

HIMES, JR., J. S. Changing Social Roles in the New South. *SSSQ*, 37:234–242.

HUGHES, E. C. Social Roles and the Division of Labor. *MS*, 17:3–7.

HYDE, R. W., M. GREENBLATT, and F. L. WELLS. The Role of the Attendant in Authority and Compliance: Notes on Ten Cases. *JGP*, 54:107–126.

JOHNSON, E. H. Role Adjustment of the Novice College Teacher. *AKD*, 26:11–17.

KENKEL, W., and D. K. HOFFMAN. Real and Conceived Roles in Family Decision Making. *MFL*, 18:311–316.

KING, B. T., and I. L. JANIS. Comparison of the Effectiveness of Improvised versus Non-Improvised Role-Playing in Producing Opinion Change. *HR*, 9:177–186.

LANG, G. The Concepts of Status and Role in Anthropology: Their Definition and Use. *ACSR*, 17:206–218.

LIDZ, T., B. PARKER, and A. CORNELISON. The Role of the Father in the Family Environment of the Schizophrenic Patient. *AJ. Psychiatry*, 113:126–132.

LIEBERMAN, S. The Effects of Changes in Roles on the Attitudes of Role Occupants. *HR*, 9:385–402.

1956 (cont.)

LINDESMITH, A., and A. STRAUSS. *Social Psychology*. N.Y.: Dryden Press.

LOCKE, H. J., G. SABAGH, and M. M. THOMES. Correlates of Primary Communication and Empathy. *RSSCW*, 24:116–124.

LYNSTAD, M. H., and R. C. STONE. Bureaucratic Mass Media: A Study in Role Definitions. *SF*, 34:356–361.

McCORMACK, T. The Druggists' Dilemma: Problems of a Marginal Occupation. *AJS*, 61:308–315.

McEWEN, W. J. Position Conflict and Professional Orientation in a Research Organization. *ASQ*, 1:208–224.

MACK, R. Occupational Determinateness: A Problem and Hypothesis in Role Theory. *SF*, 35:20–25.

MIYAMOTO, S. F., and S. F. DORNBUSCH. A Test of Interactionist Hypotheses of Self-Perception. *AJS*, 61:399–403.

MONK, M., and T. M. NEWCOMB. Perceived Consensus Within and Among Occupational Classes, *ASR*, 21:71–79.

MORRIS, R. T. A Typology of Norms. *ASR*, 21:610–613.

MYRDAL, A., and V. KLEIN. *Women's Two Roles: Home and Work*. N.Y.: Humanities Press.

NAEGELE, K. Clergymen, Teachers and Psychiatrists: A Study in Roles and Socialization. *CJEPS*, 22:46–62.

NATANSON, M. *Social Dynamics of George H. Mead*. Wash., D.C.: Public Affairs Press.

OHLIN, L. E. *Sociology and the Field of Corrections*. N.Y.: Russell Sage Foundation.

PARSONS, T. Suggestions for a Sociological Approach to the Theory of Organization. *ASQ*, 1:63–85.

PATTERSON, F. K. Adult Role in Adolescent Subculture Innovation: A Case Study. *JES*, 30:58–74.

PIERCE, A. On the Concepts of Role and Status. *Sociologus*, 6:29–34.

POWELL, R. M., *et al.* An Experimental Study of Role Taking, Group Status, and Group Formation. *SSR*, 40:159–165.

RABINOWITZ, W. A Note on the Social Perception of Authoritarians and Non-Authoritarians. *JASP*, 53:384–386.

RODGERS, D. A. Personality Correlates of Successful Role Behavior. *JSP*, 46:111–117.

SACHS, B. M. "Flexibility" and "Rigidity" in the Role Perception of Selected Administrators with Regard to Vocation. *EAS*, 42:46–53.

SCODEL, A., and M. L. FREEDMAN. Additional Observations on the Social Perceptions of Authoritarians and Non-Authoritarians. *JASP*, 52:92–95.

SCOTT, E. L. Leadership and Perceptions of Organization. Columbus, O.: Ohio State University *Bureau of Business Research Monograph No. 82.*

SEEMAN, M. Intellectual Perspective and Adjustment to Minority Status. *SP*, 3:142–153.

SPIVACK, S. S. A Study of a Method of Appraising Self Acceptance and Self Rejection. *JGP*, 88:183–202.

STANTON, H., K. BACK, and E. LITWAK. Role-Playing in Survey Research. *AJS*, 62:172–176.

STEINER, I. D., and J. S. DODGE. Interpersonal Perception and Role Structure as Determinants of Group and Individual Efficiency. *HR*, 9:467–480.

STOGDILL, R. M., E. L. SCOTT, and W. E. JAYNES. Leadership and Role Expectations. Columbus, O.: OSU *BBRM No. 86.*

STOGDILL, R. M., and C. L. SHARTLE. Patterns of Administrative Performance. Columbus, O.: OSU *BBRM No. 81.*

STOGDILL, R. M., and O. S. GOODE. Effects of the Interactions of Superiors upon the Performances and Expectations of Subordinates. *Int. J. Sociom. Sociat.*, 1:133–145.

STOGDILL, R. M., *et al.* A Predictive Study of Administrative Work Patterns. Columbus, O.: Ohio State University *Bureau of Business Research Monograph No. 85.*

STRAUSS, A. L. The Learning of Roles and of Concepts as Twin Processes. *JGP*, 88:211–217.

STRODTBECK, F. L., and R. MANN. Sex Role Differentiation in Jury Deliberations. *Sociom.*, 19:3–11.

STRYKER, S. Relationships of Married Offspring and Parent: A Test of Mead's Theory. *AJS*, 62:308–319.

SUTCLIFFE, J. P., and M. HABERMAN. Factors Influencing Choice in Role Conflict Situations. *ASR*, 21:695–703.

THIBAUT, J. W., and L. H. STRICKLAND. Psychological Set and Social Conformity. *J. Pers.*, 25:115–129.

TRICE, H. M. The "Outsider's" Role in Field Study. *SSR*, 41:27–32.

TURNER, R. Role Taking, Role Standpoint, and Reference Group Behavior. *AJS*, 61:316–328.

WILENSKY, H. L. *Intellectuals in Labor Unions: Organizational Pressures on Professional Roles.* Glencoe, Ill.: Free Press.

1957

ANDERSON, A. R., and O. K. MOORE. The Formal Analysis of Normative Concepts. *ASR*, 22:9–17.

ARGYLE, M. Social Pressure in Public and Private Situations. *JASP*, 54:172–175.

1957 (cont.)

BALES, R., and P. SLATER. Notes on "Role Differentiation in Small Decision Making Groups": A Reply to Dr. Wheeler. *Sociom.*, 20:152–155.

BARCH, A. M., D. TRUMBO, and J. NANGLE. Social Setting and Conformity to a Legal Requirement. *JASP*, 55:396–398.

BATES, F. L. A Conceptual Analysis of Group Structure. *SF*, 36:103–111.

BERNARD, J. Parties and Issues in Conflict. *J. Conflict Resol.*, 1:111–121.

———. *Social Problems at Midcentury: Role, Status, and Stress in a Context of Abundance*. N.Y.: Dryden Press.

BIDWELL, C. E. Some Effects of Administrative Behavior: A Study in Role Theory. *ASQ*, 2:163–181, 1957–58.

BLAKE, R. R., *et al*. The Generality of Conformity Behavior as a Function of Factual Anchorage, Difficulty of Task, and Amount of Social Pressure. *J. Pers.*, 25:294–316.

BORGATTA, E. F., and L. S. COTTRELL. Directions for Research in Group Behavior. *AJS*, 63:42–48.

BRIM, JR., O. G. The Parent-Child Relation as a Social System: I. Parent and Child Roles. *CD*, 28:343–364.

BROWN, D. G. The Development of Sex-Role Inversion and Homosexuality. *J. Pediatrics*, 50:613–619.

BROWN, J. S. Principles of Intrapersonal Conflict. *J. Conflict Resol.*, 1:135–154.

CARPER, J. W., and H. S. BECKER. Adjustment to Conflicting Expectations in the Development of Identification with an Occupation. *SF*, 36:51–56.

CATTELL, R. B. A Mathematical Model for the Leadership Role and Other Personality-Role Relations, in M. SHERIF and M. O. WILSON (eds.), *Emerging Problems in Social Psychology*. Norman, Okla.: University Book Exchange Duplicating Service.

CHANCE, E. Mutual Expectations of Patients and Therapists in Individual Treatment. *HR*, 10:167–178.

CROW, W. J., and K. R. HAMMOND. The Generality of Accuracy and Response Sets in Interpersonal Perception. *JASP*, 54:384–390.

DODGE, J. S., and I. D. STEINER. A Comparison of Two Techniques Employed in the Study of Interpersonal Perception. *Sociom.*, 20:1–7.

ERIKSON, K. T. Patient Role and Social Uncertainty—A Dilemma of the Mentally Ill. *Psychiatry*, 20:263–274.

EXLINE, R. V. Group Climate as a Factor in the Relevance and Accuracy of Social Perception. *JASP*, 55:382–388.

FESTINGER, L. *A Theory of Cognitive Dissonance*. Evanston, Ill.: Row, Peterson.

FICHTER, J. H. *Sociology*. Chicago: University of Chicago Press.

GERARD, H. Some Effects of Status, Role Clarity, and Group Goal Clarity upon the Individual's Relations to Group Process. *J. Pers.*, 25:475–488.

GETZELS, J., and E. GUBA. Social Behavior and the Administrative Process. *School R.*, 65:423–441.

GILBERT, D., and D. J. LEVINSON. Role Performance, Ideology and Personality in Mental Hospital Aides, in M. GREENBLATT *et al.* (eds.) *The Patient and the Mental Hospital.* Glencoe, Ill.: Free Press.

GOULDNER, A. W. Cosmopolitans and Locals: Toward an Analysis of Latent Social Roles, Part One. *ASQ*, 2:281–306.

GREENBLATT, M., D. J. LEVINSON, and R. H. WILLIAMS (eds.) *The Patient and the Mental Hospital.* Glencoe, Ill.: Free Press.

GRUSKY, O. A Case for the Theory of Familial Role Differentiation in Small Groups. *SF*, 35:209–217.

HAMAMSY, L. S. The Role of Women in Changing Navaho Society. *AA*, 59:101–111.

HARTLEY, R. E. Personal Characteristics and Acceptance of Secondary Groups as Reference Groups. *Journal of Individual Psychology*, 13:45–55.

HENRY, A. F. Sibling Structure and Perception of the Disciplinary Roles of Parents. *Sociom.*, 20:67–74.

JESSOR, R., and J. READIO. Influence of the Value of an Event Upon the Expectancy of Its Occurrence. *JGP*, 56:219–228.

KAPLAN, B. Personality and Social Structure, in J. GITTLER (ed.), *Review of Sociology.* N.Y.: Wiley.

KATZ, R. L. The Role of the Father. *MH*, 41:517–524.

KENKEL, W. F. Influence Differentiation in Family Decision Making. *SSR*, 42:18–25.

KLAPP, O. E. Concept of Consensus and Its Importance. *SSR*, 41:336–342.

LADD, J. *The Structure of a Moral Code.* Cambridge, Mass.: Harvard University Press.

MACK, R. W. Occupational Ideology and the Determinate Role. *SF*, 36:37–44.

MANGUS, A. R. Role Theory and Marriage Counseling. *SF*, 35:200–209.

MARTIN, J. G., and C. W. HOBART. The Marginal Academic Man. *AKD*, 27:38–45.

MELTZER, M. L. *Role Variability as a Function of the Understanding of Others.* Wash., D.C.: Catholic University Press.

MERTON, R. K. *Social Theory and Social Structure.* Glencoe, Ill.: Free Press (rev. and enlarged ed.), chs. 5–11.

———. The Role Set: Problems in Sociological Theory. *BJS*, 8:106–120.

——— *et al.* (eds.) *The Student-Physician.* Cambridge, Mass.: Harvard University Press.

MONEY, J., J. G. HAMPSON, and J. L. HAMPSON. Imprinting and the Establishment of Gender Role. *AMAANP*, 77:333–336.

NADEL, S. F. *The Theory of Social Structure.* Glencoe, Ill.: Free Press.

OLMSTED, D. W. Intergroup Similarities of Role Correlates. *Sociom.*, 20:8–20.

1957 (cont.)

OLMSTED, M. S. Character and Social Role. *AJS*, 63:49–57.

PHILLIPS, B. S. A Role Theory Approach to Adjustment in Old Age. *ASR*, 22:212–217.

PINE, F., and D. J. LEVINSON. Two Patterns of Ideology, Role Conception, and Personality Among Hospital Aides, in M. GREENBLATT, D. J. LEVINSON, and R. H. WILLIAMS (eds.), *The Patient and the Mental Hospital.* N.Y.: Free Press.

POLANSKY, N. A., R. B. WHITE, and S. C. MILLER. Determinants of the Role-Image of the Patient in a Psychiatric Hospital, in *The Patient and the Mental Hospital.*

RAPOPORT, R., and I. ROSOW. An Approach to Family Relationships and Role Performance. *HR*, 10:209–221.

RAVEN, B. H., and J. R. P. FRENCH, JR. An Experimental Investigation of Legitimate and Coercive Power. *AP*, 12:393.

REED, C. F. The Role-Taking Hypothesis in Delinquency. *J. Consult. Psychol.*, 21:386–390.

ROSOW, I. Issues in the Concept of Need-Complementarity. *Sociom.*, 20:216–233.

SCHAAR, J. H. *Loyalty in America.* Los Angeles: University of California Press.

SCHER, J. M. Diffusion of Communication and Role Exchange in the Treatment of Schizophrenia, in *The Patient and the Mental Hospital.*

SCHWARTZ, C. G. Problems for Psychiatric Nurses in Playing a New Role on a Mental Hospital Ward, in *The Patient and the Mental Hospital.*

SHARAF, M. R., and D. J. LEVINSON. Patterns of Ideology and Role Definition among Psychiatric Residents, in *The Patient and the Mental Hospital.*

SHERIF, M., and M. O. WILSON (eds.) *Emerging Problems in Social Psychology.* Norman, Okla.: University Book Exchange Duplicating Service.

SIEGEL, A. E., and S. SIEGEL. Reference Groups, Membership Groups, and Attitude Change. *JASP*, 55:360–364.

SMITH, E. E. Effects of Clear and Unclear Role Expectations on Group Productivity and Defensiveness. *JASP*, 55:213–217.

SOLEM, A. R. An Experimental Test of Two Theories of Involvement in Role Playing. *Int. J. Sociom. Sociat.*, 1:163–170.

SPIEGEL, J. P. The Resolution of Role Conflict within the Family. *Psychiatry*, 20:1–16.

STILES, L. J. (ed.) *The Teacher's Role in American Society.* N.Y.: Harper.

STOGDILL, R. M. Leadership and Structures of Personal Interaction. Columbus, O.: Ohio State University *Bureau of Business Research Monograph No. 84.*

STRYKER, S. Role-Taking Accuracy and Adjustment. *Sociom.*, 20:286–296.

SUPER, D. E. *The Psychology of Careers.* N.Y.: Harper.

TALLAND, G. A. Role and Status Structure in Therapy Groups. *J. Clin. Psychol.*, 13:27–33.

THEODORSON, G. A. The Relationship between Leadership and Popularity Roles in Small Groups. *ASR*, 22:58–67.

VERNON, G. M., and R. L. STEWART. Empathy as a Process in the Dating Situation. *ASR*, 22:48–52.

VOLKART, E. Bereavement and Mental Health, in A. LEIGHTON, J. A. CLAUSEN, and R. N. WILSON (eds.), *Exploration in Social Psychiatry*. N.Y.: Basic Books.

WEINER, M., *et al.* Some Determinants of Conformity Behavior. *JSP*, 45:289–297.

WHEELER, D. Notes on "Role Differentiation in Small Decision Making Groups." *Sociom.*, 20:145–151.

WILKENING, E. The County Extension Agent in Wisconsin: Perceptions of Role Definitions as Viewed by Agents. *AESRB*, No. 203 (University of Wisconsin).

WISPE, L. G., and P. W. THAYER. Role Ambiguity and Anxiety in an Occupational Group. *JSP*, 46:41–48.

ZANDER, A. F., A. R. COHEN, and E. STOTLAND. *Role Relations in the Mental Health Professions*. Ann Arbor, Mich.: Research Center for Group Dynamics, Institute for Social Research, University of Michigan.

ZETTERBERG, H. Compliant Actions. *AS*, 2:179–201.

1958

ABRAMSON, E., H. A. CUTLER, R. W. KAUTZ, and M. MENDELSON. Social Power and Commitment: A Theoretical Statement. *ASR*, 23:15–22.

BALES, R. F. Task Roles and Social Roles in Problem-Solving Groups, in E. E. MACCOBY, T. M. NEWCOMB, and E. L. HARTLEY (eds.), *Readings in Social Psychology*. N.Y.: Holt.

BECK, D. R. The Dynamics of Group Psychotherapy as Seen by a Sociologist, Part I. *Sociom.*, 21:98–127.

———. The Dynamics of Group Psychotherapy as Seen by a Sociologist, Part II. *Sociom.*, 21:180–198.

BEN–DAVID, J. The Professional Role of the Physician in Bureaucratized Medicine. *HR*, 11:255–274.

BENNIS, W. G., N. BERKOWITZ, M. AFFINITO, and M. MALONE. Authority, Power and the Ability to Influence. *HR*, 11:143–155.

BENNIS, W. G., *et al.* Reference Groups and Loyalties in the Out-Patient Department. *ASQ*, 2:481–500.

BLIZZARD, S. W. The Parish Minister's Self-Image of His Master Role. *PP*, 9:25–32.

———. The Protestant Parish Minister's Integrating Roles. *RE*, 53:374–380.

BRIM, JR., O. G. *Sociology and the Field of Education*. N.Y.: Russell Sage Foundation.

———. Family Structure and Sex Role Learning by Children: A Further Analysis of Helen Koch's Data. *Sociom.*, 21:1–16.

1958 (cont.)

BRONFENBRENNER, U., J. HARDING, and M. O. GALLWEY. The Measurement of Skill in Social Perception, in D. C. McCLELLAND *et al.* (eds.), *Talent and Society*. Princeton, N.J.: Van Nostrand.

BROWN, D. Sex Role Development in a Changing Culture. *PB*, 55:232–242.

CONNOR, R., H. GREENE, and J. WALTERS. Agreement of Family Member Conceptions of Good Parent and Child Roles. *SF*, 36:353–358.

COUCH, C. J. The Use of the Concept "Role" and Its Derivatives in a Study of Marriage. *MFL*, 20:353–357.

DIAMOND, M. Role-Taking Ability and Schizophrenia. *J. Clin. Psychol.*, 14: 321–324.

EMPEY, L. T. Role Expectations of Young Women Regarding Marriage and a Career. *MFL*, 20:152–155.

FOA, U. G. Behavior, Norms and Social Rewards in a Dyad. *BS*, 3:323–334.

FOOTE, N. N. Anachronism and Synchronism in Sociology. *Sociom.*, 21:17–29.

GOFFMAN, E. The Characteristics of Total Institutions, in *Symposium on Preventive and Social Psychiatry*. Wash., D.C.: Walter Reed Institute of Research.

GOLD, R. L. Roles in Sociological Field Observations. *SF*, 36:217–223.

GOULDNER, A. W. Cosmopolitans and Locals: Toward an Analysis of Latent Social Roles, Part II. *ASQ*, 2:444–480.

GROSS, E. *Work and Society*. N.Y.: Crowell.

GROSS, N., W. MASON, and W. McEACHERN. *Explorations in Role Analysis: Studies of the School Superintendency Role*. N.Y.: Wiley.

HATCH, M. G., and D. L. HATCH. Problems of Married Working Women as Presented by Three Popular Working Women's Magazines. *SF*, 37:148–153.

HOBART, C. W. Some Effects of Romanticism during Courtship upon Marriage Role Opinions. *SSR*, 42:336–343.

HOLLANDER, E. P. Conformity, Status and Idiosyncrasy Credit. *Psychol. R.*, 65:117–127.

HUGHES, E. C. *Men and Their Work*. Glencoe, Ill.: Free Press.

—— *et al. 20,000 Nurses Tell Their Stories*. Philadelphia: Lippincott.

HUNT, R. G., S. GOLDBERG, A. MEADOW, and W. COHEN. Some Demographic Factors in Conforming Behavior. *SSR*, 42:196–198.

JACKSON, J. M., and H. D. SALTZSTEIN. Effect of Person-Group Relationships on Conformity Processes. *JASP*, 57:17–24.

JOHNSON, M. M., and H. W. MARTIN. A Sociological Analysis of the Nurse Role. *AJN*, 58:373–377.

KIMBROUGH, E. The Role of the Banker in a Small City. *SF*, 36:316–322.

KLAPP, O. E. Social Types: Process and Structure. *ASR*, 23:674–678.

McCandless, B. D., and M. Weinstein. The Relation of Student Anxiety to Concepts of Role in Medical Care. *JME*, 33:144–151.

McCord, J., and W. McCord. The Effects of Parental Role Model on Criminality. *JSI*, 14:66–74.

Mann, J. H., and C. H. Mann. The Effect of Role Playing Experience on Self-Ratings of Inter-Personal Adjustment. *GP*, 11:27–32.

Mann, J. W. Group Relations and the Marginal Personality. *HR*, 11:77–92.

Mitchell, W. C. Occupational Role Strains: The American Elective Public Official. *ASQ*, 3:210–228.

Moreno, J. L., and L. D. Zeleny. Role Theory and Sociodrama, in J. S. Roucek (ed.), *Contemporary Sociology*. N.Y.: Philosophical Library.

Patchen, M. The Effect of Reference Group Standards on Job Satisfactions. *HR*, 11:303–314.

Phillips, L., and M. S. Rabinovitch. Social Role and Patterns of Symptomatic Behaviors. *JASP*, 57:181–186.

Powell, R. M., and L. La Fave. Some Determinants of Role-Taking Accuracy. *SSR*, 42:319–326.

Raven, B. H., and J. R. P. French, Jr. Group Support, Legitimate Power, and Social Influence. *J. Pers.*, 26:400–409.

———. Legitimate Power, Coercive Power, and Observability in Social Influence. *Sociom.*, 21:83–97.

Sargent, S. S., and R. C. Williamson. *Social Psychology*. N.Y.: Ronald Press.

Schelling, T. C. The Strategy of Conflict: Prospectus for a Reorientation of Game Theory. *J. Conflict Resol.*, 2:203–264.

Schon, D. Ultimate Rules and the Rational Settlement of Ethical Conflicts. *PPR*, 19:53–64.

Schulman, S. Basic Functional Roles in Nursing: Mother Surrogate and Healer, in E. G. Jaco (ed.), *Patients, Physicians and Illness*. N.Y.: Free Press.

Schutz, W. C. *FIRO-B: A Three-Dimensional Theory of Interpersonal Behavior*. N.Y.: Rinehart.

Sherwood, R. The Bantu Clerk: A Study of Role Expectations. *JSP*, 47:285–316.

Siegel, A. E. The Influence of Violence in the Mass Media upon Children's Role Expectations. *CD*, 29:35–56.

Solomon, D. Professional Persons in Bureaucratic Organizations, in *Symposium on Preventive and Social Psychiatry*. Wash., D.C.: Walter Reed Institute of Research.

Tagiuri, R., and L. Petrullo (eds.) *Person Perception and Interpersonal Behavior*. Stanford, Calif.: Stanford University Press.

Tupes, E. C., A. Carp, and W. R. Borg. Performance in Role Playing Situations as Related to Leadership and Personality Measures. *Sociom.*, 21:165–179.

1958 (cont.)

VIDEBECK, R. Dynamic Properties of the Concept Role. *MS*, 20:104–108.

WEISS, R. S., and N. M. SAMELSON. Social Roles of American Women, Their Contribution to a Sense of Usefulness and Importance. *MFL*, 20:358–366.

WILKENING, E. Consensus in Role Definitions of County Extension Agents between the Agents and the Local Sponsoring Committee Members. *RS*, 23:184–197.

—— and R. SMITH. Perception of Functions, Organizational Orientation, and Role Definition of a Group of Special Extension Agents. *MS*, 21:19–28.

1959

BIERI, J., and R. LOBECK. Acceptance of Authority and Parental Identification. *J. Pers.*, 27:74–86.

BLIZZARD, S. W. The Parish Minister's Self-Image and Variability in Human Culture. *PP*, 10:27–36.

BOWEN, M., R. H. DYSINGER, and B. BASAMANIA. The Role of the Father in Families with a Schizophrenic Patient. *AJ. Psychiatry*, 115:1017–1020.

BROPHY, A. L. Self, Role, and Satisfaction. *GPM*, 59:263–308.

BRUNN, K. The Significance of Roles and Norms in the Small Group for Individual Behavioral Changes while Drinking. *Quarterly J. Studies on Alcohol*, 20:53–64.

COLLEY, T. The Nature and Origin of Psychological Sexual Identity. *Psychol. R.*, 66:165–177.

DANIELS, M. J. Relational Status and the Role Concept. *PSR*, 2:41–48.

DAVIS, F. The Cabdriver and His Fare: Facets of a Fleeting Relationship. *AJS*, 65:158–165.

DUNNING, R. W. Ethnic Relations and the Marginal Man in Canada. *HO*, 18:117–122.

EMMERICH, W. Young Children's Discriminations of Parent and Child Roles. *CD*, 30:403–419.

EULAU, H., *et al.* The Role of the Representative: Some Empirical Observations on the Theory of Edmund Burke. *APSR*, 53:742–756.

FRANKIEL, R. V. *A Review of Research on Parent Influences on Child Personality.* N.Y.: Family Service Association of America.

GOFFMAN, E. The Presentation of Self in Everyday Life. *SSRM*, No. 2, University of Edinburgh Press, 1956; also N.Y.: Doubleday, 1959.

GRIFFITHS, W. A Study of Work Role Perceptions: The Community Health Worker on the Navajo Indian Reservation. *J. Psychol.*, 48:167–180.

GRUSKY, O. Role Conflict in Organization: A Study of Prison Camp Officials. *ASQ*, 3:452–472.

HARARY, F. Status and Contra-status. *Sociom.*, 22:23–43.

HARTLEY, R. E. Sex-Role Pressures and the Socialization of the Male Child. *PR*, 5:457–468.

——— and A. KLEIN. Sex-Role Concepts among Elementary-School-Age Girls. *MFL*, 21:59–64.

HELSON, H. Adaptation-Level Theory, in S. KOCH (ed.), *Psychology: A Study of a Science*, Vol. 1. N.Y.: McGraw-Hill.

HOLLANDER, E. P. Some Points of Reinterpretation Regarding Social Conformity. *Sociol. R.*, 7:159–168.

INKELES, A. Personality and Social Structure, in R. K. MERTON *et al.* (eds.), *Sociology Today*. N.Y.: Basic Books.

JACKSON, J. M. A Space for Conceptualizing Person-Group Relationships. *HR*, 12:3–15.

JANIS, I. L. Decisional Conflicts: A Theoretical Analysis. *J. Conflict Resol.*, 3:6–27.

JANOWITZ, M. *Sociology and the Military Establishment*. N.Y.: Russell Sage Foundation.

KAUSLER, D. H. Aspiration Level as a Determinant of Performance. *J. Pers.*, 27:346–351.

KOOS, E. L. *The Sociology of the Patient*. N.Y.: McGraw-Hill.

LEVINSON, D. J. Role, Personality, and Social Structure in the Organizational Setting. *JASP*, 58:170–180.

LEWIS, D. J. Stimulus, Response, and Social Role. *JSP*, 50:119–127.

LIGON, E. M. *Parent Roles: His and Her*. Schenectady, N.Y.: Character Research Project.

MACCOBY, E. E. Role-Taking in Childhood and Its Consequences for Social Learning. *CD*, 30:239–252.

MANN, J. H., and C. H. MANN. The Effect of Role-Playing Experience on Role-Playing Ability. *Sociom.*, 22:64–74.

MASON, W., R. J. DRESSEL, and R. K. BAIN. Sex Role and the Career Orientations of Beginning Teachers. *HER*, 29:370–382.

MASSARIK, F., and I. R. WESCHLER. Empathy Revisited: The Process of Understanding People. *CMR*, 1:36–46.

NEWCOMB, T. The Study of Consensus, in R. K. MERTON *et al.* (eds.), *Sociology Today: Problems and Prospects*. N.Y.: Basic Books.

PERRY, S. E., and L. C. WYNNE. Role Conflict, Role Redefinition, and Social Change in a Clinical Research Organization. *SF*, 38:62–65.

RANKIN, J. H. Psychiatric Screening of Police Recruits. *P. Pers. R.*, 20:191–196.

RIESMAN, D. Permissiveness and Sex Roles. *MFL*, 21:211–217.

RODGERS, D. A. Spontaneity and Specificity in Social Role Relationships. *J. Pers.*, 27:300–310.

RYKOFF, I., J. DAY, and L. C. WYNNE. Maintenance of Stereotyped Roles in the Families of Schizophrenics. *AGP*, 1:93–98.

1959 (cont.)

SOUTHALL, A. An Operational Theory of Role. *HR*, 12:17–34.

STEWART, D., and T. HOULT. A Social Psychological Theory of the Authoritarian Personality. *AJS*, 65:274–279.

STOGDILL, R. M. *Individual Behavior and Group Achievement*. N.Y.: Oxford.

STRAUSS, A. *Mirrors and Masks: The Search for Identity*. Glencoe, Ill.: Free Press.

THIBAUT, J. W., and H. H. KELLEY. *The Social Psychology of Groups*. N.Y.: Wiley.

THOMAS, E. J. Role Conceptions and Organizational Size. *ASR*, 24:30–37.

VIDEBECK, R., and A. P. BATES. An Experimental Study of Conformity to Role Expectations. *Sociom.*, 22:1–11.

WILSON, B. R. The Pentecostalist Minister: Role Conflicts and Status Contradictions. *AJS*, 64:494–504.

1960

ADAMS, J. B. Effects of Reference Group and Status on Opinion Change. *JQ*, 37:408–412.

BECKER, H. Normative Reactions to Normlessness. *ASR*, 25:803–810.

BECKER, H. S. Notes on the Concept of Commitment. *AJS*, 66:32–40.

BEN-DAVID, J. Roles and Innovation in Medicine. *AJS*, 65:557–568.

BERKOWITZ, J. E., and N. H. BERKOWITZ. Nursing Education and Role Conception. *NR*, 9:218–219.

BIDDLE, B. J., E. F. RANKIN, and H. A. ROSENCRANZ. *Bibliographies on Role Theory and the Role of the Teacher*. Columbia, Mo.: University of Missouri Press.

BORG, W. R. Prediction of Small Group Role Behavior from Personality Variables. *JASP*, 60:112–116.

BRIM, JR., O. G. Personality Development as Role Learning, in I. ISCOE and H. STEVENSON (eds.), *Personality Development in Children*. Austin, Tex.: University of Texas Press.

BROWN, D. G. Psychosexual Disturbances: Transvestism and Sex-Role Inversion. *MFL*, 22:218–226.

BURCHARD, W. W. The Status of Status. *SSR*, 44:417–423.

CORWIN, R., *et al*. Social Requirements of Occupational Success: Internalized Norms and Friendships. *SF*, 39:135–140.

DAKIN, R. E. Cultural Occasions and Group Structures: A Photographic Analysis of American Social Situations. *ASR*, 25:67–74.

DANIELS, M. Affect and Its Control in the Medical Intern. *AJS*, 66:259–267.

DAVID, H. P., and J. C. BRENGELMANN (eds.) *Perspectives in Personality Research*. N.Y.: Springer.

DAVIE, J. The Role of the Nurse in a Student Health Service. *SSR*, 45:66–70.

FARNSWORTH, P. R. The Effects of Role-Taking on Artistic Achievement. *JAAC*, 18:345–349.

FEFFER, M. H., and V. GOUREVITCH. Cognitive Aspects of Role-Taking in Children. *J. Pers.*, 28:383–396.

GIEBER, W. The "Lovelorn" Columnist and Her Social Role. *JQ*, 37:499–514.

GOMPERTZ, K. The Relation of Empathy to Effective Communication. *JQ*, 37:533–546.

GOODE, W. J. A Theory of Role Strain. *ASR*, 25:483–496.

———. Norm Commitment and Conformity to Role-Status Obligations. *AJS*, 66:246–258.

GOULDNER, A. W. The Norm of Reciprocity: A Preliminary Statement. *ASR*, 25:161–178.

HARTLEY, R. E. Children's Concepts of Male and Female Roles. *MPQ*, 6:83–91.

———. Relationships between Perceived Values and Acceptance of a New Reference Group. *JSP*, 51:181–190.

———. Some Implications of Current Changes in Sex Role Patterns. *MPQ*, 6:153–164.

HARTUP, W. W., and E. ZOOK. Sex-Role Preferences in Three- and Four-Year-Old Children. *J. Consult. Psychol.*, 24:420–426.

HASKELL, M. R. Toward a Reference Group Theory of Juvenile Delinquency. *SP*, 8:219–230, 1960–61.

HERMAN, S. N., and E. SCHILD. Ethnic Role Conflict in a Cross-Cultural Situation. *HR*, 13:215–227.

HYMAN, H. H. Reflections on Reference Groups. *POQ*, 24:383–396.

JACKSON, J. M. Structural Characteristics of Norms, 59th Yearbook of the National Society for the Study of Education, *Dynamics of Instructional Groups*. Chicago: University of Chicago Press.

JOHNSON, H. M. *Sociology*. N.Y.: Harcourt, Brace.

JOHNSON, P. A. The Marginal Man Revisited. *PSR*, 3:71–74.

KNAPP, D. L., and E. W. DENNY. The Counselor's Responsibility in Role Definition. *PGJ*, 40:48–50, 1960–61.

KOGAN, L. (ed.) *Social Science Theory and Social Work Research*. N.Y.: National Association of Social Workers.

LITWAK, E. Occupational Mobility and Extended Family Cohesion. *ASR*, 25:9–21.

———. Reference Group Theory, Bureaucratic Career, and Neighborhood Primary Group Cohesion. *Sociom.*, 23:27–84.

LOOMIS, C. P. *Social Systems*. Princeton, N.J.: Van Nostrand.

MADDEN, L. A. Role Definitions of Catholic Sister Educators and Expectations of Students, Their Parents, and Teaching Sisters in Selected Areas of the United States. *CUASS*, No. 14.

MASUOKA, J. Conflicting Role Obligations and Role Types: With Special Reference to Race Relations. *Japanese Sociological Review*, 11:76–108.

1960 (cont.)

MENZEL, H. Innovation, Integration, and Marginality: A Survey of Physicians. *ASR*, 25:704–713.

MILGRAM, N. A. Cognitive and Empathic Factors in Role-Taking by Schizophrenic and Brain-Damaged Patients. *JASP*, 60:219–224.

NAEGELE, K. D. Superintendency versus Superintendents: A Critical Essay. *HER*, 30:372–393.

REISSMAN, L., and R. V. PLATOU. The Motivation and Socialization of Medical Students. *JHHB*, 1:174–182.

ROSENGREN, W. R. Role Determinateness in Hospital Administrations. *Hospital Administration*, 5:46–57.

SARGENT, S. S., and K. P. BEARDSLEY. Social Roles and Personality Traits. *IJSP*, 6:66–70.

SEEMAN, M. *Social Status and Leadership: The Case of the School Executive.* Columbus, O.: Ohio State University, Bureau of Educational Research and Service.

SHERWOOD, C. E., and W. S. WALKER. Role Differentiation in Real Groups. *SSR*, 45:14–17.

SHIMADA, K. Social Role and Role Conflicts of the Protestant Parish Minister: Focused on S. W. Blizzard's Study. *Japanese Sociological Review*, 10:29–50.

SJOBERG, G. Contradictory Functional Requirements and Social Systems. *J. Conflict Resol.*, 4:198–208.

SLATER, C. Class Difference in Definition of Role and Membership in Voluntary Associations among Urban Married Women. *AJS*, 65:616–619.

SOMMER, R., H. OSMOND, and L. PANCYR. Problems of Recognition and Identity. *International Journal of Parapsychology*, 2:99–119.

STEIN, M. R., A. J. VIDICH, and D. M. WHITE. *Identity and Anxiety.* Glencoe, Ill.: Free Press.

STEINER, I. D., and W. L. FIELD. Role Assignment and Interpersonal Influence. *JASP*, 61:239–245.

SYSIHARJU, A.-L. *Equality, Home, and Work: A Socio-Psychological Study of Finnish Student Women's Attitudes towards the Woman's Role in Society.* Helsinki: University of Helsinki.

WAHLKE, J. C., *et al.* American State Legislators' Role Orientations Toward Pressure Groups. *J. Politics*, 22:203–227.

WILSON, R. N. The Physician's Changing Hospital Role. *HO*, 18:177–183.

1961

ALDOUS, J. A Study of Parental Role Functions. *Family Life Coordinator*, 10:43–44.

ASCH, S. E. Issues in the Study of Social Influences on Judgment, in I. A. BERG and B. M. BASS (eds.), *Conformity and Deviation.* N.Y.: Harper.

BASS, B. M. Conformity, Deviation and a General Theory of Interpersonal Behavior, in I. A. BERG and B. M. BASS (eds.), *Conformity and Deviation*. N.Y.: Harper.

BECKER, H. S., B. GEER, E. C. HUGHES, and A. L. STRAUSS. *Boys in White: Student Culture in Medical School*. Chicago: University of Chicago Press.

BERGEN, B. J. Comment (P. E. SLATER, Parental Role Differentiation). *AJS*, 67:308–311.

BERLEW, D. E. Interpersonal Sensitivity and Motive Strength. *JASP*, 63:390–394.

BIBLE, B. L., F. L. NOLAN, and E. J. BROWN. Consensus on Role Definition of the County Extension Executive Committee Member. *RS*, 26:146–156.

BIDDLE, B. J. *The Present Status of Role Theory*. Columbia, Mo.: University of Missouri Press.

—— et al. *Studies in the Role of the Public School Teacher*. Columbia, Mo.: University of Missouri Press.

BIDWELL, C. E. The Young Professional in the Army: A Study of Occupational Identity. *ASR*, 26:360–372.

BLACK, M. (ed.) *The Social Theories of Talcott Parsons*. Englewood Cliffs, N.J.: Prentice-Hall.

BLOCK, J. Ego Identity, Role Variability and Adjustment. *J. Consult. Psychol.*, 25:392–397.

BLOOM, B. L., and A. ARKOFF. Role Playing in Acute and Chronic Schizophrenia. *J. Consult. Psychol.*, 25:24–28.

BORGATTA, E. F. Role-Playing Specification, Personality and Performance. *Sociom.*, 24:218–233.

BUERKLE, J. V., T. R. ANDERSON, and R. F. BADGLEY. Altruism, Role-Conflict, and Marital Adjustment: A Factor Analysis of Marital Interaction. *MFL*, 23:20–26.

BURNHAM, D. L. Identity Definition and Role Demand in the Hospital Careers of Schizophrenic Patients. *Psychiatry*, 24:96–122.

CORWIN, R. G. The Professional Employee: A Study of Conflict in Nursing Roles. *AJS*, 66:604–615.

——. Role Conception and Career Aspiration: A Study of Identity in Nursing. *SQ*, 2:69–86.

COSER, R. L. Insulation from Observability and Types of Social Conformity. *ASR*, 26:28–39.

DAVIS, J. A. Compositional Effects, Role Systems, and the Survival of Small Discussion Groups. *POQ*, 25:574–584.

DE VOS, G., and H. WAGATSUMA. Value Attitudes toward Role Behavior of Women in Two Japanese Villages. *AA*, 63:1204–1230.

EMMERICH, W. Family Role Concepts of Children Ages Six to Ten. *CD*, 32:609–624.

1961 (cont.)

Eron, L. D., J. H. Laulicht, L. O. Walder, I. E. Farber, and J. P. Spiegel. Application of Role and Learning Theories to the Study of the Development of Aggression in Children. *Psychol. Rep.*, 9:291–334.

Etzioni, A. *A Comparative Analysis of Complex Organizations: On Power, Involvement, and Their Correlates.* Glencoe, Ill.: Free Press.

Fallding, H. The Family and the Idea of a Cardinal Role: A Sociological Study. *HR*, 14:329.

Fulton, R. L. The Clergyman and the Funeral Director: A Study in Role Conflict. *SF*, 39:317–323.

Gioscia, V. A Perspective for Role Theory. *ACSR*, 22:142–150.

Goffman, E. *Encounters: Two Studies in the Sociology of Interaction.* Indianapolis: Bobbs-Merrill.

Goldstein, B., and P. Dommermuth. The Sick Role Cycle: An Approach to Medical Sociology. *SSR*, 46: 36–47.

Gusfield, J. R. Occupational Roles and Forms of Enterprise. *AJS*, 66:571–580.

Hartley, R. E. Current Patterns in Sex Roles: Children's Perspectives. *JNAWDC*, 25:3–13.

Hawkes, R. W. The Role of the Psychiatric Administrator. *ASQ*, 6:89–106.

Herman, S. N., and E. O. Schild. The Stranger-Group in a Cross-Cultural Situation. *Sociom.*, 24:165–176.

Hoffman, L. W. The Father's Role in the Family and the Child's Peer-Group Adjustment. *MPQ*, 7:97–105.

Hollander, E. P. Some Effects of Perceived Status on Responses to Innovate Behavior. *JASP*, 63:247–250.

Homans, G. C. *Social Behavior: Its Elementary Forms.* N.Y.: Harcourt, Brace.

Johnson, R. C., *et al.* Authoritarianism, Occupation, and Sex-Role Differentiation of Children. *CD*, 32:271–276.

Jones, E. E., K. E. Davis, and K. J. Gergen. Role Playing Variations and Their Informational Value for Person Perception. *JASP*, 63:302–310.

Knoff, W. F. Role: A Concept Linking Society and Personality. *AJ. Psychiatry*, 17:1010–1015.

Lu, Yi-Chuang. Mother-Child Role Relations in Schizophrenia: A Comparison of Schizophrenic Patients with Nonschizophrenic Siblings. *Psychiatry*, 24:133–142.

Lynd, H. M. *On Shame and the Search for Identity.* N.Y.: Science Editions.

Maccoby, E. E. The Taking of Adult Roles in Middle Childhood. *JASP*, 63:493–503.

McGuire, C. Sex Role and Community Variability in Test Performances. *J. Educ. Psychol.*, 52:61–73.

Mann, J. H. Studies of Role Performance. *GPM*, 64:213–307.

MAXWELL, P. H., *et al.* Family Member Perceptions of Parent Role Performance. *MPQ*, 7:31–37.

MECHANIC, D. Role Expectations and Communication in the Therapist-Patient Relationship. *JHHB*, 2:190–198.

—— and E. H. VOLKART. Stress, Illness Behavior, and the Sick Role. *ASR*, 26:51–58.

MILGRAM, N. A. Role-Taking in Female Schizophrenic Patients. *J. Clin. Psychol.*, 17:409–411.

MONGEAU, B. B., H. L. SMITH, and A. C. MANEY. The "Granny" Midwife: Changing Roles and Functions of a Folk Practitioner. *AJS*, 66:497–505.

MOSS, C. S., and J. F. CLARK. Role Satisfaction of Psychologists in State Hospitals. *AP*, 16:523–528.

MOSS, H. A., and J. KAGAN. Stability of Achievement and Recognition Seeking Behaviors from Early Childhood through Adulthood. *JASP*, 62:504–513.

NELSON, H. A. Tentative Foundation for Reference Group Theory. *SSR*, 45:274–280.

NEWCOMB, T. M. *The Acquaintance Process.* N.Y.: Holt, Rinehart & Winston.

QUARANTELLI, E. L. School-Learned Adjustments to Negative Self-Images in High-Status Occupational Roles: The Dental Student Example. *JES*, 35:165–171.

RAULET, H. M. The Health Professional and the Fluoridation Issue: A Case of Role Conflict. *JSI*, 17:45–54.

ROSEN, H. Managerial Role Interaction: A Study of Three Managerial Levels. *JAP*, 45:30–34.

ROSENGREN, W. R. Status Stress and Role Contradictions: Emergent Professionalization in Psychiatric Hospitals. *MH*, 45:28–39.

ROY, P. Maternal Employment and Adolescent Roles: Rural-Urban Differentials. *MFL*, 23:340–349.

SCHACHTEL, E. On Alienated Concepts of Identity. *AJ. Psychoanalysis*, 21:120–121.

SLATER, P. E. Parental Role Differentiation. *AJS*, 67:296–308.

SMELSER, W. T. Dominance as a Factor in Achievement and Perception in Co-operative Problem Solving Interactions. *JASP*, 62:535–542.

SMITH, V. I. Role Conflicts in the Position of a Military Education Adviser. *SF*, 40:176–178.

TALBOT, E., S. C. MILLER, and R. B. WHITE. Some Aspects of Self-Conceptions and Role Demands in a Therapeutic Community. *JASP*, 63:338–345.

TURNER, R. H. The Problem of Social Dimensions in Personality. *PSR*, 4:57–62.

WRONG, D. H. The Oversocialized Conception of Man in Modern Sociology. *ASR*, 26:183–193.

WURSTER, C. R., B. M. BASS, and W. ALCOCK. A Test of the Proposition: We Want to be Esteemed Most by Those We Esteem Most Highly. *JASP*, 63:650–653.

1962

ABLESSER, H. "Role Reversal" in a Group Psychotherapy Session. *GP*, 15:321-325.

ANDERSON, A. R. Logic, Norms, and Roles, in J. H. CRISWELL *et al.* (eds.), *Mathematical Methods in Small Group Processes*. Stanford, Calif.: Stanford University Press.

ANGELL, R. C. Preferences for Moral Norms in Three Problem Areas. *AJS*, 67:650-660.

ARNOLD, M. F. Perception of Professional Role Activities in the Local Health Departments. *PHR*, 77:80-88.

BATES, F. L. Some Observations Concerning the Structural Aspect of Role Conflict. *PSR*, 5:75-82.

BELL, R. R., and J. V. BUERKLE. The Daughter's Role during the "Launching Stage." *MFL*, 24:384-388.

BIDDLE, B. J., J. P. TWYMAN, and E. F. RANKIN, JR. The Role of the Teacher and Occupational Choice. *School R.*, 70:191-206.

BLAKE, R. R., and J. S. MOUTON. Comprehension of Points of Communality in Competing Solutions. *Sociom.*, 25:56-63.

BLAU, P. M. Patterns of Choice in Interpersonal Relations. *ASR*, 27:41-55.

BLUMER, H. Society as Symbolic Interaction, in A. M. ROSE (ed.), *Human Behavior and Social Processes*. Boston: Houghton Mifflin.

CATTELL, R. B. Group Theory, Personality and Role: A Model for Experimental Researches, in F. GELDARD (ed.), *Defense Psychology*. London: Pergamon.

COHEN, B. P. The Process of Choosing a Reference Group, in *Mathematical Methods in Small Group Processes*.

CONRAD, F. A. Sex Roles as Factors in Longevity. *SSR*, 46:195-202.

COSER, L. Some Functions of Deviant Behavior and Normative Flexibility. *AJS*, 63:172-181.

DANIELS, M. J. Levels of Organization in the Role Position of the Staff Nurse. *SF*, 40:242-248.

DE LAUWE, M. J. CHOMBART (ed.) Images of Women in Society. *ISSJ*, Vol. 16 (entire issue).

DIGGORY, J. C. Sex-Differences in Judging the Acceptability of Actions. *JSP*, 56:107-114.

DINITZ, S., S. ANGRIST, M. LEFTON, and B. PASAMANICK. Instrumental Role Expectations and Posthospital Performance of Female Mental Patients. *SF*, 40:248-254.

EHRLICH, H. J., J. W. RINEHART, and J. C. HOWELL. The Study of Role Conflict: Explorations in Methodology. *Sociom.*, 25:85-97.

EVAN, W. M. Role Strain and the Norm of Reciprocity in Research Organizations. *AJS*, 68:346-354.

FARBER, B. Elements of Competence in Interpersonal Relations: A Factor Analysis. *Sociom.*, 25:30–47.

FORM, W. H., and J. A. GESCHWENDER. Social Reference Basis of Job Satisfaction. *ASR*, 27:228–237.

GLASSER, P. H., and L. N. GLASSER. Role Reversal and Conflict between Aged Parents and Their Children. *MFL*, 24:46–50.

HANSON, R. C. The Systemic Linkage Hypothesis and Role Consensus Patterns in Hospital-Community Relations. *ASR*, 27:304–313.

HARTLEY, R., F. HARDESTY, and D. GORFEIN. Children's Perceptions and Expressions of Sex Role Preferences. *CD*, 33:221–227.

HEISS, J. S. Degree of Intimacy and Male-Female Interaction. *Sociom.*, 25:197–208.

HOROWITZ, I. L. Consensus, Conflict and Cooperation: A Sociological Inventory. *SF*, 41:177–188.

ISHIYAMA, T., J. M. DENNY, R. PRADA, and R. VESPE. The Role of the Psychologist on Mental Hospital Wards as Defined by the Expectant-Others. *J. Clin. Psychol.*, 18:3–10.

JANOSKA–BENDL, J. Probleme Der Freizheit in Der Rollenanalyse (Problems of Freedom in Role Analysis). *Koelner Zeitschrift fuer Soziolgie und Sozialpsychologie*, 14:459–475.

KLARE, H. Correctional Staff Roles and Perception of Authority. *Journal of Offender Therapy*, 6:44–46.

KOTLAR, S. L. Instrumental and Expressive Marital Roles. *SSR*, 46:186–194.

LEFKOWITZ, M. M. Some Relationships between Sex Role Preferences of Children and Other Parent and Child Variables. *Psychol. Rep.*, 10:43–53.

LOCKWOOD, D. H., and B. GUERNEY, JR. Identification and Empathy in Relation to Self-Dissatisfaction and Adjustment. *JASP*, 65:343–347.

LONG, H. H. Marginal Men and the New Negro Identity. *NS* (April), 6–12.

LU, YI-CHUANG. Contradictory Parental Expectations in Schizophrenia. *AGP*, 6:219–234.

LYNN, D. B. Sex-Role and Parental Identification. *CD*, 33:555–564.

MACCOBY, E. E. Class Differences in Boys' Choices of Authority Role Conflict Resolution. *Sociom.*, 25:117–119.

MADIGAN, F. C. Role Satisfactions and Length of Life in a Closed Population. *AJS*, 67:640–649.

MESSINGER, S. L. Life as Theater: Some Notes on the Dramaturgic Approach to Social Reality. *Sociom.*, 25:98–110.

MILLER, D. C., and F. A. SHULL, JR. The Prediction of Administrative Role Conflict Resolution. *ASQ*, 7:143–160.

MITCHELL, B. D. Role Reversal in Musical Training. *GP*, 15:154–158.

MIZRUCHI, E. H., and R. PERRUCCI. Norm Qualities and Differential Effects of Deviant Behavior: An Exploratory Analysis. *ASR*, 27:391–399.

1962 (cont.)

NALL, F. C. II. Role Expectations: A Cross-Cultural Study. *RS*, 27:28–41.

NIX, H. L., and F. L. Bates. Occupational Role Stresses: A Structural Approach. *RS*, 27:7–17.

OESER, O. A., and F. HARARY. A Mathematical Model for Structural Role Theory. *HR*, 15:89–109.

OPLER, M. K. Industrial Societies and the Changing Role of Doctors. *J. Occupational Medicine*, 4:237–241.

OSSENBERG, R. J. The Experience of Deviance in the Patient-Role: A Study of Class Differences. *JHHB*, 3:277–282.

OWEN, C. Feminine Roles and Social Mobility in Women's Weekly Magazines. *Sociol. R.*, 10:283–296.

PARK, P. Problem Drinking and Role Deviation: A Study in Incipient Alcoholism, in D. J. PITTMAN and C. R. SNYDER (eds.), *Society, Culture, and Drinking Patterns*. N.Y.: Wiley.

PECK, R. F., and C. GALLIANI. Intelligence, Ethnicity and Social Roles in Adolescent Society. *Sociom.*, 25:64–72.

PLOTNICOV, L. Fixed Membership Groups: The Locus of Culture Processes. *AA*, 64:97–103.

ROSENGREN, W. R. Social Instability and Attitudes toward Pregnancy as a Social Role. *SP*, 9:371–378.

SEEMAN, M., and J. W. EVANS. Apprenticeship and Attitude Change. *AJS*, 67:365–378.

SEGAL, B. E. Male Nurses: A Case Study in Status Contradiction and Prestige Loss. *SF*, 41:31–38.

SHERIF, M. The Self and Reference Groups: Meeting Ground of Individual and Group Approaches. *Annals of the New York Academy of Sciences*, 96:797–813.

SHIBUTANI, T. Reference Groups and Social Control, in A. M. ROSE (ed.), *Human Behavior and Social Processes*. Boston: Houghton Mifflin.

SKIPPER, J. K. Functional Significance of the Nurse Role: An Evaluation. *JHHB*, 3:41–45.

SOMMER, R. The Distance for Comfortable Conversation: A Further Study. *Sociom.*, 25:111–116.

SPERGEL, I. Role Behavior and Supervision of the Untrained Group Work. *Social Work*, 7:69–76.

STONE, G. Appearance and the Self, in A. ROSE (ed.), *Human Behavior and Social Processes*. Boston: Houghton Mifflin.

STRAUS, M. A. Work Roles and Financial Responsibility in the Socialization of Farm, Fringe, and Town Boys. *RS*, 27:257–274.

STRYKER, S. Conditions of Accurate Role-Taking: A Test of Mead's Theory, in A. M. ROSE (ed.), *Human Behavior and Social Processes*. Boston: Houghton Mifflin.

TAIETZ, P. Conflicting Group Norms and the "Third" Person in the Interview. *AJS*, 68:97–104.

TURK, T., and H. TURK. Group Interaction in a Formal Setting: The Case of the Triad. *Sociom.*, 25:48–55.

TURNER, R. H. Role-Taking: Process versus Conformity, in A. M. ROSE (ed.), *Human Behavior and Social Processes*. Boston: Houghton Mifflin.

———. Primary and Secondary Group Moral Responsibility Roles. *Mens en Maatschappj* (The Netherlands), 37:335–346.

———. Some Family Determinants of Ambition. *SSR*, 46:397–411.

WARSHAY, L. H. Breadth of Perspective, in A. M. ROSE (ed.), *Human Behavior and Social Processes*. Boston: Houghton Mifflin.

WILSON, B. R. The Teacher's Role—A Sociological Analysis. *BJS*, 13:15–32.

YOUNG, F. W., and R. C. YOUNG. Occupational Role Perceptions in Rural Mexico. *RS*, 27:42–52.

1963

ALLEN, L. A., and R. L. SUTHERLAND. *Role Conflict and Congruences Experienced by New Faculty Members as they Enter the Culture of a College Community*. Austin, Tex.: Hogg Foundation for Mental Health, University of Texas.

ARKOFF, A., G. MEREDITH, and J. DONG. Attitudes of Japanese-American and Caucasian-American Students toward Marriage Roles. *JSP*, 59:11–15.

ARTHUR, B. Role Perceptions of Children with Ulcerative Colitis. *AGP*, 8:536–545.

AXELSON, L. J. The Marital Adjustment and Marital Role Definitions of Husbands of Working and Nonworking Wives. *MFL*, 25:189–195.

BARRET, R. S. Performance Suitability and Role Agreement, Two Factors Related to Attitudes. *Pers. Psychol.*, 16:345–357.

BELL, R. R., and J. V. BUERKLE. Mothers and Mothers-in-Law as Role Models in Relation to Religious Background. *MFL*, 25:485–486.

BERNSTEIN, R. The Maternal Role in the Treatment of Unmarried Mothers. *Social Work*, 8:58–66.

BIBLE, B. L., and J. D. McCOMAS. Role Consensus and Teacher Effectiveness. *SF*, 42:225–233.

BRANDZEL, R. Role Playing as a Training Device in Preparing Multiple-Handicapped Youth for Employment. *GP*, 16:16–21.

BURSCHE, K., and G. POMIAN. The Role and Social Position of Foremen in Industrial Works. *Polish Sociological Bulletin*, 1:93–94.

CLAESSENS, D. Rolle und Verantwortung (Role and Responsibility). *Soziale Welt*, 14:1–13.

1963 (cont.)

DAVIS, F., and V. L. OLESEN. Initiation into a Woman's Profession: Identity Problems in the Status Transition of Coed to Student Nurse. *Sociom.*, 26:89–101.

DAVIS, J. A. Structural Balance, Mechanical Solidarity, and Interpersonal Relations. *AJS*, 68:444–462.

DE FLEUR, M. L. Children's Knowledge of Occupational Roles and Prestige: Preliminary Report. *Psychol. Rep.*, 13:760.

DE LANGE, W. H. Patient Role Conflict and Reactions to Hospitalization. *JHHB*, 4:113–118.

DE LUCIA, L. A. The Toy Preference Test: A Measure of Sex-Role Identification. *CD*, 34:107–117.

ENOCH, R. The Role of the Participant Observer in Social Research. *Proceedings of the Southwestern Sociological Association*, 13:105–114.

EPSTEIN, R., S. LIVERANT. Verbal Conditioning and Sex-Role Identification in Children. *CD*, 34:99–106.

EVANS, T. Q. The Brethren Pastor: Differential Conceptions of an Emerging Role. *Journal for the Scientific Study of Religion*, 3:43–51.

GOFFMAN, E. *Stigma: Notes on the Management of Spoiled Identity*. Englewood Cliffs, N.J.: Prentice-Hall.

GULLAHORN, J. T., and J. E. GULLAHORN. Role Conflict and Its Resolution. *SQ*, 4:32–48.

HALL, E. T. A System for the Notation of Proxemic Behavior. *AA*, 65:1003–1006.

HELLER, K., R. A. MEYERS, and L. V. KLINE. Interviewer Behavior as a Function of Standardized Client Roles. *J. Consult. Psychol.*, 27:117–122.

INKELES, A., and D. J. LEVINSON. The Personal System and the Sociocultural System in Large-Scale Organizations. *Sociom.*, 26:217–229.

JOHNSON, M. M. Sex Role Learning in the Nuclear Family. *CD*, 34:319–333.

KAVOLIS, V. A Role Theory of Artistic Interest. *JSP*, 60:31–37.

KILBRICK, A. K. Dropouts in Schools of Nursing: The Effect of Self and Role Perception. *NR*, 12:140–149.

KINCH, J. W. A Formalized Theory of the Self-Concept (Research Note). *AJS*, 68:481–486.

KOGAN, K. L., and J. K. JACKSON. Conventional Sex Role Stereotypes and Actual Perception. *Psychol. Rep.*, 13:27–30.

―――. Role Perceptions in Wives of Alcoholics and of Nonalcoholics. *Quarterly J. Studies on Alcohol*, 24:627–639.

KUETHE, J. L., and G. STRICKER. Man and Woman: Social Schemata of Males and Females. *Psychol. Rep.*, 13:655–661.

LANSKY, L. M. The Family Structure Also Affects the Model: Sex Role Identification in Parents of Pre-School Children. *MPQ*, 10:39–50.

LANSKY, L. M., and G. McKAY. Sex Role Preferences of Kindergarten Boys and Girls: Some Contradictory Results. *Psychol. Rep.*, 13:415–421.

LESLIE, G. R., and K. P. JOHNSEN. Changed Perceptions of the Maternal Role. *ASR*, 28:919–928.

LEVEEN, L., and D. PRIVER. Significance of Role Playing in the Aged Person. *Geriatrics*, 18:57–63.

LYNN, D. B. Learned Masculine and Feminine Roles. *MFL*, 25:103–105.

MARTIN, R. M. Performance, Purpose, and Permission. *Phil. Sci.*, 30:122–137.

MEDINNUS, G. R. The Relation between Parental Prescriptions for Child and Parent Roles. *JSP*, 60:101–106.

MILGRAM, S. Behavioral Study of Obedience. *JASP*, 67:371–378.

MILLER, D. R. The Study of Social Relationships: Situation, Identity, and Social Interaction, in S. KOCH (ed.), *Psychology: A Study of a Science*, Vol. 5. N.Y.: McGraw-Hill.

MOMENT, D., and A. ZALEZNIK. *Role Development and Interpersonal Competence.* Boston: Division of Research, Harvard Business School.

MUSSEN, P., and E. RUTHFORD. Parent-Child Relations and Parental Personality in Relation to Young Children's Sex-Role Preferences. *CD*, 34:589–607.

OMARI, T. P. Role Expectation in the Courtship Situation in Ghana. *SF*, 42:147–156.

OSSENBERG, R. J. The Experience of Deviance in the Patient-Role: A Study of Class Differences. *JHHB*, 3:277–282.

RAJOGOPALAN, C. Social Change: An Analysis of Role Conflict and Deviation. *Indian Journal of Social Work*, 24:11–18.

RETTIG, S., and H. E. RAWSON. The Risk Hypothesis in Predictive Judgments of Unethical Behavior. *JASP*, 66:243–248.

ROBINSON, G. A New Theory of Empathy and Its Relation to Identification. *Journal of Asthma Research*, 1:49–114.

SCHROEDER, W. W. Lay Expectations of the Ministerial Role. *J. Scientific Study Religion*, 2:217–227.

SHERLOCK, B. J. Acquisition of the Nursing Role and the Transmission of Non-therapeutic Orientations. *NR*, 12:182–184.

SHUVAL, J. T. Perceived Role Components of Nursing in Israel. *ASR*, 28:37–46.

SMELSER, N. J., and W. T. SMELSER (eds.) *Personality and Social Systems.* N.Y.: Wiley.

SORENSON, G. A., T. R. HUSEK, and C. YU. Divergent Concepts of Teacher Role: An Approach to the Measurement of Teacher Effectiveness. *J. Educ. Psychol.*, 54:287–294.

STEINMANN, A. A Study of the Concept of the Feminine Role of 51 Middle-Class American Families. *GPM*, 67:275–352.

STOTLAND, E., and J. A. WALSH. Birth Order and an Experimental Study of Empathy. *JASP*, 66:610–614.

1963 (cont.)

STOTLAND, E., and R. E. DUNN. Empathy, Self-Esteem, and Birth Order. *JASP*, 66:532–540.

STUCKERT, R. P. Role Perception and Marital Satisfaction—A Configurational Approach. *MFL*, 25:415–419.

TAVES, M. J., R. G. CORWIN, and J. E. HAAS. *Role Conception and Vocational Success and Satisfaction: A Study of Student and Professional Nurses*. Columbus, O.: Ohio State University Bureau of Business Research Monograph.

TAYLOR, C. C., and D. ENSMINGER. Role and Status Relationships in Program Administration. *International Review of Community Development*, No. 12, pp. 89–108.

THARP, R. G. Dimensions of Marriage Roles. *MFL*, 25:389–404.

TURK, H. Social Cohesion through Variant Values: Evidence from Medical Role Relations. *ASR*, 28:28–37.

—— and T. INGLES. *Clinic Nursing: Explorations in Role Innovation*. Philadelphia: F. A. Davis.

TWYMAN, J. P., and B. J. BIDDLE. Role Conflict of Public School Teachers. *J. Psychol.*, 55:183–198.

——. *The Uses of Role Conflict*. Stillwater, Okla.: Oklahoma State University Monographs in Social Science.

USEEM, J., R. USEEM, and J. DONOGHUE. Men in the Middle of the Third Culture: The Roles of American and Non-Western People in Cross-Cultural Administration. *HO*, 22:169–179.

WARD, B. E. (ed.) *Women in the New Asia: The Changing Social Roles of Men and Women in South and South-East Asia*. Amsterdam: UNESCO.

WEBB, A. Sex-Role Preferences and Adjustment in Early Adolescence. *CD*, 34:609–618.

WEINSTEIN, E. A., and P. DEUTSCHBERGER. Some Dimensions of Altercasting. *Sociom.*, 26:454–466.

WEINSTOCK, S. A. Role Elements: A Link between Acculturation and Occupational Status. *BJS*, 14:144–149.

WEISMAN, C. B. Social Structure as a Determinant of the Group Worker's Role. *Social Work*, 8:87–94.

WHATLEY, JR., C. D. Status, Role and Vocational Continuity of Discharged Mental Patients. *JHHB*, 4:105–112.

WHITLOCK, G. E. Role and Self Concepts in the Choice of the Ministry as a Vocation. *J. Pastoral Care*, 17:208–212.

WILLIAMS, JR., D. T. *The Concepts, Status and Role, as They Affect the Study of Higher Education*. Stanford, Calif.: Stanford University Press.

WILLIAMSON, H. M., W. E. EDMONSTON, and J. A. STERN. Use of the EPPS for Identifying Personal Role Attributes Desirable in Nursing. *JHHB*, 4:266–277.

WILLISTON, G. C. The Foster-Parent Role. *JSP*, 60:263–272.

Theses and Dissertations

ADAMS, F. Values, Managers and Workers Role and Status in a Modern State Mental Hospital (Ph.D., Tulane University, 1958).

ANGUS, A. J. A Sociological Interpretation of the Changing Role and Status of the Nurse Anesthetist (M.A., University of Pittsburgh, 1956).

ASHTON, M. K. An Exploratory Investigation of the Student Role in the Self Conception of University Freshmen (M.A., University of North Dakota, 1959).

AXELSON, L. J. A Study of the Marital Adjustment and Role Definitions of Husbands of Working and Non-Working Wives (Ph.D., Washington State University, 1963).

BAILEY, L. V. The Role Conflict of American Career Housewives (M.A., University of Oklahoma, 1958).

BEALL, H. A. Administrative Succession: A Study of Role Acquisition and Maintenance (Ph.D., University of Oregon, 1962).

BECHILL, V. C. A Comparison of Role Incongruity in Married and Divorced Couples (Ph.D., Vanderbilt University, 1962).

BECKER, H. S. Role and Career Problems of the Chicago Public School Teacher (Ph.D., University of Chicago, 1951).

BENNETT, JR., W. S. Motivational Structure and Perceived Role Disparities (M.A., University of Missouri, 1961).

BERNSTEIN, M. R. A Study of Teachers' Role-Expectations and Role-Perceptions of a Principal, Superintendent, and Board of Education, and the Relationship between Convergence and Divergence of Role-Expectation and Role-Perception and Teacher Morale (Ph.D., New York University, 1959).

BERRY, P. M. Consensus of Role Perceptions in a Welfare Planning Council (Ph.D., University of Southern California, 1960).

BIBLE, B. L. Role Expectations of County Executive Committee Members in the Cooperative Agricultural and Home Economics Extension Service of Pennsylvania (Ph.D., Pennsylvania State University, 1959).

BIDDLE, B. J. An Application of Social Expectation Theory to the Initial Interview (Ph.D., University of Michigan, 1955).

BINSTOCK, J. S. Status and Role of the Aged in Three Generation Jewish Families of Eastern European Origin (M.A., University of Chicago, 1952).

BLOOMBAUM, M. S. Resolution of Role Conflict (Ph.D., University of California, 1961).

BOCK, E. W. Correlates of the Accuracy of Role-Taking and the Congruence of Self–Other Images among Married Couples. (Ph.D., Iowa State University, 1961).

BOGUSLAW, R. Role Tension and Role Perception: An Approach to the Analysis of Labor-Management Relations (Ph.D., New York University, 1954).

Theses and Dissertations (cont.)

BOOKBINDER, L. J. Self Perception, Social Perception and Response Sets in High and Low Authoritarians (Ph.D., Northwestern University, 1959).

BRADSHAW, B. R. Role Conflict and Personality: A Replication Study (M.A., Northwestern University, 1956).

BREER, JR., P. E. Predicting Interpersonal Behavior from Personality and Role (Ph.D., Harvard University, 1960).

BROIDA, H. An Empirical Study of Sex-Role Identification and Sex-Role Preference in a Selected Group of Stuttering Male Children (Ph.D., University of Southern California, 1962).

BROWN, B. M. The Clergyman's Role as Premarital and Marital Counselor (M.A., University of North Carolina, 1951).

BRUHN, J. G. The Sick Role: Initial Conceptions Related to the Length and Success of Psychotherapy (Ph.D., Yale University, 1961).

BURCHARD, W. The Role of the Military Chaplain (Ph.D., University of California, 1953).

BURTNER, F. A. The Vo-Ag Teacher: An Inquiry into the Status and Role of an Emergent Profession (Ph.D., University of North Carolina, 1958).

BUSCAGLIA, L. F. An Experimental Study of the Sarbin-Hardyck Test as Indexes of Role Perception for Adolescent Stutterers (Ph.D., University of Southern California, 1963).

CALLAWAY, A. B. Some Environmental Factors and Community Influences Brought to Bear upon the Personal Lives of Missouri Teachers and Administrators (Ed.D., University of Missouri, 1951).

CARLIN, J. The Rabbi: A Sociological Study of a Religious Specialist (M.A., University of Chicago, 1951).

CATES, J. N. Role, Role Conflict, and Resolution in a Mental Hospital (Ph.D., Yale University, 1961),

CHAIKLIN, H. The House Staff of a University Teaching Hospital: A Study of Conflicting Norms (Ph.D., Yale University, 1961).

CHANELES, S. The Concert Pianist: The Study of the Social Roles and Functions of the Artist in American Society (Ph.D., New York University, 1960).

CHARTERS, W. A Study of Role Conflict among Foremen in Heavy Industry (Ph.D., University of Michigan, 1952).

CLOYD, J. S. Patterns of Role Behavior in Small-Group Social Systems (Ph.D., University of Nebraska, 1963).

CONRAD, R. The Administrator Role: A Sociological Study of Leadership in a Public School System (Ph.D., Stanford University, 1951).

CORWIN, R. G. Role Conception and Mobility Aspiration: A Study in the Formation and Transformation of Bureaucratic, Professional, and Humanitarian Nursing Identities (Ph.D., University of Minnesota, 1960).

COSER, R. L. The Role of the Patient in a Hospital Ward (Ph.D., Columbia University, 1957).

COUCH, C. J. A Study of the Relationships between Self-Views and Role-Taking Accuracy (Ph.D., University of Iowa, 1955).

COWAN, P. H. Teacher Role Perception in Colleges and Universities (Ph.D., Stanford University, 1956).

CROOK, R. K. Role Differentiation and Functional Integration: A Structural Model of a Mental Hospital Ward (Ph.D., Princeton University, 1963).

CURWOOD, S. Role Expectation as a Factor in the Relationship between Mother and Teacher (Ph.D., Radcliffe College, 1956).

DAVIS, R. C. Commitment to Professional Values as Related to the Role Performance of Research Scientists (Ph.D., University of Michigan, 1956).

DERMAN, S. The Conflict of Church and Sect Role in the Southern Baptist Ministry (Ph.D., Duke University, 1956).

DEUTSCHBERGER, P. Role and Feedback in the Management of the Social Encounter (Ph.D., Vanderbilt University, 1962).

DIANA, J. The Visiting Teacher: A Study in Status Dilemma and Professionalization (Ph.D., University of Pittsburgh, 1956).

DICK, F. Professionalization of the Retail Credit Executive Role (Ph.D., University of Texas, 1956).

DODD, P. C. Role Conflicts in the School Principalship (Ph.D., Harvard University, 1962).

DOLAN, R. J. An Analysis of the Role Structure of a Complex Occupation with Special Emphasis on the Value- and Role-Orientations Associated with the County-Agent Situs (Ph.D., Louisiana State University, 1963).

DRABICK, L. W. Perception of the Public School Teacher's Role as a Correlate of Social Position (Ph.D., Pennsylvania State University, 1960).

DYER, D. A. Self-Concept, Role Internalization, and Saliency in Relation to Four-H Leader Effectiveness (Ph.D., Michigan State University, 1963).

DYER, E. Roles and Role Expectations in the Two-Income Family (Ph.D., University of Wisconsin, 1955).

DYMOND, R. F. Empathic Ability: An Exploratory Study (Ph.D., Cornell University, 1949).

EHRLICH, H. J. The Analysis of Role Conflicts in a Complex Organization: The Police (Ph.D., Michigan State University, 1959).

EPLEY, D. Adolescent Role Relationships in the Dynamics of Prejudice (Ph.D., Michigan State University, 1954).

ERIKSON, K. T. Drama and the Role of the Patient: Rehearsal for Normalcy (M.A., University of Chicago, 1955).

EVANS, T. The Psychological Induction of Nurses into the Professional Work Group (M.A., University of Chicago, 1953).

Theses and Dissertations (cont.)

FALK, L. L. The Minister's Responses to His Perceptions of Conflict between Self-Expectations and Parishioners' Expectations of His Role (Ph.D., University of Nebraska, 1962).

FATHI, A. Role Conflict and Marginality: A Study of Jewish High-School Students (M.A., University of Washington, 1959).

FEELEY, A. L. Administration Leadership: A Study of Role Expectations and Perceptions in the Areas of Public Relations and Curriculum Development by Secondary School Principals and Staff Members (Ph.D., University of Pittsburgh, 1962).

FELLIN, P. A. A Study of the Effects of Reference Group Orientations and Bureaucratic Careers on Neighborhood Cohesion (Ph.D., University of Michigan, 1962).

FISHBURN, C. E. Teacher Role Perception in the Secondary Schools of One Community (Ed.D., Stanford University, 1955).

FISHER, L. A. The Function of Role Expectations of Superiors, Colleagues, and Students in the Evaluation of Effectiveness of Instructors (Ph.D., University of Chicago, 1954).

FOLTA, J. R. Nurses' Perceptions of Role Requirements and Role Action in Situations Involving Death in Hospitals (Ph.D., University of Washington, 1963).

FOREST, C. A. Sisters as Graduate Students: The Integration of the Roles of the Religious Teacher, Student, and Scholar (M.A., Fordham University, 1959).

FOUNTAIN, JR., B. E. A Study of the Role of Selected North Carolina School Superintendents in School-Community Relations (Ph.D., University of North Carolina, 1958).

GARDNER, R. V. An Investigation of the Role Convergence of the City Planner and City Manager (Ph.D., University of Illinois, 1959).

GEORGOPOULOS, B. S. The Normative Structure of Social Systems (Ph.D., University of Michigan, 1956).

GERSTL, J. The Social Role of the Atomic Scientist (Ph.D., Columbia University, 1955).

GIELE, J. Z. Social Change in the Feminine Role: A Comparison of Women's Suffrage and Women's Temperance, 1870–1920 (Ph.D., Radcliffe College, 1961).

GOFFMAN, I. W. Self–Other Differentiation and Role Performance: A Study of Professional Agents of Social Control (Ph.D., University of Michigan, 1959).

GOLDBERG, D. Family and Role Structure and Fertility (Ph.D., University of Michigan, 1958).

GOLDSTEIN, R. The Professional Nurse in the Hospital Bureaucracy (Ph.D., University of Chicago, 1954).

GORDON, G. A Delineation of the Sick Role (Ph.D., New York University, 1962).

Goss, L. C. Parent and Teacher Perceptions of the Role of the Elementary School Teacher (Ph.D., Stanford University, 1959).

Goss, M. E. Physicians in Bureaucracy: A Case Study of Professional Pressures on Organizational Roles (Ph.D., Columbia University, 1958).

Griff, M. Role Conflict and the Career Development of the Commercial Artist (Ph.D., University of Chicago, 1958).

Habenstein, R. The American Funeral Director (Ph.D., University of Chicago, 1954).

Hall, M. J. The Social Performance of a College Minister: Role, Status, and Function (M.A., Florida State University, 1957).

Hall, R. L. Social Influence on Role Behavior of a Designated Leader (Ph.D., University of Nebraska, 1953).

Hamilton, P. A. The Influence of Social Factors on Religious Role Perception and Behavior (Ph.D., University of Notre Dame, 1961).

Haskell, M. R. The Relationship of Changes in Role-Playing Ability to Changes in Certain Social Values (Ph.D., New York University, 1957).

Hatch, R. S. An Evaluation of a Forced-Choice Differential Accuracy Approach to the Measurement of Supervisory Empathy (Ph.D., University of Minnesota, 1962).

Hays, D. Positional Experience and Accuracy of Role Cognition (M.A., University of Missouri, 1961).

Heer, D. M. The Role of the Working Wife in Catholic Families (Ph.D., Harvard University, 1958).

Henderhan, R. C. The Relationship of Several Social-Psychological Variables to Empathic Ability (Ph.D., Ohio State University, 1963).

Herman, R. D. Segmentation of Bureaucratic and Familial Roles among Business Executives (Ph.D., University of Wisconsin, 1959).

Hilmar, N. A. Conflicting Social Norms in a Formal Organization: A Study of Interpersonal Expectations (Ph.D., Cornell University, 1955).

Hoffman, R. E. The Doctor's Role: A Study of Consensus, Congruence, and Change (Ph.D., University of Nebraska, 1958).

Howard, S. J. Determinants of Sex-Role Identification of Homo-Sexual Female Delinquents (Ph.D., University of Southern California, 1962).

Hudson, J. B. A Study of the Social Interactionist View of Role Taking and the Self (M.A., University of Washington, 1955).

———. Feminine Roles and Family Norms in a Small City (Ph.D., Cornell University, 1963).

Hurlburt, J. K. Role Expectations and the Self: An Empirical Study of Their Relationship to Marital Adjustment (Ph.D., State University of Iowa, 1960).

Hurvitz, N. Marital Roles and Adjustment in a Middle-Class Group (Ph.D., University of Southern California, 1958).

Theses and Dissertations (cont.)

ISTIPHAN, I. Role Expectations of American Undergraduate College Women in a Western Coeducational Institution (Ph.D., University of Southern California, 1962).

JAMBOR, H. Discrepancies in Role Expectations for the Supervisory Position—A Concern of Social Work Administration (Ph.D., University of Minnesota, 1954).

JAMMOS, J. M. The Priest's Clientele: Expectations, Criticism, Mistakes (Ph.D., University of Chicago, 1954).

JOHNSON, J. G. An Analysis and Description of Role Expectations for Ministers of the Southern California District of the Lutheran Church—Missouri Synod (Ph.D., University of Southern California, 1961).

JONES, F. E. Sociological Aspects of Role Acquisition among Infantry Recruits (Ph.D., Harvard University, 1945).

KATZ, B. Predictive and Behavioral Empathy and Client Change in Short-Term Counseling (Ph.D., New York University, 1962).

KLAUSNER, S. Z. Role Adaptation of Ministers and Psychiatrists in the Religio-Psychiatric Movement (Ph.D., Columbia University, 1963).

KORSTVEDT, A. J. Role-Taking Behavior in Normal and Disturbed Children: A Developmental Analysis of Cognitive Processes (Ph.D., Clark University, 1962).

KOTLAR, S. L. Middle-Class Marital Roles—Ideal and Perceived in Relation to Adjustment in Marriage (Ph.D., University of Southern California, 1961).

KRAFT, E. D. Construction of a Movie Test to Measure the Ability to Understand Others (Ph.D., Columbia University, 1962).

KROHN, R. G. The Social Role of the Revolutionary Hero (M.A., University of Minnesota, 1957).

LACOGNATA, A. Role Expectations of University Faculty and Students: A Social-Psychological Analysis (Ph.D., Michigan State University, 1962).

LAMB, H. E. Self and Role Concepts Related to Behavior, Intelligence and Academic Achievement (Ph.D., University of Maryland, 1963).

LAULICHT, J. A Scale Analysis of Criteria for the Resolution of Role Conflict Situations (Ph.D., University of Kentucky, 1954).

LAZURE, J. M. The Definition of the Priest-Teacher's Role (Ph.D., Harvard University, 1963).

LIEBERMAN, S. The Relationship between Attitudes and Roles: A Natural Field Experiment (Ph.D., University of Michigan, 1954).

LOPEZ, JR., F. M. A Psychological Analysis of the Relationship of Role Consensus and Personality Consensus to Job Satisfaction and Job Performance (Ph.D., Columbia University, 1962).

LORTIE, D. Doctors without Patients: The Anesthesiologist—A New Medical Specialist (M.A., University of Chicago, 1949).

McCollum, J. W. The Chicago Electrical Apprentice: Conception of Role (M.A., University of Chicago, 1953).

McCray, J. S. The Role, Status, and Participation of the Aged in a Small Community (Ph.D., Washington University, 1956).

McDowell, H. Osteopathy: A Study of a Semi-Orthodox Healing Agency (M.A., University of Chicago, 1950).

———. The Principal's Role in a Metropolitan School System (Ph.D., University of Chicago, 1954).

McKinley, D. G. Social Status and Parental Roles (Ph.D., Harvard University, 1960).

McNamara, J. A. The Modern Jazz Musician and His Relation to His Audience: Role Conflict in the Pattern Variable Schema (M.A., University of California, 1958).

Maranell, G. M. Role-Taking: Empathy and Transparency (Ph.D., University of Iowa, 1959).

Martin, H. W. Physician Role Conflict in Community Participation (Ph.D., University of North Carolina, 1957).

Mennis, M. A. An Analysis and Evaluation of the Treatment of Women's Social Roles in American Research from 1945 to 1956 (M.A., Catholic University, 1957).

Menzel, H. The Social Psychology of Occupations: A Synthetic Review (M.A., Indiana University, 1950).

Miller, R. Teacher Role and the Rural-Urban Continuum (M.A., University of Missouri, 1961).

Mondlane, E. C. Role Conflict, Reference Group, and Race (Ph.D., Northwestern University, 1961).

Moss, L. W. The Master Plumber in Detroit: A Study of Role Adjustment (Ph.D., University of Michigan, 1955).

Moyer, L. N. Occupational Variables and the Role of the Sick (Ph.D., Ohio State University, 1963).

Murphy, G. L. The Social Role of the Prison Chaplain (Ph.D., University of Pittsburgh, 1956).

Murphy, R. J. Mobility and Occupational Role: A Comparative Analysis (Ph.D., Northwestern University, 1955).

Naboisek, H. Validation of a Method for Predicting Role Expectations in Group Therapy (Ph.D., University of California, 1953).

Nathanson, C. A. Learning the Doctor's Role: A Study of First and Fourth Year Medical Students (M.A., University of Chicago, 1958).

Nelson, H. E. Occupational Self-Images of Teachers: A Study of the Occupational Involvements and Work-Role Orientations of Michigan Industrial Education Teachers (Ph.D., Michigan State University, 1963).

Theses and Dissertations (cont.)

ORLINSKY, N. Patients' and Therapists' Definitions of Therapist's Role in Relation to Outcome of Therapy (Ph.D., University of Chicago, 1959).

O'TOOLE, R. Experiments in George Herbert Mead's "Taking the Role of the Other" (Ph.D., University of Oregon, 1963).

PALMORE, E. G. Some Functions of the Active Therapist Role (Ph.D., Columbia University, 1959).

PALOLA, E. G. Organization Types and Role Strains: A Laboratory Study of a Complex Organization (Ph.D., University of Washington, 1962).

PENDLETON, P. W. Academic Role of the College Student (Ph.D., Ohio State University, 1956).

PETERS, M. An Investigation of Attitudes of Purdue University Students toward Woman's Roles (M.A., Purdue University, 1955).

PETERSON, W. A. Career Phases and Interage Relationships: The Female High School Teacher in Kansas City (Ph.D., University of Chicago, 1956).

PHILLIPS, B. S. A Role Theory Approach to Predicting Adjustment of the Aged in Two Communities (Ph.D., Cornell University, 1956).

PLYLER, H. E. Variation of Ministerial Roles by Size and Location of Church (Ph.D., University of Missouri, 1961).

POINTEU, M. B. Perception of Social Norms by Role Types (M.A., Fisk University, 1955).

POWNALL, G. A. An Analysis of the Role of the Parole Supervision Officer (Ph.D., University of Illinois, 1963).

QUARANTELLI, E. L. The Dental Student: A Social-Psychological Study (Ph.D., University of Chicago, 1959).

REISSMAN, L. The Civil Servant and a Study of Role Conception in Bureaucracy (M.A., University of Wisconsin, 1947).

RITTENHOUSE, R. R. The Role of Conscientious Objectors in American Prisons (M.A., University of Illinois, 1958).

ROBERTS, E. J. Marginal Woman: Application of the Marginal Concept to the Status and Social Role of the Modern Woman in the U.S. (M.A., University of North Carolina, 1950).

ROBIN, S. A Comparison of Male-Female Roles in Engineering (Ph.D., Purdue University, 1963).

ROSENSTEIN, A. J. A Comparative Study of the Role Conflict, Marital Adjustment and Personality Configuration of Private Adoptive and Agency Adoptive Parents (Ph.D., University of Southern California, 1959).

ROSS, I. Role Specialization and Supervision (Ph.D., Columbia University, 1956).

RUDERMAN, D. L. An Exploration of Empathic Ability in Children and Its Relationship to Several Variables (Ph.D., Columbia University, 1962).

SANTOPOLA, F. A. The Priest: A Projective Analysis of Role (Ph.D., Fordham University, 1956).

SEBALD, H. Parent-Peer Control and Masculine-Marital Role Perceptions of Adolescent Boys (Ph.D., Ohio State University, 1963).

SHARPE, R. F. Differences between Perceived Administrative Behavior and Role-Norms as Factors in Leadership Evaluation and Group Morale (Ph.D., Stanford University, 1954).

SHERLOCK, B. J. Role Acquisition in a State Mental Hospital (Ph.D., University of Colorado, 1961).

SHIMADA, K. Role Conflict and Authoritarianism in a Sample of Protestant Parish Ministers (M.A., Pennsylvania State University, 1958).

SILVERMAN, L. J. Social Role of a Salesman (M.A., New School for Social Research, 1956).

SIMPSON, I. H. The Socialization of Student Nurses: A Study of the Development of a Professional Self-Image (Ph.D., University of North Carolina, 1956).

SLUDER, L. A. The Changing Role of the Protestant Minister in the United States (M.A., University of Texas, 1956).

SMITH, R. T. A Study of the Professional Role of Dentists (Ph.D., University of Wisconsin, 1960).

SMITH, T. E. An Analysis of the Role of the School Psychologist in the State of California (Ph.D., University of Southern California, 1962).

SOMMERFELD, R. E. Role Conceptions of Lutheran Ministers in the St. Louis Area (Ph.D., Washington University, 1957).

SPRAY, S. L. Behavioral Mix in Role Performances: A Study of Executive Behavior (Ph.D., University of Oregon, 1962).

STEMPHENS, R. The Academic Administrator: The Role of the University President (Ph.D., University of North Carolina, 1956).

STERNBERG, D. S. The Growth of Empathy: An Investigation of the Relationship between Sensitivity to the Self-Perception of Others as a Function of Frequency of Interpersonal Contact and Certain Selected Personality Variables (Ph.D., New York University, 1962).

SUNDHEIM, B. J. M. The Relationships Among n Achievement, n Affiliation, Sex-Role Concepts, Academic Grades, and Curricular Choice (Ph.D., Columbia University, 1963).

SYNDER, N. The Scientist's Conception of His Role in American Society (M.A., University of Buffalo, 1951).

THOMES, M. M. Parents of Schizophrenic and Normal Children: A Comparison of Parental Attitudes, Marital Adjustment, Role Behavior and Interaction (Ph.D., University of Southern California, 1959).

THRASHER, J. H. The Role-Set and Socialization of the Psychiatric Patient (Ph.D., University of North Carolina, 1961).

Theses and Dissertations (cont.)

TOWNER, S. B. Roles Student Nurses Desire or Expect to Perform and Roles Achieved by Graduate Nurses from the Same Selected School of Nursing (Ph.D., University of Southern California, 1957).

TUMBLIN, J. The Professional Role of the Southern Baptist Missionary (Ph.D., Duke University, 1956).

TWYMAN, J. P. Role Conflict Incidence in the Teaching Profession (Ph.D., University of Kansas City, 1961).

VAZ, E. The Metropolitan Taxi Driver: His Work and Self Conception (M.A., McGill University, 1955).

WAIK, E. Becoming a Nurse—Socialization into an Occupational Role (M.A., University of British Columbia, 1957).

WALDMAN, H. Correlates of Empathy in Family Life Teachers (Ph.D., Columbia University, 1962).

WEIL, M. W. A Study of the Factors Affecting the Role and Role Expectations of Women Participating or Planning to Participate in the Labor Force (Ph.D., New York University, 1959).

WHEELER, L. S. Desire: A Determinant of Self-Evaluation through Social Comparison (Ph.D., University of Minnesota, 1963).

WIGGINS, J. A. Role Differentiation (M.A., University of Washington, 1959).

WILEY, R. W. A Comparative Evaluation of the Roles of Ministers, School Counselors, Parents, and Others in Assisting Youth with Life-Work Selection Problems (Ph.D., Pennsylvania State University, 1963).

WILLIAMS, D. M. A Study of the Relative Effectiveness of Selected Teaching Procedures in the Modification of Children's Attitudes toward the Negro (Ph.D., New York University, 1946).

WILSON, R. N. The American Poet: A Role Investigation (Ph.D., Harvard University, 1952).

YASIN, S. Opinion Responses as Role Behavior: A Social Psychological Study in Race Relations (M.A., Michigan State University, 1954).

YOURGLICH, A. A Study of Role Consensus in the Family System (Ph.D., University of Oregon, 1961).

Index